Florentine Histories

FLORENTINE HISTORIES

by

NICCOLÒ MACHIAVELLI

A New Translation by

LAURA F. BANFIELD

and

HARVEY C. MANSFIELD, JR.

With an Introduction by Harvey C. Mansfield, Jr.

PRINCETON UNIVERSITY PRESS

PRINCETON, NEW JERSEY

COPYRIGHT © 1988 BY PRINCETON UNIVERSITY PRESS

PUBLISHED BY PRINCETON UNIVERSITY PRESS,

41 WILLIAM STREET, PRINCETON, NEW JERSEY 08540

IN THE UNITED KINGDOM:

PRINCETON UNIVERSITY PRESS, OXFORD

LIBRARY OF CONGRESS CATALOGING-IN-PUBLICATION DATA

MACHIAVELLI, NICCOLÒ, 1469–1527.

FLORENTINE HISTORIES.

TRANSLATION OF: ISTORIE FIORENTINE.

BIBLIOGRAPHY: P.

INCLUDES INDEX.

I. FLORENCE (ITALY)—HISTORY—TO 1421. 2. FLORENCE

(ITALY)—HISTORY—1421–1737. I. TITLE.

DG736.3.M3313 1988   945'.51   87–38503

(ALK. PAPER)

ISBN 0–691–05521–1

ISBN 0–691–00863–9 (PBK.)

FIRST PRINCETON PAPERBACK PRINTING, 1990

THIS BOOK HAS BEEN COMPOSED IN LINOTRON BEMBO

CLOTHBOUND EDITIONS OF

PRINCETON UNIVERSITY PRESS BOOKS

ARE PRINTED ON ACID-FREE PAPER, AND BINDING

MATERIALS ARE CHOSEN FOR STRENGTH AND DURABILITY.

PAPERBACKS, ALTHOUGH SATISFACTORY FOR

PERSONAL COLLECTIONS, ARE NOT

USUALLY SUITABLE FOR

LIBRARY REBINDING

PRINTED IN THE UNITED STATES OF AMERICA

BY PRINCETON UNIVERSITY PRESS, PRINCETON, NEW JERSEY

10 9 8 7 6 5 4 3

CONTENTS

WE have translated Machiavelli's title for this work as *Florentine Histories* rather than the more usual, and less accurate, *History of Florence*. This choice accords with our general inclination to literalness in translation, but it is also intended to indicate a specific doubt as to whether Machiavelli is writing "history" as we know it in the *Florentine Histories*.

Machiavelli's work does resemble a present-day history book in certain respects. It selects an object of narration, Florence; it describes a particular period, from the origins of the city to the death of Lorenzo de' Medici in 1492; and it presents a problem or theme, the causes of the remarkable hatreds and divisions within Florence. But it is not a history of Florence in the sense we are accustomed to, which requires that Florence have or have had a history. Machiavelli does not use the word *istoria* to refer to an object of study; he uses it to mean only the study itself. Whereas for us history is both the object of study and the study itself, for Machiavelli history is a study, apparently, of something other than history. Thus, when he speaks of "our history" or "my history," he refers to a study or an inquiry that he also calls "my narrations" or "my description" or "my undertaking" (see the Letter dedicatory). And since he does not have in mind history as an object, he can say "Florentine histories" in the plural if he wishes, contrary to usage today, which admits that many histories of Florence have been written but denies that Florence could have had more than one history. Further contrary to current practice, Machiavelli does not speak of "historiography": for him, history *is* historiography.

Machiavelli's usage of the word "history," therefore, is enough to make us doubt that the *Florentine Histories* is history as we know it. But perhaps history as we know it would never have allowed us to suppose otherwise. History as we know it, in the sense of an object as well as a study, embraces Machiavelli in a context that could not fail to differ profoundly from our context, from our history. His historical context includes both the facts of his time, which would have influenced his writing of history, and the historiography characteristic of his time, together with the conception of history underlying those historiographic methods.

To begin with the latter, we find humanist historians (as well as chroniclers) preceding Machiavelli who titled their works *histories* in the plural, above all, Leonardi Bruni's *Historiae Florentini Populi*. More important, their histories incorporate certain features that do not appear in today's history books: the division of the history into books with general, non-historical introductions; invented speeches presented as if they were actual speeches taken down verbatim or paraphrased; and the presentation of a political history so much to the neglect of economic, cultural, social, and intellectual history as to imply that political history is the chief or even the only history. Machiavelli's adoption of these conventions of humanist historiography suggests that his conception of history and even of historical context differs from ours.

In the Preface, Machiavelli says that his purpose in this work is "to write down the things done at home and abroad [or, inside and outside] by the Florentine people." In the first book, as he says in the Preface, he narrates "all the unforeseen events in Italy following upon the decline of the Roman Empire up to 1434." He shows how Italy from the time of the barbarian invasions "came to be under those powers that governed it" in 1434. Florence had its origin earlier than the barbarian invasions, we learn in II 2, at the time when the Roman Republic was dissolving; but we would say, and Machiavelli seems to mean, that his first book sets Florence "in context." The difficulty is that he calls this context "our universal treatise" (II 2). Although the first book appears to be merely a narration of events in Italy, Machiavelli invests it with a significance more than historical. Also, each of the following seven books begins with a chapter that discusses some general topic nonhistorically: colonies, natural enmities between men of the people and the nobles, liberty and license, the natural cycle of order and disorder, the advantage of victory in war, the difference between divisions with "sects" and those without them, and conspiracies. To be sure, Machiavelli typically contrasts the ancients and the moderns in each regard in a way that might seem historical, but he does so to explain the superior virtue of the ancients, not merely to adduce a difference in historical context.

In the broad sweep of his outlook, and in his attention both to the rise and fall of states and to their internal divisions, Machiavelli is alive to the fact of "historical change," as we would say. But he interprets it differently. For him, historical change is either the motion of nature—not perhaps random but not intended by men—or the order and ordering ("orders and modes" in the Preface and VIII 29) that men intend. Since nature's motions do not make men feel safe or grateful, they appear to men as "fortune," sometimes good and sometimes bad but never reliable. Because nature looks to us like fortune, it is in effect reducible to fortune. Instead of the classical opposition, first discerned by philosophers, between nature as unchanging and fortune as fickle, Machiavelli adopts the popular attitude, as he sees it, that neither nature nor fortune can be trusted. And since human order made by human virtue is designed to overcome this sense of lack of support, and to create reliable principles and states, the context of history must be understood as a contest between virtue and fortune. Possibly this contest may be won definitively by virtue, that is, at some historical time. But the contest itself, because it explains history, is not historical and will not be decided by history. If the contest between virtue and fortune is the context of history, then the context of history is not history. That is why the word "history" for Machiavelli means a study or an inquiry and does not refer to history as an object.

To vaunt the worth of his history, Machiavelli makes a statement in the Preface that we would regard today as unhistorical, but one that fits the practices of humanist historiography. "And if every example of a republic is moving," he says, "those which one reads concerning one's own are much more so and much more useful; and if in any other republic were there ever notable divisions, those of Florence are most notable. . . ." He offers a practical and a theoretical inducement to his readers, neither of which resembles a question of historical interest in our regard. A historian, for us, is supposed to be above concern for "one's own" and would not admit to choosing a topic for its utility to his own country. Yet he is not so abstracted from historical fact as to believe that his topic is a mere "example" out of some general category, whose selection must be justified by a theoretical interest, say, in republics. If Florence is merely an example of a republic, then it is hard to find a boundary between the *Florentine Histories* and Machiavelli's apparently more theoretical works, *The Prince* and the *Discourses on Livy*—that is, between history and political science. True, the *Florentine Histories* is devoted mainly to a republic, not to both republics and principalities as a work of political science might require. But the *Discourses on Livy* is also devoted mainly to a republic (the Roman), and *The Prince* is mainly about principalities. More important, the reader soon discovers that the Florentine republic, whose leaders are frequently called "princes" by Machiavelli and which is once referred to as a principality (I 26), shares many of the institutions and much of the behavior of principalities. It is no wonder that many scholars have sought to find Machiavelli's political science in his *Florentine Histories*: it is left quite visible in the beginning chapters of its books and in many pungent judgments throughout. In VIII 1 Machiavelli refers his readers to the *Discourses on Livy* for a longer discussion of conspiracies, not for a more abstract or scientific one.

Thus Machiavelli, as author of the *Florentine Histories* and in common with humanist historians, has two different but not exclusive motives— practical and theoretical—the first of which seems to us beneath history and the second above it. From this double motive for history, Machiavelli's concentration on the political can be derived. Historians today, rightly doubting that politics can explain all human activities, are drawn beyond political history to establish and investigate social, economic, cultural, and intellectual history. Confident that history exists as an object, they look for another kind of history if the dominant one seems unsatisfactory. But for Machiavelli, as we have seen, history is not an object; rather, the object of history is the contest between virtue and nature or fortune. To go beyond or beneath political history is to leave the realm of what we can do with "our own arms" and to enter that of nature or fortune, where we seem powerless. Machiavelli would want to know from the modern historian whether social, economic, cultural, and intellectual history could come under human control, that is, under politics. He would want to know whether the other kinds of history could become political history by being raised to our awareness or lowered to our reach.

In the *Florentine Histories* Machiavelli does not disregard the other kinds so much as he politicizes them. In what might be social history, he considers divisions among various classes of the "people" and dwells on the rise of the guilds (Book II) and the revolt of the plebs (Book III), but always for their political consequences. For economic history, he discusses the opening of an alum mine in Volterra (VII 29) as the cause of war and the operations of the bank of San Giorgio in Genoa (VIII 29) as an instance of free government amidst corruption. To keep up with culture, he mentions the "most excellent" architect Brunelleschi (IV 23), but then relates how an experiment of his at a siege of Lucca backfired (or backwatered) against the Florentine army (see also his political comment on the architecture of the Pitti Palace in VII 4). Marsilio Ficino, Pico della Mirandola, and some others are mentioned as recipients of Medici patronage and thus as occasions of praise for the Medici (VII 6, VIII 36). Dante appears in the role of historian of Florence's origins and of the cause of its parties (II 2), as the man who had the prudence to call the people to arms (II 18), and as one of those expelled from Florence (II 24)—whether justly or not, Machiavelli does not say. Donato Acciaiuoli, "a man very learned in Greek and Latin," is mentioned as spokesman for the Florentines on one occasion (VIII 14).

Besides the uncertainty as to whether his work is history or political science, and in addition to the concentration on politics, Machiavelli shares with humanist historians the device of inventing speeches. Even though he was not present and could not have been present, he puts appropriate speeches into the mouths of actual historical figures as if they were characters in a play of his. In "my history," as he calls it, he even provides "private reasonings" that no one could have overheard (Letter dedicatory). Sometimes he introduces the speeches with the formula "in this sense"; often there is no such announcement. Sometimes the speeches are given indirectly, sometimes directly, as if these were the exact words. Such license on Machiavelli's part seems to defy the obligation binding historians to respect historical fact and to leave his history to wander in the neighborhood of poetry and rhetoric. But Machiavelli is so far from casual or forgetful in his use of invented speeches that this technique appears to be one of his themes or preoccupations. The phrase "in the mouth of" someone, though not occurring in the *Florentine Histories*, is one of his favorites elsewhere. In the *Discourses on Livy* he refers nearly a dozen times to instances in which Livy makes someone say or do something. The practice he discovers in the historian Livy seems difficult to distinguish from that of the poet Virgil, who, according to Machiavelli in *The Prince* (ch. 17), says something interesting "in the mouth of Dido."

And yet Machiavelli prides himself on "the dignity and truthfulness of the history" (Letter dedicatory), as did the humanist historians, who expressly claimed to be speaking truth. It might be better to infer, then, that Machiavelli and the humanists have a notion of the truth of history that does not concede the sovereignty of historical fact. Fact, in their view, needs to be filled out with opinion, and it is the duty of the historian, in the absence of scribes and witnesses, to infer human intention and to make it explicit in speeches, adding sense to actions in order to arrive at truth. And if the speeches had been recorded, he might even have been compelled to change them for their own good. Thus, in the humanist (as well as the classical) conception, historical truth is not only compatible with patriotism and rhetoric but in need of them. Historical truth is not simply opposed to what historians today call "myth"; somehow it must be reconciled with myth because everyone, even the historian, has a fatherland (*patria*) and because all facts need to be interpreted with speech to gain significance. On behalf of truth, the historian may—or must—criticize the actions he relates. But if his criticism is to serve a practical end and is to be accepted by the citizens to whom it is directed, it must appear to be patriotic. Judged by the sovereignty of historical fact, this conception does not allow, much less encourage, historical research as practiced today. But before dismissing this conception of historical truth as odd and primitive, we should be sure that our historians can meet, or successfully evade, the requirements that history be patriotic and interpretive.

The facts of Machiavelli's time—the pressures and influences of power bearing on his writing—are the other element of his historical context, in addition to the dominant forms of discourse. These facts come to a focus in Machiavelli's relationship with the Medici, the ruling family in Florence when he wrote the *Florentine Histories*. Machiavelli was commissioned to write this work on November 8, 1520, at the instance of Cardinal Giulio de' Medici, who had become Pope Clement VII by the time Machiavelli finished. When Machiavelli presented eight books of the *Florentine Histories* to the pope in May 1525 (from the second sentence of the Letter dedicatory it seems he may have intended to write more), he was paying homage to the ruling power in both his city and the Church. In his Letter dedicatory, introducing himself as a humble servant, Machiavelli acknowledges the problem of flattery when one writes by commission. He nonetheless proudly proclaims "the dignity and the truthfulness of the history." He begins the Letter by saying that he was commissioned for the work, at the end he calls it "my undertaking," and next he begins the Preface very firmly in his own name: "My purpose, when I first decided to write. . . ." Then, grasping his commission as if it were his own idea, he proceeds to reveal in the outline of his history that it centers on "the year of the Christian religion 1434," the year when the Medici family gained the greatest authority in Florence. Machiavelli is so far from unaware of his historical context that he makes it the crux of his work, and we learn of his context from the text. Indeed, a survey of all his works might lead one to say that the *Florentine Histories* is his most contextual work, the one where he makes the powers impinging on him, which he is neither free of nor subservient to, the subject of his reflection. That is perhaps why the *Florentine Histories*, as opposed to *The Prince* and the *Discourses on Livy*, makes so little of innovation and founding in politics and does not dwell on the "new prince" or "new modes and orders." These are the themes, respectively, of the two works into which he said he put everything he knows. In the *Florentine Histories*, by contrast, he says he has striven to satisfy everyone "while not staining the truth."

Two of Machiavelli's surviving letters contain remarks about the *Florentine Histories*, and another comment was reported after his death by his young friend Donato Giannotti. All three tell of his concern with his context and suggest how he may have dealt with it. In his letter to Guicciardini of May 19, 1521, he says:

> Concerning the *Histories* and the republic of wooden sandals [the monastery where he was staying], I do not believe I have lost anything by coming here, because I have learned of many of their institutions and orders that have good in them; so I believe I can make use of them for some purposes, especially in comparisons. For where I have to reason about silence, I will be able to say: "They stay more quiet than the brothers when they eat." And so one will be able to adduce many other things through me by the means that this bit of experience has taught me.

In a fragment of another letter to Guicciardini of August 30, 1524, Machiavelli says:

> I have been staying and stay now at the villa to write the history, and I would pay ten *soldi*, I will not say more, to have you at my side so that I could show you where I am; for, having to come to certain particulars, I would need to learn from you whether I offend too much either by exalting or by abasing things. Yet I shall keep on considering by myself and shall strive to act so that, while I am speaking the truth, no one will be able to complain.

Giannotti reports that Machiavelli said to him:

> I cannot write this History from when Cosimo took the state until Lorenzo's death as I would write it if I were free from all hesitations [*respetti*]. The actions will be true, and I shall not leave anything undone; only I shall not tell in what mode or by what means and tricks one arrives at so great a height. And whoever wants to learn this also may note very well what I will make his adversaries say, because that which I will not want to say myself, as from me, I will make his adversaries say.[1]

Thus by the first remark it would seem that Machiavelli lets actions speak louder than words; by the second, that he exaggerates and understates so as to forestall complaints; and by the third, that he criticizes indirectly by speaking through adversaries.

We cannot say, however, that Machiavelli was unwilling to flatter the Medici because he put virtue above power and success. For him truth was not so distant from flattery as to leave him serenely unconcerned with the causes of greatness. Nor can we say that Machiavelli's attention to his own city comes from a desire, both responsible and patriotic, to improve its virtue, as virtue is ordinarily understood. It is time to take notice of Machiavelli's rebellious criticism of his two humanist predecessors as historians of the Florentine people, Leonardo Bruni and Poggio Bracciolini. They were, he says in the Preface, "two very excellent historians" and "very diligent" in describing the wars of the Florentine people. But they went wrong in regard to "civil discords and internal enmities, and the effects arising from them." Believing that these divisions were unimportant and that to describe them might offend the living, they failed to see that discord revealed the greatness of Florence, and they failed to understand that greatness. For they did not consider that "actions that have greatness in themselves, as do those of governments and states, however they are treated, or whatever end they may have, always appear to bring

---

[1] L. A. Ferrai, "Lettere inedite di Donato Giannotti," *Atti del R. Istituto Veneto di Scienze, Lettere ed Arti*, ser. 6, 3 (1884–1885), 1582.

men more honor than blame" (Preface). In cruder words, Bruni and Poggio overestimated the power of morality in determining reputation, and the particular inadequacy of their histories in regard to civil discords is the result of a deep and general mistake that infected their work as a whole and rendered them incapable of understanding human ambition and the desire men have to perpetuate their names.

However much Machiavelli's methods resemble those of the humanist historians, he separates himself deliberately and decisively from them by basing his advice on what is done rather than what should be done. (He took the same departure in Chapter 15 of *The Prince*.) When reading the humanist historians, one breathes the spirit of Cicero, and one is particularly reminded of the second book of *De Republica* (a work they did not know), where Cicero, with fine irony and careful responsibility, blends an account of the origin of his own republic with the development of the features of the best regime. This kind of history is both theoretical and practical because it supposes that nature and virtue are not so much in contest as in cooperation. Machiavelli, on the other hand, who did not think highly of Cicero (see especially *Discourses on Livy* I 52), was no mere observer of the contest between nature or fortune and virtue; he was no Stoic nobly but passively resigned to the limits of politics. For him the end and consequence of theory are to expand the possibilities of practice. To attempt this "undertaking," he opposed himself to the entire tradition preceding him—classical, medieval, and humanist—as too dependent on the force of morality. Whatever he borrowed from that tradition was used against it.

To conclude, we may briefly suggest what follows upon Machiavelli. If Machiavelli does not accept the sovereignty of historical fact, he does appear to set forth the sovereignty of historical *effects*. When virtue is understood not as acting in accordance with moral precepts but as producing impressive effects, we are, perhaps, on the way toward the sovereignty of fact and the study of history as an object. As long as Machiavelli's effects are products of human virtue and his "actions that have greatness in themselves" are human actions, then what men do matters more than what happens to them. And Machiavelli's peculiar humanism, however morally dubious, survives. But as soon as the effects are thought to come from forces larger than human, though less than divine, then human fortune subsumes human virtue and acquires patterns of its own. In these patterns the historian's facts come to life and quickly learn to speak for themselves. History is no longer an opposition between virtue and fortune; it has become a mixture of the two, in which virtue is diminished by its historical conditions and fortune is enhanced by a new predictability, even rationality, when seen in the guise of those same conditions. With a view to Machiavelli, one might be induced to doubt that our notion of history was made for us by history.

It is enough for an introduction to introduce; to begin here an interpretation of this marvelously intricate work would in some degree usurp the right of the reader. Having seen that the *Florentine Histories* is not the sort of history we today might expect, we are left in pleasurable bewilderment as to what sort of history it may be. To echo the recent question of one scholar: What, then, did Machiavelli want to teach with his *Florentine Histories?*

HARVEY C. MANSFIELD, JR.

A NOTE ON THE TRANSLATION

IN this translation we have sought to be as literal and exact as is consistent with *readable English*. We consider readable English to be language that is perfectly well understood today even if particular words and expressions are not familiar. For example, we translate *ragionare* as "reason about" and *modo* as "mode" instead of the usual "discuss" and "way." The reason for this departure is precisely to enable the reader to recognize that Machiavelli used these words differently from us. Yet since these words and their context are still understandable, the reader can ponder, as well as register, the difference.

With other words of obvious importance, where the discrepancy between the familiar and the readable is not so great—such as "nature," "sect," "order," "form," "matter," "spirit," and "state"—we have done our best to be consistent; occasionally we have stated our decision in a footnote. Above all, we have translated *virtù* as "virtue," so that the reader can form his own opinion of Machiavelli's meaning and not have to remain a captive of the translator's.

We have also resisted the temptation to indulge in elegant variation. Since Machiavelli does not define his key terms explicitly and systematically, it is often as difficult to know which they are as what they mean. But he sometimes indicates the importance of a word in a certain context by using it densely there (for example, *chiamare*, "to call" or "to call in," in Book 1). These indications must not be covered over with fussy translation. We know that certain theories (which in effect deny the possibility of translation) regard these practices as unsophisticated. With us, they are intended simply to show respect for a great writer and thinker whom we wish to make accessible to readers of English without legislating the terms under which he will be accessible. Most bad translation results from feelings of superiority, whether innocent or unintentional, on the part of translators—superiority toward the original author and toward the reader.

In the same spirit of caution, we have provided only slight and occasional historical annotation. As explained in the introduction, it would be hasty to assume that Machiavelli shares our appetite and esteem for historical information. He even appears to have departed sometimes from the facts available to him from his own sources. Likewise, we did not want to distract the reader by frequently whispering dates in his ear when Machiavelli does not provide them. We did not want to distract him, that is, from noticing when and how Machiavelli gives dates and from thinking over the modern "mode" of dating, in which Machiavelli takes an obvious interest.

We have followed the text of the *Florentine Histories* in the Casella edition, but with constant reference to the Carli edition. We have profited from the annotation by Franco Gaeta and from the translation by Allan Gilbert. We would like to acknowledge the help of Mary C. Mansfield, Dain Trafton, and Elizabeth Vangel, and a fellowship granted to Mansfield at the National Humanities Center. The map was contributed by Elliott Banfield.

H. C. M.

ABBREVIATIONS

AW   *The Art of War*

D   *Discourses on Livy*

FH   *Florentine Histories*

NM   Niccolò Machiavelli

P   *The Prince*

Florentine Histories

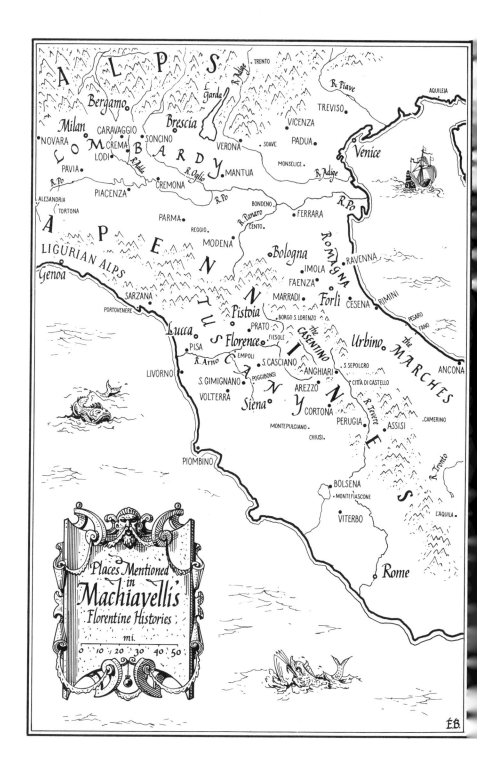

Places Mentioned in Machiavelli's Florentine Histories

mi.

0 10 20 30 40 50

TO THE MOST HOLY

AND BLESSED

FATHER

OUR LORD CLEMENT

THE SEVENTH:

HIS HUMBLE SERVANT

NICCOLÒ MACHIAVELLI

AFTER I was commissioned by your Holiness, Most Blessed and Holy Father, when your fortune was lower,[1] that I might write about the things done by the Florentine people, I used all the diligence and art lent to me by nature and experience to satisfy you. And since I have come now, in my writing, to those times which, through the death of the Magnificent Lorenzo de' Medici,[2] brought a change of form in Italy, and because the things that followed afterwards were higher and greater and are to be described in a higher and greater spirit, I judged it would be well to reduce to one volume all that I had described up to those times and to present it to Your Most Holy Blessedness, so that you may begin to taste in some part the fruits of your seeds and of my labors.

So in reading this, Your Holy Blessedness will see first, after the Roman Empire began to lose its power[3] in the West, with how many disasters and how many princes over many centuries Italy overturned its states.[4] You will see how the pontiff, the Venetians, the kingdom of Na-

---

[1] This work was commissioned on November 8, 1520, by Pope Leo X (Giovanni de' Medici) through the intervention of Giulio de' Medici, then a cardinal, who became Pope Clement VII in 1523. Eight books of the *Florentine Histories* (no more were completed) were presented to Clement VII in Rome by Machiavelli in May 1525.

[2] In 1492; see *FH* VIII 36, the last chapter.

[3] NM does not use one word for "power," such as *potere* in modern Italian; rather, he uses two words, *potestà* and *potenza*. In this he follows the Latin usage of Thomas Aquinas and Marsilius, as well as the Italian of Dante. In their writings *potestà* and *potestas* appear to mean a power (sometimes legal) that may be exercised, as opposed to *potenza* and *potentia* for power that must be exercised. In this translation the less frequent *potestà* will be footnoted.

[4] *Stato* means both status and state, as today, but the meanings are more closely con-

3

ples, and the duchy of Milan took the first ranks and commands in the land;[5] you will see how your fatherland, which had removed itself because of its division from submission to the emperors, remained divided until the time when it began to govern itself under the shelter of Your House.[6] And because I was particularly charged and commanded by Your Holy Blessedness that I write about the things done by your ancestors in such a mode that it might be seen I was far from all flattery (for just as you like to hear true praise of men, so does feigned praise presented for the sake of favor[7] displease you), I very much fear that in describing the goodness of Giovanni, the wisdom of Cosimo, the humanity of Piero, and the magnificence and prudence of Lorenzo,[8] it may appear to Your Holiness that I have transgressed your commands. For this I excuse myself to you and to anyone to whom such descriptions are displeasing as hardly faithful, because, when I found that the records of those who described them at various times were full of praise for them, I was obliged either to describe them as I found them, or out of envy to be silent about them. And if under those remarkable deeds of theirs was hidden an ambition contrary to the common utility, as some say, I who do not know it am not bound to write about it; for in all my narrations I have never wished to conceal an indecent deed with a decent cause, or to obscure a praiseworthy deed as if it were done for a contrary end.

But how far I am from flattery may be known from all parts of my history, and especially in speeches and in private reasonings, direct as well as indirect, which with their judgments and their order preserve the proper humor of the person speaking without any reservation. I shun hateful words in all places as of little need to the dignity and truthfulness of the history. Thus no one who correctly considers my writings can reproach me as a flatterer, especially when they see how I have not said very much in memory of the father of Your Holiness,[9] the cause of this being his short life, during which he could not have made himself known; nor could I have rendered him illustrious by writing. Nonetheless, his deeds

---

nected. *Stato* is the status of a person or group while dominating someone else (in this case, the states of Italy dominating Italians). Although NM sometimes speaks of "the state," he always means someone's state and does not refer to an impersonal state. See Harvey C. Mansfield, Jr., "On the Impersonality of the Modern State: A Comment on Machiavelli's Use of *Stato*."

5 Lit.: province.

6 The Medici House; see *FH* IV 11, 16.

7 Lit.: grace.

8 On Giovanni de' Medici (1360–1429), see *FH* IV 16; on Cosimo de' Medici (1389–1464), *FH* VII 5; on Piero de' Medici (1416–1469), *FH* VII 5, 10, 23; on Lorenzo de' Medici (1448–1492), *FH* VIII 36.

9 Giuliano de' Medici (1453–1478), killed in the Pazzi conspiracy; see *FH* VIII 6.

were sufficiently great and magnificent for having fathered Your Holiness—a deed which outweighs those of his ancestors by a great deal and which will add more centuries to his fame than his stingy fortune denied him years of life. I have striven, meanwhile, Most Holy and Blessed Father, in this description of mine, while not staining the truth, to satisfy everyone; and perhaps I will not have satisfied anyone; nor would I wonder if this were to be the case, because I judge it impossible without offending many to describe things in their times. Nonetheless, I come happily to the task, hoping that just as I am honored and nourished by the humanity of Your Blessedness, so will I be helped and defended by the armed legions of your most holy judgment; and with the same spirit[10] and confidence with which I have written until now will I pursue my undertaking,[11] so long as life does not leave me and Your Holiness does not abandon me.

[10] *Animo* refers to the "spirit" with which human beings defend themselves, as opposed to the "higher and greater spirit" (*spirito*) they may rise to; see the first paragraph above and P, Let. Ded. *Animo* can also mean "mind" in the sense of "intent," but not in the sense of "intellect"; see the first words of the Preface, below.

[11] *Impresa* will be translated as "undertaking," "enterprise," or "campaign."

PREFACE

MY intent, when I at first decided to write down the things done at home and abroad[1] by the Florentine people, was to begin my narration with the year of the Christian religion 1434, at which time the Medici family, through the merits of Cosimo and his father Giovanni, gained more authority than anyone else in Florence; for I thought that Messer Leonardo d'Arezzo and Messer Poggio, two very excellent historians, had told everything in detail that had happened from that time backwards.[2] But when I had read their writings diligently so as to see with what orders and modes they proceeded in writing, so that by imitating them our history might be better approved by readers, I found that in the descriptions of the wars waged by the Florentines with foreign princes and peoples they had been very diligent, but as regards civil discords and internal enmities, and the effects arising from them, they were altogether silent about the one and so brief about the other as to be of no use to readers or pleasure to anyone. I believe they did this either because these actions seemed to them so feeble that they judged them unworthy of being committed to memory by written word, or because they feared that they might offend the descendants of those they might have to slander in their narrations. These two causes (may it be said by their leave) appear to me altogether unworthy of great men, for if nothing else delights or instructs in history, it is that which is described in detail; if no other lesson is useful to the citizens who govern republics, it is that which shows the causes of the hatreds and divisions in the city, so that when they have become wise through the dangers of others, they may be able to maintain themselves united. And if every example of a republic is moving, those which one reads concerning one's own are much more so and much more useful; and if in any other republic there were ever notable divisions, those of Florence are most notable. For most other republics about which we have any information have been content with one division by which, depending on accidents, they have sometimes expanded and sometimes ruined their city; but Florence, not content with one, made many. In Rome, as everyone knows, after the kings were driven out, disunion between the

[1] Lit.: inside and outside.
[2] Leonardo Bruni of Arezzo (1374–1444) and Poggio Bracciolini (1380–1454), authors of histories of Florence; see the introduction.

nobles and the plebs arose and Rome was maintained by it until its ruin.[3]
So it was in Athens, and so in all the other republics flourishing in those
times. But in Florence the nobles were, first, divided among themselves;
then the nobles and the people; and in the end the people and the plebs:
and it happened many times that the winning party was divided in two.
From such divisions came as many dead, as many exiles, and as many
families destroyed as ever occurred in any city in memory. And truly, in
my judgment no other instance appears to me to show so well the power
of our city as the one derived from these divisions, which would have had
the force to annihilate any great and very powerful city. Nonetheless
ours, it appeared, became ever greater from them; so great was the virtue
of those citizens and the power of their genius and their spirit to make
themselves and their fatherland great that as many as remained free from
so many evils were more able by their virtue to exalt it, than could the
malice of those accidents that had diminished it overwhelm it. And there
is no doubt that had Florence enjoyed such prosperity after it had freed
itself from the Empire as to have obtained a form of government to maintain it united, I know no republic either modern or ancient that would
have been its superior, so full of virtue, of arms, and of industry would it
have been. For one sees that after it had driven out the Ghibellines in such
numbers that Tuscany and Lombardy were filled with them, the Guelfs,
together with those who remained inside, drew off 1,200 men of arms
and 12,000 infantry from the city's own citizens in the war against
Arezzo, a year before the battle of Campaldino.[4] Afterwards in the war
waged against Filippo Visconti, duke of Milan, when the Florentines had
to make trial of their industry rather than rely on their own arms (for
these had been exhausted at the time), one may see that in the five years
the war lasted,[5] they spent 3,500,000 florins. When it was over, they were
not content with peace, and to show further the power of their city, they
went into the field at Lucca.[6]

I do not know, therefore, what cause would make these divisions unworthy of being described in detail. And if those very noble writers were
restrained so as not to offend the memories of those whom they had to
reason about, they were deceived and showed they knew little about the
ambition of men and the desire they have to perpetuate the name of their
ancestors as well as their own: nor did they remember that many who
have not had the opportunity to acquire fame through some praiseworthy
deed have contrived to acquire it with despicable things. Nor did they

---

[3] See *D* I 4–6.

[4] A victory of the Guelfs in Florence over the Ghibellines in Arezzo, June 11, 1289.

[5] 1423–1428; see *FH* IV 15.

[6] 1430–1438.

7

consider that actions that have greatness in themselves, as do those of governments and states, however they are treated or whatever end they may have, always appear to bring men more honor than blame. When I had considered these things, they made me change my plan, and I decided to begin my history from the beginning of our city. And because it is not my intention to take the place of others, I will describe in detail until 1434 only things happening inside the city, and of those outside I will tell only what is necessary to a knowledge of the things inside. After having passed 1434, I will write in detail about both. Furthermore, in order that this history may be better understood in all times, before I deal with Florence I will describe by what means Italy came to be under those powers that governed it in that time. All of these things, Italian as well as Florentine, will take up four books. The first will narrate briefly all the unforeseen events[7] in Italy following upon the decline of the Roman Empire up to 1434. The second will carry the narration from the beginning of the city of Florence to the war which, after the expulsion of the duke of Athens, was waged against the pontiff.[8] The third will end in 1414 with the death of King Ladislas of Naples; and with the fourth we will come to 1434,[9] from which time onward the things that happened inside Florence and outside, until our present times, will be described in detail.

[7] Lit.: accidents. *Accidenti* will be translated as "accidents" or as "unforeseen events."

[8] The duke of Athens was expelled from Florence in 1343, and the war of the Otto Santi took place in 1375. It is described not in Book II but in *FH* III 7.

[9] The date of the return of Cosimo de' Medici to Florence.

BOOK I

I

THE peoples who live in northern parts beyond the Rhine and the Danube rivers, having been born in a productive and healthful region, often increase to such a multitude that it becomes necessary for a part of them to abandon their fathers' lands and to seek new countries to inhabit. The order they follow, when one of those provinces wishes to unburden itself of inhabitants, is to divide into three parts and assign each person a place so that each part may be equally supplied with nobles and base, with rich and poor; then the part to which the lot falls goes to seek its fortune, and the two parts, unburdened of the third, remain to enjoy their fathers' goods. These are the populations that destroyed the Roman Empire; the opportunity was given to them by the emperors when they abandoned Rome, the ancient seat of the Empire, and retired to live in Constantinople. The emperors had weakened the western part of the Empire because they watched over it less and left it more exposed to pillage by their ministers and their enemies. And truly, for the ruin of such an empire founded on the blood of so many virtuous men, there could not have been less indolence in princes nor less infidelity in ministers, nor less force nor less obstinacy in those who attacked it; for not one but many populations conspired in its ruin. The first from these northern parts to come against the Empire, after the Cimbri, who were defeated by the Roman citizen Marius,[1] were the Visigoths—whose name means in their language no otherwise than in ours, Western Goths. After some engagements at the borders of the Empire, they held their seat on the Danube for a long time by permission of the emperors. Then it happened that for various causes and at various periods they attacked the Roman provinces many times but were nonetheless always checked by the power of the emperors. The last who defeated them gloriously was Theodosius:[2] so much so that since they were reduced to obedience to him they did not again choose a king to rule them but, remaining content with the stipend allowed them, lived and fought under his government and his ensigns.

But when death came to Theodosius, and his sons Arcadius and Hon-

---

[1] The Cimbri invaded Italy in 102 B.C. and were defeated by Marius the next year.
[2] In A.D. 382.

9

orius were left heirs of his empire but not of his virtue and fortune, the times changed with the prince. Theodosius had placed three governors over the three parts of the Empire: Rufinus in the East, in the West Stilicho, and Gildo in Africa. All of them, after the death of the prince, thought not of governing their parts but of possessing them as princes. Gildo and Rufinus were crushed right at the beginning; but Stilicho, who knew better how to conceal his intent, sought on the one hand to acquire the trust of the new emperors and on the other to stir up the state so that it would be easier afterwards for him to seize it. And to make the Visigoths enemies of the emperors, he advised the emperors not to give the Visigoths their accustomed subsidy. Furthermore, as it appeared to him that these enemies would not be enough to stir up the Empire, he ordered that the Burgundians, Franks, Vandals, and Alans—likewise northern peoples and already on the move to seek new towns[3]—should attack the Roman provinces. Since the Visigoths were deprived now of their subsidy, they made Alaric their king so as to be in better order to seek revenge for their injury. They attacked the Empire and after many unforeseen events devastated Italy, and seized and sacked Rome.[4] After this victory Alaric died and was succeeded by Ataulf, who took for his wife Placidia, sister of the emperors;[5] and because of this relationship he agreed with them to go to the aid of Gaul and Spain, provinces that had been attacked by the Vandals, Burgundians, Alans, and Franks for the causes given above. From this it followed that the Vandals, who had occupied that part of Spain called Betica,[6] were fought strongly by the Visigoths and, having no recourse, were called by Boniface, who was governing Africa for the Empire, to come and occupy that province. For Boniface, having rebelled himself, feared lest his error be noticed by the emperor. The Vandals took up this enterprise willingly for the causes given and, under their king Genseric, made themselves lords of Africa. In the meantime, Theodosius son of Arcadius succeeded to the Empire;[7] and because he thought little about things in the West, he made these populations think that they could keep the things they had acquired.

2

AND thus the Vandals were lords of Africa, the Alans and the Visigoths of Spain; the Franks and the Burgundians not only took Gaul but also

---

[3] *Terre* will be translated "towns" throughout.
[4] In 410.
[5] Gallia Placidia, sister of Honorius, in 414.
[6] Now called Andalusia.
[7] Theodosius II (408–450).

gave their own names to those parts they had occupied, whence one part is called France and the other Burgundy. Their prosperous successes spurred new populations to the destruction of the Empire; and other peoples called Huns occupied Pannonia, situated on the far shore of the Danube River, a province which having taken its name from the Huns is today called Hungary. The emperor added to these disorders, as he saw himself attacked on so many sides; so as to have fewer enemies, he began to make accords, now with the Vandals, now with the Franks, things which increased the authority and the power of the barbarians and diminished those of the Empire. Nor was the island of Britain, which today is called England, secure from much ruin, because the Britons, fearing the peoples who had occupied France and not seeing how the emperor could defend them, called the Angles, peoples of Germany, to their aid. The Angles accepted the undertaking under Vortigern their king; first they defended the Britons and then expelled them from their island, remaining to live there themselves, and they called it Anglia after their name. But the [former] inhabitants, dispossessed of their fatherland, became ferocious through necessity and thought that although they had not been able to defend their own country they might seize one belonging to others. Thus they crossed the sea with their families and seized those places which they found nearest the shore and called that country Brittany after their name.

3

THE Huns, who as we said above had occupied Pannonia, mingled together with other peoples termed[1] Gepidae, Heruli, Thuringi, and Ostrogoths (for so the Eastern Goths are called in their language) and set out to seek new countries; and since they could not enter France, which was defended by barbarian forces, they came to Italy under Attila their king. A short time before, he had killed his brother Bleda so as to be alone in the kingdom.[2] Since he became very powerful through this thing, Andaric, king of the Gepidae, and Gelimer, king of the Ostrogoths, were left his subjects. When Attila had come thus to Italy, he besieged Aquileia, where he stayed for two years without hindrance; and during the siege he laid waste all the surrounding countryside and dispersed all its inhabitants. This, as we shall tell in its place,[3] gave the city of Venice its beginning. After the capture and ruin of Aquileia and of many other cities, he turned toward Rome, but refrained from ruining it because of the

---

[1] *Detto* will be translated "termed" or "dubbed," as distinguished from *nominato*, "named," and *chiamato*, "called."

[2] See *D* 1 9, 18, for another instance of killing one's brother in order to "be alone."

[3] *FH* 1 29.

prayers of the pontiff,[4] reverence for whom had such power over Attila that he left Italy and withdrew to Austria, where he died. After his death, Gelimer, king of the Ostrogoths, and other heads of other nations took up arms against Henry and Euric, Attila's sons: they killed one and forced the other to go with the Huns back across the Danube to return to their fatherland. The Ostrogoths and the Gepidae settled in Pannonia, and the Heruli and Thuringi remained on the other bank of the Danube. Attila having left Italy, Valentinian, the Western emperor, decided to restore it; and to make it more convenient for him to defend it from the barbarians, he abandoned Rome and located his residence in Ravenna.

These adversities, which the Western Empire had suffered, had been the cause that the emperor, living in Constantinople, had many times yielded possession of the Empire to others, as a thing full of dangers and expense. And many times even without his permission the Romans, seeing themselves abandoned, would themselves create an emperor for their own defense; or someone on his own authority would usurp the Empire. So it happened in these times that the Empire was seized by the Roman Maximus after the death of Valentinian,[5] and he forced Valentinian's widow Eudoxia to take him for a husband. Desiring to avenge such an injury, since she was born of imperial blood and could not suffer marriage to a private citizen, she secretly exhorted Genseric, king of the Vandals and lord of Africa, to come to Italy, pointing out to him the ease and usefulness of acquiring it. He, enticed by the booty, came quickly and, finding Rome abandoned, sacked it and stayed for fourteen days. He also seized and sacked still more towns in Italy; then with himself and his army stuffed with booty, he returned to Africa. The Romans returned to Rome and, Maximus having died, created the Roman Avitus Emperor. Then, after many things took place inside Italy and outside, and after the deaths of more emperors, the Empire of Constantinople came to Zeno and the Roman Empire to Orestes and his son Augustulus, who seized it by deceit. While they were planning to hold it by force, the Heruli and Thuringi, who I said had been settled after the death of Attila on the other bank of the Danube, leagued together and under Odovacar, their captain, came into Italy; and into the places left vacant by them came the Longobards, likewise northern peoples, led by their king Godogo; and they were, as we shall say in its place,[6] the last plague in Italy. Thus Odovacar came into Italy, conquered and killed Orestes near Pavia, and Augustulus fled. After this victory, so that Rome might change its title with the

---

[4] Leo I (440–461).

[5] In 455.

[6] *FH* 1 8.

change of power, Odovacar dropped the name of empire and had himself called king of Rome. And of all the heads of the peoples that were overrunning the world at that time, he was the first to settle down to live in Italy; for the others, either from fear of being unable to hold it because it could be helped easily by the Eastern emperor or for some other hidden cause, had despoiled it and afterwards sought other countries in which to establish their seats.

4

IN these times, therefore, the ancient Roman Empire was brought under these princes: Zeno, reigning in Constantinople, commanded the whole Eastern Empire; the Ostrogoths were lords of Moesia and Pannonia; the Visigoths, the Suevi, and the Alans held Gascony and Spain; the Vandals, Africa; the Franks and the Burgundians, France; the Heruli and the Thuringi, Italy. The kingdom of the Ostrogoths had come to Theodoric, nephew of Gelimer, who kept up a friendship with Zeno, the Eastern emperor, and wrote to him that it appeared to his Ostrogoths an unjust thing that they who were superior in virtue to all other peoples should be inferior in empire, and that it would be impossible for him to be able to restrain them within the confines of Pannonia. And so, seeing how it was necessary for him to allow them to take up arms and to go to seek new towns, he wished to let Zeno know first so that he might be able to provide for them by ceding to them some country where, by his good grace, they could live more decently and more comfortably. So Zeno, partly from fear and partly from his desire to expel Odovacar from Italy, allowed Theodoric to attack Odovacar and take possession of Italy. Theodoric quickly departed from Pannonia, where he left behind his friends, the Gepidae peoples; and coming into Italy, he killed Odovacar and his son and, following the example of Odovacar, took the title of king of Italy. He established his seat in Ravenna, moved by the same causes that had already made Emperor Valentinian live there.

Theodoric was in war and peace a most excellent man, for in the one he was always the victor, in the other he benefited greatly his cities and peoples. He distributed the Ostrogoths throughout the towns with their own heads so that he might command them in war and correct them in peace; he enlarged Ravenna, restored Rome, and, except for military training, allowed the Romans every other honor. He contained within their borders all the barbarian kings living in the Empire without the tumult of war, but by his authority alone; he built towns and fortresses from the head of the Adriatic Sea to the Alps in order to impede more easily the passage of new barbarians who might wish to attack Italy. And if so many virtues had not been sullied at the end of his life by some cruelties[1] caused by various suspicions about his kingdom—as the deaths of Symmachus and Boethius, most holy men, demonstrate—his memory would be in every way worthy of any honor whatever from every side, because through his virtue and goodness not only Rome and Italy but all the other parts of the Western Empire, free of the continual battering they had suffered for so many years from so many barbarian inundations, recovered and settled down into good order and a very prosperous state.

5

AND truly, if ever times were miserable in Italy and in the provinces overrun by the barbarians, they were those from Arcadius and Honorius until Theodoric.[1] For if one considers how much harm is caused to a republic or a kingdom by a change of prince or government, and not through any extrinsic force but solely through civil discords (where one sees how a few changes ruin every republic and every kingdom, even the most powerful), it can easily be imagined how much Italy and the other Roman provinces suffered in those times; for not only did the government and princes vary, but the laws, the customs, the mode of life, the religion, the language, the dress, the names. Each one of these things by itself, to say nothing of all of them together, would terrify every firm and steady spirit thinking about them, to say nothing of seeing and enduring them. From this arose the ruin, the birth, and the expansion of many cities: Among those that were ruined were Aquileia, Luni, Chiusi, Popolonia, Fiesole, and many others; among the new cities built were Venice, Siena, Ferrara, l'Aquila, and many other towns and fortified places[2] omitted for brevity; those which became great from small were Florence, Genoa, Pisa, Milan, Naples, and Bologna. To all of these must be added the destruction and remaking of Rome and many that were varyingly unmade and remade. From among these ruins and new peoples sprang new languages, as appears in the speech used now in France, Spain, and Italy: the native language of the new peoples mixed with the ancient Roman to make a new order of speech. Moreover, not only have the names of provinces changed, but the names of lakes, rivers, seas, and men: for France, Italy, and Spain are filled with new names altogether foreign to the ancient. Thus one

---

[1] Cf. *P* 8, 17, on the relationship between virtue and cruelty.

[1] From A.D. 395 to 493.

[2] *Castella* (*castello*) will be translated "fortified place," "fortified town," or occasionally "castle."

sees, leaving aside many others, that the Po, Garda, the Archipelago[3] do not conform to the old names; men too, once Caesars and Pompeys, have become Peters, Johns, and Matthews.

But among so many changes, change of religion was not of lesser moment, because in the struggle between the custom of the ancient faith and the miracles of the new, the gravest tumults and discords were generated among men. If indeed the Christian religion had been united, fewer disorders would have followed; but the struggles among the Greek Church, the Roman Church, and the Church at Ravenna—and even more, the struggle between the heretical and the catholic sects—afflicted the world in many modes. Witness to this is Africa, which suffered more anguish on account of the Arian sect believed in by the Vandals than through their avarice or natural cruelty. Living thus, among so many persecutions, men bore the terror of their spirit written in their eyes, because, aside from the infinite evils they endured, for a good part of them the possibility of seeking refuge in God, in whom all the miserable are wont to hope, was lacking. Therefore, as the greater part of them were uncertain as to which God they ought to turn to, they died miserably, deprived of all help and all hope.

6

THEODORIC, therefore, merited no small praise for having been the first one to still so many evils. In consequence, during the thirty-eight years he reigned in Italy,[1] he brought it to such greatness that the former afflictions[2] were no longer known there. But when he died, the kingdom was left to Athalaric, born of his daughter Amalasuntha, and in a little while, fortune being not yet played out, Italy returned to its former anxieties. For Athalaric died shortly after his grandfather, and the kingdom was left to his mother; she was betrayed by Theodatus, whom she had called upon to help her govern it. But when he had killed her and made himself king—for which he became hated by the Ostrogoths—he inspired in Emperor Justinian the belief that he could drive Theodatus out of Italy. As captain of this undertaking the emperor appointed Belisarius, who had already conquered Africa, driven out the Vandals, and brought it back into the Empire. Belisarius then took Sicily; from there he passed into Italy and seized Naples and Rome. The Goths, having seen this dis-

---

[3] The Tuscan Archipelago.

[1] In fact, thirty-three years: 493–526.

[2] Lit.: battering; see *FH* I 4, end.

aster, killed their king Theodatus as the cause of it, and in his place they elected Witigis, who, after some engagements, was besieged and taken in Ravenna by Belisarius. Before his victory was complete, however, Belisarius was recalled by Justinian, who replaced him with Giovanni and Vitales. They were altogether unlike him in virtue and customs, so that the Goths recovered their spirits and created Hildibad, then governor of Verona, their king.

After Hildibad—for he was killed—the kingdom came to Totila. He crushed the emperor's men, then recovered Tuscany and Naples and drove back their captains almost to the last of all the states that Belisarius had recovered. Because of this, it appeared to Justinian that he should send Belisarius back into Italy. But as Belisarius returned with scanty forces, he lost the reputation for the things he had done there first instead of acquiring any more; for when Belisarius was with his men at Ostia, Totila snatched Rome away right before his eyes. And seeing that he could neither let it go nor hold it, Totila destroyed the greater part, drove out the people, and led the senators out with them. Then, as he deemed Belisarius of little account, he led his army away to Calabria to engage the men who were coming from Greece in aid of Belisarius. Meanwhile, Belisarius, seeing that Rome had been abandoned, turned to an honorable enterprise: for he entered Rome, now in ruins, and, as quickly as he could, rebuilt the walls of the city and summoned its inhabitants back in. But fortune was opposed to this praiseworthy enterprise, for Justinian was attacked just then by the Parthians and recalled Belisarius; and he, so as to obey his lord, abandoned Italy, leaving that province to the discretion of Totila, who again took Rome. But Rome was not treated with the same cruelty as before because, at the prayer of Saint Benedict, who at that time had a very great reputation for holiness, Totila turned to rebuilding it instead. Justinian, meanwhile, had made an accord with the Parthians, and just as he was thinking that he might send new men to the aid of Italy, he was prevented by the Slavs, new northern peoples who had crossed the Danube and attacked Illyria and Thrace; so Totila occupied nearly the whole of Italy. But when Justinian had conquered the Slavs, he sent the eunuch Narses into Italy with armies. A most excellent man in war, Narses arrived in Italy, crushed and killed Totila; and the remnants of the Goths left after that defeat withdrew to Pavia, where they created Teias their king. Narses for his part took Rome after the victory and in the end came to battle with Teias near Nocera, and killed and crushed him. By this victory the name of the Goths was altogether eliminated from Italy, where they had ruled for seventy years[3] from their king Theodoric through Teias.

[3] In fact, sixty years: 493–553.

7

BUT hardly was Italy freed from the Goths when Justinian died and left as his successor his son Justin.[1] Acting on the advice of his wife Sophia, he recalled Narses from Italy and sent Longinus as his successor. Longinus followed the order of the others by living in Ravenna, but aside from this he gave Italy a new form; for he did not appoint provincial governors as had the Goths, but in all the cities and towns of any importance he made heads whom he called dukes. Nor in this distribution did he do more honor to Rome than to other towns, for he abolished the consuls and the senate, names which had been maintained there until that time, put Rome under one duke who was sent there every year from Ravenna, and called it the duchy of Rome. To the one who stayed in Ravenna on behalf of the emperor to govern all Italy, he gave the name exarch. This division made easier the ruin of Italy and gave opportunity more quickly to the Longobards to occupy it.

8

NARSES was highly indignant at the emperor for having taken from him the government of that province, which he had acquired by his own virtue and his own blood, for Sophia, not satisfied with injuring him by having him recalled, had to add words full of insult, saying that she wanted him back to spin with the other eunuchs. So, overflowing with indignation, Narses persuaded Alboin, king of the Longobards, then reigning in Pannonia, to come and occupy Italy. The Longobards, as was shown above,[1] had moved into those places near the Danube that had been abandoned by the Heruli and Thuringi when they had been led into Italy by their king Odovacar. The Longobards stayed there for some time until Alboin, a savage and bold man, acceded to their kingdom, and they crossed the Danube, came to battle with Kunimund, king of the Gepidae, who held Pannonia, and defeated him. Finding Rosamund, the daughter of Kunimund, among the spoils, Alboin took her for his wife and made himself lord of Pannonia. Moved by his savage nature, he made a cup of Kunimund's skull, from which he used to drink in memory of that victory. But when he was called into Italy by Narses, with whom he had been friends during the Gothic war, he left Pannonia to the Huns, who, as we said,[2] had returned to their fatherland after the death of Attila and

[1] Justin II (565–578).
[1] FH I 3.
[2] FH I 3.

had come from there into Italy. When he found Italy divided into so many parts, he in one stroke occupied Pavia, Milan, Verona, Vicenza, all Tuscany, and the larger part of Flaminia today called Romagna. Because he had acquired so much so quickly, it appeared to him that victory over Italy was already his, and he celebrated with a feast in Verona. And when he had drunk much he became merry; as Kunimund's skull was filled with wine, he had it offered to Queen Rosamund, who was eating across from him, and in a loud voice so that she could hear he said that amidst such merriment he wanted her to drink with her father. That speech was like a stab in the breast of the woman, and she decided to get revenge. Knowing that Helmechis, a noble Lombard, young and fierce, loved her maidservant, Rosamund arranged with her that she would secretly see to it that Helmechis sleep with the queen in her place. Helmechis, coming according to plan[3] to find her in the dark, and believing himself to be with the maidservant, lay with Rosamund. After the fact, she revealed herself to him and showed him that it was now his choice either to kill Alboin and ever after enjoy her and the kingdom or to be killed by him as the violator of his wife. Helmechis agreed to kill Alboin. But after they had killed him they saw that they would not succeed in seizing the kingdom; and indeed, not doubting that they would be killed by the Longobards for the love the Longobards bore to Alboin, they fled with the royal treasure to Ravenna and to Longinus, who received them honorably. During these travails Emperor Justin died, and in his place was put Tiberius, who was engaged in a war with the Parthians and was unable to assist Italy. Therefore, to Longinus the time seemed opportune for him, through Rosamond and her treasure, to become king of the Longobards and of all Italy; he discussed his design with her and persuaded her to kill Helmechis and take himself for a husband. Having accepted the plan, she ordered a goblet of poisoned wine, which she gave from her own hand to Helmechis, thirsty as he was leaving the bath. He had drunk half of it when he felt his insides turn over, and realizing what it was, he forced Rosamund to drink the rest; and so in a few hours, both of them died, and Longinus was deprived of the hope of becoming king.

The Longobards meanwhile gathered in Pavia, which they had made the chief seat of their kingdom, and appointed Cleph to be their king. He rebuilt Imola, which had been destroyed by Narses, and occupied nearly every place from Rimini as far as Rome, but in the course of his victories he died. This Cleph was so cruel, not only to outsiders but even to his own Longobards, that, frightened by royal power,[4] they desired to have kings no longer. Instead, they appointed thirty dukes from among them-

---

[3] Lit.: her order.
[4] *Potestà*.

selves to govern the rest. This council was the cause that the Longobards never occupied all of Italy, that their rule was never to extend beyond Benevento, and that Rome, Ravenna, Cremona, Mantua, Padua, Monselice, Parma, Bologna, Faenza, Forlì, Cesena might at times have to defend themselves but would never be occupied by them. For not having a king made them less ready for war; and after they reinstated one, they became, since they had been free for a time, less submissive and more inclined toward discords among themselves: it was this which at first delayed their victory and finally drove them out of Italy. As the Longobards stayed within these limits, the Romans and Longinus made an accord with them that everyone should lay down his arms and enjoy what he possessed.

9

IN these times the pontiffs began to come into greater authority than they had ever had before. For the first ones after Saint Peter had been revered by men for the holiness of their lives and for the miracles, and their examples so extended the Christian religion that princes had necessarily to submit to it so as to dispel the great confusion abroad in the world. Thus, since the emperor had become Christian, left Rome, and gone off to Constantinople, it followed, as we said at the beginning,[1] that the Roman Empire fell more quickly into ruin and the Roman Church grew more quickly. Still, as the whole of Italy was subject to either emperors or kings until the arrival of the Longobards, the pontiffs never obtained during those times any other authority than reverence for their customs and their learning gave them; in other things they submitted to either the emperors or the kings, and sometimes were killed by them and sometimes used by them as ministers in their actions. But the one who made the pontiffs become of greater moment in the affairs of Italy was Theodoric, king of the Goths, when he established his seat in Ravenna. Since Rome was left without a prince, the Romans for their own safety had cause to give greater obedience to the pope. Nonetheless, their [his] authority did not increase much by this, except that it did gain for the church of Rome a place ahead of the one in Ravenna. But when the Lombards[2] came and divided Italy into more parts, they gave the pope cause to be more active. Because he was now almost the head of Rome, the emperor of Constantinople and the Lombards respected him, so that the Romans, through the pope, joined not as subjects but as partners with the Longobards and

[1] *FH* I I.
[2] The Longobards; NM uses both names in this chapter and the next; see *FH* I I I.

Longinus. And thus as the popes continued to be friends now of the Lombards, now of the Greeks, they added to their dignity.

But then, after the ruin of the Eastern Empire (which took place in these times under Emperor Heraclius[3] because the Slavic peoples, of whom we made mention above,[4] attacked Illyria again; and when they had occupied it, they called it Slavonia after their name; and the other parts of that empire were attacked first by the Persians, then by the Saracens, who came out of Arabia under Mohammed, and finally by the Turks, who took Syria, Africa, and Egypt from it), there no longer remained to the pope, because of the impotence of the Empire, any opportunity to find refuge in it in his own oppressions.[5] And on the other side, as the forces of the Longobards were growing, he decided he needed to seek new support, and he had recourse to those kings in France. So henceforward, all the wars waged by the barbarians in Italy were for the most part caused by the pontiffs, and all the barbarians who invaded it were most often called in by them. This mode of proceeding continues still in our times; it is this that has kept and keeps Italy disunited and infirm.[6] Therefore, in describing what has happened from those times until our own, no more will be shown about the ruin of the Empire, which is all in dust, but rather the expansion of the pontiffs and of the other principalities that governed Italy afterwards until the arrival of Charles VIII will be shown. And you will see how the popes—first through censures, then by censures and arms together, mixed with indulgences—were terrible and awesome; and how, for having used them both badly, they have lost the one altogether and as regards the other remain at the discretion of others.

10

BUT returning now to our order, I am going to tell how the papacy had come to Gregory III and the kingdom of the Longobards to Aistulf, who, contrary to agreements that had been made, seized Ravenna and began war on the pope. Consequently, Gregory, for the causes described above,[1] having no longer any confidence in the emperor of Constantinople because he was weak, nor wishing to trust in the faith of the Lombards because they had so many times broken it, had recourse in France to Pepin II. From having been a lord in Austrasia and Brabant, he had become

[3] 610–641.
[4] FH I 6.
[5] Probably refuge from those oppressing him, but the ambiguity is in NM's text.
[6] See D I 12.
[1] FH I 9.

king of France, not so much through his own virtue as through that of Charles Martel, his father, and Pepin, his grandfather. For it was Charles Martel, when he was governor of that kingdom, who gave that memorable defeat to the Saracens near Tours on the river Loire, where more than two hundred thousand of them were slain,[2] after which his son Pepin became king of that kingdom through the reputation and virtue of his father. It was to him, as was said, that Pope Gregory sent for help against the Longobards. Pepin promised to send it to him, but first desired to see him and to honor him in person.

Therefore Gregory went to France, passing through the towns of the Lombards, his enemies, without being hindered by them: such was the reverence they had for religion. When he had gone thus into France, Gregory was honored by that king and sent back into Italy with his armies, which then besieged the Longobards in Pavia. Thus was Aistulf constrained by necessity to come to an accord with the French, who made the accord at the urging[3] of the pope, who did not want the death of his enemy but rather that he be converted and live. Under this accord Aistulf promised to give back to the Church all the towns he had occupied. But when Pepin's troops had returned to France, Aistulf did not observe the accord, and the pope again had recourse to Pepin. Again he sent his armies into Italy, conquered the Longobards, and took Ravenna; and contrary to the will of the Greek emperor, he gave Ravenna to the pope with all the other towns that were under his exarchate, and added to them the territory of Urbino and the Marches.[4] But while consigning these towns, Aistulf died, and Desiderius, a Lombard who was duke of Tuscany, took up arms so as to seize the kingdom.[5] He asked the pope for help while promising his friendship, and the pope granted it to him so that other princes also granted it. Desiderius kept his faith in the beginning and continued to consign towns to the pontiff in accordance with the treaties made by Pepin. Nor did any other exarch come from Constantinople to Ravenna, which was now governed instead according to the will of the pontiff.

I I

AFTER Pepin died, his son Charles succeeded to the kingdom—he who, because of the greatness of the things he did, was named "the Great."

---

[2] At Poitiers in 732.
[3] Or prayer.
[4] In 756.
[5] The kingdom of the Longobards.

Meanwhile the successor to the papacy was Theodore I.[1] He came into conflict with Desiderius and was besieged by him in Rome; so the pope sought help from Charles, who crossed the Alps, besieged Desiderius in Pavia, captured him and his sons, and sent them to prison in France. Then he went to visit the pope in Rome, where he judged that the pope as Vicar of God could not be judged by men; and the pope and the Roman people made him emperor.[2] And thus Rome began again to have an emperor in the West; and whereas the pope used to be confirmed by the emperors, the emperor began in his election to have need of the pope. As the Empire was coming to lose its privileges, the Church acquired them, and by these means it kept increasing its authority over the temporal princes. The Longobards had been in Italy for two hundred and thirty-two years,[3] and by now they retained nothing of the foreigner other than the name, and since Charles wanted to reorder Italy—it was now in the time of Pope Leo III— he was content that they live in the places where they had been raised and that the province be called Lombardy after their name. And that they might have reverence for the Roman name, he desired that all that part of Italy next to them which had been under the exarchate of Ravenna be called Romagna. Besides this, he created his son Pepin king of Italy. His jurisdiction extended as far as Benevento, and all the rest was possessed by the Greek emperor with whom Charles had made an accord.

In these times Paschal I came to the pontificate; and, because the priests of the churches of Rome were nearer to the pope and were present at his election, so as to crown their power[4] with a splendid title they began to call themselves cardinals. They claimed so much reputation for themselves, especially after they excluded the Roman people from electing the pontiff, that only rarely was the election of one from outside their number; thus when Paschal died, Eugene II, a titular of St. Sabina, was created.[5] And Italy, after falling into the hands of the French, changed partly in form and order, because the pope had obtained more authority in temporal things and the French had introduced the names of counts and marquesses, just as previously the names of the dukes had been put there by Longinus, exarch of Ravenna. After some other popes the papacy came to Osporco, a Roman, who because of the ugliness of his name had him-

---

[1] Not Theodore but Paul I (757–767). Adrian I (772–795) was the pope who called in Charlemagne in 772.

[2] NM appears to confound the earlier visit of Charlemagne to Rome in 772, after his defeat of Desiderius, with his coronation by Leo III in Rome in 800.

[3] Since 568.

[4] *Potestà*.

[5] The parish of St. Sabina in Rome.

self called Sergius, which began the changing of names that the pontiffs practice upon their election.[6]

I 2

MEANWHILE, Emperor Charles had died and was succeeded by his son Louis. After Louis's death so many differences arose among his sons that in the time of his grandsons the Empire was taken away from the house of France and brought to Germany; the first German emperor was called Arnulf. Not only did the family of the Charleses lose the Empire because of its discords, but it lost the kingdom of Italy as well, for the Lombards regathered their forces and attacked[1] the pope and the Romans; and it was thus that the pontiff, not seeing with whom he might seek refuge, out of necessity created Berengar, duke of Friuli, king of Italy. These unforeseen events inspired the Huns, who were in Pannonia, to attack Italy; and when they came to grips with Berengar, they were forced to return to Pannonia, or Hungary, which is what their province was named by them.

In these times the emperor in Greece was Romanus, who as prefect of his armed force had taken the empire from Constantine. And because Puglia and Calabria had rebelled at such a change—for they had submitted to Constantine's empire, as we said above[2]—Romanus was outraged by such rebellion and allowed the Saracens to pass through these places; they came, and having taken those provinces, tried to storm Rome. But the Romans, since Berengar was busy defending himself from the Huns, made Alberic, duke of Tuscany, their captain and through his virtue saved Rome from the Saracens. Having left that siege, the Saracens built a fortress on Mount Gargano and from there made themselves lords of Puglia and Calabria while fighting the rest of Italy. And so in these times Italy came to be marvelously afflicted, embattled from the direction of the Alps by the Huns and from that of Naples by the Saracens.

Italy suffered in these travails for many years under three Berengars who succeeded one another.[3] During this time the pope and the Church were disturbed every hour and had nowhere to turn because of the disunity among the Western princes and the impotence of the Eastern ones. The city of Genoa and all its coasts were destroyed in these times by the Saracens, whence arose the greatness of the city of Pisa, in which many peoples, driven from their fatherlands, took refuge. These things hap-

[6] In fact, the usage began with Octavian (955–963), who called himself John XII.
[1] Lit.: offended.
[2] *FH* I 8.
[3] Two, not three: Berengar I (888–924) and Berengar II (950–963).

pened in the year of the Christian religion 931. But when Otto, duke of
Saxony, son of Henry and Matilda, a prudent man of great reputation,
became emperor, Pope Agapetus set to urging him to come to Italy to
pull it out from under the tyranny of the Berengars.

13

THE states of Italy in these times were ordered in this way: Lombardy
was under Berengar III and his son Albert; Tuscany and Romagna were
governed by a minister of the Western emperor; Puglia and Calabria
obeyed partly the Greek emperor and partly the Saracens; in Rome every
year two consuls were created from among the nobility, who according
to the ancient custom governed it, and in addition there was a prefect who
dispensed justice[1] to the people; and they had a council of twelve men
who every year assigned rectors to the towns put under them. The pope
had more or less authority in Rome and in all Italy according to whether
he had the favor of the emperors or of those who were more powerful
there. Emperor Otto came, then, to Italy and took the kingdom from the
Berengars, who had reigned there for fifty-five years,[2] and restored to the
pontificate its dignities. This emperor had a son and a grandson also
called Otto who succeeded, one after the other, to the Empire. At the
time of Otto III, Pope Gregory V was driven out by the Romans; and so
Otto came into Italy and restored him to Rome; and the pope, so as to
have revenge on the Romans, deprived them of their authority to create
the emperor and gave it to six princes of Germany: three bishops—
Mainz, Treves, and Cologne—and three princes—Brandenburg, Pala-
tine, and Saxony. This took place in 1002. After the death of Otto III, the
electors created Henry, duke of Bavaria, as emperor, and after twelve
years he was crowned by Stephen VIII.[3] Henry and his wife Simeonda[4]
lived a very holy life, as is seen by the many churches furnished and built
by them, among which was the Church of San Miniato, near the city of
Florence. Henry died in 1024 and was succeeded by Conrad of Swabia
and then he by Henry II. This last came to Rome, and because there was
a schism in the Church of three popes, he deposed them all and brought
about the election of Clement II, by whom he was crowned emperor.

[1] Lit.: reason.
[2] Otto came into Italy three times, in 951, 961, and 966; Berengar I became king of Italy
in 888 and emperor in 915.
[3] In fact, by Benedict VIII in 1014.
[4] In fact, Kunigunda (Gunnhild).

14

ITALY was then governed partly by peoples, partly by princes, and partly by those sent by the emperor, of whom the greatest, to whom the others deferred, was called Cancellarius. Among the princes the most powerful were Godfrey and his wife, the Countess Matilda, daughter of Beatrice, the sister of Henry II. She and her husband held Lucca, Parma, Reggio, and Mantua, with all of what today is called the Patrimony.[1]

At that time the ambition of the Roman people was much at war with the pontiffs. That people had at first used their authority to free themselves from the emperors; but then, when the pontiffs had taken dominion over the city and reformed it according to their views, that people immediately became an enemy of the pontiffs, and the latter received many more injuries from that people than from any other Christian prince. And in times when the popes with their censures made the whole West tremble, they had the Roman people in rebellion, and neither one of them had any other intention than to take away reputation and authority from the other. Then Nicholas II came to the pontificate, and just as Gregory V had deprived the Romans of the power to create the emperor, so did Nicholas deprive them of participation in the creation of the pope, and he willed that that election belong only to the cardinals.[2] Nor was he content with this: since, having made a convention with the princes who governed Calabria and Puglia, for causes that will soon be told, he forced all the officials sent by the Romans throughout their jurisdiction to render obedience to the pope, and some of them he deprived of their offices.

15

AFTER the death of Nicholas, there was a schism in the Church because the clergy of Lombardy were not willing to render obedience to Alexander II, elected in Rome, and they created Cadalus of Parma antipope. Henry, who regarded the power of the pontiffs with hatred, gave Pope Alexander to understand that he should renounce the pontificate, and the cardinals to understand that they should go to Germany to create a new pontiff.[1] And thus was he the first prince who began to feel of what importance spiritual wounds might be, because the pope held a council at

---

[1] The patrimony of St. Peter around Rome, south of Tuscany, from Radicofani to Ceperano.

[2] In the Lateran Council of 1059.

[1] Henry IV called the Diet of Worms in 1076 to depose Gregory VII, not Alexander II.

Rome and deprived Henry of the Empire and the kingdom. Some Italian peoples followed the pope and some followed Henry; this was the seed of the Guelf and Ghibelline humors, for the sake of which Italy, when it lacked barbarian invasions, was torn apart by internal wars. Thus, when Henry was excommunicated, he was compelled by his people to come to Rome and to kneel barefooted before the pope to ask forgiveness. This happened in the year 1080.[2] Nonetheless, a new discord arose shortly thereafter between the pope and Henry; so the pope excommunicated him again; and the emperor sent his own son, also called Henry, with an army into Rome and, with the help of the Romans who held the pope in hatred, besieged him in his fortress. Then Robert Guiscard came from Puglia to rescue him, and Henry did not wait for him but returned to Germany. Only the Romans stood firm in their obstinacy, so that Rome was again sacked by Robert and returned to the ancient ruins from which it had been restored before by many pontiffs. And because the ordering of the kingdom of Naples came from this Robert, it does not seem superfluous to me to speak in detail about his actions and his origin.

16

WHEN disunion arose among the heirs of Charlemagne, as we showed above,[1] opportunity was given to new northern peoples called Normans to come and attack France; and they occupied that country which today is termed Normandy after them. Some part of these peoples came from there into Italy in the times when that province was infested by the Berengars, by the Saracens, and by the Huns, and they occupied some towns in Romagna, where during those wars they virtuously maintained themselves. To Tancred, one of those Norman princes, were born many sons, among whom were William, named Ferebac,[2] and Robert, dubbed Guiscard. The principality had come to William, and the tumults in Italy had ceased to some degree; nonetheless, the Saracens held Sicily, and every day they would raid the shores of Italy. Because of this, William agreed with the princes of Capua and Salerno and with Maniaces, the Greek who governed Puglia and Calabria on behalf of the Greek emperor, to attack Sicily; and should victory follow, they agreed that each of them would receive a quarter share of the spoils and the state. The enterprise was successful: the Saracens were driven out, and they occupied Sicily. After this

[2] Actually, in 1077.
[1] FH I 12.
[2] Bras de Fer.

victory Maniaces secretly had men come from Greece, took possession of the island for the emperor, and divided only the booty. William was malcontent with this but waited for a more convenient time to show it, and he left Sicily together with the princes of Salerno and Capua. As soon as these princes left him to return to their homes, William did not return to Romagna but turned about with his men toward Puglia and quickly occupied Melfi, and thus in a short time against the forces of the Greek emperor made himself lord of almost the whole of Puglia and Calabria, the provinces of which Robert Guiscard, his brother, was lord at the time of Nicholas II. And because he had had many differences with his nephews over the inheritance of those states, he used the authority of the pope to settle them. This was a favor executed willingly by the pope, as he was desirous of gaining over Robert so that Robert might defend him against the German emperors and against the insolence of the Roman people with the effect, as we showed above,[3] that at the instance of Gregory VII, Robert drove Henry from Rome and subdued the people there. Robert was succeeded by his sons Roger and William, to whose state was added Naples and all the towns between Naples and Rome, and afterwards Sicily, over which Roger made himself lord. But then William, while on his way to Constantinople so as to take the daughter of the emperor for his wife, was attacked by Roger, who took his state from him. And Roger, made proud by this acquisition, at first had himself called king of Italy; but later, content with the title of king of Puglia and Sicily, he was the first to give a name and order to that kingdom which still today is maintained within its ancient limits in spite of the many changes that have taken place there not only in bloodline but in nation. For when the Norman stock diminished, the kingdom was changed into a German one, from that into French, from that into Aragonese, and today it is held by the Flemings.

17

URBAN II, who was hated in Rome, had come to the pontificate. And as it appeared to him that because of the disunities in Italy he could not be secure, he turned to a generous enterprise, went away to France with all the clergy, and in Auvergne gathered up many peoples to whom he made a speech against the infidels.[1] This speech so inflamed their spirits that they decided to make a campaign[2] in Asia against the Saracens. This cam-

---

[3] *FH* I 15.

[1] Urban II's speech was at Clermont in 1095.

[2] Or enterprise; NM uses the same word, *impresa*, for each crusade and for all of them together.

paign along with all the others like it were later called the Crusades because all those who went on them had their arms and clothing marked with a red cross. The princes of this enterprise were Godfrey, Eustace, and Baldwin of Bouillon, counts of Boulogne, and one Peter the Hermit, celebrated for his holiness and prudence. Many kings and many peoples participated in it with money, and many private individuals fought without any pay—so great a power did religion have then on the spirits of men, moved by the example of those who were the heads of it. This enterprise was glorious in the beginning because all Asia Minor, Syria, and a part of Egypt came under the power[3] of the Christians; and through it the Order of the Knights of Jerusalem was born, which still rules today[4] and holds the island of Rhodes, the single remaining obstacle to the power of the Mohammedans. Also born of it was the Order of the Templars, which shortly after disappeared on account of their bad customs. There followed at various times various unforeseen events in which many nations and particular men were celebrated. The king of France and the king of England came to the aid of the enterprise, and the Pisan, the Venetian, and the Genoese peoples acquired very great reputation there; they fought with varying fortune until the times of the Saracen Saladin.[5] His virtue and the discords of the Christians in the end took from them all the glory they had acquired in the beginning, and after ninety years the Christians were driven out of the place they had successfully recovered with such honor.[6]

18

AFTER the death of Urban, Paschal II was created pontiff and Henry IV succeeded to the Empire. Henry came to Rome pretending friendship with the pope; later he sent the pope and all the clergy to prison, not ever to be freed unless he was first given permission to be able to dispose of the churches in Germany as he saw fit. In these times the Countess Matilda died and left the Church heir to her whole state.[1]

After the deaths of Paschal and Henry IV, there followed more popes and emperors until finally the papacy came to Alexander III and the Em-

---

[3] *Potestà*. The "power" of the Mohammedans in the next clause is *potenzia*.

[4] Rhodes fell to the Turks in 1522, while NM was writing the *Florentine Histories*. For what might be made of this fact for the dating of NM's work, see Dionisotti, "Machiavelli Storico," and Gilbert, *Machiavelli and Guicciardini*.

[5] Saladin ruled from 1173 to 1193.

[6] Jerusalem, taken by the Crusaders in 1099 and lost to Saladin in 1187.

[1] Matilda of Tuscany (1046–1115).

pire to Frederick the Swabian, dubbed Barbarossa. The pontiffs in those times had had many difficulties with both the Roman people and the emperors; these increased greatly in the time of Barbarossa. Frederick was an excellent man in war but full of such pride that he could not bear to have to yield to the pontiff; nonetheless, upon his election he came to Rome to be crowned and peacefully returned to Germany. But he remained in this state of mind briefly, for he returned to Italy so as to subdue some towns in Lombardy that were not obeying him, and it happened at this time that the cardinal of San Clemente,[2] of Roman birth, separated himself from Pope Alexander and was made pope by some cardinals. As Emperor Frederick was in the field at Crema at the time, Alexander came to him to complain about the antipope; and Frederick answered that they should both come to visit him and that he would then judge which of them was to be pope. This answer did not please Alexander; and because he saw that Frederick was inclined to favor the antipope, he excommunicated him and fled to Philip, king of France. Meanwhile, Frederick, carrying on the war in Lombardy, took and destroyed Milan, which caused Verona, Padua, and Vicenza to unite against him for common defense. In the meantime, the antipope had died; so Frederick created Guido da Cremona[3] in his place. The Romans during these times, because of the absence of the pope and because of the hindrances the emperor was meeting in Lombardy, had retaken a certain amount of authority in Rome, and they went about reclaiming obedience from those towns which used to be subject to them. As the Tusculans were unwilling to yield to their authority, they went after them with their people, who were given help by Frederick; and they cut down the Roman army with such massacre that Rome was never afterward either populous or rich. Meanwhile, Pope Alexander had returned to Rome, as it appeared to him that he could be safe there because of the hostility the Romans had for Frederick and the enemies he had in Lombardy. But Frederick, setting aside every hesitation, went into the field in Rome, where Alexander did not wait for him but fled to William, king of Puglia, who had been left heir to that kingdom after the death of Roger.[4] But as Frederick was driven away by the plague, he let go the siege and returned to Germany; and the towns of Lombardy, which had taken a common oath against him, so as to be able to fight Pavia and Tortona, which the imperial parties held, built a city that would be the seat of that war and named it Alessandria in honor of Pope Alexander and in scorn of Frederick. Then Guido the anti-

[2] The antipope Victor IV (1159–1164), opposed to Pope Alexander III (1159–1181).
[3] In fact, Guido da Crema, who became the antipope Paschal III (1164–1168).
[4] William II (1166–1189) succeeded William I, not Roger II.

pope died, and in his place was put Giovanni da Fermo,[5] who stayed in Montefiasconi through the favors of the parties of the emperor.

19

POPE Alexander, in the midst of this, had gone to Tusculum, called there by that people so that he with his authority might defend it from the Romans. There spokesmen sent by Henry, king of England, came to him to inform him that in regard to the death of the blessed Thomas, archbishop of Canterbury, their king was not at all at fault, although indeed he had been publicly defamed for it. At this, Pope Alexander sent two cardinals to England to find out the truth of the matter; and although they did not find the king manifestly guilty, nonetheless, because of the infamy of the sin and because he had not honored the pope as he deserved, they required of him as penance that all the barons of the kingdom must be called together and that by an oath he must beg forgiveness in their presence. Furthermore, he must send immediately two hundred soldiers to Jerusalem, paid for one year; he himself would be obliged to go there personally, with as large an army as he could muster, before three years had passed; he must annul all the things done in his reign that were unfavorable to ecclesiastical freedom; and he must agree that anyone of his subjects could, if he wished, appeal to Rome. All these things were accepted by Henry: thus did such a king submit to a judgment to which today a private man would be ashamed to submit. Nonetheless, while the pope had so much authority among princes far away, he could not make himself obeyed by the Romans, whom he could not entreat to let him stay in Rome even though he promised he would not busy himself with anything but ecclesiastical things: thus are appearances[1] feared more when they are far away than when nearby.

Frederick had returned to Italy at this time, and, while he was preparing to start a new war against the pope, all his prelates and barons gave him to understand that they would abandon him unless he became reconciled with the Church; so he was constrained to go and do honor to the pope in Venice, where together they made their peace. In the accord the pope deprived the emperor of all authority he might have over Rome and named William, king of Sicily and Puglia, to be his ally. And Frederick, who could not bear not making war, joined the enterprise in Asia in order to vent against Mohammed the ambition that he had not been able to vent

---

[5] Giovanni da Struma, who took the name Callistus III (1168–1178).

[1] Lit.: things that appear.

against the vicars of Christ; but having arrived at the river [Cidnus],[2] he
was lured by the clarity of its waters into washing himself in them, from
which disorder he died. And thus were the waters more favorable to the
Mohammedans than were excommunications to the Christians, for
whereas the excommunications only checked his pride, the waters
quenched it.

20

WHEN Frederick died, the pope had only to subdue the insubordination
of the Romans; and after many disputes over the creation of the consuls,
they agreed that the Romans would, according to their custom, elect
them but that the consuls could not take office without first swearing to
maintain faith with the Church. This accord made John, the antipope,
flee to Mount Albano, where after a short time he died. In these times
William, king of Naples, died, and the pope schemed to seize that kingdom because the king had left no sons other than Tancred, his natural
son. The barons did not yield to the pope in this but rather wanted Tancred to be king. The pope at that time was Celestine III,[1] and as he desired
to take the kingdom out of the hands of Tancred, he arranged that Henry,
son of Frederick, be made emperor and promised him the kingdom of
Naples with the proviso that he restore to the Church the towns that
belonged to it. And to make the thing easier, he took Constance, the
daughter of William and already old, out of a monastery and gave her to
him as wife. And thus did the kingdom of Naples pass from the Normans, who had been its founders, to the Germans. As soon as the affairs
of Germany were settled, Emperor Henry came to Italy with his wife
Constance and his four-year-old son called Frederick and seized the
Kingdom[2] without much difficulty because Tancred had already died,
leaving a young son dubbed Roger.[3] Henry died in Sicily after some time,
and he was succeeded in the Kingdom by Frederick and in the Empire by
Otto, duke of Saxony, made emperor through the favors that Pope Innocent III did for him. But as soon as the crown was gained, Otto became, contrary to every expectation, an enemy of the pope, occupied
Romagna, and was ordering an assault on the Kingdom; for this the pope

[2] Now called Saleph. The name is lacking in all the manuscripts and in the Giunta edition;
it is supplied only in the Blado edition.
[1] At the time of William II's death, the pope was Clement III (1187–1191), not Celestine
III (1191–1198).
[2] NM, as was customary, refers to the kingdom of Naples simply as "the Kingdom."
[3] Not Roger but William.

excommunicated him so that he was abandoned by everyone, and the electors elected Frederick king of Naples. Frederick came to Rome for the crown, but the pope was unwilling to crown him because he feared his power and so sought to draw him out of Italy as he had Otto. Frederick was so outraged that he went off to Germany, where he made war again on Otto and defeated him. In the meantime, Innocent died. Besides his remarkable works, he built the hospital of Santo Spirito in Rome. He was succeeded by Honorius III, during whose time the orders of Saint Dominic and Saint Francis emerged in 1218. This pontiff crowned Frederick; and John, a descendant of Baldwin, king of Jerusalem,[4] who was with remnants of the Christians in Asia and still bore the title, gave him one of his daughters as wife and included in the dowry the title of that kingdom: from here it began that any king of Naples is titled the king of Jerusalem.

21

IN Italy at that time they lived in this mode: the Romans no longer made consuls, but in their place they made with the same authority sometimes one and sometimes more senators. The league that the cities of Lombardy had made against Frederick Barbarossa still lasted—the cities being Milan, Brescia, Mantua, and the greater part of the cities of Romagna, as well as Verona, Vicenza, Padua, and Treviso; in the party of the emperor were Cremona, Bergamo, Parma, Reggio, Modena, and Trento; the other cities and fortified towns of Lombardy, Romagna, and the Trevisan March favored sometimes one party and sometimes the other, according to necessity. There had come to Italy at the time of Otto III one Ezzelino, to whom, while he remained in Italy, a son was born who fathered another Ezzelino. This last, being rich and powerful, attached himself to Frederick II, who, as has been said,[1] had become an enemy of the pope; and as he came into Italy, through the deeds and favor of Ezzelino, Frederick took Verona and Mantua, destroyed Vicenza, seized Padua, and defeated the army of the allied towns; and after this he came toward Tuscany. Ezzelino, meanwhile, had subjugated the whole Trevisan March; he was not able to take Ferrara because it was defended by Azzo d'Este and by men the pope had in Lombardy. Thus, when the siege was lifted, the pope gave the city in fief to Azzo d'Este, from whom were descended those who are its lords still today. Frederick stopped at Pisa, desirous of making himself lord of Tuscany; and by acknowledging the friends and

---

[4] John was not descended from Baldwin.
[1] *FH* I 20.

enemies of that province, he sowed such discord as caused the ruin of all Italy. For the Guelf and Ghibelline parties multiplied, those who followed the Church being called Guelfs and those who followed the emperors, Ghibellines; and in Pistoia this name was heard for the first time. By the time Frederick left Pisa, he had attacked and laid waste the towns of the Church in so many ways[2] that the pope, having no other remedy, proclaimed a crusade against him, as his predecessors had done against the Saracens. And Frederick, lest he be abandoned by his own men at a stroke, as Frederick Barbarossa and his other ancestors had been, hired many Saracens; and to oblige them to him and to make a firm bulwark against the Church in Italy that would not fear papal maledictions, he gave them Nocera[3] in the Kingdom so that, having a refuge of their own, they could serve him with greater security.

22

INNOCENT IV had come to the pontificate. Fearing Frederick, he went to Genoa and from there to France, where he ordered a council at Lyons, which Frederick decided to attend. But he was prevented by the rebellion of Parma; and having been repulsed in that enterprise, he went to Tuscany and from there to Sicily, where he died. He left his son, Conrad, in Swabia, and in Puglia he left Manfred, born of a concubine, whom he had made duke of Benevento. Conrad came to take possession of the Kingdom, but when he arrived in Naples he died, leaving of himself Conradin, a small boy, who was in Germany. Therefore Manfred seized that state, first as the tutor of Conradin; then, spreading the rumor[1] that Conradin was dead, he made himself king against the wishes of the pope and the Neapolitans, whom he made to consent by force. While these things were troubling the Kingdom, in Lombardy many movements were stirring within the Guelf and Ghibelline parties. On the Guelf side was a legate of the pope; on the Ghibelline side, Ezzelino, who had possession of nearly the whole of Lombardy on the other side of the Po. And because during the course of the war Padua rebelled against him, he had twelve thousand Paduans killed; and he himself died before the war was ended, when he was at the age of eighty years. After his death all the towns he had held became free.

Manfred, king of Naples, was pursuing his enmities against the Church

[2] Lit.: modes.
[3] Actually, Lucera.
[1] Lit.: name.

as his forefathers had done, and he kept the pope, who was called Urban IV, in constant anxieties; so the pontiff, in order to subdue him, proclaimed a crusade against him, and he went to wait for his men in Perugia. And as it appeared to him that when his men came they might be few, weak, and late, he decided that to defeat Manfred would require surer help; and he turned to France for favor and created Charles of Anjou, brother of King Louis of France, the king of Sicily and Naples, and pressed him to come to Italy to take over that kingdom. But before Charles could come to Rome, the pope died, and Clement IV was put in his place. In his time[2] Charles came to Ostia with thirty galleys and arranged that his other men come by land. During his stay in Rome the Romans made him senator in order to ingratiate themselves with him, and the pope invested him with the Kingdom with the obligation that he pay fifty thousand florins a year to the Church, and he also made a decree that in the future neither Charles nor anyone else who might hold that kingdom could be emperor. And when Charles went up against Manfred, he crushed and killed him near Benevento and made himself lord of Sicily and the Kingdom. But Conradin, to whom this state belonged by the testament of his father, gathered many men in Germany and came into Italy against Charles, with whom he fought at Tagliacozzo; and Conradin was first defeated and then, as he fled unrecognized, was taken and killed.

23

ITALY remained quiet until Adrian V succeeded to the pontificate. And since Charles was in Rome, governing it through the office he held as senator, the pope could not endure his power, and he went to live in Viterbo and entreated Emperor Rudolf to come into Italy against Charles. Thus the pontiffs, now for the sake of religion, now for their own ambition, never ceased calling new men into Italy and inciting new wars; and after they had made one prince powerful, they repented it and sought his ruin. Nor would they allow any province that they out of weakness were unable to possess to be possessed by others. And the princes feared them because, whether fighting or fleeing, they always won, unless they had been oppressed with some deceit, as were Boniface VIII and some others, who under color of friendship were captured by the emperors. Rudolf did not come into Italy, as he was restrained by the war he was waging with the king of Bohemia. In the meantime, Adrian died and Nicholas III, of the house of Orsini, was made pontiff—a bold and ambitious man

[2] 1264–1268.

who pondered every mode of diminishing Charles's power. He arranged[1] that Emperor Rudolf complain that Charles kept a governor in Tuscany favorable to the Guelf party, which he had restored in that province after the death of Manfred. Charles yielded to the emperor and withdrew his governors, and the pope sent one of his nephews there, a cardinal, as governor of the Empire; as a result, the emperor, for the honor done him, restored Romagna to the Church, which had been taken from it by his predecessors, and the pope made Bertoldo Orsini duke of Romagna. And as it seemed to him that he had become powerful and that he could show his face openly to Charles, Nicholas deprived him of the office of senator and decreed that no one of royal blood could ever be a senator in Rome. He had it in mind also to snatch Sicily from Charles, and to this end he secretly set in motion a plan with Peter, king of Aragon, which was effected later in the time of his successor. He was scheming further to make two kings from his own house, one in Lombardy and the other in Tuscany, whose power would defend the Church from Germans who might want to come into Italy and from the French who were in the Kingdom. But he died with these thoughts. He was the first of the popes to show his own ambition openly and to scheme, under the guise of making the Church great, to honor and benefit his own. And as until this time no mention was ever made of nephews and relatives of any pontiff, so henceforward the history will be full of them, so that we shall come to mention even sons: nor is there anything left for the pontiffs to try unless it be that while up to our times they have schemed to leave their sons as princes, so for the future they may plan to leave them a hereditary papacy. It is certainly true that until now the principalities ordered by them have had short lives because most times the pontiffs, by living a short time, either do not provide for planting their plants or, if they do plant them, leave them with roots so few and weak that they wither at the first wind, when the virtue that sustains them is gone.[2]

24

TO Nicholas III succeeded Martin IV, who being of French birth favored Charles's party; in his favor, Charles sent his men to Romagna to help him when Romagna rebelled against him. Guido Bonato, an astrologer,[1] was in the field at Forlì, and he ordered that at a time given by him the

[1] Lit.: ordered.
[2] See NM's discussion of Cesare Borgia and Pope Alexander VI in *P* 7, 11.
[1] Mentioned by Dante in *Inferno*, xx 118.

people should attack them; so all the French were taken and killed. At this time the plan made by Pope Nicholas with Peter, king of Aragon, was put into effect, by which the Sicilians killed all the French they found on the island;[2] and Peter made himself lord of the island, saying that it belonged to him through his wife Constance, the daughter of Manfred. But Charles died while reordering a war to recover the island, and he was survived by Charles II, who had been a prisoner in Sicily in the former war. And in order to win his freedom he promised that he would return as a prisoner if within three years he had not got the pope to invest the royal family of Aragon with the kingdom of Sicily.

25

EMPEROR Rudolf, instead of coming to Italy to restore the reputation of the Empire there, sent one of his spokesmen with authority to be able to set free all those cities that would pay ransom. Hence many cities did pay it, and with liberty they changed their mode of living. Adolf of Saxony succeeded to the Empire, and Peter Murrone to the pontificate. He was named Pope Celestine, and since he was a hermit and full of holiness, he renounced the pontificate after six months; and Boniface VIII was elected. The heavens (who knew that there must come a time when the French and the Germans would move out of Italy and that that province would then remain altogether in the hands of the Italians), so that the pope, when free of ultramontane hindrances, would be able neither to consolidate nor to enjoy his power, made two very powerful families rise in Rome, the Colonna and the Orsini, so that with their power and proximity they would keep the pontificate weak. Whence Pope Boniface, who understood this, decided he would eliminate the Colonna; and besides having them excommunicated, he proclaimed a crusade against them. If this offended them much, it offended the Church even more; for arms which had been used virtuously for the love of the faith, when used for his own ambition against Christians, began not to cut. Thus did too great a desire to vent their appetites cause the pontiffs little by little to disarm themselves. Furthermore, Boniface deprived two members of that family who were cardinals of their cardinalates. And Sciarra, head of that house, while fleeing from him, was taken unrecognized by Catalan pirates and put to the oar; but afterwards he was recognized in Marseilles and sent to King Philip of France, who had been excommunicated by Boniface and deprived of the kingdom. As Philip considered that in a war waged

---

[2] See *FH* I 23. These were the Sicilian Vespers of 1282.

against pontiffs one either ended a loser or ran into many dangers, he turned to trickery; and pretending that he wished to come to an accord with the pope, he sent Sciarra to Italy secretly. Sciarra arrived in Anagni, where the pope was, and having gathered his friends together at night, captured him; and although the pope was set free by the people of Anagni soon after, nonetheless, because of his grief at that injury, he died insane.

26

IT was Boniface who ordered the jubilee in 1300 and who provided that it be celebrated every hundred years. In these times there were many travails between the Guelf and Ghibelline parties; and because Italy had been abandoned by the emperors, many towns became free and many were seized by tyrants. Pope Benedict restored their hats to the Colonna cardinals[1] and restored Philip, king of France, to communion with the Church. He was succeeded by Clement V, who, as he was French, moved the court to France in the year 1305.[2] Meanwhile, Charles II, king of Naples, died and was succeeded by his son Robert. Henry of Luxembourg had attained to the Empire, and he came to Rome to be crowned, notwithstanding that the pope was not there. His coming was followed by many movements in Lombardy because he sent all the exiles, whether Guelf or Ghibelline, back to their towns, from which it followed that by their driving one another out, that province was filled with war; nor, for all his exertion, could the emperor prevent it. He left Lombardy and came to Pisa by way of Genoa. There he strove to take Tuscany away from King Robert; and, as he was getting no profit by it, he left for Rome, where he stayed a few days because he was driven out by the Orsini with the approval of King Robert. He returned to Pisa, and so as to make war against Tuscany more securely and to take it from the government of King Robert, he had it attacked by King Frederick of Sicily. But while he was hoping at once to seize Tuscany and take King Robert's state from him, he died. Ludwig of Bavaria succeeded him to the Empire. Meanwhile, John XXII attained to the papacy, and in his time the emperor never ceased persecuting the Guelfs and the Church, which were for the most part defended by King Robert and the Florentines. From this arose many wars waged in Lombardy by the Visconti against the Guelfs, and in Tuscany by Castruccio of Lucca against the Florentines. But because the Visconti family was the one that gave a beginning to the duchy of

---

[1] In fact, Jacopo and Pietro Colonna did not get their hats back.
[2] Actually, in 1309.

Milan, one of the five principalities that later governed Italy, it seems proper for me to recount their condition from an earlier time.[3]

27

AFTER the league in Lombardy of those cities that we made mention above[1] came about for the purpose of defense against Frederick Barbarossa, Milan, having recovered from its ruin and to get revenge for the injuries it had received, joined it. The league did restrain Barbarossa and kept alive the parties of the Church in Lombardy for a time, and, in the travails of the wars that then followed, the della Torre family became very powerful in that city. From then on, its reputation kept growing, while the emperors had little authority in that province. But when Frederick II came into Italy and the Ghibelline party became powerful through the work of Ezzelino, Ghibelline humors rose in every city; and in Milan, among those who took the Ghibelline side was the Visconti family, which had driven the della Torre out of Milan. But they stayed out only a short while because, through accords made between the emperor and the pope, they were restored to their fatherland. But when the pope went to France with his court and Henry of Luxembourg came into Italy so as to go to Rome for his crown, he was received in Milan by Matteo Visconti and Guido della Torre, who were then the heads of their families. But Matteo was scheming to make use of the emperor to expel Guido; and, judging that the enterprise would be easy because Guido belonged to the faction opposed to the Empire, he took advantage of the grievances of the people over the sinister behavior of the Germans. Cautiously he went about encouraging everyone and persuading them to take up arms and slough off their slavery to these barbarians. And when it appeared to him that he had arranged the matter to his purpose, he had someone in his confidence start a tumult over which all the people took up arms against the German name. The scandal had hardly begun when Matteo with his sons and all his partisans were in arms; and they were running to Henry to tell him how the tumult was started by the della Torre, who were not content to live privately in Milan and had taken the opportunity of attempting to despoil it in order to ingratiate themselves with the Guelfs in Italy and to become princes of that city. But they said that he should be of good spirit because they, on their side, if he should want to defend himself, were ready to save him by any mode. Henry believed everything Matteo said

---

[3] Lit.: from a loftier place. NM's discussion of Castruccio begins in *FH* II 26.
[1] See *FH* I 18.

to be true, and he joined his forces with those of the Visconti and they attacked the della Torre, who had run into many parts of the city in order to stop the tumults; and those whom they could have, they killed, and the others, stripped of their possessions, they sent into exile. Thus Matteo Visconti was left as a prince in Milan, and after him Galeazzo and Azzo, and after them Luchino and Giovanni. Giovanni became an archbishop in that city; and Luchino, who died before him, left Bernabò and Galeazzo;[2] but since Galeazzo also died shortly after, he left Giovan Galeazzo, dubbed Count of Virtue. After the death of the archbishop, Giovan Galeazzo killed Bernabò, his uncle, by deceit and was left alone as prince of Milan:[3] he was the first to have the title of duke. He left Filippo and Giovan Mariagnolo; and when the latter was killed by the people of Milan, the state was left to Filippo, who left no male children. Thus that state was transferred from the house of Visconti to that of the Sforza in the mode and for the causes that will be told in their place.[4]

28

BUT, returning to where I digressed, Emperor Ludwig came into Italy to give reputation to his party and to take the crown. When he reached Milan, so as to have cause for getting money from the Milanese, he made a show of leaving them free and he put the Visconti in prison; then, through the mediation of Castruccio of Lucca, he set them free. And after he had gone to Rome so that he could stir up Italy more easily, he made Piero della Corvara antipope, with whose reputation, together with the strength of the Visconti, he schemed to keep the opposing parties of Tuscany and Lombardy enfeebled. But Castruccio died, and his death was the cause of the beginning of the emperor's ruin, for Pisa and Lucca rebelled against him, and the Pisans sent the antipope as a prisoner to the pope in France; thus the emperor, despairing of things in Italy, returned to Germany. He had barely left when John, king of Bohemia, came into Italy, called in by the Ghibellines of Brescia, and made himself lord of Brescia and Bergamo. And because his coming was with the consent of the pope, although he pretended the contrary, the legate of Bologna[1] favored him, judging that this might be a good remedy for ensuring that the emperor not return to Italy. By this course, Italy changed its condi-

---

[2] Bernabò and Galeazzo II were sons of Stefano Visconti, brother of Luchino and Giovanni.

[3] See *P* 21 and *D* II 13.

[4] See *FH* VI 24.

[1] The papal legate.

tion, because, when the Florentines and King Robert saw that the legate was favoring the undertakings of the Ghibellines, they became enemies of all those who were friends of the legate and the king of Bohemia; and, without regard to Guelf and Ghibelline parties, many princes united with them, among whom were the Visconti, the della Scala, Filippo Gonzaga of Mantua, the Carrara, and the Este. As a result, the pope excommunicated them all; and the king, out of fear of this league, went back home to gather more forces; then, when he returned to Italy with more men, he realized that the undertaking was nonetheless difficult, so much so that, dismayed, he returned to Bohemia, to the displeasure of the legate. He left only Reggio and Modena defended, and he placed Parma under the protection of Marsilio and Piero de' Rossi, who were very powerful in that city. After he left, Bologna joined the league, and the allies divided among themselves four cities that remained on the side of the Church; they agreed that Parma should go to the della Scala, Reggio to the Gonzaga, Modena to the Este, and Lucca to the Florentines. But in the campaigns for these towns many wars ensued, which were in good part settled afterwards by the Venetians. And to someone it will perhaps appear not a proper thing that we have so long postponed reasoning about the Venetians, since they are a republic that for order and power ought to be celebrated above every other principality in Italy; but to remove the surprise, and to understand the cause of it, I will go further back in time so that everyone may understand what its beginnings were and why the Venetians delayed becoming involved in the affairs of Italy for so long a time.

29

AS Attila, king of the Huns, was besieging Aquileia, its inhabitants, after they had defended themselves for a long time and had become desperate for their safety, fled as best they could with their movable things to the many uninhabited reefs that were at the tip of the Adriatic Sea. The Paduans too, seeing the fire close by and fearing that with Aquileia conquered Attila might come to find them, carried all their movable things of more value to the same sea in a place dubbed Rivo Alto,[1] where they sent their women, children, and old as well; and their youth they kept in Padua to defend it. Besides these, the people of Monselice with the inhabitants of the surrounding hills, urged on by the same terror, went to the reefs in the same sea. But after Attila had taken Aquileia and laid waste Padua,

---

[1] Now Rialto.

Monselice, Vicenza, and Verona, the Paduans and those who were strongest remained to inhabit the swamps around Rivo Alto. At the same time, all the peoples surrounding that province, which in ancient times was called Vinezia, driven out by the same accidents, withdrew to these swamps. Thus constrained by necessity, they left very pleasant and fertile places to live in places that were sterile, deformed, and devoid of every comfort. And because many peoples were brought together at a stroke, in a very short time they made those places not only habitable but delightful; they established laws and orders among themselves, and amidst so much ruin in Italy, they enjoyed security.[2] In a short time they grew in reputation and forces; for in addition to the above-mentioned inhabitants, many from the cities of Lombardy, driven out especially by the cruelty of Cleph, king of the Longobards, took refuge there. This was no small addition to the city; so at the time when Pepin, king of France, came at the urging[3] of the pope to drive the Longobards out of Italy, among the agreements made between him and the emperor of the Greeks was that the duke of Benevento and the Venetians would not obey either one or the other of them but would enjoy their liberty in the middle. Besides all this, as necessity had led them to live in the waters, so it forced them to think of how they could live decently when they had no use of the land; and going in their ships throughout the world, they filled their city with a variety of merchandise. Since other men had need of this, it was advantageous for them to gather frequently at that place. Nor for many years did they think of any other dominion than of what might make the traffic of their merchandise easier. So they acquired many ports in Greece and Syria; and because in their travels to Asia the French used their ships a good deal, the island of Candia was given to them as payment. And while they lived in this form their name became terrible on the seas and venerated within Italy, so that in all the controversies that arose, they were most often the arbiters. Thus it happened that when differences arose among the allies on account of the towns that they had to divide among themselves, the cause was brought before the Venetians, and Bergamo and Brescia were left to the Visconti. But in time, after the Venetians had seized Padua, Vicenza, and Treviso, and later Verona, Bergamo, and Brescia, and many cities in the Kingdom and in Romagna, driven on by their lust for domination, they came to so great an opinion of their power that not only the Italian princes but the kings beyond the Alps were in

---

[2] Cf. D I 1, 6, on the beginnings of Venice.

[3] Lit.: prayer. NM confuses here the Pepin who was the father of Charlemagne with another Pepin, his son, who attacked Venice in 810.

terror of them. Consequently these kings and princes together conspired[4] against them and in one day[5] took from them that state which they had won for themselves in so many years with infinite expense; and even though in our more recent times they have reacquired something, yet since they have reacquired neither their reputation nor their forces, they live, as do all the other Italian princes, at the discretion of others.

30

BENEDICT XII had attained to the pontificate. Because it appeared to him that he had lost possession of Italy altogether and because he feared that Emperor Ludwig might make himself lord of it, he decided to make friends in it of all those who had usurped the towns that used to obey the emperor, so that they would have cause to fear the Empire and draw together with him for the defense of Italy. And he issued a decree that all the tyrants of Lombardy should keep the towns they had usurped with just titles. But with this concession the pope died and was replaced by Clement VI. The emperor, seeing with how much liberality the pontiff had given away towns belonging to the Empire, so as not to be any less liberal with the things of others than the pope had been, gave to all the tyrants in the towns of the Church their own towns, so that they might possess them by imperial authority. Because of this, Galeotto Malatesti and his brothers became lords of Rimini, Pesaro, and Fano; Antonio da Montefeltro, of the Marches and Urbino; Gentile da Varano, of Camerino; Guido da Polenta, of Ravenna; Sinibaldo Ordelaffi, of Forlì and Cesena; Giovanni Manfredi, of Faenza; Ludovico Alidosi, of Imola; and besides these many others in many other towns, so that of all the towns of the Church, few were left without a prince. It was this that kept the Church weak until Alexander VI in our time, by ruining their descendants, returned its authority to it. The emperor was in Trent when he made this concession, and he let it be known[1] that he wanted to come into Italy, whence many wars followed in Lombardy, by which the Visconti made themselves lords of Parma.

At this time, Robert, king of Naples, died, leaving only two granddaughters born of his son Charles, who had died some time earlier; and he bequeathed that the elder, called Giovanna, should be heir to the King-

---

[4] Lit.: swore an oath. Cf. *D* III 11 for another "conspiracy of all Italy" against the Venetians.

[5] Allusion to the battle of Vailà, also known as the battle of Agnadello (1509). See *P* 12, 20, 26; *D* I 6, 53, II 10, III 31. Also NM's *Decennale*, II 175–193; *Asino d'Oro*, V 49–56.

[1] Lit.: gave out the name.

dom and that Andrew, his nephew and son of the king of Hungary, should take her for his wife. Andrew did not remain with her for long, as she had him killed and married another cousin, called Ludovico, prince of Taranto. But Ludwig, king of Hungary and brother of Andrew, came into Italy with his men in order to avenge his brother's death, and he drove Queen Giovanna and her husband from the Kingdom.

3 1

AT this time a memorable thing happened in Rome: one Niccolò di Lorenzo,[1] chancellor at the Capitol, drove out the Roman senators and made himself, with the title of tribune, head of the Roman Republic, which he restored in its ancient form with such a reputation for justice and virtue that not only the towns nearby but all Italy sent ambassadors to him. So the old provinces, seeing how Rome had been reborn, lifted their heads; and some being moved by fear and some by hope, they honored him. But Niccolò, notwithstanding so much reputation, abandoned himself in his first beginnings: for he turned coward under so great a burden and fled in disguise without being driven out by anyone; and he went to meet Charles, king of Bohemia, who had been elected emperor by order of the pope in contempt of Ludwig of Bavaria. To ingratiate himself with the pontiff, Charles sent Niccolò to him as a prisoner. Then it happened later, after some time, that in imitation of Niccolò, one Francesco Baroncegli seized the tribunate of Rome and drove out the senators. In consequence, the pope, as the quickest remedy to repress him, took Niccolò out of prison, sent him to Rome, and gave him the office of tribune. So Niccolò retook his state and had Francesco killed. But since the Colonna had become his enemies, he too was killed not long after and the office restored to the senators.

3 2

IN the meantime, the king of Hungary, having driven out Queen Giovanna, returned to his own kingdom. But the pope, who desired to have the queen near Rome rather than that king, worked it out that he was content to restore the Kingdom to her provided that her husband, Ludovico, content with his title of Taranto, not be called king. The year 1350 had come, so it appeared to the pope that the jubilee ordered by Pope

[1] Better known as Cola di Rienzo.

Boniface VIII for every hundred years could be reduced to fifty years. When he accomplished this by decree, the Romans, because of this benefit, were content to have him send four cardinals to Rome to reform the state of the city and to appoint senators of his own choice. The pope again proclaimed Ludovico of Taranto king of Naples; and for this benefit Queen Giovanna gave the Church Avignon, which was part of her patrimony. Luchino Visconti died in these times, and as a result, Giovanni, archbishop of Milan, was left alone as lord. He waged many wars on Tuscany and its neighbors, by which he became very powerful. When he died, he was survived by his nephews, Bernabò and Galeazzo; but shortly after, Galeazzo died and left Giovan Galeazzo, who shared that state with Bernabò.[1] In these times Charles, king of Bohemia, was emperor, and Innocent VI was pontiff. The latter sent into Italy Egidio, a cardinal of Spanish birth, who by his virtue restored the reputation of the Church not only in Romagna and in Rome but throughout Italy; he recovered Bologna, which had been seized by the archbishop of Milan; he forced the Romans to accept a foreign senator to be sent there each year by the pope; he made honorable accords with the Visconti; he crushed and captured the Englishman John Hawkwood, who with four thousand Englishmen fought in aid of the Ghibellines in Tuscany.[2] Thus, when Urban V succeeded to the pontificate and learned of these victories, he decided to visit Italy and Rome, where Emperor Charles also came; and after a few months Charles went back to his kingdom and the pope to Avignon. After the death of Urban, Gregory XI was created; and because Cardinal Egidio had also died, Italy returned to its former discords caused by the peoples leagued together against the Visconti. So the pope first sent a legate to Italy with six thousand Bretons; then he came in person and moved the court back to Rome in 1376,[3] after the seventy-first year that it had been in France. But after his death he was replaced by Urban VI, and shortly afterwards, at Fondi, Clement VII was created by ten cardinals who said Urban had not been elected properly.

In these times, the Genoese, who had lived for many years under the government of the Visconti, rebelled. And between the Venetians and them, many very important wars arose over the island of Tenedos, on account of which all Italy became divided. During this war artillery was seen for the first time, a new instrument invented by the Germans. And although the Genoese were for a time on top and kept Venice besieged for many months, nonetheless at the end of the war the Venetians won

[1] Cf. *FH* I 27 (end).
[2] Egidio Albornoz neither defeated Hawkwood nor took him prisoner.
[3] By our dating, 1377.

out. Through the mediation of the pontiff, peace was made in the year 1381.

33

THERE had arisen, as we have said,[1] a schism in the Church, in which Queen Giovanna favored the schismatic pope. For this, Urban had a campaign made against her into the Kingdom by Charles of Durazzo, a descendant of the kings of Naples. When he came, he took her state from her and made himself lord of the Kingdom, and she fled to France. The king of France, angered by this, sent Louis of Anjou to Italy to recover the Kingdom for the queen, to drive Urban out of Rome, and to make the antipope lord of it. But in the middle of this undertaking Louis died, and his men, having been defeated, returned to France. Meanwhile, the pope went to Naples, where he put nine cardinals in prison for having followed the party of France and the antipope. Then he became angry with the king[2] for refusing to make one of his nephews prince of Capua; and, pretending not to care about it, he asked the king to grant him Nocera as a place to live. There he made himself strong and prepared to deprive the king of the Kingdom. For this, the king came to battle with him, and the pope fled to Genoa, where he had the cardinals whom he had imprisoned put to death. From there he went to Rome, and to make reputation for himself he created twenty-nine cardinals. At this time Charles, king of Naples, went to Hungary, where he was made king and shortly after was killed. In Naples he left his wife with his children, Ladislas and Giovanna.

At this time also, Giovan Galeazzo Visconti had killed his uncle Bernabò and taken over the whole state of Milan; and since it was not enough for him to have become duke of all Lombardy, he also wanted to seize Tuscany, but just when he believed he was getting dominion over it, after which he would be crowned king of Italy, he died. Urban VI was succeeded by Boniface IX. At the same time, in Avignon, the antipope Clement VII died and was replaced by Benedict XIII.

34

IN these times there were many soldiers in Italy—English, German, and Breton—some led by those princes who at various times had come to

---

[1] *FH* I 32.
[2] Charles of Durazzo.

Italy, and some sent by the pontiffs when they were in Avignon. All the Italian princes made their wars with them for a long time, until there emerged Ludovico da Conio,[1] from the Romagna, who formed a company of Italian soldiers named for Saint George. In a short time its virtue and discipline took away the reputation of foreign arms and returned it to Italian arms, which the princes of Italy used afterwards in the wars they fought together. The pope, because of his discord with the Romans, went to Assisi, where he stayed so long that the jubilee of 1400 came, at which time the Romans, that he might return to Rome for the advantage of that city, were content to accept again a foreign senator sent by him, and they let him fortify the Castel Sant'Angelo. With these conditions he returned; and to enrich the Church, he ordered that for vacant benefices anyone might pay a year's income to the Camera. Although when Giovan Galeazzo, duke of Milan, died, he left two sons, Giovan Mariagnolo and Filippo, that state divided into many parts; and in the troubles that followed there, Giovanmaria was killed and Filippo was locked up for a time in the fortress of Pavia, where, because of the trust and virtue of the castellan, he was saved. Among others who seized cities once possessed by their father was Guglielmo della Scala, who, when exiled, found himself in the hands of Francesco da Carrara, lord of Padua, through whom he regained the state of Verona, where his stay was short because, by Francesco's order, he was poisoned and the city taken from him. On account of this, the inhabitants of Vicenza, who had been living safely under the ensigns of the Visconti, became fearful of the greatness of the lord of Padua and gave themselves to the Venetians; and through them the Venetians began a war against him, and from him they took first Verona and then Padua.

35

IN the meantime, Pope Boniface died, and Innocent VII was elected. To him the Roman people petitioned that he give up the fortresses and restore their freedom to them. The pope did not want to agree to this, so the Roman people called Ladislas, king of Naples, to their aid. Afterwards, when an accord had been reached between them, the pope returned to Rome; he had fled to Viterbo out of fear of the people and there made Ludovico, his nephew, count of the Marches. After he died, Gregory XII was created with the obligation to renounce the papacy at any time the antipope might also renounce it. And through the urging of the

[1] Alberigo da Conio; see *P* 12.

cardinals that an attempt be made to see if the Church could be reunited, Benedict, the antipope, came to Porto Venere and Gregory to Lucca, where they discussed many things and concluded none. So the cardinals of both popes abandoned them, and, as for the popes, Benedict went to Spain and Gregory to Rimini. The cardinals, for their part, with the favor of Baldassarre Cossa, cardinal and legate of Bologna, ordered a council in Pisa, where they created Alexander V. He quickly excommunicated King Ladislas and invested Louis of Anjou with the Kingdom. Then, together with the Florentines, Genoese, and Venetians, and with the legate Baldassarre Cossa, they assaulted Ladislas and took Rome from him. But in the heat of this war Alexander died, and Baldassarre Cossa was created pope and had himself called John XXIII. He left Bologna, where he had been created, and went to Rome, where he found Louis of Anjou, who had come with the army of Provence, and in a skirmish with Ladislas, they defeated him. By the fault of the condottieri, however, they were unable to follow up the victory, so that the king in a little while regained his forces and retook Rome; and the pope fled to Bologna, and Louis to Provence. Then the pope, thinking how he might diminish the power of Ladislas, arranged to have Sigismund, king of Hungary, elected emperor and persuaded him to come to Italy and conferred with him in Mantua. They agreed to hold a general council in which the Church would be reunited, for united it could easily oppose the forces of its enemies.

36

THERE were three popes at that time—Gregory, Benedict, and John—who kept the Church weak and without reputation. Constance, a city in Germany, was chosen against the will of Pope John as the site of the council. And although the death of Ladislas had eliminated the cause that made the pope promote the business of the council, nonetheless, since he had obligated himself, he could not refuse to go there. Not many months after, when he was brought to Constance, he recognized his error late and tried to flee, for which he was put in prison and forced to resign the papacy. Gregory, also one of the antipopes, renounced through a messenger of his, and Benedict, the other antipope, who was unwilling to renounce, was condemned as a heretic. In the end, abandoned by his cardinals, he too was forced to renounce, and the Council created Oddo, from the house of Colonna, as pontiff, thereafter called Martin V. Thus the Church was united after forty years in which it had been divided among many pontiffs.

37

AT this time, as we have said,[1] Filippo Visconti was in the fortress of Pavia. But when death came to Facino Cane, who during the travails in Lombardy had become lord of Vercelli, Alessandria, Novara, and Tortona and had accumulated much wealth, he left the inheritance of his states to Beatrice, his wife, as he had no children; and he ordered his friends to arrange that she be married to Filippo. Filippo, having become powerful by this marriage, reacquired Milan and the whole state of Lombardy. Afterwards, so as to be grateful for great benefits in the way that all princes almost always are, he accused his wife Beatrice of adultery and had her put to death. Having therefore become very powerful, he began to think about wars in Tuscany so as to pursue the designs of his father Giovan Galeazzo.

38

WHEN Ladislas, king of Naples, died, he left to his sister Giovanna, aside from the Kingdom, a great army captained by the chief condottieri of Italy, among the first of whom was Sforza of Cotignuola, reputed valorous by these armed men. The queen, so as to escape the infamy of having kept a certain Pandolfello whom she had raised, took for a husband James of La Marche, a Frenchman of royal lineage, with these conditions: that he would be content to be called prince of Taranto and that he would leave to her the title and the government of the Kingdom. But as soon as he arrived in Naples, the soldiers called him king; so great discords arose between husband and wife, each getting the better of the other many times; but in the end, the queen retained her estate. Then she became an enemy of the pontiff, and thus Sforza, so as to bring her into necessity and so that she would have to throw herself into his lap, resigned from her service against her expectation.[1] Because of this, she found herself disarmed at a stroke; and having no other remedies, she turned for assistance to Alfonso, king of Aragon and Sicily, whom she adopted as a son; and she hired Braccio da Montone, who had as high a reputation in arms as did Sforza and was an enemy of the pope because he had seized Perugia from him as well as some other towns of the Church. Then there was peace between her and the pope; but King Alfonso, suspecting that she might deal with him as she had with her husband, sought cautiously to

[1] See *FH* I 34.
[1] See *P* 12; *AW* I.

secure mastery of the fortresses. But she, who was astute, foresaw this and made herself strong in the fortress in Naples. Thus, as they grew more suspicious of each other, they came to arms; and the queen, with the help of Sforza, who had returned to her services, overcame Alfonso, drove him from Naples, deprived him of his adoption, and adopted Louis of Anjou. As a result, war arose again between Braccio, who had taken the side of Alfonso, and Sforza, who favored the queen. In carrying on the war, Sforza was drowned while crossing the Pescara River, so that the queen was again left disarmed; and she would have been driven out of the Kingdom had she not been helped by Filippo Visconti, duke of Milan, who forced Alfonso to turn back to Aragon. But Braccio, undismayed by Alfonso's having abandoned himself, continued his campaign against the queen; and when he besieged l'Aquila, the pope judged that Braccio's greatness did not suit the Church, and he took to its[2] service Francesco, Sforza's son. Francesco went to meet Braccio at l'Aquila, where he killed and crushed him. Among the survivors of Braccio's party was his son Oddo; the pope deprived him of Perugia but left him the state of Montone. But shortly after, he was killed fighting in Romagna for the Florentines, so that of those who fought together with Braccio, Niccolò Piccinino held the highest reputation.

39

BUT because we have come in our narrative nearly to those times that I planned[1]—for what remains to be dealt with is not important for the most part, other than the wars that the Florentines and Venetians had with Filippo, duke of Milan, which will be told of when we deal particularly with Florence[2]—I do not want to proceed further. I will only call to mind briefly in what straits Italy found itself, in regard to both princes and arms, in the times at which we have arrived in our writing. Of the principal states, Queen Giovanna II held the kingdom of Naples; in the Marches, the Patrimony, and Romagna, some of the towns obeyed the Church, and some were held by their vicars or tyrants: as Ferrara, Modena, and Reggio by the Este; Faenza by the Manfredi; Imola by the Alidosi; Forlì by the Ordelaffi: Rimini and Pesaro by the Malatesti; and Camerino by the da Varano. As for Lombardy, part obeyed Duke Filippo and part the Venetians, since all those who used to hold their own partic-

---

[2] Or his.
[1] See *FH*, Preface.
[2] In *FH*, Book IV.

ular states there had been eliminated, except for the house of Gonzaga, which was lord of Mantua. The Florentines were lords of the greater part of Tuscany: only Lucca and Siena lived under their own laws—Lucca was under the Guinigi, Siena was free. The Genoese, who were sometimes free and sometimes slaves either of the kings of France or of the Visconti, lived in dishonor and were numbered among the lesser powers. All these principal powers were not armed with arms of their own. Duke Filippo, shut up in his rooms and not letting himself be seen, directed his wars through commissioners; the Venetians, as they turned to the land, threw aside the arms that had made them glorious on the seas and, following the custom of the other Italians, administered their armies under the government of others. The pope, because arms did not befit him as a man of religion, and Queen Giovanna of Naples, because she was a woman, did from necessity what the others had done by bad choice; the Florentines also obeyed the same necessities because, having eliminated their nobility by frequent divisions, the republic was left in the hands of men nurtured in trade and thus continued in the orders and fortune of the others. The arms of Italy, therefore, were in the hands either of lesser princes or of men without a state; for the lesser princes, unmoved by any glory, wore them so as to live either more rich or more secure, and the others, nurtured in them since childhood and not knowing any other art, sought to be honored for them by having them or by power. Among these, the most famous were: Carmignuola; Francesco Sforza; Niccolò Piccinino, an apprentice to Braccio; Agnolo della Pergola; Lorenzo and Micheletto Attenduli; Tartaglia;[3] Jacopaccio;[4] Ceccolino da Perugia; Niccolò da Tolentino; Guido Torello; Antonio dal Ponte ad Era; and many others similar to these. Along with these were those lords of whom I spoke above,[5] to whom were added the barons of Rome, the Orsini, and the Colonna, with other lords and gentlemen of the Kingdom and of Lombardy. Since they depended on war, they had made a sort of bond and understanding together and had reduced war to an art in which they would temporize, so that most times both one side and the other of those who were waging war would lose; and in the end, they reduced it to such vileness that any mediocre captain in whom only a shadow of ancient virtue had been reborn would have despised them, to the astonishment[6] of all Italy, which, because of its lack of prudence, honored them. Of these lazy princes, therefore, and these very vile arms, my history will be filled. But before

[3] Angelo Lavello, dubbed il Tartaglia (the stutterer).
[4] Jacopo Caldora.
[5] The lesser princes.
[6] Lit.: admiration.

I come to that, it is necessary for me, as I promised in the beginning, to turn back and to recount the origin of Florence, and to make everyone clearly understand what was the state of that city in those times, and by what means it came to that state among so many travails that had fallen upon Italy for a thousand years.

BOOK II

I

AMONG the other great and marvelous orders of the ancient republics and principalities that in our times have been eliminated was that by which they used to build many towns and cities anew and at all times. For no single thing is more worthy of an excellent prince and of a well-ordered republic, nor more useful to a province, than building new towns where men can settle for the convenience of defense or cultivation. The ancients were able to do this easily, as it was their practice to send new inhabitants into conquered or vacant countries, which they called colonies.[1] For besides being the cause of building new towns, this order made the conquered country more secure for the victor, filled vacant places with inhabitants, and kept men well distributed in the provinces. From this it arose that, living more comfortably in a province, men multiplied more there and were more ready for offense and more secure in defense. As this custom has been eliminated today through the bad practice of republics and princes, ruin and weakness have arisen in the provinces; for this order alone is what makes empires more secure and, as has been said, maintains countries as abundantly inhabited. Security arises because the colony that is settled by a prince in a country newly seized by him stands as a fortress and guard to keep the rest faithful. Besides, one cannot maintain a province as inhabited or preserve the inhabitants well distributed within it without this order. For all places in it are not either productive or healthy; hence it arises that men abandon the latter and are wanting in the former; and if there is no mode of getting men back to what they abandoned or to go where they are wanting, the province will in a short time be spoiled: for one part becomes deserted from too few inhabitants, another part poor from too many. And because nature cannot compensate for this disorder, it is necessary that industry compensate for it: for unhealthy countries become healthy by means of a multitude of men that seizes them at a stroke; they cleanse the earth by cultivation and purge the air with fires, things that nature could never provide.[2] This is demonstrated by the city of Venice, put in a swampy and diseased place; nonetheless, the many

[1] On colonies, see *P* 3; *D* I 1, II 6, 9, 10, 19, III 24, 32.
[2] See *FH* I 29; and *D* I 1, II 5.

inhabitants who gathered there at a stroke rendered it healthy. Pisa too, because of the foulness of the air, was never filled with inhabitants until Genoa and its coasts were destroyed by the Saracens; this made those men, driven from their earthly fatherlands, gather there at a stroke in such numbers that they made it populous and powerful. When the order of sending out colonies has been lacking, conquered countries are held with greater difficulty and vacant countries never fill up, while those that are too full do not relieve themselves. As a result, many parts of the world, and especially of Italy, have become deserted by comparison to ancient times; and it all happened and happens because in the princes there is no appetite for true glory and in the republics no order that deserves to be praised. In ancient times, therefore, by virtue of these colonies, either new cities arose frequently or those already begun grew; and among these was the city of Florence, which had its beginning from Fiesole and its growth from colonies.

2

IT is a thing very true, as Dante and Giovanni Villani have shown,[1] that, since the city of Fiesole had been placed on the summit of a mountain, to make its markets more frequented and more convenient for those who might want to come to them with their merchandise it had ordered the place for them not on the hillside but in the plain between the foot of the mountain and the Arno River. These markets, I judge, were the cause of the first buildings that were put up in those places, as the merchants were moved by the wish to have convenient shelters to hold their merchandise, which in time became solid buildings. Afterwards, when the Romans had conquered the Carthaginians, rendering Italy safe from foreign wars, the buildings multiplied to a great number. For men never maintain themselves in difficulties unless maintained there by some necessity; so whereas the fear of war may force them to live willingly in formidable and harsh places, when the war ends, beckoned[2] by convenience, they live more willingly in domestic and easy places. Thus, the security that was born in Italy through the reputation of the Roman Republic enabled the dwellings, already begun in the mode stated, to increase to such number that they took on the form of a town, which from the beginning was named Villa Arnina. Afterwards, civil wars began in Rome, first between

---

[1] Dante, *Inferno* xv 61–63, and *Paradiso* xv 124–126; Giovanni Villani, *Cronica* I 35; and see *D* 1. For recent historical scholarship, see Rubinstein, "Il Poliziano e la questione delle origini di Firenze," and idem, "Machiavelli e le origini di Firenze."

[2] Lit.: called.

Marius and Sulla, then between Caesar and Pompey, and later between the killers of Caesar and those who wanted to avenge his death. Thus first by Sulla,[3] and later by those three Roman citizens who divided up the empire after the revenge they had for Caesar,[4] colonies were sent to Fiesole; either all or some of these located their dwellings in the plain near the town already begun; and by this increase the place became so full of buildings, men, and every other civil order that it could be counted among the cities of Italy. But as to how the name of Florence might have been derived, there are various opinions. Some would have it called for *Florino*, one of the heads of the colony;[5] others would have it not *Florenzia* but *Fluenzia* in the beginning because it was located next to the flowing Arno, and as a witness they cite Pliny, who says, "the Fluentini are by the Flowing Arno."[6] This could be false because Pliny in his text shows where the Florentines were located, not what they were called; and the word *Fluentini* may well be corrupt because Frontinus and Cornelius Tacitus, who wrote almost in Pliny's time, called them *Florenzia* and *Florentini*.[7] For already in the time of Tiberius they governed themselves by the custom of the other Italian cities, and Cornelius refers to Florentine spokesmen as having come to the emperor to beg that water from the Chiana not be emptied onto their country.[8] Nor is it reasonable that the city should have had two names at the same time. I believe, therefore, that it was always called *Florenzia* for whatever cause it was so named; and so from whatever cause the origin might have been, it was born under the Roman Empire and in the time of the first emperors began to be recorded by writers. And when that Empire was afflicted by the barbarians, Florence was destroyed by Totila, king of the Ostrogoths, and rebuilt two hundred and fifty years later by Charlemagne. From that time until the year of Christ 1215, it lived in the fortune under which those who commanded Italy lived.[9] In these times, first the descendants of Charlemagne were lords, after that the Berengars, and last, the German emperors, as we showed in our universal treatise.[10] Nor could the Florentines in those times grow or do anything worthy of memory, because of the power of

---

[3] This was the opinion of Leonardo Bruni, *Historiae florentini populi* I 1, and of Poggio Bracciolini, *Historiae florentini populi* I 1. See also Bruni's *Laudatio Florentinae Urbis*, printed in Baron, *From Petrarch to Leonardo Bruni*.

[4] The second triumvirate: Octavius, Antony, and Lapidus.

[5] G. Villani, *Cronica* I 38.

[6] Pliny, *Natural History* III 52.

[7] Tacitus, *Annals* I 79. The first book of the *Libri regionum o colonarium*, actually the work of Balbo, was mistaken for the work of Frontinus by Machiavelli's source, Poliziano.

[8] Tacitus, *Annals* I 79.

[9] Cf. *D* I 49.

[10] NM's name for Book I of *FH*.

those in the Empire to whom they were subject. Nonetheless, in 1010, on the day of Saint Romulus, a day sacred to the inhabitants of Fiesole, they seized and destroyed Fiesole; they did this either with the consent of the emperors or during that time between the death of one and the creation of another when everyone was more free. But afterwards, when the pontiffs obtained more authority in Italy and the German emperors were weakened, all the towns of that province governed themselves with less reverence for the prince, so that in 1080, at the time of Henry III,[11] Italy became openly divided between him and the Church. Notwithstanding this, the Florentines maintained themselves united until 1215, obedient to the conquerors, seeking no other empire than to save themselves. But just as in our bodies, where the later the infirmities come, the more dangerous and mortal they are, so with Florence: the later it was in joining the sects of Italy, by so much more was it afflicted by them. The cause of the first division is very well known because it was celebrated by Dante[12] and many other writers. Even so, it seems to me worth recounting briefly.

3

AMONG other very powerful families in Florence were the Buondelmonti and Uberti; near to them were the Amidei and the Donati. In the Donati family there was a rich widow who had a daughter very beautiful to see. This widow had planned by herself to marry her daughter to Messer Buondelmonte, a young knight and head of the Buondelmonti family. Either out of negligence or because she believed she could always be in time, she had not revealed her plan to anyone, when chance brought about the betrothal of Messer Buondelmonte to a young girl of the Amidei family—at which that woman was very malcontent. And as she was hoping that by means of her daughter's beauty she could upset the wedding before it should be celebrated, she saw Messer Buondelmonte coming alone toward her house and went downstairs leading her daughter behind her. As he was passing by she managed to meet him and she said, "I am truly very happy that you have chosen a wife, although I had saved for you this daughter of mine"; and pushing open the door, she let him see her. The knight, having seen the beauty of the girl, which was rare, and considering her bloodline and her dowry not inferior to those of the one he had taken, was inflamed with such ardor to have her that, not thinking of the faith he had pledged or the injury he did in breaking it, or

[11] Henry IV; see *FH* I 15.
[12] *Paradiso* XVI 136–150.

of the evils he might encounter from breaking faith, he said, "Since you have saved her for me and there is still time, I would be ungrateful to refuse her," and without letting any time pass, he celebrated the marriage. As soon as this thing became known, the Amidei and Uberti families, which were related by marriage, were filled with indignation. Gathering together with many other relatives, they concluded that this injury could not be tolerated without shame and that they could avenge it with no other revenge than the death of Messer Buondelmonte. Although there were some who dwelt on the evils that might follow such a course, Mosca Lamberti said that he who thought over many things never concluded any one of them, and he repeated that trite and famous phrase, "A thing done is ended."[1] Thereupon they entrusted this homicide to Mosca, Stiatta Uberti, Lambertuccio Amidei, and Oderigo Fifanti. On Easter morning these men hid in the houses of the Amidei situated between the Ponte Vecchio and Santo Stefano, and as Messer Buondelmonte passed over the river on his white horse, thinking it was as easy to forget an injury as it was to renounce a family relation, he was attacked and killed by them at the foot of the bridge beneath a statue of Mars.[2] This homicide divided the whole city, and one part stood with the Buondelmonti, the other with the Uberti. Since these families were strong in houses, towers, and men, they fought for many years without one dislodging the other. And as long as their enmities did not end in peace, truces were arranged; and in this way, depending on new accidents, their enmities were sometimes calmed and sometimes inflamed.

4

AND Florence remained in these travails until the time of Frederick II, who was convinced that because he was king of Naples,[1] he could increase his forces against the Church. To solidify his power in Tuscany he favored the Uberti and their followers, who, with his favor, drove out the Buondelmonti; and thus was our city also divided, just as Italy had been for a long time, between the Guelfs and the Ghibellines. Nor does it seem superfluous to me to recall the families who followed the one sect and the other. Those then following the Guelf party were the Buondelmonti, Nerli, Rossi, Frescobaldi, Mozzi, Bardi, Pulci, Gherardini, Foraboschi, Bagnesi, Guidalotti, Sacchetti, Manieri, Lucardesi, Chiaramontesi,

[1] Dante, *Inferno* XXVIII 103–111.
[2] Ibid., XIII 143–144; *Paradiso* XVI 140–148.
[1] See *FH* I 21.

Compiobbesi, Cavalcanti, Giandonati, Gianfigliazzi, Scali, Gualterotti, Importuni, Bostichi, Tornaquinci, Vecchietti, Tosinghi, Arrigucci, Agli, Sizi, Adimari, Visdomini, Donati, Pazzi, Della Bella, Ardinghi, Tedaldi, and Cerchi. For the Ghibelline party were the Uberti, Mannegli, Ubriachi, Fifanti, Amidei, Infangati, Malespini, Scolari, Guidi, Galli, Cappiardi, Lamberti, Soldanieri, Cipriani, Toschi, Amieri, Palermini, Migliorelli, Pigli, Barucci, Cattani, Agolanti, Brunelleschi, Caponsacchi, Elesei, Abati, Tedaldini, Giuochi, and Galigai. In addition, many men of the people joined with the noble families on one side or the other so that almost the whole city was corrupted by the division. Thus the Guelfs, having been expelled, withdrew to towns in the upper Valdarno where they had a large number of their fortresses; and in this mode they defended themselves as best they could against the forces of their enemies. But when Frederick died, those in Florence who were men of the middle and had more credit with the people thought that it might be better to reunite the city than to ruin it by keeping it divided. So they worked it out that the Guelfs, setting aside their injuries, returned, and the Ghibellines, setting aside their suspicion, received them; and when they were united, it seemed to them that the time had come to take the form of a free way of life and an order that would enable them to defend themselves, before the new emperor should acquire forces.

5

THEREFORE they divided the city into six parts and elected twelve citizens, two for each sixth, to govern it; they would be called "the Ancients" and would be replaced every year. And to remove the causes of enmities that originated from the judges, they provided for two foreign judges, one called "Captain of the People" and the other "Podestà," who were to judge cases, civil as well as criminal, arising among citizens.[1] And because no order is stable without providing itself with a defender, they established twenty banners within the city and seventy-six in the countryside and enrolled all the young men under them. They ordered that each should stand ready and armed under his banner at any time that he might be called by the Captain or the Ancients, and they varied the badges on them according to the weapons so that the crossbowmen carried one ensign and the shield-bearers another. And every year on the day of the Pentecost, with great pomp they gave the ensigns to new men and new

---

[1] See D I 49, where NM criticizes this innovation. In fact, only the Captain of the People was created in 1250; the Podestà already existed.

heads were assigned to the whole order. And to give majesty to their armies and a point² where each one who had been sent into the fray could take refuge and, having taken refuge, might again be able to face the enemy, they ordered a great wagon drawn by two oxen covered in red and on it a red-and-white ensign. Whenever they wanted the army to come forth, they brought this wagon into the Mercato Nuovo and with solemn pomp turned it over to the heads of the people. They also had a bell termed the Martinella to lend magnificence to their undertakings, which rang continuously for a month before the armies were to go forth from the city so that the enemy might have time for its defense; so much virtue was in these men then, and with such generosity of spirit did they govern themselves, that, while today an unexpected assault on the enemy is looked upon as a generous and prudent action, in those times it was reputed contemptible and false. They also took this bell with their armies and with it commanded the guards and other actions of war.

6

ON these military and civil orders the Florentines founded their freedom. Nor could one conceive how much authority and force Florence had acquired in a short time: it became not only head of Tuscany but was counted among the first cities of Italy, and it would have risen to any greatness if frequent and new divisions had not afflicted it. The Florentines lived under this government for ten years, during which time they forced the people of Pisa, Arezzo, and Siena to league with them. Returning from the field at Siena, they took Volterra, destroyed some other fortified places as well, and brought the inhabitants to Florence. These campaigns were all undertaken on the advice of the Guelfs, who were much more powerful than the Ghibellines both because the latter were hated by the people for their haughty behavior during the time of Frederick when they governed and because, being the party of the Church, the Guelfs were more loved than the party of the emperor. For with the help of the Church they hoped to preserve their freedom and were afraid of losing it under the emperor. Meanwhile, the Ghibellines, seeing that they were losing their authority, were unable to remain quiet and only waited for an opportunity to regain the state. It appeared to them to have come when they saw that Manfred, son of Frederick, had made himself lord of the kingdom of Naples and had very much shaken the power of the Church.¹

² Lit.: head.
¹ See *FH* I 22.

So they secretly laid plans with him in order to regain their authority, but they were unable to manage that their plans not be discovered by the Ancients. The Ancients then summoned the Uberti, who not only did not obey but took up arms and fortified themselves in their houses. In indignation at this the people armed themselves and with the help of the Guelfs forced the Uberti to abandon Florence and to go with the whole Ghibelline party to Siena. From there they asked for help from Manfred, king of Naples, and, through the industry of Messer Farinata degli Uberti, the king's men defeated the Guelfs near the Arbia River with such slaughter that those who were saved from that defeat, judging that their city was lost, took refuge not in Florence but in Lucca.

7

MANFRED had sent Count Giordano to the Ghibellines at the head of his troops, a man highly reputed in arms in those times. After the victory he went to Florence with the Ghibellines and brought that city to obedience entirely to Manfred by abolishing the magistrates and every other order through which any form of its freedom might appear. This injury, done with little prudence, was received universally with great hatred; and from being merely hostile to the Ghibellines, everyone became very hostile, and from all of this arose what in time was their ruin. And as Giordano had to return to Naples because of the necessities of the Kingdom, he left behind as royal vicar in Florence Count Guido Novello, a lord of Casentino. He called a council of the Ghibellines at Empoli, where it was decided by each that if they wanted to maintain the Ghibelline party powerful in Tuscany it was necessary to destroy Florence, which was alone capable, because of its Guelf people, of restoring the forces of the parties of the Church. There was neither citizen nor friend to oppose this so cruel sentence given against so noble a city, except for Messer Farinata degli Uberti.[1] He defended it openly and without any hesitation, saying that he had not undergone so many perils with so much trouble not to be able to live in his fatherland and that he would not now stop wishing for that which he had sought so long or renounce what had already been given him by fortune; rather, he would be no less an enemy to those who designed otherwise than he had been to the Guelfs. And if someone among them feared his fatherland and would ruin it, he hoped to defend it with the same virtue by which he had expelled the Guelfs. Messer Farinata was a man of great spirit, excellent in war, head of the Ghibellines, and much

[1] Dante, *Inferno* x 91–92.

esteemed by Manfred. His authority put an end to that reasoning, and they thought over other modes by which they might save the state.

8

THE Guelfs who had taken refuge in Lucca were dismissed by the Lucchese because of threats by the count; so they went to Bologna. From there they were called by the Guelfs of Parma to go against the Ghibellines; and having overcome their adversaries there by their virtue, they were given all their adversaries' possessions. Their wealth and honors had increased so much that, upon learning that Pope Clement had called upon Charles of Anjou to seize the Kingdom from Manfred, they sent spokesmen to the pontiff to offer him their forces. So the pope not only received them as friends but also gave them his ensign, which was ever after carried in war by the Guelfs and is the one still used in Florence. Afterwards, Manfred was stripped of the Kingdom by Charles and killed;[1] and since the Guelfs of Florence had intervened there, their party became bolder and that of the Ghibellines weaker. Thus the Ghibellines governing Florence together with Count Guido Novello judged that it would be well to win the people to their side, whom they had previously aggravated by every possible injury, by giving them some benefits; and if they had applied those remedies before necessity came, it would have been useful, but as they applied them now unwillingly, the remedies were not only not useful but hastened their ruin.[2] They judged, therefore, that they could make the people their friends and partisans if they returned to them some of the honors and authority that they had taken from them; and they elected thirty-six citizens from among the people, together with two knights brought in from Bologna to reform the state of the city.[3] As soon as these men met, they divided all the city into guilds,[4] and over each guild they ordered a magistrate to pass judgment[5] on those under them. Further, they assigned to each a banner under which every man would present himself armed whenever the city might have need of it. In the beginning there were twelve guilds, seven greater and five lesser, but the lesser grew to fourteen, so that altogether there were twenty-one as at present. The thirty-six reformers were to manage other things for the common benefit.

[1] See *FH* I 22.
[2] See *D* I 38.
[3] See Dante, *Inferno* XXIII 103–108.
[4] *Arti* or "arts," to be translated "guilds."
[5] Lit.: reason.

9

COUNT Guido ordered a tax to be levied on the citizens, so as to maintain his soldiers, but he met such difficulty that he did not dare to use force to collect it. And as it appeared to him that he had lost the state, he withdrew to confer with the heads of the Ghibellines; and they decided to take away from the people by force what they had given them with little prudence. And when it appeared to them that their arms were in order, while the thirty-six were assembled together, they raised a disturbance. At this, the thirty-six became frightened and retired to their homes, and immediately the banners of the guilds were brought out with many armed men behind; and when they learned that Count Guido with his party was at San Giovanni, they took their stand at Santa Trinita and gave their obedience to Messer Giovanni Soldanieri. The count, on the other side, hearing where the people were, started to go find them; the people did not flee from the conflict but advanced against the enemy, and they met where the loggia of the Tornaquinci stands today. Here the count was repulsed with the loss and death of many of his men, after which he was so dismayed that he feared the enemy would attack at night and, finding his men beaten and discouraged, might kill him. So powerful was this imagination in him that, without thinking of any other remedy, he decided to save himself by fleeing rather than fighting, and against the advice of the Rectors and of the Party[1] he left for Prato with all his men. But as soon as he found himself in a safe place, his fear left him and he realized his error. Wishing to correct it, at the break of day he returned with his men to Florence to reenter by force the city that he had abandoned out of vileness. But his plan did not succeed: for the people who had been able to drive him out only with difficulty were able to keep him out with ease. So, grieving and humiliated, he went away to the Casentino, and the Ghibellines returned to their villas. Since the people had thus been victors, to encourage those who loved the good of the republic they decided to reunite the city by calling back all the citizens, Ghibelline as well as Guelf, who might be outside. Thus the Guelfs returned, six years after they had been driven out, and for the Ghibellines, too, their recent injury was pardoned and they were restored to their fatherland. Nonetheless, the Ghibellines were strongly hated by the people and by the Guelfs because the latter were unable to erase the memory of their exile and the former remembered too well the tyranny they lived through when under their government. Because of this, neither the one party nor the other could rest its spirit. While the people lived in this form in Florence, the rumor was

---

[1] The Ghibelline party.

spread that Conradin, Manfred's nephew, was coming with his men from Germany to acquire Naples. As a result, the Ghibellines were filled with the hope of being able to regain their authority, and the Guelfs thought over what they might have to do to secure themselves against their enemies; and they asked King Charles for help to enable them to defend themselves if Conradin came through. Then, when Charles's men were coming, the Guelfs were made insolent; and they so frightened the Ghibellines that, two days before their arrival, the Ghibellines fled without being driven out.

10

WHEN the Ghibellines had left, the Florentines reordered the state of the city. They elected twelve heads who were to sit in the magistracy for two months, and they called these, not "Ancients," but "Good Men"; beside these, they elected a council of eighty citizens, which they called the "Credenza"; and after this there were one hundred and eighty of the people, thirty for each of the six sections of the city, who together with the Credenza and the twelve Good Men were called the General Council. They ordered still another council of one hundred and twenty citizens from among the people and nobles, who were to make final[1] all things deliberated in the other councils, and with that they distributed the offices of the republic. When this government had been confirmed, they further strengthened the Guelf party with magistrates and other orders so that they might be able to defend themselves from the Ghibellines with greater forces. The goods of the latter were divided into three shares, of which they made one public, another went to the magistracy of the Party[2] called the "Captains," and the third was given to the Guelfs to compensate them for the damages they had received. Also the pope, so as to keep Tuscany Guelf, made King Charles his imperial vicar there. Thus the Florentines were upholding their reputation by virtue of the new government, by laws within, and by arms without when the pontiff died; after a long dispute, lasting over two years, Pope Gregory X was elected. As he had been away in Syria for a long time and was still there at the time of his election, he was far removed from the humors of the parties and so did not regard them in the mode they had been regarded by his predecessors. Therefore, having come to Florence on his way to France, he considered it the office of an excellent shepherd to reunite the city; and he

[1] Lit.: give perfection to.
[2] The Guelf party.

worked it out so well that the Florentines were content to receive the Ghibelline syndics in Florence to negotiate the mode of their return. Although an accord was reached, the Ghibellines were so frightened that they did not want to return. The pope gave the blame to the city for this, and in anger he excommunicated it; it remained under this ban as long as the pontiff lived, but after his death it was reconsecrated by Pope Innocent V. The pontificate had come to Nicholas III, born of the Orsini house;[3] and because the pontiffs always feared one whose power had become great in Italy, even though it had grown through the favors of the Church, and because they sought to bring down that power, there arose those frequent tumults and frequent changes that occurred in Italy. For the fear of one power brought the growth of someone weak, and when that one had grown, he was to be feared, and being feared they sought to bring him down.[4] This made the Kingdom to be taken from the hands of Manfred and given to Charles; this then made others fear him and seek his ruin. Thus, Nicholas III, moved by these causes, worked it out that by means of the emperor the government of Tuscany was taken from Charles, and he sent his legate, Messer Latino, into that province in the name of the Empire.

II

FLORENCE was then in very bad condition because the Guelf nobility had become insolent and did not fear the magistrates. So every day many homicides and other acts of violence were done without any punishment for those who committed them because they were the favorites of one or another of the nobles. The heads of the people, therefore, so as to put a stop to this insolence, thought it would be well to bring back the exiles; this gave the legate an opportunity of reuniting the city, and the Ghibellines returned. In place of twelve governors they made fourteen, seven for each side, who were to govern for a year and who were to be elected by the pope. Florence remained under this government for two years, until Pope Martin, of French birth, succeeded to the pontificate and restored to King Charles all the authority that had been taken from him by Nicholas. So the parties in Tuscany immediately revived because the Florentines took up arms against the governor of the emperor; and to deprive the Ghibellines of the government as well as to keep the powerful in check, they ordered a new form of regime.

[3] See *FH* I 23.
[4] See *D* I 12.

It was the year 1282, and since the magistrates and ensigns had been given to the guild corporations, they were highly reputed; whence they, by their authority, ordered that in the place of the fourteen, three citizens be created who would be called the "Priors." They were to be in the government of the republic for two months, and they could be of the people and of the great, provided that they were merchants or practiced an art. After the first magistracy, they were raised to six so that there would be one from each sixth, and that number was kept until 1342, when the city was redivided into quarters and the Priors increased to eight. Yet during this span of time, through some accident, sometimes there were twelve. This magistracy was the cause, as will be seen in time, of the ruin of the nobles, because through various accidents they were excluded from it by the people and afterwards crushed without any respect. In the beginning the nobles consented to it because they were not united; for, as one desired too much to take away the state of another, they all lost it. They assigned a palace to this magistracy where it would reside continually, as before it had been the custom for the magistrates and councils to meet in churches; and they further honored the magistracy with sergeants and other ministers. Although at the beginning they were called only Priors, yet later, for greater magnificence, they added the name Signori. The Florentines remained quiet within for some time while they made war on the inhabitants of Arezzo for having driven out the Guelfs; and at Campaldino they succeeded in defeating them. And as the city grew in men and riches, it appeared appropriate also to extend the walls; and they widened the circle as one sees it at present, whereas before, the diameter would have been only the distance from Ponte Vecchio to San Lorenzo.

12

THE wars outside and the peace within had almost eliminated the Ghibelline and Guelf parties in Florence. Only those humors were still excited that are naturally wont to exist in all cities between the powerful and the people; for since the people want to live according to the laws and the powerful want to command by them, it is not possible for them to understand together.[1] While the Ghibellines made them fear, this humor was not discovered; but as soon as they were subdued, its power was revealed. Every day someone of the people was injured, and neither the laws nor the magistrates were sufficient to avenge him because every noble, with his relatives and friends, would defend himself against the forces of the Priors and the Captain. Therefore, the princes of the guilds, desir-

---

[1] See *P* 9; *D* I 5.

ing to remedy this inconvenience, provided that each Signoria at the beginning of its term should create a Gonfalonier of Justice, a man of the people, to whom they gave a thousand men enrolled under twenty banners. He was to be ready with his standard[2] and his armed men to favor justice at any time he might be called upon by them or by the Captain. The first to be elected was Ubaldo Ruffoli. He brought out his standard and destroyed the houses of Galletti[3] because in France one of that family had killed a man of the people.

It was easy for the guilds to make this order because of the grave enmities that remained awake among the nobles, who did not pay any attention to the provision made against them until they saw the severity of that execution. It struck them with great terror at first; yet in a short while they reverted to their insolence, for as some of them had always been from the Signori, they had the means to prevent the Gonfalonier from being able to do his duty. Furthermore, since the accuser always needed to have a witness when he received some offense, no one would be found willing to testify against the nobles. So in a brief time Florence returned to the same disorders and the people suffered the same injuries from the great because the judges were slow and their sentences lacked executions.

13

AND as the men of the people did not know what course to take, Giano della Bella, a man of very noble lineage but a lover of the freedom of the city, inspired the heads of the guilds to reform the city. On his advice it was ordered that the Gonfalonier should reside with the Priors and should have four thousand men obeying him. All the nobles were again deprived of the power to sit with the Signori; the accomplices of an offender were forced to pay the same penalty as he, and they made public report sufficient for passing judgment. By these laws, which were called the Ordinances of Justice, the people acquired much reputation, and Giano della Bella much hatred, because the powerful had a very bad opinion of him as the destroyer of their power, and the rich men of the people envied him because it appeared to them that his authority was too much. This was to be demonstrated as soon as opportunity allowed. Fate then brought it about that a man of the people was killed in a brawl in which many nobles had taken part, among whom was Messer Corso Donati. As he was bolder than the others, the blame was put on him and he was therefore arrested by the Captain of the People. And however the thing should have

[2] *Gonfalone*, from which Gonfalonier is derived.
[3] Actually, the Galli.

gone, whether Messer Corso may not have erred or the Captain was afraid to condemn him, he was absolved. This absolution so displeased the people that they took up arms and ran to the house of Giano della Bella to beg him to be the one to see to it that the laws of which he had been the inventor be observed. Giano, who desired Messer Corso to be punished, did not make them put down their arms as many judged that he ought to have done, but encouraged them to go to the Signori to complain about the case and to beg them to provide for it. Thereupon the people were filled with indignation, and as it appeared to them that they had been offended by the Captain and abandoned by Giano, they went not to the Signori but to the Captain's palace, took it, and sacked it. This act displeased all the citizens. Those who longed for the ruin of Giano accused him, putting all the blame on him; so, since there was some enemy of his among the Signori who then followed, Giano was accused to the Captain as an agitator of the people. And while his cause was being argued, the people armed themselves and ran to all his houses offering him defense against the Signori and his enemies. Giano did not want either to put these popular favors to the test or to commit his life to the magistrates, for he feared the malice of the latter and the instability of the former. Thus, to deny his enemies the opportunity of injuring him and his friends the opportunity of offending their fatherland, he decided to depart, to give way to envy and to free the citizens from the fear they had of him, and to leave that city which with his care and at his peril he had freed from the servitude of the powerful. He chose a voluntary exile.

14

AFTER his departure the nobility rose up in hope of regaining its dignity; and judging the ills to have arisen from its divisions, the nobles united together and sent two from among them to the Signoria, which they judged would be in their favor, to beg that it be content to moderate in some part the severity of the laws made against them. As soon as the request was revealed, it excited the spirits of the people because they feared that the Signori would grant it to them; and so, between the desire of the nobles and the suspicion of the people, they came to arms. The nobles made their stand in three places—at San Giovanni, in the Mercato Nuovo, and at the Piazza de' Mozzi—under three chiefs: Messer Forese Adimari, Messer Vanni de' Mozzi, and Messer Geri Spini. The men of the people assembled in very great numbers under their ensigns at the palace of the Signori, who lived then near San Brocolo. And because the people were suspicious of that Signoria, they deputed six citizens to govern with it. While the one party and the other were preparing for battle, some men of the people as well as of the nobles, along with certain men of religion of good repute, placed themselves in the middle to pacify them. They reminded the nobles that their pride and their bad government were the cause of the honors taken from them and the laws made against them, that their taking up arms now to regain by force what they had allowed to be taken from them on account of their own disunion and their evil ways[1] was nothing other than to wish to ruin their fatherland and to worsen their own condition; and they should remember that the people were far superior to them in number, riches, and hatred, and that the nobility by which it appeared to them that they were superior to others would not fight and would turn out to be, when it came to steel, an empty name that would not be enough to defend them against so many. To the people, on their side, they recalled that it was not prudent always to want the ultimate victory, and that it was never a wise course to make men desperate, because he who does not hope for good does not fear evil. They ought to think that nobility was that which had honored the city in war, and therefore it was neither a good nor a just thing to persecute it with such hatred; that as the nobles bore easily their not enjoying the supreme magistracy, they could not at all tolerate that it was in each one's power, through the orders[2] that had been made, to drive them out of their fatherland; and therefore it was good to mitigate them and by this benefit to have arms be put down; nor should they want to try the fortune of battle, trusting in their number, for many times it had been seen that the many were overcome by the few. In the people there were diverse views: many wanted to come to battle, as to a thing that must come of necessity one day; and so it was better to have it now than to wait until the enemy was more powerful; and if one believed that the nobles would rest content when the laws were mitigated, it would be well to mitigate them; but their pride was so great that they would never lay it aside unless forced to do so. To many others, wiser and of calmer spirit, it appeared that moderating the laws would not mean much but that coming to battle might mean very much; so their opinion prevailed, and they provided that in accusations against the nobles, witnesses would be necessary.

15

WHEN their arms had been put down, both parties remained full of suspicion, and each fortified itself with towers and arms. The people, moved

[1] Lit.: not good modes.
[2] The Ordinances of Justice.

by the fact that those Signori had been favorable to the nobles, reordered the government by restricting it in number; as its princes there remained the Mancini, Magalotti, Altoviti, Peruzzi, and Cerretani. The state having been strengthened, for the greater magnificence and security of the Signori they laid the foundation of a palace for them in the year 1298 and made a piazza for it where the houses of the Uberti had once been. The public prisons were also begun at the same time; these buildings were completed at the end of a few years. Never was our city in a greater and more prosperous state than in these times, when it was replete with men, riches, and reputation; there were thirty thousand citizens skilled in arms, and those in the surrounding countryside came to seventy thousand. All Tuscany, part as subjects and part as friends, obeyed it; and although there was some anger and suspicion between the nobles and the people, nonetheless they produced no bad effect, and everyone lived united in peace. If this peace had not been disturbed by new enmities within, it would not have had to fear those from the outside, for the city was in such a position that it did not fear either the empire or its own exiles; and with its forces it could have responded to all the states of Italy. That evil, therefore, which outside forces could not have done to it, was done by those from within.

16

THERE were two families in Florence, the Cerchi and the Donati, who were very powerful in wealth, nobility, and men. Between them—since they were neighbors both in Florence and in the countryside—there had been some dispute, not, however, so grave that they came to arms; and perhaps there would not have been any great effects if the malign humors had not been increased by new causes. Among the first families of Pistoia was that of the Cancellieri.[1] It happened that while Lore of Messer Guglielmo and Geri of Messer Bertacca, all of that family, were playing, they came to words and Geri was slightly wounded by Lore. The incident displeased Messer Guglielmo, and, thinking that with humanity he could take away the scandal, he increased it; for he ordered his son to go to the house of the father of the wounded one to ask his pardon. Lore obeyed his father, yet this humane act did not sweeten any part of the bitter spirit of Messer Bertacca, who had his servants seize Lore and cut off his hand,

---

[1] On parties in Pistoia, see remarks in *P* 20, and *D* II 21, 25, III 27. See also NM's brief writing on the parties in Pistoia in his own time (1502), *Ragguaglio delle cose fatte dalla repubblica fiorentina per quietare le parte di Pistoia.*

and for greater insult, on a manger, while saying to him: "Go back to your father and tell him that wounds are treated with steel and not with words." The cruelty of this deed so displeased Messer Guglielmo that he had his men take up arms to avenge it; Messer Bertacca also armed to defend himself, and thus not only that family but the whole city of Pistoia was divided. And because the Cancellieri were descended from Messer Cancelliere, who had had two wives, one of whom was named Bianca, one of the parties who were her descendants named itself "White" and the other party, so as to take a contrary name, was named "Black." As time went on, there were many fights between them, with the deaths of many men and the ruin of many houses; and since they could not unite themselves, exhausted from the evil and desiring either to bring an end to their discords or by the division of others to increase them, they came to Florence. As the Blacks were related to the Donati, they were favored by Messer Corso, the head of that family; hence the Whites, so as to have powerful support to sustain them against the Donati,[2] appealed to Messer Veri de Cerchi, a man for every quality in no way inferior to Messer Corso.

17

THIS humor, having come from Pistoia, increased the old hatred between the Cerchi and the Donati; and it was already so manifest that the Priors and the other good citizens did not doubt that it would come to arms between them at any hour, after which the whole city would become divided. Therefore, they had recourse to the pontiff, begging[1] him that he with his authority bring to bear some remedy upon these humors now in motion that they themselves were not able to do. The pope sent for Messer Veri and charged him to make peace with the Donati, at which Messer Veri showed his amazement, saying that he had no enmity toward them; and because peace presupposed war, he did not know, since there was no war between them, why peace should be necessary. Then, since Messer Veri returned from Rome without any other conclusion, the humors grew so that every little accident could make them spill over, as indeed did happen.

It was in the month of May, at a time and on holidays when throughout Florence there was public celebrating.[2] Thus some youths of the Donati

---

[2] According to Villani and Stefani, the family relationship was between the Whites and the Cerchi; NM follows Bruni. See Anna Maria Cabrini, *Per una valutazione delle "Istorie Fiorentine" di Machiavelli*, pp. 133–134.

[1] Or praying.

[2] Cf. *FH* I 26.

family with their friends, on horseback, stopped to watch the women dancing near Santa Trinita when they were joined by some of the Cerchi, they too accompanied by many nobles. As they did not recognize the Donati who were in front and as they, too, wanted to see, they urged their horses through them and pushed them. Whereupon the Donati, considering themselves offended, drew their weapons, to which the Cerchi replied valiantly, and, after many wounds given and received by each, they separated. This disorder was the beginning of much evil because the whole city was divided, the men of the people as well as the great, and the parties took the names of Whites and Blacks.

The heads of the White party were the Cerchi, and siding with them were the Adimari, Abati, some of the Tosinghi, the Bardi, the Rossi, the Frescobaldi, the Nerli and the Mannegli, all the Mozzi, the Scali, the Gherardini, the Cavalcanti, Malespini, Bostichi, Giandonati, Vecchietti, and the Arrigucci. Joining these were many popular families, together with all the Ghibellines who were in Florence; so with the great number following them, they had nearly the whole government of the city. The Donati, on the other side, were the heads of the Black party, and with them were that part of the families named above who did not join the Whites, and also all the Pazzi, the Bisdomini, the Manieri, Bagnesi, Tornaquinci, Spini, Buondelmonti, Gianfigliazzi, and Brunelleschi. Nor did this humor infect only the city, but also it divided the whole countryside; hence the captains of the Party[3] and whoever was of the Guelfs and a lover of the republic were very afraid lest this new division might by its ruin of the city cause a resurgence of the Ghibelline parties. Again they sent to Pope Boniface for him to think of a remedy if he did not want that city which had always been a shield for the Church either to be ruined or to become Ghibelline. Therefore the pope sent to Florence Matteo d'Acquasparta, a Portuguese cardinal, as legate, and because he met with difficulty in the White party, which, because it appeared more powerful was less afraid, he left Florence angrily and interdicted it. Thus he left Florence in greater confusion than it was before his coming.

18

THUS, while the spirits of all men were agitated, it happened that at a funeral where many of the Cerchi and Donati were present, they came to words and then to arms; but for the moment nothing more came of it than tumults. After everyone had gone home, the Cerchi decided to at-

---

3 The Guelf party.

tack the Donati, and with a great number of men went to find them; but by the virtue of Messer Corso they were thrown back with a large number of them wounded. The whole city was now in arms: the Signori and the laws were overcome by the fury of the powerful, while the wisest and best citizens lived full of suspicion. The Donati and their party were more fearful because they were less powerful; so to provide for their things, Messer Corso met with the other Black chiefs and the captains of the Party, and they agreed to ask the pope to send someone of royal blood to come to reform Florence, thinking that by this means it might be possible to overcome the Whites. The assembly and the decision were made known to the Priors and by the opposite party were accused as a conspiracy against free life. As both parties were in arms, the Signori, on the advice and prudence of Dante, who was one of them at the time, took up spirit and had the people armed, whom many from the countryside joined; then they forced the heads of the parties to put down their arms, and they banished Messer Corso Donati with many of the Black party; and to show they were neutral in this judgment, they also banished some of the White party, who returned a little later under color of decent causes.

19

MESSER Corso and his men, because they judged the pope favorable to their party, went to Rome; and they persuaded the pope in his presence of what they had already written to him. At the court of the pontiff was Charles of Valois, brother of the king of France, who had been called to Italy by the king of Naples to proceed to Sicily. So it appeared to the pope, especially since it had been urged[1] by the Florentine exiles, that he should send him to Florence until a convenient time for the sailing[2] should come. Thus Charles came, and although the Whites, who were then ruling, were suspicious of him, nonetheless, as he was the head of the Guelfs and had been sent by the pope, they did not dare to obstruct his coming; but, to make him a friend, they gave him authority enabling him to dispose of the city according to his own will. With this authority, Charles had all his friends and partisans armed, which so aroused the suspicions of the people, who did not want their freedom taken from them, that everyone took up arms and stayed at home in order to be ready if Charles should make any move.

[1] Lit.: prayed for.
[2] To Sicily.

The Cerchi and the heads of the White party, since they had been heads of the republic for some time and had behaved proudly, had come to be universally hated. This fact inspired Messer Corso and the other Black exiles to come to Florence, especially as they knew that Charles and the captains of the Party favored them. And when the city was in arms because of its fear of Charles, Messer Corso, with all the exiles and many others who were his followers, entered Florence without being impeded by anyone. Although Messer Veri de' Cerchi was urged to go out against him, he was unwilling to do so, saying that he wished the people of Florence, against whom Messer Corso was coming, to punish him. But the contrary happened, for he was received and not punished by them; and Messer Veri found it appropriate to flee, if he wanted to save himself. For when Messer Corso had forced the Pinti gate, he made a stand at San Piero Maggiore, a place near his own house, and he gathered many friends and people desiring new things, who assembled there. The first thing he did was to let out of prison anyone who for either public or private cause had been detained there. He forced the Signori to return to their homes as private men and elected new men who were men of the people and of the Black party; and for five days he set about plundering those who were the leaders[3] of the White party. The Cerchi and other princes of their sect had left the city and retired to their strongholds when they saw that Charles was against them and the greater part of the people hostile; and whereas before they had never wished to follow the advice of the pope, they were forced to resort to him for help, showing him that Charles had come to disunite, not to unite, Florence. Whereupon the pope again sent his legate, Messer Matteo d'Acquasparta, who made peace between the Cerchi and the Donati, and strengthened it with marriages and new weddings. And though he wanted the Whites also to participate in office, the Blacks who held the state would not permit this; so the legate departed neither more satisfied nor less irate than the other time, and he left the city, for its disobedience, interdicted.

20

BOTH parties were still in Florence, therefore, and each one malcontent: the Blacks, seeing the enemy party nearby, feared it would retake its lost authority to their ruin; and the Whites saw themselves lacking their authority and honors. To these irritations and natural suspicions new injuries were added. Messer Niccola de' Cerchi, accompanied by many of his

---

[3] Lit.: the first.

friends, was on his way to his properties and had reached the bridge over the river Affrico when he was assaulted by Simone, [son] of Messer Corso Donati. The fight was heavy and had a lamentable end for each side because Messer Niccola was killed and Simone so wounded that he died the following night. This case agitated the whole city once again; and although the Black party was more to blame, it was, nonetheless, defended by those who governed. And before a judgment had been given, it was discovered that the Whites had carried on a conspiracy with Messer Piero Ferrante, one of Charles's barons, with whom they negotiated to get themselves put back in government. This affair came to light through letters written by the Cerchi to him, notwithstanding the opinion that the letters were forged and found by the Donati to conceal the infamy they had acquired by the death of Messer Niccola.

Thus all the Cerchi with their followers in the White party, among whom was the poet Dante, were banished, their goods confiscated, and their homes destroyed. Together with many Ghibellines who had sided with them, they scattered in many places, seeking new fortune with new trials. Charles, having done what he came to do in Florence, left and returned to the pope to carry out his campaign in Sicily, where he was neither wiser nor better than he had been in Florence; so disgraced was he that after the loss of many of his men he returned to France.

21

AFTER Charles's departure life went very quietly in Florence; only Messer Corso was restless, because it did not appear to him that he held the rank in the city which he believed was his due. Indeed, as it was a popular government, he saw the republic being administered by many inferior to himself. Moved by these passions, therefore, he thought he would make the indecency of his intent appear decent with a decent cause, and he slandered many citizens who had administered public money, saying that they had used it for private comforts and that it would be well to find them out and punish them. This opinion of his was taken up by many who had the same desire as he, to which was added the ignorance of many others who believed Messer Corso to be moved by love for his fatherland. For their part, the slandered citizens, having the favor of the people, defended themselves; and so great was this dispute that after civil modes were used it came to arms. In one party were Messer Corso and Messer Lottieri, bishop of Florence, with many of the great and some of the people; in the other were the Signori with the greater part of the people; and so there was fighting in many parts of the city. When the Signori saw the great danger they were in, they sent to the Lucchese for help, and suddenly all the people of Lucca were in Florence. Through their authority things were settled for the time being, and the tumults ceased; and the people kept their state and freedom without otherwise punishing the movers of the scandal.

The pope had heard about the tumults in Florence, and to stop them he sent Messer Niccolao da Prato as his legate. Since he was a man of great reputation for his rank, learning, and breeding, he quickly acquired such trust that he had authority given to him enabling him to establish a state to suit himself. And because he was of Ghibelline origin, he had it in mind to repatriate the exiles; but he wanted first to gain the people over to himself, and to this end he reinstated the old companies of the people,[1] an order that greatly increased the power of the people and decreased that of the great. Thus, when it appeared to the legate that he had the multitude obliged to him, he planned to have the exiles brought back; and in trying various ways, not only did none succeed, but they ended in his becoming so suspect to those who were ruling that he was compelled to depart. Filled with indignation, he returned to the pontiff, leaving Florence in complete confusion and interdicted. And the city was agitated not only by one humor but by many, there being enmities in it between the people and the great, the Ghibellines and the Guelfs, the Whites and the Blacks. Thus all the city was in arms and full of fighting, for many were malcontent at the departure of the legate, they too desiring that the exiles return. First among those provoking the scandal were the Medici and the Giugni, who had shown themselves to the legate as favorable to the rebels. There was fighting, therefore, in many parts of Florence.

To these ills was added a fire that broke out first in Orto San Michele in the houses of the Abati, from which it leapt to those of the Caponsacchi, burning them as well as the houses of the Macci, the Amieri, Toschi, Cipriani, Lamberti, Cavalcanti, and the whole Mercato Nuovo; it passed from there to Porta Santa Maria and burned it entirely; and circling from the Ponte Vecchio, it burned the houses of the Gherardini, Pulci, Amidei, and Lucardesi, and so many others as well that their number reached seventeen hundred or more. It was the opinion of many that the fire had been started by chance in the heat of battle. Some others asserted that the fire was set by Neri Abati, prior of San Piero Scheraggio, a dissolute man eager for evil, who, seeing the people engaged in fighting, thought he could do some wicked thing that men could not remedy while they were engaged; and that it might turn out better for him, he set the fire in the house of his companions, where he could do it more conveniently. It was

[1] See *FH* II 5.

in the year 1304 and in the month of July[2] that Florence was agitated by fire and steel. Only Messer Corso Donati did not arm himself amidst all the tumults, for he judged that thus he could more easily become arbiter of both parties when, exhausted from fighting, they would turn to accords.[3] Nonetheless, they put down their arms more from satiety with evil than for the unity that might be born among them: the only thing that came of it was that the rebels did not return, and the party that favored them remained inferior.

22

WHEN the legate had returned to Rome and heard about the new scandals going on in Florence, he persuaded the pope that if he wanted to unite Florence it was necessary to have twelve of the first citizens of the city come to him. Afterwards, with the nourishment of the evil removed, it would be easy to think about how to eliminate it. This advice was accepted by the pontiff, and the citizens who were called in obeyed. Among them was Messer Corso Donati. After the departure of these men [from Florence] the legate let the exiles know that, as Florence was without its heads, now was the time for them to return. So the exiles, having put together their force, came to Florence, and, entering the city through walls not yet complete, they got as far as the Piazza San Giovanni.

It was a notable thing that those who had fought earlier for the exiles' return, when they were unarmed and praying to be restored to their fatherland, should later take up arms against them, when they saw them armed and ready to seize the city by force (so much more did they value the common utility than private friendship). They joined with all the people to force the exiles to return where they had come from.[1] The exiles failed in their undertaking because they left part of their men at Lastra and because they did not wait for Messer Tolosetto Uberti, who was to come from Pistoia with three hundred cavalry. For they supposed that speed rather than strength would bring them victory. And indeed, it does often happen in such undertakings that tardiness takes away opportunity from you and speed takes away strength. When the rebels had departed, Florence returned again to its old divisions. To take authority from the family of the Cavalcanti, the people forcibly seized from them le Stinche, a fortified place in the Val di Grieve, which had belonged to that family of old.

[2] On June 10.
[3] Villani says merely that Messer Corso stayed in the middle because he was ill with gout; Giovanni Villani, *Cronica* VIII 71.
[1] See Dante, *Paradiso* XVII 49–63.

And because those who were taken within it were the first ones to be put into the newly built prison,[2] the prison was called after the fortified place from which they had come and is still called le Stinche.

The first men of the republic again revived the companies of the people and gave them the ensigns under which the men of the guilds used to assemble previously. They called the heads Gonfaloniers of the companies and Collegi of the Signori,[3] and they wanted these men to help the Signoria with arms during riots[4] and with advice in time of peace. They added an executor to the two rectors,[5] who was to act together with the Gonfaloniers against the insolence of the great.

Meanwhile, the pope had died, and Messer Corso and the other citizens had returned from Rome. Life would have gone on quietly if the city had not been agitated again by the restless spirit of Messer Corso. To get reputation for himself, he always held opinions contrary to the most powerful men; and whichever way he saw the people inclined, he too turned so that his authority would be more welcome to them. So he was at the head of all the disputes and novelties, and all those who desired to obtain some extraordinary thing resorted to him. As a result, many citizens of repute hated him, and as this hatred was seen to be growing, the party of the Blacks was coming to open division. For Messer Corso made use of his private forces and authority, and his adversaries, those of the state; but so great was the authority he carried in his person that everyone feared him. Nonetheless, to take from him the popular favor that can easily be eliminated in this way, they spread it about that he wished to establish a tyranny. It was easy to persuade the people of this because his mode of living overstepped all civil bounds. This opinion grew greatly after he had taken as a wife the daughter of Uguccione della Faggiuola, head of the Ghibelline party and a White and a man very powerful in Tuscany.

23

AS soon as this marriage came to notice, it inspired his adversaries, and they took up arms against him. The people, for the same causes, did not defend him, and indeed the greater part of them agreed with his enemies. At the head of his adversaries were Messer Rosso della Tosa, Messer Pazzino de' Pazzi, Messer Geri Spini, and Messer Berto Brunelleschi. These men, with their followers and the greater part of the people, gathered in

---

[2] See *FH* II 15.
[3] Lit.: colleagues of the Signori, members of a college associated with the Signori.
[4] Lit.: scandals.
[5] The Podestà and the Captain of the People.

arms at the foot of the palace of the Signori. By their order a charge was made to Messer Piero Branco, Captain of the people,[1] against Messer Corso, as a man who with the help of Uguccione wanted to make himself tyrant. After this he was cited and then judged a rebel for his defiance; nor was there more than the space of two hours from the accusation to the sentence. When their judgment had been given, the Signori together with the companies of the people gathered under their ensigns and went to find him. Messer Corso for his part was frightened neither by seeing himself abandoned by many of his own people nor by the sentence given, nor by the authority of the Signori, nor by the multitude of his enemies. He fortified himself in his houses in the hope that he could defend himself until Uguccione, whom he had sent for, would come to his aid. His houses and the streets around them were blockaded by him and then manned by his partisans, who defended them in such a way that the people, despite their great number, were unable to overcome them. Thus, the fighting was heavy, with deaths and wounds on every side; and when the people saw that they could not overcome Messer Corso through the open routes, they seized the houses near his, and after these were broken through, they entered his house by unexpected routes. As Messer Corso saw himself thus encircled by enemies, and trusting no longer in the aid of Uguccione, he decided, since he despaired of victory, to see if he could find a remedy to bring safety. He and Gherardo Bordoni, at the head of many others of his strongest and most trusted friends, made a dash against the enemy, who opened up in a manner that enabled them to fight their way through. They got out of the city through the Porta alla Croce. Nonetheless, they were pursued by many men, and Gherardo was killed at the Affrico[2] by Boccaccio Cavicciuli. Messer Corso too was overtaken and seized at Rovezzano by some Catalan knights, soldiers of the Signoria. But in coming toward Florence, so as not to look at his victorious enemies in the face and be tortured by them, he let himself fall off his horse; and when he was on the ground, his throat was cut by one of the men leading him. His body was picked up by the monks of San Salvi and buried without any honor. Such was the end of Messer Corso, from whom his fatherland and the party of the Blacks realized many goods and many evils; and had he been of a quieter spirit, his memory would be more prosperous. Nonetheless, he deserves to be numbered among the rare citizens our city has had. It is true that his restlessness made his fatherland and his party not remember the obligations they owed to him, and in the end it brought about his death and many evils to both. Uguc-

---

[1] Actually Podestà at the time, October 1308.
[2] The river Affrico.

cione, while coming to the aid of his son-in-law, heard when he reached Remoli that Messer Corso had been attacked by the people. As he thought he could do him no favor and did not want to harm himself without helping him, he turned back.

24

WITH the death of Messer Corso, which happened in the year 1308, the tumults ceased and life went on quietly until it was learned that Emperor Henry was coming into Italy with all the Florentine rebels whom he had promised he would restore to their fatherland. To the heads of the government, consequently, it appeared that it would be well to reduce the number of rebels so as to have fewer enemies. So they decided that all the rebels should be restored except those mentioned by name in the law, to whom return was forbidden. As a result, the greater part of the Ghibellines and some of those in the party of Whites, among whom were Dante Alighieri, the sons of Messer Veri de Cerchi and of Giano della Bella, remained outside. Besides this, they sent to Robert, king of Naples, for aid; and since they were unable to obtain it as friends, they gave him the city for five years so that he would have to defend them as his men. On his way the emperor took the road from Pisa and went through the marshes to Rome, where he was crowned in the year 1312. Then, having decided to subdue the Florentines, he came from there by way of Perugia and Arezzo to Florence. He took up a position with his army in the monastery of San Salvi, a mile away from the city, where he stayed for fifty days without any profit. So much did he despair of being able to disturb the state of the city that he went away to Pisa, where he agreed with Frederick, king of Sicily, to attempt a campaign against the Kingdom. He advanced with his men, and while he was hoping for victory and King Robert was fearing ruin, he arrived in Buonconvento and died.[1]

25

IT happened a short time later that Uguccione della Faggiuola became lord of Pisa and soon after of Lucca, having been put there by the Ghibelline party. With the support[1] of these cities he did very serious damage

---

[1] Cf. *FH* I 26, where these events are narrated without reference to Florence and where the emperor's attack on Tuscany is said, incorrectly, to have been mounted by Frederick alone.

[1] Lit.: favor.

to those nearby. To free themselves from this, the Florentines asked King Robert for Piero, his brother, to direct their armies. Uguccione for his part never ceased increasing his power. He had seized many fortified places in the Valdarno and the Val di Nievole by force and deceit; but when he went on to besiege Montecatini, the Florentines judged that it was necessary for them to go to its aid if they did not want that fire to burn their whole country. After they gathered a large army they went into the Val di Nievole, where they came to battle with Uguccione, and after much fighting they were defeated. There died Piero, the king's brother, whose body was never found; and with him more than two thousand men were slain. Nor was the victory a happy one for Uguccione's side, because a son of his died there with many other heads of the army.

After this defeat, the Florentines fortified their towns around them, and King Robert sent as their captain Count d'Andria, dubbed Count Novello. Because of his behavior or else because it is natural to the Florentines that every state annoys them and every accident divides them, the city became divided between friends and enemies of the king, notwithstanding the war it was waging against Uguccione. The heads of the enemies were Messer Simone della Tosa, the Magalotti, with certain other men of the people who were superior to the others in the government. These men arranged to send to France and afterwards to Germany to get heads and men so that when they arrived, these men could drive out the count, governor for the king. But fortune prevented them from getting any one of them. Nonetheless, they did not abandon their undertaking, and as they were seeking for one to adore and could not get him from France or from Germany, they got him from Gubbio; and after they had first driven out the count, they had Lando da Gubbio[2] come as executive, or indeed as sheriff, to whom they gave full power[3] over the citizens. He was a rapacious and cruel man who went about the town accompanied by many armed men and took the life of this one or that according to the will of those who had elected him. His insolence became so great that he struck false money with the Florentine stamp without anyone's daring to oppose him: to such greatness had the discords of Florence brought him! Truly a great and wretched city, which neither the memory of past divisions, nor fear of Uguccione, nor the authority of a king had been able to keep firm, so that it found itself in a very bad state for being plundered outside by Uguccione and inside by Lando da Gubbio. Those who were friends of the king and against Lando and his followers were the noble

[2] Lando de' Becchi, da Gubbio.
[3] Potestà.

families and the great men of the people, and all the Guelfs. Nonetheless, since the state was in the hands of their adversaries, they could not reveal themselves without great peril. Yet having decided to free themselves from such an indecent tyranny, they wrote secretly to King Robert to ask him to make Count Guido da Battifolle his vicar in Florence. This was immediately ordered by the king; and the enemy party, even though the Signori were against the king, did not dare to oppose the count, because of his good qualities. Nonetheless, he did not have much authority because the Signori and Gonfaloniers of the companies favored Lando and his party. And while Florence was living through these travails, the daughter of King Albert of Germany came through on her way to meet Charles, son of Robert, her intended husband. She was greatly honored by the friends of the king, and they lamented to her the condition of the city and the tyranny of Lando and his partisans. So, before she left, through her support[4] and that brought in from the king, the citizens united and Lando's authority was taken from him; and he was sent back to Gubbio full of booty and blood. Lordship for the king was prolonged for three years to reform the government, and because seven Signori from the party of Lando had already been elected, six from those of the king were elected. There followed some magistracies with thirteen Signori, but afterwards they were reduced to seven in accordance with former custom.

26

IN these times lordship over Pisa and Lucca was taken from Uguccione, and Castruccio Castracani, from citizen of Lucca, became lord of it.[1] Since he was young, daring, and fierce, and fortunate in his undertakings, in a very short time he became prince of the Tuscan Ghibellines. Because of this, the Florentines, after their civil discords had been put down, for many years thought, first, that Castruccio's forces would not grow, but then, when they did grow despite their wishes, they thought of what they might have to do to defend themselves against them. And so that the Signori might deliberate with better advice and execute with greater authority, they created twelve citizens whom they named "Good Men," without whose advice and consent the Signori could not act on any important thing. Meanwhile, the end of King Robert's lordship had come; the city, having become prince of itself, reordered itself with the custom-

---

4 Lit.: favors.
1 On Castruccio, see NM's *The Life of Castruccio Castracani of Lucca* and *D* II 9, 12.

ary rectors and magistrates; and the great fear it had of Castruccio kept it united. Castruccio, after having done many things against the signori of Lunigiana, attacked Prato, whereupon the Florentines decided to go to its aid, closed up their shops, and went there as a people.[2] Twenty thousand on foot and fifteen hundred on horse gathered there. And to take forces from Castruccio and add them to themselves, the Signori made it known through a decree that any Guelf rebel coming to the aid of Prato would be restored to his fatherland after the campaign; so more than four thousand rebels came over to them. This great army, brought with such speed to Prato, so frightened Castruccio that, without wishing to try the fortune of battle, he withdrew to Lucca. This gave rise to dispute in the Florentine camp between the nobles and the people: the people wanted to follow him and fight him so as to eliminate him, while the nobles wanted to return, saying that it was enough to have put Florence in peril in order to free Prato. It had been well when they were compelled by necessity, but now that necessity was absent, when they could acquire little and lose much, it was no time to tempt fortune. As they were unable to agree, the judgment was put to the Signori, who found the same dispute between the people and the great in the councils. When this was heard through the city, it brought many people together in the piazza uttering words full of menace against the great: so the great yielded out of fear. Such a course, taken late and by many unwillingly, gave the enemy time to retire safely to Lucca.

27

THIS disorder made the people so indignant against the great that the Signori were unwilling to honor the faith pledged by their own order and encouragement to the exiles. Having a presentiment of this, the exiles decided to forestall it. They went ahead of the army so as to be the first to enter Florence and presented themselves at the gates of the city. Because this action had been foreseen, it did not succeed for them, and they were repulsed by those who had remained in Florence. But to see if they could have by agreement what they had not been able to obtain by force, they sent eight men as ambassadors to remind the Signori of the faith pledged to them and the dangers they had run under it, hoping for the reward that had been promised to them. And although the nobles felt themselves to be indebted by this obligation since they in particular had promised what the Signori had obligated themselves to, and although

---

[2] Lit.: popularly.

they very much exerted themselves for the benefit of the exiles, nonetheless, because of the indignation the generality of people,[1] which was not as it could have been if the campaign against Castruccio had been won,[2] they did not obtain it. The result was blame and dishonor for the city. When many of the nobles became indignant because of this, they tried to obtain by force what they had asked for and had been denied. They made an agreement with the exiles, who were to come armed to the city while inside they would take up arms to help them. The thing was discovered before the designated day; so the exiles found the city in arms and organized[3] to stop those outside and to frighten those inside so that no one dared to take up arms. Thus, without gaining any profit, they pulled out of the enterprise. After their departure it was desired to punish those who were to blame for having had them come; but though everyone knew who the culprits were, no one dared to name them, to say nothing of accusing them. Therefore, to learn the truth regardless, it was provided that in the councils anyone might denounce the culprits in writing, and that those written up should be presented to the Captain secretly. In consequence, Messer Amerigo Donati, Messer Tegghiaio Frescobaldi, and Messer Lotteringo Gherardini were accused. Since they had a judge more favorable perhaps than their offenses deserved, they were sentenced only to pay a fine.

28

THE tumults that arose in Florence because of the arrival of the rebels at the gates showed that for the companies of the people, a single head was not enough. They therefore wanted each company to have three or four heads in the future, and they added to each Gonfalonier two or three whom they called Pennonieri,[1] so that when there was no necessity for the whole company to convene, a part of it might be engaged under one head. As happens in all republics, always after an unforeseen event some old laws are annulled and others are renewed. So, whereas earlier the Signoria had been made over from time to time, the then Signori and Collegi, because they had much power, had themselves given authority to make Signori that were to sit for the next forty months. They put these

[1] Lit.: the universality. NM, in accord with the usage of his time, says "universal" in cases where we would expect him to use "general," since he apparently does not mean "everyone."

[2] That is, the follow-up campaign proposed by the people; see the end of *FH* II 26.

[3] Lit.: ordered.

[1] Flag bearers.

names into a bag and every two months drew them out. But before the end of the forty months had come, new baggings were held because many citizens doubted that their names had been put into the bag. From this beginning the order arose of putting into the bag for a longer time the names of all the magistrates, both those of the inside and those of the outside,[2] whereas earlier the successors to the councils were elected at the end of magistracies. These baggings were later called "squittini." Because the squittini were held every three or, at the most, five years, it appeared that they would relieve the city of the annoyance and remove the cause of tumults that arose at the creation of every magistrate because there were so many competitors. Since they did not know how else to correct it, they took this way and did not understand the defects that were hidden under this small advantage.

29

IT was the year 1325, and Castruccio, having seized Pistoia, had become so powerful that the Florentines, fearing his greatness, decided to attack him before he should get complete dominion over that city and to remove it from obedience to him. And from among their citizens and friends they gathered twenty thousand foot soldiers and three thousand cavalry, and with this army they encamped at Altopascio so as to seize it and in that way hinder him from being able to come to the aid of Pistoia. The Florentines succeeded in taking that place and afterwards went toward Lucca, laying waste the countryside; but because of the little prudence and less faith of the captain, not much progress was made.

Their captain was Messer Ramondo di Cardona. This man had seen before how liberal the Florentines had been with their liberty, how they gave it now to the king, now to the legates, now to other men of lesser quality. He thought that if he led them into some necessity, it could easily happen that they would make him prince. Nor did he fail to mention it frequently, and he asked to have the same authority in the city that they had given him in the army, without which, he pointed out, he could not get the obedience necessary to a captain. As the Florentines would not consent to this, he went about wasting time while Castruccio was gaining[1] it. For the assistance that had been promised by the Visconti and the other tyrants of Lombardy was on its way to him. Though Messer Ramondo was strong in men, still, just as before, through little faith, he

---

[2] Inside and outside the city.
[1] Lit.: acquiring.

did not know how to win, so afterwards, through little prudence, he did not know how to save himself, but, proceeding slowly with his army, he was attacked by Castruccio near Altopascio and defeated after a great battle in which many citizens were taken or slain and together with them, Messer Ramondo. For his slight faith and evil advice he received from fortune the punishment he deserved to have from the Florentines. The harm that Castruccio inflicted on the Florentines after his victory in booty, prisoners, ruin, and arson could not possibly be told. For he rode and ranged for months wherever he wished without any man to oppose him; and for the Florentines after such a defeat, it was much merely to save the city.

30

YET the Florentines did not become so vile that they failed to provide large sums of money, hire men, and send to their friends for help. Nonetheless, to check such an enemy, no provision was enough; so they were forced to elect as their lord, Charles, duke of Calabria and son of King Robert, if they wanted him to come to their defense.[1] For as these were accustomed to lording it over Florence, they would rather have its obedience than its friendship. But because Charles was engaged in the wars in Sicily and was therefore unable to come and take the lordship,[2] he sent Walter, a man of French birth and duke of Athens. He took possession of the city as vicar of the lord and ordered the magistrates according to his will. His bearing was nonetheless so modest, and so contrary to his nature, that everyone loved him.

When the wars in Sicily had been settled, Charles came to Florence with a thousand cavalry, making his entrance in July of the year 1326. His arrival prevented Castruccio from freely plundering the Florentine countryside. Nonetheless, the reputation he had acquired outside was lost inside, and what damage had not been inflicted by enemies had to be endured at the hands of its friends, for the Signori did nothing without the consent of the duke. At the end of one year he had extracted four hundred thousand florins from the city, notwithstanding that by the agreements made with him he was not to have more than two hundred thousand. Such were the charges with which every day either he or his father burdened the city. To this damage were added other new suspicions and new

[1] See *D* II 9, 12.
[2] "Lordship" is *signoria*, the name for the very council by which Florence governed itself; see *FH* II 26.

enemies. The Ghibellines in Lombardy became suspicious on account of Charles's coming to Tuscany, so that Galeazzo Visconti and the other tyrants of Lombardy, with money and promises, had Ludwig of Bavaria come into Italy.[3] Ludwig had been elected emperor against the wish of the pope. He came to Lombardy and from there into Tuscany, where with the help of Castruccio he became lord of Pisa. From Pisa, with his money replenished, he went off toward Rome. This made Charles leave Florence out of fear for the Kingdom, and he left behind Messer Filippo da Saggineto as his vicar. After the departure of the emperor, Castruccio made himself lord of Pisa, and the Florentines by negotiation took Pistoia away from him. Castruccio went to encamp at Pistoia, and remained there with such virtue and obstinacy that, although the Florentines attempted many times to rescue it and attacked first his army and then his countryside, they were never able to deter him from his campaign either by force or by industry. So great was his thirst to punish the Pistolese and to get the better of the Florentines! Thus the Pistolese were compelled to accept him as lord. Although this affair brought much glory to him, it also brought so much hardship that on his return to Lucca, he died. And because it rarely happens that fortune does not accompany a good or an evil with another good or evil, Charles, duke of Calabria and lord of Florence, also died, in Naples, so that in a little while the Florentines were, beyond their every expectation, freed from the lordship of one and from the fear of the other. When they were left free, they reformed the city and annulled the entire order of the old councils; and they created two of them, one of three hundred popular citizens, the other of two hundred and fifty great and popular. The first they called Council of the People and the other Council of the Commune.

3 1

WHEN the emperor arrived in Rome, he created an antipope, ordered many things against the Church, and attempted many others without effect.[1] So in the end he departed in shame and came to Pisa, where either out of indignation or because they had not been paid, about eight hundred German cavalry rebelled against him and marshaled their forces in Montecarlo above the Ceruglio. As soon as the emperor left Pisa to go to Lombardy, these men occupied Lucca and drove out Francesco Castra-

[3] See *FH* I 26, 28.
[1] See *FH* I 28.

canni, who had been left there by the emperor. Thinking that they might extract some profit from their prey, they offered the city to the Florentines for eighty thousand florins—which was refused on the advice of Messer Simone della Tosa. This course would have been very advantageous to our city if the Florentines had maintained that wish, but as they changed their minds soon after, it was very damaging. For if before they could have had it peaceably for so low a price and did not want it, later when they did want it they did not get it even though they would have bought it for a much higher price. This was the cause that Florence changed its government so many times to its very great harm. Lucca, thus refused by the Florentines, was bought by Messer Gherardino Spinoli, a Genoese, for thirty thousand florins. And because men are slower to take what they can have than to desire what they cannot get, as soon as this purchase made by Messer Gherardino was revealed and for how low a price he had had it, the people of Florence were inflamed by an extreme desire to have the city, reproaching themselves and the one who had dissuaded them from it. And to get it by force, since they had not wanted to buy it, Florence sent its men to plunder and overrun the people of Lucca.

In the meantime, the emperor had left Italy, and the antipope, by order of the Pisans, had gone to prison in France. The Florentines, from the death of Castruccio, which happened in 1328, until 1340 remained quiet inside and attended only to the affairs of their state outside. They carried on many wars in Lombardy because of the coming of King John of Bohemia and in Tuscany on account of Lucca. They also adorned the city with new buildings; for they built the tower of Santa Reparata[2] with the advice of Giotto, a very famous painter in those times. Because of a flood in 1333, the waters of the Arno rose in some places in Florence more than twelve fathoms, thus ruining some bridges and many buildings; and they restored the ruined objects with great care and expense.

32

BUT when the year 1340 came, new causes of change arose. The powerful citizens had two ways of increasing or maintaining their power: one was to restrict the baggings of the magistrates so that they would always come either to themselves or to their friends;[1] and the other was for them to be the heads of the election of the rectors so as then to have judges favorable

---

[2] The campanile of the cathedral, now called Santa Maria del Fiore.

[1] The lot would be taken from among the "powerful citizens" and their friends—a way of manipulation, in contrast to the second and third ways, which were open domination. See *FH* II 28.

to them. And so highly did they value this second policy that when the ordinary rectors were not enough for them, they sometimes added a third. Thus at this time they added Messer Jacopo Gabrielli da Gubbio extraordinarily under the title of Captain of the Guard and gave him all authority over the citizens. Every day this man inflicted many injuries as contemplated by whoever was governing, and among the injured were Messer Piero de' Bardi and Messer Bardo Frescobaldi. As they were nobles and naturally arrogant, they could not bear being offended by a foreigner wrongfully and as contemplated by a few powerful men. They conspired to get revenge against him and whoever was governing, a conspiracy in which were many noble families and some popular that were displeased with the tyranny of whoever was governing.

The plan[2] made among them was that each would gather many armed men at home, and the morning after the solemn day of All Saints, when everyone was in the churches praying for their dead, they would take up arms to kill the Captain and the first among those who were ruling, and afterwards reform the state with new Signori and a new order. But because the more that dangerous courses are considered, the less willingly they are undertaken, it always happens that conspiracies that allow an interval of time before their execution are discovered.[3] Among the conspirators was Messer Andrea Bardi; in thinking the thing over, fear of punishment became more powerful in him than hope of revenge. He revealed everything to Jacopo Alberti, his brother-in-law, who informed the Priors, and the Priors, those in the regime. As the thing was almost at hazard, All Saints' Day being near, many citizens met at the palace, and judging that there was danger in delay, they wanted the Signori to ring the alarm and call the people to arms. The Gonfaloniers were Taldo Valori and Francesco Salviati, one of the Signori. Because they were relatives of the Bardi, it did not please them to sound the alarm. They argued that it was not good to have the people arm for every slight occasion, for authority given to a multitude not tempered by any check never did any good; that it was easy to start riots[4] but difficult to stop them, and so the better course would be to learn the truth of the thing first and to punish it by civil means than to try to correct it by a tumult on the basis of mere report, with the ruin of Florence. These words were not listened to on any side, and, amidst insulting gestures[5] and coarse words, the Signori were compelled of necessity to sound the alarm, at which the whole people ran with arms to the piazza. When the Bardi and Frescobaldi for their

[2] Lit.: order.
[3] See *D* III 6.
[4] Lit.: scandals.
[5] Lit.: modes.

part saw themselves discovered, they took up arms so as to win with glory or die without shame, hoping to defend the part of the city south of the river where they had their houses. They fortified the bridges, while hoping for the aid they expected from the nobles in the countryside and others of their friends. This design was spoiled for them by the men of the people who were living with them in that part of the city and who took up arms in favor of the Signori. Consequently, finding themselves isolated, they abandoned the bridges and withdrew to the street where the Bardi lived, as being stronger than any other, and that they defended virtuously. Messer Jacopo da Gubbio, knowing that the whole conspiracy was against him, fearful of death, altogether foolish and frightened, placed himself near the palace of the Signori in the midst of his armed men. But in the other rectors, in whom there was less to blame, there was more spirit, especially in the Podestà, who was called Messer Maffeo da Carradi. He appeared where the fighting was and, without fearing anything, crossed the Rubaconte Bridge, put himself among the swords of the Bardi, and signaled that he wanted to speak to them. Hence reverence for the man, for his manners, and for all his other great qualities made them lay down their arms at a stroke and listen to him quietly. With modest and grave words he censured their conspiracy and pointed out the danger in which they would find themselves if they did not yield to the popular impulse. He gave them hope that they would afterwards be heard and judged with mercy, and promised he would work it out that there would be compassion for their reasonable indignation. Then, turning to the Signori, he persuaded them that they would not want to prevail with the blood of their citizens and that they would not wish to judge those whom they had not heard. He worked it out well that, with the consent of the Signori, the Bardi and the Frescobaldi with their friends abandoned the city and without being impeded returned to their castles.

When they had departed and the people had disarmed, the Signori proceeded only against those of the Bardi and Frescobaldi families who had taken up arms. To strip them of power they bought the castles of Mangono and of Vernia from the Bardi, and they provided by law that no citizen could own a castle nearer than twenty miles to Florence. A few months later Stiatta Frescobaldi was beheaded and many others of that family declared rebels. It was not enough for those who were governing to have overcome and tamed the Bardi and Frescobaldi; but as men do almost always, the more authority they have, the worse they use it and the more insolent they become. Whereas at first it was one Captain of the Guard that afflicted Florence, they elected another in the countryside, and with very great authority so that men suspect to them could live neither in Florence nor outside. They were so stirred up against all the nobles that they were prepared to sell the city and them so as to avenge themselves. And as they waited for the opportunity, it came up well and they used it better.

33

BECAUSE of the many travails there had been in Tuscany and Lombardy, the city of Lucca had come under the lordship of Mastino della Scala, lord of Verona. Although he had received Lucca with the obligation to consign it to the Florentines, he had not done so because, being lord of Parma, he judged that he could keep it and so did not care about the faith he had pledged. For this the Florentines joined with the Venetians for revenge, and they waged such a war against him that he was about to lose his whole state. Nonetheless, they got no more advantage from having beaten Mastino than a little satisfaction of mind, because the Venetians, as do all those who ally with the less powerful, made peace without any regard for the Florentines as soon as they had won Treviso and Vicenza. But shortly after, the Visconti, lords of Milan, took Parma from Mastino; and as he judged that because of this he could no longer hold Lucca, he decided to sell it. The competitors were the Florentines and the Pisans, and in the press of bargaining the Pisans saw that the Florentines, being richer, were about to get it. Therefore they resorted to force, and with the help of the Visconti they went into the field. The Florentines did not on that account hold back on their purchase but closed their contract with Mastino, paying in part with money and in part by giving hostages. They sent Naddo Ruccellai, Giovanni di Bernardino de' Medici, and Rosso di Ricciardo de' Ricci there to take possession. These men entered Lucca by force, and the city was turned over to them by Mastino's men. The Pisans nonetheless continued their campaign and with all industry sought to have it by force, and the Florentines wanted to free Lucca from siege. After a long war the Florentines were driven off with loss of money and acquisition of shame, and the Pisans became its lords. The loss of this city, as always happens in similar cases, made the people of Florence indignant against those who were governing, and in all places and through all the piazzas they defamed them publicly, accusing them of avarice and wicked counsel.

At the beginning of this war, authority had been given to twenty citizens to carry it on; they had elected Messer Malatesta da Rimini to be captain of the campaign. He had governed it with little spirit and less prudence, and as they had then sent to Robert, king of Naples, for help, the king had sent Walter, duke of Athens, to them. Since the heavens willed that things prepare for future evil, he arrived in Florence precisely at the time when the campaign at Lucca had been lost completely. So these Twenty, seeing the people indignant, thought to renew their hope by electing a new captain and with that election either to check or to remove the causes for the slanders against themselves. And so that the people might still have cause to fear and that the duke of Athens might defend them with greater authority, they elected him first as protector, then as captain of their men-at-arms. The great, for the causes given earlier, lived malcontented, and many of them, having known Walter when at another time he had governed Florence in the name of Charles, duke of Calabria,[1] thought that the time had come when by the ruin of the city they could put out the fire burning within them. They judged that they had no other mode of subduing the people that had afflicted them than to put themselves under a prince who, since his virtue was known to one party and his insolence to the other, might check the one and reward the other. To this they added the hope of the good their merits would deliver when by their deeds he should acquire the principality. Therefore, they were often with him secretly, and they persuaded him to take lordship over everything, offering him the greatest help they could. To the authority and encouragements of these men was added that of certain popular families, which were the Peruzzi, Acciaiuoli, Antellesi, and Buonaccorsi. They were burdened by debts, and being without means of their own, they were desirous of having those debts satisfied by others, and thus by the enslavement of their fatherland to free themselves from slavery to their creditors. These persuasions inflamed the ambitious spirit of the duke to a greater desire to rule; and to give himself the reputation of a severe and just man, and in this way to increase his favor[2] with the plebs, he prosecuted those who had directed the war against Lucca, took the lives of Messer Giovanni de' Medici, Naddo Rucellai, and Guglielmo Altoviti and condemned many to exile and many to fines.

34

THESE executions frightened the middle citizens very much; they satisfied only the great and the plebs—the latter because their nature is to rejoice in evil and the former so as to see themselves avenged for the many injuries received from the people. And when the duke passed through the

---

[1] In 1326; see II 30.
[2] Lit.: grace.

streets, the frankness of his spirit was praised with loud voices, and every-one encouraged him publicly to find out frauds among the citizens and punish them. The office of the Twenty had come to less, and the reputa-tion of the duke had become great and fear of him very great, so that everyone was having his coat of arms[1] painted on their houses to show him they were his friends; nor did he lack anything as prince but the title.[2] And as it appeared to him that he could attempt anything safely, he gave the Signori to understand that he judged it necessary for the good of the city that free lordship[3] be given to him. Since the whole city was con-senting to it, he desired, then, that they too should consent to it. The Signori, as it happened, having long ago foreseen the ruin of their father-land, were all agitated by this request, and for all that they recognized their own danger; still, lest they fail their fatherland, they spiritedly re-fused.

The duke, so as to give himself a greater mark of religion and human-ity, had chosen the convent of Fra Minori di Santa Croce for his dwelling. Desiring to give effect to his evil thought, he had it publicly proclaimed that on the following morning all the people should appear in the piazza of Santa Croce before him. This proclamation frightened the Signori much more than the words that had been spoken before, and they con-ferred with those citizens whom they judged to be lovers of the fatherland and of freedom. Nor, since they recognized the duke's forces, were they able to think of any other remedy than to pray to him and to see, since their forces were insufficient, if their prayers were enough either to deter him from his enterprise or to make his lordship less harsh. A part of the Signori went to find him, therefore, and one of them spoke in this sense:

"We have come, lord, to you, moved first by your requests and then by the commands you have made to gather the people, for it appears certain to us that you want to obtain extraordinarily that which we have not granted to you in the ordinary way. Nor is it our intention to oppose your designs with any force, but only to point out to you how heavy a weight you are taking on your back, and how dangerous the course you are se-lecting, so that you can always remember our advice and that of those who counsel you otherwise, not for your advantage but to vent their rage. You are seeking to enslave a city which has always lived free; for the lordship which we did indeed yield to the kings of Naples was in alliance and not in slavery. Have you considered how important this is in a city like this, and how vigorous is the name of freedom, which no force can

[1] Lit.: ensign.
[2] For this phrase in Latin, applied to Hiero of Syracuse, see *P* 6.
[3] Or the Signoria.

subdue, no time consume, and no merit counterbalance? Think, lord, how much force will be necessary to keep such a city enslaved. Foreign forces, which you can always keep, are not enough; those from inside you cannot trust because those who are your friends now and who encourage you to select this course, just as they will have fought their enemies with your authority, will seek as they can to eliminate you and make themselves princes. The plebs in whom you trust will for any accident, though the slightest, reverse itself. So in a short time you may fear to have the whole city hostile, which will be the cause of its ruin and yours. Nor will you be able to find a remedy for the evil, because those lords can make their lordship safe who have few enemies, whom either by death or by exile it is easy to eliminate; but amidst universal hatred one never finds any security, because you[4] never know from whence evil may spring, and he who fears every man cannot secure himself against anyone. If indeed you try to do it, you aggravate the dangers, because those who remain burn more with hatred and are readier for revenge. That there is not enough time to consume the desires for freedom is most certain, for freedom, one knows, is often restored in a city by those who have never tasted it but who loved it only through the memories of it left to them by their fathers; and thus, once recovered, they preserve it with all obstinacy and at any peril. And even if their fathers had not recalled it to them, the public palaces, the places of the magistrates, the ensigns of the free orders recall it. These things must be recognized with the greatest desire by citizens. Which deeds of yours do you[5] want to be a counterweight to the sweetness of free life or to make men lose their desire for present conditions? Not if you were to add all Tuscany to this empire, and if every day you were to return to the city in triumph over our enemies; for all the glory would not be its but yours, and the citizens would not acquire subjects but fellow slaves in whom they would see their own slavery aggravated. And even if your habits were saintly, your modes benign, your judgments upright, they would not be enough to make you loved; and if you believe that they would be, you would be deceiving yourself, for to a man used to living unshackled every chain weighs and every link binds him. Besides, to find a violent state with a good prince is impossible, for of necessity either they must become alike or the one quickly ruins the other. Thus, you have to believe either that you have to hold this city with the greatest violence (for such a thing the citadels, the guards, and friends from outside many times are not enough), or that you have to be content with the authority that we have given you. And we urge you to this,

---

[4] The speaker shifts from the formal to the familiar "you."
[5] The speaker shifts back to the formal "you."

reminding you that that dominion is alone lasting which is voluntary. Nor should you, blinded by a little ambition, be led to place yourself where, unable either to rest or to rise higher, you must necessarily fall with the greatest harm to yourself and to us."

35

THESE words did not move the obdurate spirit of the duke in any part, and he said it was not his intention to take freedom away from the city but to restore it; for only disunited cities were enslaved and united ones free. And if Florence, by his ordering, should rid itself of sects, ambition, and enmities, he would be giving it liberty, not taking that away. It was not his ambition but the prayers of many citizens that led him to take on this charge; so they would do well to content themselves with what contented the others. As for those dangers he might incur on account of this, he did not regard them, because it was the office of a man not good to set aside the good for fear of evil, and of a pusillanimous man not to pursue a glorious undertaking because the end was doubtful; and he believed he could conduct himself so that in a short time they would realize they had trusted him little and feared him too much. Thus the Signori agreed, seeing that they could do no further good, that the following morning the people would gather at their own piazza,[1] and that by their authority lordship[2] would be given to the duke under the same conditions that it had been given already to Charles, duke of Calabria.

It was the eighth day of September and in the year 1342 when the duke, accompanied by Messer Giovanni della Tosa and all his companions, and by many other citizens, came to the piazza. Together with the Signoria he climbed to the rostrum, which is what the Florentines call those steps that are at the foot of the palace of the Signori; there they read out to the people the agreements made between the Signoria and him. And when in the reading it came to that part where lordship was to be given to him for one year, there was a shout from among the people, "For life!" As Messer Francesco Rustichelli, one of the Signori, rose to speak and calm the tumult, his words were interrupted by shouts, so that with the consent of the people, the duke was elected lord not for one year but in perpetuity, and his name was picked up and carried around the piazza by the shouting multitude. It is the custom that the one put in charge of the palace guard in the absence of the Signori be locked inside; this office was entrusted

---

[1] The Piazza della Signoria, not the Piazza di Santa Croce, where the duke lived.
[2] Or the Signoria.

then to Rinieri de Giotto. Corrupted by friends of the duke, and without waiting for any force to be used, he put the duke inside; the frightened and dishonored Signori returned to their houses, and the palace was sacked by the family of the duke, the standard of the people torn apart, and his ensign raised above the palace. This was received with the inestimable sorrow and affliction of good men, and with great pleasure by those who either in ignorance or out of wickedness had consented to it.

36

NOW that the duke had acquired lordship, so as to take away the authority of those who were accustomed to being defenders of freedom, he prohibited the Signori from gathering at the palace and consigned them to a private house. He took away the ensigns from the Gonfaloniers of the companies of the people; he removed the orders of justice[1] against the great, freed the prisoners from the jails, had the Bardi and the Frescobaldi returned from exile, forbade anyone to carry arms; and to defend himself better from those inside, he made himself a friend to those outside. He greatly benefited the Aretines, therefore, and all others subject to the Florentines; he made peace with the Pisans, even though he had been made prince so as to make war on them; he canceled the bills of those merchants who had lent money to the republic in the war against Lucca, increased the old taxes and created new ones, took all authority away from the Signori and sought advice from Messer Baglione da Perugia and Messer Guglielmo d'Assisi, his rectors, and Messer Cerrettieri Bisdomini. The assessments he levied on citizens were heavy and his sentences unjust, and the severity and humanity that he had feigned were converted into arrogance and cruelty, whence many great citizens and popular nobles were either fined or killed, or tortured in new modes. And, lest he behave better outside than inside, he ordered six rectors for the countryside, who beat and despoiled the peasants. He kept the great under suspicion even though he had been benefited by them and had returned to many of them their fatherland, for he could not believe that the generous spirits usually found in the nobility could be content in obedience to him; and so he turned to benefiting the plebs, thinking that with their favors and with foreign arms he could preserve the tyranny. Therefore, when the month of May came, a time in which peoples are wont to celebrate, he made more companies of the plebs and the lesser people, to which, honored with splendid titles, he gave ensigns and money: so one part of

[1] The Ordinances of Justice; see *FH* II 13.

them went about the city celebrating and the other accepted the celebrations with very great pomp. As the fame of his new lordship spread, many of French blood came to seek him out, and he gave them all positions as his most trusted men, so that Florence in a short time became subject not only to the French but to their customs and their dress; for the men and women imitated them without any regard to civil life or to any shame. But above all else, what displeased was the violence that he and his men did, without any respect, to the women.

Thus did citizens live full of indignation as they saw the majesty of their state ruined, the orders laid waste, the laws annulled, every decent being corrupted, all civil modesty eliminated; for those accustomed to not seeing any regal pomp were unable to meet him without sorrow, surrounded by his armed satellites on foot and on horse. For when they saw their shame nearer, they were compelled of necessity to honor the one they especially hated. To this was added fear as they saw the frequent deaths and continuing assessments with which he impoverished and consumed the city. Such indignation and fears were known to the duke and feared by him; nonetheless, he wished to show everyone he believed himself loved. Thus it happened that when Matteo di Morozzo, either to ingratiate himself with him or to free himself from danger, revealed to him that the Medici family with some others had conspired against him, the duke not only did not investigate the thing but had the discloser put to death miserably. With this course he took away spirit from those who might seek to warn him for his safety and gave it to those who might wish his ruin.[2] He also had the tongue of Bettone Cini cut out with such cruelty that he died of it, for having censured the assessments that were levied on the citizens. This increased the indignation of the citizens and their hatred of the duke, for the city was accustomed to do and to speak about everything and with every license and could not bear to have its hands tied and its mouth sealed. Thus the indignation and hatred grew to such a degree that they would have inflamed not only the Florentines, who do not know how to maintain freedom and are unable to bear slavery, but any servile people to recover their freedom. Wherefore many citizens of every quality resolved to lose their lives or get back their freedom; and in three parties of three sorts of citizens three conspiracies were made: the great, the people, and the artisans. They were moved, apart from universal causes, because it appeared to the great that they were not getting back the state; to the people, that they had lost it; and to the artisans, that they were losing their earnings.

The archbishop of Florence, Messer Agnolo Acciaiuoli, had already

[2] See *D* III 6 (end).

exalted the deeds of the duke in his sermons and had got great favors from the people for him. But after he saw him a lord and recognized his tyrannical ways, it appeared to him that he had deceived his fatherland; and to amend the error he had committed, he thought he had no other remedy than to have the hand that had inflicted the wound heal it. He made himself head of the first and strongest conspiracy, in which were the Bardi, Rossi, Frescobaldi, Scali, Altoviti, Magalotti, Strozzi, and Mancini. Messers Manno and Corso Donati were princes of one of the other two, and with them were the Pazzi, Cavicciuli, Cerchi, and Albizzi. In the third, Antonio Adimari was first, and with him were the Medici, Bordoni, Rucellai, and Aldobrandini. These men thought about killing the duke in the house of the Albizzi, where they believed he might go on the day of San Giovanni to see the horse races, but since he did not go, they did not succeed. They thought of attacking him as he went for a walk in the city, but they saw that this mode was difficult because he went about well accompanied and armed and always varied his route so that there could be no certain place to wait for him. They reasoned about killing him at the councils, but it appeared to them that even if they killed him they would be left at the discretion of his forces. While these things were being discussed among the conspirators, Antonio Adimari revealed himself to some of his Sienese friends so as to get men from them by showing them a part of the conspirators and affirming that the whole city was prepared to free itself. Whereupon one of them passed the thing along to Messer Francesco Brunelleschi, not to expose it but in the belief that he too was one of the conspirators. Messer Francesco, either out of fear for himself or out of the hatred he bore for the others, revealed everything to the duke; hence Pagolo del Mazzeca and Simone da Monterappoli were taken. They frightened the duke by revealing the quality and quantity of the conspirators, and he was advised to summon them rather than arrest them, because if they should flee, it would be possible to secure himself against them without scandal by their exile. So the duke had Antonio Adimari summoned, who, trusting in his companions, immediately appeared. He was detained. The duke was advised by Messer Francesco Brunelleschi and Messer Uguccione Buondelmonte to ride through the town armed and to have those who had been arrested put to death, but this was not agreeable to him as it appeared to him that for so many enemies his forces were small. Yet he took another course by which, if it had succeeded, he would have secured himself against his enemies and provided himself with forces. The duke was accustomed to summon citizens to advise him on current cases; so having sent outside to provide men, he made a list of three hundred citizens and had his sergeants summon them under color of wanting to consult with them. Then, when they would have been brought together, he planned to eliminate them either by death or by prison. The capture of Antonio Adimari and the sending for men, which could not be done secretly, had frightened the citizens, especially the guilty ones, hence the boldest refused to obey. And because each had read the list, they sought each other out and inspired each other to take up arms, preferring to die like men, arms in hand, than to be led like cattle to the slaughterhouse. Thus, in a few hours, all three conspiracies were revealed to each other and they resolved to start a tumult in the Mercato Vecchio on the following day, which was the 26th of July, 1343, and after that to arm themselves and to call the people to freedom.

37

WHEN the next day came, at the sound of noon, according to the order given, they took up arms; and the whole people armed with a cry for liberty. Each person prepared himself in his own district under ensigns with the arms of the people, which had been made secretly by the conspirators. All the heads of families, noble as well as popular, met and swore an oath both for their defense and for death to the duke, except for some of the Buondelmonti and Cavalcanti and the four popular families who had contributed to making him lord.[1] They, together with the butchers and others of the basest plebs, ran armed to the piazza in favor of the duke. At this noise the duke armed the palace, and his men, who had been lodged in different places, mounted their horses to go to the piazza. On the way they were fought in many places and killed, but about three hundred cavalry got there. The duke was in doubt whether he should go out to fight the enemy or defend the palace from within. On the other side, the Medici, Cavicciuli, Rucellai, and other families who had been more offended by him were doubtful whether, if he should come out, many who had taken up arms against him might not reveal themselves to be his friends; and desiring to deny him the opportunity of coming out and of increasing his forces, they took the lead and attacked the piazza. On their arrival those popular families who had come out for the duke, seeing themselves openly attacked, changed their minds now that the duke's fortune had changed, and all took the side of the citizens, except for Messer Uguccione Buondelmonte, who went into the palace, and Messer Giannozzo Cavalcanti, who, having withdrawn with some of his companions to the Mercato Nuovo, climbed up on a bench and begged the people who were going armed into the piazza to go there in

[1] The Peruzzi, Antellesi, Acciaiuoli, and Buonaccorsi; see *FH* II 33.

favor of the duke. To frighten them he exaggerated the size of the duke's forces, and he threatened that they would all be killed if they should obstinately pursue an undertaking against their lord. Finding no man either to follow him or to castigate him for his insolence, and seeing that he labored in vain, he withdrew to his house so as not to try fortune further. Meanwhile, the battle in the piazza between the people and the duke's troops was great; and although the palace helped the latter, they were overcome. Part of them submitted themselves to the Podestà of the enemy; part, leaving their horses behind, fled into the palace. While the fighting was going on in the piazza, Corso and Messer Amerigo Donati[2] with part of the people broke into the Stinche, burned the papers of the Podestà and the public chamber, sacked the houses of the rectors, and killed all the duke's ministers whom they could get. The duke, for his part, seeing that he had lost the piazza and that the whole city was hostile, and without hope of any aid, tried to see if he could win the people over with some humane act. He had the prisoners come to him, and with loving and gracious words he freed them; and although Antonio Adimari was displeased with it, he made him a knight. He had his own ensigns taken down from the palace and raised those of the people. These things, done late and out of season, because they were forced and done without dignity, served him little. Thus he remained, malcontent, besieged in his palace; and he saw that for having wanted too much, he was losing everything. He feared that in a few days he would have to die either of hunger or by the sword. The citizens withdrew to Santa Reparata to give form to the state. They created fourteen citizens, half from the great and half popular, who with the bishop would have whatever authority would enable them to reform the state of Florence. They elected six more, who were to have the authority of the Podestà until the one who had been elected should come. Many men had come to Florence in aid of the people, among whom were the Sienese with six ambassadors, men much honored in their fatherland. These men carried on negotiations between the people and the duke, but the people refused any discussion[3] on accord unless first Messer Guiglielmo d'Assisi and his son, together with Messer Cerrettieri Bisdomini, were put in their power.[4] The duke did not want to grant this; yet, as he was being threatened by the men shut in with him, he let himself be coerced. Without doubt, indignation appears greater and wounds are graver when liberty is being recovered than when it is being defended. Messer Guglielmo and his son were placed among thousands of their enemies, and the son was not yet eighteen years old;

[2] In fact, one man, Messer Corso di Amerigo Donati.
[3] Lit.: reasoning.
[4] *Potestà*.

nonetheless, his age, his form, and his innocence could not save him from the fury of the multitude. Those whom they could not wound living, they wounded when dead, and not satisfied with cutting them to pieces with their swords, they tore them apart with their hands and their teeth. And so that all their senses might be satisfied in revenge, having first heard their wails, seen their wounds, and handled their torn flesh, they still wanted their taste to relish them; so as all the parts outside were sated with them, they also sated the parts within. As much as this rabid fury harmed[5] Messer Guglielmo and his son, it was useful to Messer Cerrittieri; for the multitude, wearying of cruelty to these two, did not remember him. As he was not asked for, he remained in the palace, from which, later in the night, he was taken away safely by certain of his relatives and friends. The multitude having purged itself with the blood of these two, an accord was concluded. The duke was to depart with his men and his things in safety and to renounce all his rights[6] over Florence; and then, outside the domain, he was to ratify his renunciation in the Casentino. After this accord, on the sixth day of August, he left Florence accompanied by many citizens; and having arrived in the Casentino, he ratified the renunciation, though still unwillingly. Nor would he have kept his faith if Count Simone had not threatened to take him back to Florence. As his governing demonstrated, this duke was avaricious and cruel, difficult in audiences, arrogant in replies; he wanted the slavery and not the good will of men; and for this he desired to be feared rather than loved.[7] Nor was his person less hateful than his habits, for he was small, black, and had a long and sparse beard, so that in every way he deserved to be hated. Thus at the end of ten months his wicked habits took from him the lordship that the wicked advice of others had given him.

38

THESE unforeseen events occurring in the city inspired all the towns subject to the Florentines to get back their own freedom. Arezzo, Castiglione, Pistoia, Volterra, Colle, and San Gimignano rebelled, so that with one stroke Florence was left deprived of its tyranny and its dominion. In recovering its freedom, it taught its subjects how to recover theirs. Thus, just after the expulsion of the duke and the loss of their dominion, the fourteen citizens and the bishop thought it preferable to placate their subjects with peace than to make enemies of them by war, and to show them

---

[5] Lit.: offended.
[6] Lit.: reasons.
[7] See *P* 18.

that they were as glad of their subjects' freedom as of their own.[1] Therefore, they sent spokesmen to Arezzo to renounce the empire they had over that city and to sign an accord with them, so that, since they could no longer have them as subjects, they might profit from them as friends of their city. With the other towns also they made agreements as best they could, provided that they keep the Florentines as friends, so that, being free, the other towns could help maintain the Florentines' own freedom. This course, prudently adopted, had a very prosperous result; for Arezzo, after not many years, returned to the empire of the Florentines, and the other towns were reduced to their former obedience within a few months. And thus many times things are obtained more quickly and with fewer dangers and less expense by avoiding them than by pursuing them with all force and obstinacy.

39

SINCE things outside were settled, they turned to those inside; and after some debate between the great and the popular, it was concluded that the great should have one-third of the Signoria and half of the other offices. The city, as we showed above,[1] was divided into sixths, from which six Signori, one from each sixth, had been elected, except when by some accidents for a time twelve or thirteen were created; but shortly after, they returned to six. That it should be reformed in this part, therefore, became apparent as much because the sixths were unequally divided as because, if they wanted to give a part to the great, it was needful to increase the number of Signori. So they divided the city into quarters and from each created three Signori; they left out the Gonfaloniers of Justice and those of the companies of the people; and in place of the twelve Good Men they made eight councilors, four of each sort. The government having been established with this order, the city would have settled down if the great had been content to live with that modesty which is required by civil life; but they acted in a contrary way, for as private individuals they did not want companions, and in the magistracies they wanted to be lords. Every day produced some example of their insolence and arrogance. This displeased the people, and they lamented that from one tyrant who had been eliminated a thousand had been born. Thus instances of insolence grew on one side and indignation on the other, so that the heads of the popular side pointed out to the bishop that the great were indecent and not good companions to the people; and they persuaded him to see to it that the

[1] See D II 21.
[1] See FH II 11.

great contented themselves with taking part in the other offices and left to the people alone the magistracy of the Signori.

The bishop was naturally good, but it was easy to turn him first to one side, then to another. The result of this was that, at the instance of his consorts, he had at first favored the duke of Athens and then, by the advice of other citizens, had conspired against him. He had favored the great in reform of the state, and so now he appeared to favor the people, having been moved by the reasons submitted to him by these popular citizens. And believing that he would find in others as little stability as was in himself, he persuaded himself to conduct the affair by accord. He convened the Fourteen, who had not yet lost authority, and with the best words he knew he urged them to yield the rank of the Signoria to the people, promising quiet for the city from it, otherwise their ruin and undoing. These words strongly excited the spirits of the great. Messer Ridolfo di Bardi rebuked him with bitter words, calling him a man of little faith and reproaching him as frivolous for his friendship with the duke and as a betrayer for expelling him; and he concluded by telling him that the honors they had acquired at their peril they were willing to defend at their peril. And having departed with the others, angered by the bishop, he let his consorts and all the noble families hear about it. The popular side also told others what they had in mind, and while the great ordered themselves with help for the defense of their Signori, it did not appear to the people that they should wait until the great were in order, and they ran to the palace, armed and shouting that the great should give up the magistracy. The noise and tumult were great. The Signori saw themselves abandoned because the great, seeing the whole people armed, did not dare to take up arms, and each stayed inside his house. Thus the popular Signori, who had made a first attempt to calm the people by assuring them that their companions were modest and good men and had been unable to succeed in this, as the less evil course sent them back to their houses, to which they were with trouble led safely. After the great had left the palace, the office of the four great councilors was also taken away, and in their stead twelve popular ones were made. The eight Signori who were left chose one Gonfalonier of Justice and sixteen Gonfaloniers of the companies of the people, and they reformed the councils so as to put the whole government in the will of the people.

40

WHILE these things were going on, there was a great scarcity in the city, so that the great and the lesser people were malcontent—the latter because of hunger, the former for having lost their dignities. This gave Messer Andrea Strozzi the inspiration that he could take over the freedom of the city. He sold his wheat at a lower price than others, for which many people gathered at his houses, so many that one morning he dared to mount his horse and with several of those people behind him to call the people to arms. In a short time he had gathered together more than 4,000 men, with whom he went into the piazza of the Signori and asked that the palace be opened to them. But the Signori, with threats and arms, moved them off the piazza, and then with proclamations so frightened them that little by little everyone returned to his house. Thus Messer Andrea, finding himself alone, was able to save himself only with trouble from the hands of the magistrates. This unforeseen event, though it was rash and had the ending that like motions usually have, gave hope to the great that they could compel the people, since they saw that the lesser plebs was in disaccord with it. So as not to lose this opportunity, they decided to arm themselves with every sort of help so as to regain by force, reasonably, that which had been unjustly taken from them by force. And they grew so confident of victory that they openly provided themselves with arms, fortified their houses, sent to friends as far away as Lombardy for help. The people too, together with the Signori, made their own provisions by arming themselves and by asking for help from the Perugians and the Sienese. Indeed, help had already arrived for both parties, and the whole city was in arms. The great had taken up positions on this side of the Arno in three places: at the houses of the Cavicciulli near San Giovanni, at the houses of the Pazzi and the Donati at San Piero Maggiore, and at those of the Cavalcanti in the Mercato Nuovo. Those on the other side of the Arno had fortified themselves at the bridges and in the streets of their houses: the Nerli were defending the bridge at Carraia, the Frescobaldi and Mannegli at Santa Trinita, the Rossi and Bardi at the Ponte Vecchio and Rubaconte. The popular side, for their part, were gathering under the Standard of Justice[1] and under the ensigns of the companies of the people.

41

WHILE standing in this manner, it did not appear to the people that they should hold off the engagement any longer, and the first to move were the Medici and Rondinegli, who attacked the Cavicciulli on that side of the piazza of San Giovanni which gives entrance to their houses. Here the engagement was great because they were struck by stones from the tow-

[1] See *FH* II 12.

ers and wounded by crossbows from below. The battle lasted for three hours, and the people kept gaining, so that the Cavicciulli, seeing themselves overwhelmed by the multitude and lacking help, became frightened and submitted themselves to the Podestà of the people, who saved their houses and property for them. He took from them only their weapons and commanded them to disperse and go unarmed to the houses of those on the popular side who were their relatives and friends.

The first attack having won,[1] the Donati and the Pazzi too were easily conquered because they were less powerful than the others. There remained on this side of the Arno only the Cavalcanti, who were strong both in men and in position. Nonetheless, when they saw all the Gonfaloni[2] against them and that the others had been overcome by only three Gonfaloni, they surrendered without putting up much defense. Already three parts of the city were in the hands of the people; only one[3] remained in the power of the great, but it was the most difficult both because of the power of those defending it and because of the site, which was protected by the Arno River. Thus one needed to win the bridges that were being defended in the modes shown above. The Ponte Vecchio was the first to be attacked; it was hardily defended because the towers were armed, the streets barricaded, and the barricades guarded by very fierce men. So the people were repulsed with serious loss. Recognizing therefore that here they were struggling in vain, they tried to cross the Rubaconte bridge, and finding the same difficulties there, they left four Gonfaloni on guard at those two bridges and with the others attacked the bridge at the Carraia. And although the Nerli defended themselves manfully, they were unable to withstand the fury of the people, both because the bridge (having no towers to defend it) was weaker and because the Capponi and the other popular families, their neighbors, attacked them. Struck thus on every side, they abandoned the barricades and gave way to the people, who then conquered the Rossi and the Frescobaldi because all the popular side on the other side of the Arno joined with the victors. There remained only the Bardi, whom neither the ruin of the others nor the union of the people against them nor the slight hope of help could frighten. They would rather fight and either die or see their houses burned and sacked than voluntarily submit themselves to the will of their enemies. They so defended themselves, therefore, that the people tried many times in vain to conquer them either from the Ponte Vecchio or from the Rubaconte bridge, and always they were repulsed with death

[1] *Vincere* is translated "win" or "conquer."
[2] The standards of the companies of the people; that is, those companies.
[3] The Oltrarno, across the river.

and wounds for many. Some time ago, a road had been built by which, from the via Romana, passing through the houses of the Pitti, one could reach the walls on the hill of San Giorgio. The people sent six Gonfaloni by this route with orders to attack the houses of the Bardi from the rear. This attack made the Bardi lose their spirit and allowed the people to win the campaign; for as soon as those who guarded the barricades in the streets heard their own houses being attacked, they abandoned the engagement and ran to their defense. This allowed the barricades of the Ponte Vecchio to be conquered, and the Bardi were put to flight from every side; they were received by the Quaratesi, Panzanesi, and Mozzi. Meanwhile, the people, and of these the most ignoble part, thirsting for booty, looted and sacked all their houses, pulled down and burned their palaces and towers with such rage that the cruelest enemy to the Florentine name would have been ashamed of such ruin.

42

THE great having been conquered, the people reordered the state; and because the people were of three sorts—powerful, middle, and low—it was ordered that the powerful should have two Signori, the middle people three, and the low three, and that the Gonfalonier should be first from one and then from another. Besides this, all the Orders of Justice[1] against the great were resumed; and to make them even weaker, many of them were mixed among the popular multitude. The ruin of the nobles was so great and afflicted their party so much that they never again dared to take up arms against the people; indeed, they became continually more humane and abject. This was the cause by which Florence was stripped not only of its arms but of all generosity. After this downfall, the city maintained its quiet until the year 1353, during which time occurred that memorable pestilence celebrated with such eloquence by Messer Giovanni Boccaccio,[2] by which more than ninety-six thousand souls in Florence were lost. The Florentines also waged their first war against the Visconti, caused by the ambition of the archbishop,[3] then prince in Milan. As soon as this war was finished, parties started up inside the city, and although the nobility had been destroyed, nonetheless fortune did not lack for ways to revive new trials through new divisions.

[1] The Ordinances of Justice; see *FH* II 13, 36.
[2] The plague of 1348 is described in the introduction to the First Day of Boccaccio's *Decameron*.
[3] Archbishop Giovanni Visconti.

BOOK III

I

THE grave and natural enmities that exist between the men of the people and the nobles, caused by the wish of the latter to command and the former not to obey, are the cause of all evils that arise in cities.[1] For from this diversity of humors all other things that agitate republics take their nourishment. This kept Rome disunited, and this, if it is permissible to compare little things with great, has kept Florence divided, although diverse effects were produced in one city and the other. For the enmities between the people and the nobles at the beginning of Rome that were resolved by disputing were resolved in Florence by fighting. Those in Rome ended with a law, those in Florence with the exile and death of many citizens; those in Rome always increased military virtue, those in Florence eliminated it altogether; those in Rome brought the city from equality in the citizens to a very great inequality, those in Florence reduced it from inequality to a wonderful equality. This diversity of effects may have been caused by the diverse ends these two peoples had, for the people of Rome desired to enjoy the highest honors together with the nobles, while the people of Florence fought to be alone in the government without the participation of the nobles. And because the desire of the Roman people was more reasonable, offenses to the nobles came to be more bearable, so that the nobility would yield easily and without resorting to arms. Thus, after some differences, they would come together to create a law whereby the people would be satisfied and the nobles retain their dignities. On the other side, the desire of the Florentine people was injurious and unjust, so that the nobility readied greater forces for its own defense; and that is why it came to the blood and exile of citizens, and the laws that were made afterwards were not for the common utility but were all ordered in favor of the conqueror. From this it also followed that in the victories of the people the city of Rome became more virtuous, for as men of the people could be placed in the administration of the magistracies, the armies, and the posts of empire together with the nobles, they were filled with the same virtue as the nobles, and that city, by growing in virtue, grew in power. But in Florence, when the people conquered,

---

[1] See *P* 9; *D* I 5; *FH* II 12.

the nobles were left deprived of the magistracies, and if they wanted to regain them, it was necessary for them not only to be but to appear similar to men of the people in their conduct, spirit, and mode of living. From this arose the variations in coats of arms[2] and the changes of family titles that the nobles made so as to appear as the people. So the virtue in arms and the generosity of spirit that were in the nobility were eliminated, and in the people, where they never had been, they could not be rekindled; thus did Florence become ever more humble and abject. And whereas Rome, when its virtue was converted into arrogance, was reduced to such straits that it could not maintain itself without a prince, Florence arrived at the point that it could easily have been reordered in any form of government by a wise lawgiver. These things can be clearly recognized in part through the reading of the preceding book, which showed the birth of Florence and the beginning of its freedom, with the causes of its divisions, and how the parties of the nobles and the people ended with the tyranny of the duke of Athens and the ruin of the nobility. It remains now to tell about the enmities between the people and the plebs, and the various accidents they produced.

2

THE power of the nobles having been tamed and the war with the archbishop of Milan ended, it appeared that no cause of scandal remained in Florence. But the evil fortune of our city and its own orders, which were not good, gave rise to enmity between the family of the Albizzi and that of the Ricci, which divided Florence just as at first that between the Buondelmonti and the Uberti and afterwards that between the Donati and the Cerchi had done. The pontiffs, who were then in France, and the emperors, who were in Germany, so as to maintain their reputations in Italy, had sent to it at various times a number of soldiers of various nations; so in these times Englishmen, Germans, and Bretons were there. As these men were left without pay when the wars ended, under an ensign of adventure they laid an assessment on one or another prince. Thus, in the year 1353 one of these companies came to Tuscany captained by Monreale, a Provençal.[1] His arrival frightened all the cities of that province, and not only did the Florentines provide themselves with men by public means but many citizens, among them the Albizzi and the Ricci, armed themselves for their own safety.

[2] Lit.: ensigns.
[1] Monreale of Albano, a Provençal and Knight of Jerusalem, who in 1354, not 1353, laid assessments on Perugia, Siena, Florence, Arezzo, and Pisa.

These families were full of hatred for each other, and each was thinking how it could crush the other so as to obtain the principality in the republic. They had not yet, however, come to arms but had only encountered each other in the magistracies and in the councils. Thus, when the whole city found itself armed, a quarrel[2] arose by chance in the Mercato Vecchio; and many people gathered, as they are wont to do in such unforeseen events. As the rumor of it spread, it was reported to the Ricci that the Albizzi were attacking them and to the Albizzi that the Ricci were coming to seek them out. At this the whole city rose up, and the magistrates were able with trouble to check both families, so that in fact the conflict, which had been spread about by chance and not by the fault of either of them, did not take place. Though this accident was slight, it rekindled their spirits further, and each sought with greater diligence to acquire partisans. But as the citizens had already attained such equality through the ruin of the great that the magistrates were more revered than they used to be in the past, they planned to prevail by the ordinary way and without private violence.

3

WE have told before[1] how after the victory of Charles I the magistracy of the Guelf party was created and how it was given great authority over the Ghibellines. Time, various accidents, and new divisions had pushed this authority into oblivion, so that many descendants of the Ghibellines now exercised the first magistracies.[2] Uguccione de' Ricci, head of that family, therefore arranged to have renewed the law against the Ghibellines, among whom, in the opinion of many, were the Albizzi, who had been born many years ago in Arezzo and had come to live in Florence. Hence Uguccione thought that by renewing this law he could deprive the Albizzi of the magistracies, providing by it that any descendant of the Ghibellines would be condemned if he exercised any magistracy. This design of Uguccione's was disclosed to Piero di Filippo degli Albizzi, and he thought he would favor it, judging that if he opposed it he would declare himself a Ghibelline. This law, therefore, renewed through the ambition of these men, did not subtract but gave reputation to Piero degli Albizzi and was the beginning of many evils: nor can a law be made more damaging to a republic than one that looks back a long time.[3] Since Piero had

[2] Lit.: question.
[1] *FH* II 10, 11.
[2] This was not in fact the case.
[3] See *D* I 37.

thus favored the law, that which had been found by his enemies to impede him was the way to his greatness; for when he had made himself prince of this new order, he obtained ever more authority because he was favored by this new sect of Guelfs above any other. And because no magistrate was found to seek out who might be Ghibellines—which is why the law was not of much value—he provided that authority be given to the captains[4] to declare who were Ghibellines and, when declared, to notify them and admonish them not to take any magistracy; and if they did not obey the admonition, they would be condemned. From this it arose afterwards that all those in Florence who are deprived of the power to exercise magistracies are called "the admonished." Thus the captains, their boldness increasing with time, admonished without any respect not only those who merited it but anyone they pleased, moved by whatever avaricious or ambitious cause; and from 1357, when the order began, until '66, already more than two hundred citizens were admonished. Consequently, the captains and the sect of the Guelfs became powerful, since everyone, for fear of being admonished, honored them, and especially their heads, who were Piero degli Albizzi, Messer Lapo da Castiglionchio, and Carlo Strozzi. Although this insolent mode of proceeding displeased many, the Ricci were the least content of any others, as it appeared to them that they had been the cause of the disorder through which they saw the republic being ruined and their enemies the Albizzi, counter to their schemes, become very powerful.

4

THEREFORE, when Uguccione de' Ricci found himself one of the Signori, he wanted to bring an end to the evil of which he and his associates had been the beginning; and with a new law he provided that to the six captains of the party three should be added, two of them from the lesser guildsmen. He also wanted to have those declared Ghibellines to be confirmed as such by twenty-four Guelf citizens deputed for that purpose. This provision tempered for the time being a good part of the power of the captains, so that admonishing was in great part abandoned, and if they still admonished some, these were few. Nonetheless, the sects of Albizzi and Ricci were watchful, and each out of hatred for the other would oppose the other's alliances, undertakings, and decisions. So they lived with such troubles from 1366 to '71, during which time the sect of Guelfs regained its forces.

[4] Of the Guelf party.

In the Buondelmonti family there was a knight called Messer Benchi, who because of his merits in a war against the Pisans had been made a man of the people and by this had become eligible to be one of the Signori. While he was waiting to take his seat in the magistracy, a law was made that no great man who had been made a man of the people be allowed to exercise the office. This act offended Messer Benchi very much, and, foregathering with Piero degli Albizzi, they decided to strike at the lesser people through admonishing and to be alone in the government. And through the favor Messer Benchi had among the ancient nobility and that which Piero had with the greater part of the powerful among the people, they enabled the Guelf sect to regain its forces, and with the new reforms made in the party they ordered things so that they could dispose the captains and the twenty-four citizens to suit themselves. Hence, there was a return to admonishing with more boldness than before, and the house of the Albizzi, as head of this sect, grew steadily. On the other side, the Ricci and their friends did not fail to impede their designs as much as they could; so they lived in very great suspicion, each fearing every sort of ruin for himself.

5

AFTER this, many citizens, moved by love of their fatherland, met in San Piero Scherragio and, having reasoned much about these disorders among themselves, went to the Signori, to whom one of them with more authority spoke in this sense: "Many of us feared, magnificent Signori, to meet together by private order even for a public cause, as we judged we could either be considered presumptuous or be condemned as ambitious. But when we considered that every day and without heed many citizens meet in the loggias or in their houses, not for any public utility but for their own ambition, we judged that since those who gather for the ruin of the republic have no fear, those who meet for the public good and utility ought also not to have fear. Nor do we care about what others judge of us, since others do not value what we can judge of them. The love that we bear, magnificent Signori, for our fatherland first made us gather and now makes us come to you to reason about the evil that one sees already great and yet keeps growing in this republic of ours, and to offer ourselves ready to help you eliminate it. You could succeed in this, though the undertaking may seem difficult, if you will put aside private considerations and with public forces use your great authority. The common corruption of all the Italian cities, magnificent Signori, has corrupted and still corrupts your city, for ever since this province extricated itself from under the forces of the empire, its cities have had no powerful check to restrain them and have ordered their states and governments so as not to be free but divided into sects. From this have arisen all the other evils and all the other disorders that appear in it. First, there is neither union nor friendship among the citizens, except among those who have knowingly committed some wickedness either against their fatherland or against private persons. And because religion and fear of God have been eliminated in all, an oath and faith given last only as long as they are useful; so men make use of them not to observe them but to serve as a means of being able to deceive more easily. And the more easily and surely the deception succeeds, the more glory and praise is acquired from it; by this, harmful men are praised as industrious and good men are blamed as fools. And truly, in the cities of Italy all that can be corrupted and that can corrupt others is thrown together: the young are lazy, the old lascivious; both sexes at every age are full of foul customs, for which good laws, because they are spoiled by wicked use, are no remedy. From this grows the avarice that is seen in our citizens and the appetite, not for true glory, but for the contemptible honors on which hatreds, enmities, differences, and sects depend; and from these arise deaths, exiles, persecution of the good, exaltation of the wicked. For good men, trusting in their innocence, do not seek out, as do the wicked, those who will defend them and honor them extraordinarily, and so they fall undefended and unhonored. From this example arises the love of party and the power of parties, because bad men out of avarice and ambition, and good men out of necessity, participate in them. And what is most pernicious is to see how the promoters and princes of parties give decent appearance to their intention and their end with a pious word; for always, although they are all enemies of freedom, they oppress it under color of defending the state either of the best[1] or of the people. For the prize they desire to gain by victory is not the glory of having liberated the city but the satisfaction of having overcome others and of having usurped the principality of the city. Having been led to this point, there is nothing so unjust, so cruel, or mean that they do not dare to do it. Hence orders and laws are made not for the public but for personal utility; hence wars, pacts, and friendships are decided not for the common glory but for the satisfaction of few. And if other cities are filled with these disorders, ours is stained with them more than any other; for the laws, the statutes, and the civil orders have always been and still are ordered not in accordance with free life but by the ambition of that party which has come out on top. Whence it arises that always when one party is driven out and one division eliminated,

[1] The *Ottimati*.

another emerges. For in the city that prefers to maintain itself with sects rather than with laws, as soon as one sect is left there without opposition, it must of necessity divide from within itself, because the city cannot defend itself by those private modes that it had ordered in the first place for its own safety. And that this is true, both the ancient and the modern divisions of our city demonstrate. Everyone believed that when the Ghibellines were destroyed, the Guelfs would then live for a long time happily and respected; nonetheless, in a little while they divided into the Whites and the Blacks. After the Whites were conquered, the city was never again without parties: now to favor the exiles, now because of the enmities of the people and the great, always we fought; and by giving to others what we either would not or could not keep among ourselves by accord, we subjected our freedom now to King Robert, now to his brother, now to his son, and at the last to the duke of Athens. Nonetheless, we were never at rest in any state, as we were never in accord to live free and were not content to be slaves. Nor did we hesitate, so much were our orders disposed to divisions even while living in obedience to the king, to substitute for his majesty a very vile man born in Gubbio.[2] For the honor of this city one ought not even to remember the duke of Athens, whose bitter and tyrannical spirit should have made us wise and taught us how to live. Nonetheless, he had hardly been driven out when we had our arms in hand, and we fought with more hatred and greater rage than we had ever fought together, any other time, so that our ancient nobility was left conquered and again put under the will of the people.[3] Nor did many believe that any cause of scandal or party would ever arise again in Florence, since a check had been put on those who by their pride and unbearable ambition appeared to have been the cause. But now it is seen through experience how mistaken the opinion of men is and how false their judgment, for the pride and ambition of the great was not eliminated but taken from them by our men of the people, who now, by the wont of ambitious men, seek to obtain the first rank in the republic. Having no other modes of seizing it than by discords, they have divided the city again; and they have revived the names of Guelf and Ghibelline, which had been eliminated and had better never existed in this republic. And it has been given from above, so that there be nothing perpetual or quiet in human things, that in all republics there be fatal families that are born for their ruin. With these, our republic has been more abundant than any other, for not one but many have agitated and afflicted it as did first the Buondelmonti and the Uberti, then the Donati and the Cerchi, and

[2] See *FH* II 25.
[3] See *FH* II 42.

now—how shameful and ridiculous!—the Ricci and Albizzi agitate and divide it. We have not reminded you of our corrupt habits and our old and continuing divisions to frighten you, but to remind you of their causes and to show you that as you yourselves can remember them, so can we, and to tell you that the example of those old divisions ought not to make you diffident about stopping these. For so great was the power in those ancient families and so great were the favors they had from princes that civil orders and modes were not enough to check them; but now the empire has no force here, the pope is not feared, and all Italy and this city have been brought to such equality that for it to be able to rule itself is not very difficult for us. And this republic of ours especially can not only maintain itself united, notwithstanding former examples to the contrary, but reform itself with good customs and civil modes, providing that you, Signori, prepare yourselves to will to do it. To this we urge you, moved by charity for our fatherland, not by any private passion. And although its corruption be great, eliminate now the evil that affects us, the rage that consumes us, the poison that kills us; and credit the ancient disorders not to the nature of men but to the times, which having changed, you can hope for better fortune for our city through better orders. The malignity of fortune can be overcome with prudence by putting a check on the ambition of those ones,[4] by annulling the orders that nourish sects, and by adopting those that do in truth conform to a free and civil life. May you be pleased rather to do now, with the benignity of laws, that which, after deferring, men may be required by necessity to do with the support of arms."

6

THE Signori, moved first by what they knew themselves and then by the authority and urgings of these men, gave authority to fifty-six citizens to see to the safety of the republic. It is very true that most men are more apt to preserve a good order than to know how to find one for themselves. These citizens gave more thought to eliminating the present sects than to taking away the causes of future ones; so they achieved neither the one nor the other. For they did not remove the causes of the new ones, and of those they were watchful of, they made one more powerful than the other, with greater danger to the republic. They therefore excluded from all magistracies, except those of the Guelf party, for three years, three of the Albizzi family and three of the Ricci family, among whom

4 The Ricci and the Albizzi.

were Piero degli Albizzi and Uguccione de' Ricci. They forbade all citizens to enter the palace except at times when the magistrates were sitting. They provided that anyone who might be assaulted or kept from possession of his goods could with one petition accuse the offender to the councilors and have him declared as among the great and, so declared, brought under their charges. This provision took away the boldness of the Ricci sect and increased that of the Albizzi; for though they were equally marked, nonetheless the Ricci suffered much more by it because, if the palace of the Signori was closed to Piero, the palace of the Guelfs, where he had very great authority, remained open to him. And if at first he and those who followed him were hot for admonishing, after this injury they became very hot. To this ill will more new causes were added.

7

SITTING in the pontificate was Pope Gregory XI, who, while located in Avignon, governed Italy through legates as his predecessors had done. Full of avarice and pride, they had afflicted many cities. One of the legates, who was in Bologna at the time, took the occasion of a famine that year in Florence and thought to make himself lord of Tuscany. Not only did he not help the Florentines with provisions but, to take from them the hope of future harvests, he attacked them with a great army at the first appearance of spring, hoping to overcome them easily by finding them unarmed and starving. And he might perhaps have succeeded if the men with whom he made the attack had not been unfaithful and venal; for the Florentines, having no better remedy, gave his soldiers one hundred and thirty thousand florins and made them abandon the campaign. Wars begin at the will of anyone, but they do not end at anyone's will. This war, begun because of the ambition of the legate, was continued by the indignation of the Florentines; they made an alliance with Messer Bernabò[1] and with all the cities hostile to the Church, and they created eight citizens to administer it with authority to be able to act without appeal and to spend without rendering account.[2]

This war begun against the pontiff enabled those who had followed the sect of the Ricci to rise again, notwithstanding Uguccione's death.[3] Contrary to the Albizzi, they had always favored Messer Bernabò and disfavored the Church, and all the more because the Eight were all enemies of

[1] Bernabò Visconti.
[2] These eight were called the Otto Santi, and the war, that of the Otto Santi (1375–1378).
[3] Uguccione de' Ricci died in 1383.

the Guelf sect. This made Piero degli Albizzi, Messer Lapo da Castiglion-chio, Carlo Strozzi, and the others draw closer together for the harming[4] of their adversaries, and while the Eight were making war, they were admonishing. The war lasted three years and did not end before the death of the pontiff. It was administered with such virtue and with such universal satisfaction that the magistracy was extended to the Eight every year; and they were called Saints even though they had little regard for censures, had despoiled the churches of their goods, and had compelled the clergy to celebrate the offices—so much more did those citizens then esteem their fatherland than their souls.[5] And they showed the Church that just as before they had defended it as friends, so now as enemies they could afflict it; for they made all Romagna, the Marches, and Perugia rebel.

8

NONETHELESS, while they carried on so great a war against the pope, they could not defend themselves either from the captains of the Party[1] or from their sect, because the envy the Guelfs bore toward the Eight increased their boldness, and they did not refrain from injuring not only the other noble citizens but even some of the Eight. To such arrogance did he not help the Florentines with provisions, but, to take from them Signori, and one went with less reverence to the latter than to the former. The palace of the Party was respected more than their own, so much that no ambassador came to Florence who did not have a commission to the captains. And so with Pope Gregory dead, the city was left without war outside, and people lived in great confusion inside; for on the one hand, the boldness of the Guelfs was unbearable, and on the other hand, no one saw any mode by which it could be defeated. Even so, it was judged that they would necessarily have to come to arms to see which of the two seats should prevail. On the side of the Guelfs were all the ancient nobles with the greater part of the most powerful men of the people, among whom, as we said,[2] Messer Lapo, Piero, and Carlo were princes. On the other side were all the popular men of the lesser sort, whose heads were the Eight of War, Messer Giorgio Scali, Tommaso Strozzi, with whom the Ricci, Alberti, and Medici were joined. The rest of the multitude, as almost always happens, adhered to the side of the malcontents. To the

[4] Lit.: offending.
[5] See NM's letter to Vettori of April 16, 1527.
[1] The Guelf party.
[2] See *FH* III 3 (end).

heads of the Guelf sect the forces of their adversaries appeared vigorous and a great danger to them any time a Signoria hostile to them should want to bring them down; and thinking it would be well to provide against this, they gathered together to examine the condition of the city as well as their own state. It appeared to them that the admonished, by having grown to so great a number, might have brought them so much blame that the whole city had become their enemy. And they saw no other remedy for this than that, having taken their honors from them, they should also take away their city, seizing the palace of the Signori by force and returning the whole state to their sect[3] in imitation of the ancient Guelfs, who lived securely in the city only by having driven all their adversaries from it. Everyone agreed to this but disagreed about the time.

<h1 style="text-align:center">9</h1>

IT was then the year 1378 and the month was April, and to Messer Lapo it did not appear right to delay, as he asserted that nothing was so harmful to time as time itself,[1] and especially to them, since Salvestro de' Medici, who they knew was opposed to their sect, could easily be the Gonfalonier in the next Signoria. To Piero degli Albizzi, on the other hand, delay appeared right, because he judged that they would need forces, that it would not be possible to gather them without exposing themselves, and that when they were discovered they would be in clear danger. He judged it necessary, therefore, to wait for the next day of San Giovanni,[2] at which time, since that was the most solemn day in the city, a great multitude would gather there, among which they could then hide as many men as they wished; and to remedy what they feared from Salvestro, he would be admonished. And if this did not seem the thing to do, they would admonish one of the college from his quarter;[3] and, since the bags were empty, when a substitute was drawn they could easily produce the chance that he or some relative of his would be drawn, which would take from Salvestro the possibility of being able to sit as Gonfalonier.[4] So they resolved on this decision, although Messer Lapo consented unwillingly. He judged that delay was harmful and that the time for doing a thing is never

[3] The new sect of Guelfs; see *FH* III 3.
[1] See *FH* VII 3; *P* 3.
[2] June 24.
[3] One of the Twelve.
[4] A new lot could be manipulated so that Salvestro or one of his family would be selected one of the Twelve. Then, since the law prohibited a single family from holding more than one office at a time, Salvestro could not be elected Gonfalonier.

altogether convenient, so that anyone who waits for all conveniences either never tries anything or, if he tries, does it more often to his disadvantage. They admonished one of the college, but they did not succeed in hindering Salvestro, because when the causes were discovered by the Eight, they arranged it so that the substitute was not drawn. Thus Salvestro, son of Messer Alamanno de' Medici, was drawn as Gonfalonier.

This man, born of a very noble popular family, could not bear that the people should be oppressed by a few powerful men. He had thought about how to bring an end to this insolence, and, seeing himself favored by the people and by many noble popular companions, he shared his designs with Benedetto Alberti, Tommaso Strozzi, and Messer Giorgio Scali, who promised every aid to further them. Thus they secretly resolved on a law to renew the Orders[5] of Justice against the great, to diminish the authority of the captains of the Party, and to give to the admonished a mode of being recalled to their dignities. And so that the law might be proposed and enacted[6] at almost the same time, and as it had to be deliberated upon first among the Collegi and then in the councils, Salvestro, who found himself provost (which rank for the time it lasts makes one almost a prince of the city), had the college and the council assemble on the same morning. First he proposed to the Collegi, who were separated from the council, the planned[7] law, which, as something new, found such disfavor in the few[8] that it was not approved. Consequently, Salvestro, seeing that the first ways of getting it enacted were cut off to him, pretended to leave the place to attend to his necessities; and, without anyone's being aware of it, he went to the council. There, having climbed up high where everyone could see and hear him, he said he believed he had been made a Gonfalonier not to be a judge of private causes, which had their own ordinary judges, but to watch over the state—to correct the insolence of the powerful and to temper those laws by the use of which one would see the republic ruined. And he said that he had thought diligently about both these things and had provided for them as far as it had been possible for him, but the malignity of men so opposed his just enterprises that the way to doing good had been taken from him, and the way not only to deliberating on it but to hearing about it had been taken from them.[9] Hence, seeing that he was no longer able to be of any use in anything to the republic or to the universal good, he did not know for what cause he should any longer keep his magistracy, which either he did not deserve or someone else believed he did not deserve. On this account

[5] Ordinances.
[6] Lit.: obtained.
[7] Lit.: ordered; the proposed law.
[8] Lit.: in the number of the few.
[9] Since the Collegi had rejected his proposal, it could not be heard by the council.

he wanted to go home so that the people could put another in his place who would have either greater virtue or better fortune than he. And having said these words, he left the council to go home.

10

THOSE in the council who were aware of this and others who desired innovation raised an uproar, to which the Signori and the Collegi ran; and when they saw their Gonfalonier taking his leave, they restrained him with entreaties[1] and by authority, and brought him to the council, which was in full tumult. There many noble citizens were threatened with very abusive words, among them Carlo Strozzi, who was taken around the chest by an artisan who wished to kill him but was defended by the effort of bystanders. Still, the one who excited greater tumult and put the city under arms was Benedetto degli Alberti, who at the top of his voice, from the windows of the palace, called the people to arms; and the piazza was quickly filled with armed men—so that which the Collegi had been unwilling to do when they were begged at first, they did when threatened and frightened. At the same time the captains of the Party had assembled many citizens in their palace to be advised on how to defend themselves against the order of the Signori; but as soon as the uproar was heard and what the councilors had decided was understood, everyone took refuge in his own home. No one should make a change in a city believing that he can stop it at his convenience or regulate it in his mode. It was the intention of Salvestro to create that law and put the city to rest, and the thing went otherwise because the humors set in motion had changed everyone so that the stores did not open, the citizens fortified themselves in their homes, many hid their movable goods in the monasteries and churches, and it appeared that each one feared some evil nearby. The guild corporations met, and each made a syndic; then the Priors called together the Collegi and these syndics, and they debated for a whole day how the city might be quieted to everyone's satisfaction. But being of diverse opinions, they did not agree.

The day after, the guilds brought out their banners. The Signori, hearing of this and fearing what would happen, called upon the council to provide a remedy. Hardly had it assembled when an uproar was heard, and quickly the ensigns of the guilds with a large number of armed men behind them were in the piazza. Then, so as to give the guilds and the people hope of being content and to take from them the opportunity for

[1] Lit.: prayers.

evil, the council gave a general power,[2] which in Florence is called balìa, to the Signori, Collegi, the Eight, the captains of the Party, and the guild syndics, enabling them to reform the state of the city for its common benefit. And while this was being ordered, some ensign bearers from the guilds and from those of lesser quality, moved by those who wanted to get revenge for the recent injuries they had received from the Guelfs, detached themselves from the others, and they sacked and burned the house of Messer Lapo da Castiglionchio. As soon as he learned that the Signoria had taken a stand[3] against the orders of the Guelfs and saw the people in arms, and having no remedy other than to hide or flee, he first hid in Santa Croce, then, dressed as a friar, fled to the Casentino, where he was heard many times lamenting for himself for having consented to Piero degli Albizzi and for Piero for having wanted to wait until San Giovanni's Day to secure the state for themselves. But Piero and Carlo Strozzi hid at the first alarms, believing that when these had ceased they could be secure in Florence because they had many relatives and friends. When Messer Lapo's house had been burned—because evils begin with difficulty and grow with ease—many other houses were sacked and burned out of either universal hatred or private enmities. And so that they might have company with more thirst than theirs for stealing the goods of others, they broke open the public prisons and then sacked the monastery of the Agnoli and the convent of Santo Spirito, where many citizens had hidden their movables. Nor would the public treasury have been safe from the hands of these predators if it had not been defended by their reverence for one of the Signori who, on horse, with many armed men behind him, opposed the rage of the multitude in whatever mode he could. The popular fury was mitigated both by the authority of the Signori and by nightfall, and the next day the balìa offered grace to the admonished with the proviso that for three years they could not hold any magistracy. They annulled laws prejudicial to citizens made by the Guelfs, declared Messer Lapo de Castiglionchio and his associates rebels, and, with him, many others who were universally hated. After these decisions, new Signori were announced, of whom Luigi Guicciardini was Gonfalonier; through them, hope of stopping the tumults was raised because it seemed to everyone that these were peaceful men and lovers of common quiet.

II

NONETHELESS, the stores did not open, the citizens did not put away their arms, and there were heavy guards throughout the city. Because of

---

[2] *Potestà.*
[3] Lit.: made an undertaking.

this, the Signori did not assume the magistracy outside the palace with the usual pomp, but did so inside without observing any ceremony. These Signori judged that nothing was more useful to do at the beginning of their magistracy than to pacify the city; and so they had arms put away, stores opened; they had many of those from the countryside who had been called in by citizens in their favor leave Florence; they ordered a watch by day in many places of the city. So if the admonished could have been kept quiet, the city would have been quieted. But they were not content to wait three years to regain their honors; so for their satisfaction the guilds assembled again and requested the Signori, for the good and quiet of the city, to order that any citizen who at whatever time had been one of the Signori, Collegi, captains of the Party, or consul of any guild could not be admonished as a Ghibelline; further, that new baggings be held in the Guelf party and that the old bags be burned. These demands were accepted not only by the Signori but immediately by all the councilors, to whom it appeared that the tumults, which had already begun again, would be stopped. But because it is not enough for men to get back their own but they want also to seize what belongs to others and get revenge, those who put their hopes in disorders pointed out to the artisans that they would never be safe if their many enemies were not driven out and destroyed. Apprehensive of these things, the Signori had the magistrates of the guilds, together with their syndics, come before them; and Luigi Guicciardini, the Gonfalonier, spoke to them in this form: "If these Signori, and I together with them, had not known, and for a good time, the fortune of this city, which is such that when wars outside are ended, those inside begin, we would have marveled more at the tumults that have continued and they would have brought us more displeasure. But because things we are accustomed to bring less anxiety with them, we have suffered the recent riots with patience, especially as they were begun without blame on our part, and as we hoped that in accordance with past examples they would come to an end sooner or later, since so many and such grave demands have been granted you. But as we apprehend that you have not become quiet, that indeed you want new injuries to be done to your citizens and new exiles to be condemned, our displeasure grows with your indecency. And truly, if we had believed that during our magistracy our city had to be ruined, either by opposing you or by gratifying you, we would have avoided these honors with flight or exile; but as we hoped to have to do with men who might have in them some humanity and some love for their fatherland, we accepted the magistracy willingly, believing that with our humanity we could conquer your ambition by any mode. But we see now by experience that the more humbly we behave, the more we concede, the more you grow proud and the more indecent things you demand. And if we speak thus, we do it not to offend you but to make you repent. For we want someone else to tell you what pleases you; we want to tell you what is useful to you. Tell us, by your faith, what more can you decently desire from us? You wanted to take authority away from the captains of the Party: it was taken from them. You wanted that their bags be burned and that new reforms be made: we have consented to it. You wanted the admonished restored to their honors: this was permitted. By your urging[1] we have pardoned those who burned houses and despoiled churches, and many honored and powerful citizens have been exiled to satisfy you; the great, in contemplation of you, have been restrained by new orders. What end will these demands of yours have, or how long will you abuse our liberality? Do you not see that we tolerate being conquered with more patience than you tolerate victory? To what will your disunions lead this city of yours? Do you not remember that when it was disunited Castruccio, a vile citizen of Lucca, defeated it? That a duke of Athens, one of your private condottieri, subjugated it? But when it was united, neither an archbishop of Milan nor a pope could defeat it, and after many years of war they were left in shame. Why, then, do you want your discords to make a slave of a city in peace that so many powerful enemies left free in war? What do you get out of your disunion other than servitude? Or of the goods that you have stolen or would steal from us other than poverty? For those are the things that, with our industry, nourish the whole city; and if it is despoiled of them, they cannot nourish it; and those who will seize them, as things ill acquired, will not know how to preserve them: from this, hunger and poverty will come to the city. These Signori and I command you, and if decency permits it, we pray you to still your spirits for once and be content to rest quietly with the things that have been ordered through us, and if ever you wish something new, be pleased to ask for it with civility and not with tumult and arms. For if they are decent things, you will always be granted them, and you will not give occasion to wicked men, at your charge and to your cost, to ruin your fatherland on your shoulders." These words, because they were true, moved the spirits of those citizens very much, and they thanked the Gonfalonier courteously[2] for having done his duty to them as a good Signore and to the city as a good citizen. They offered themselves ready to obey as much as had been commissioned to them. And the Signori, so as to give them cause for it, deputed two citizens for each of the greater magistrates, who together with the syndics of the guilds were to act together should there be anything to reform for the common quiet and to report it to the Signori.

[1] Lit.: prayers.
[2] Lit.: humanely.

12

WHILE these things were proceeding, another tumult arose that hurt[1] the republic a good deal more than the first. The greater part of the arson and robbery that took place in the preceding days had been done by the lowest plebs of the city, and those among them who had shown themselves the boldest feared that with the greater differences quieted and composed, they would be punished for the mistakes committed by them and that, as always happens to them, they would be abandoned by those who had incited them to do evil. Added to this was the hatred that the lesser people had for the rich citizens and princes of the guilds, since it did not appear to them that they had been satisfied for their labor as they believed they justly deserved. For when the city had been divided into guilds in the time of Charles I,[2] each one was given a head and a government, and it was provided that the subjects of each guild were to be judged by their own heads in civil matters. The guilds, as we have already said, were twelve at the beginning but then, in time, grew until they reached twenty-one; and their power was such that in a few years they had taken over the whole government of the city. And because among them some were more and some less honored, they divided themselves into greater and lesser; seven of them were called "greater" and fourteen "lesser." From this division and from the causes we have narrated above arose the arrogance of the captains of the Party, because those citizens who had been Guelfs of old, in whose governance that magistracy always revolved, favored the people of the greater guilds and persecuted those in the lesser guilds together with their defenders: hence arose the many tumults against them that we have narrated. But in the ordering of the guild corporations, many of those occupations in which the lesser people and the lowest plebs were engaged were left without guild corporations of their own, but were subordinated under various guilds appropriate to the character of their occupation. In consequence, when they were either not satisfied for their labor or in some mode oppressed by their masters, they had no other place of refuge than the magistracy of the guild that governed them, from which it did not appear to them that they got the justice they judged was suitable. And of all the guilds, the one that had and has the most dependents under it was and is the Wool Guild.[3] This guild, because it was the most powerful and the first, by authority of all sustained and still sustains with its industry the greater part of the plebs and the lesser people.

[1] Lit.: offended.
[2] See *FH* II 8.
[3] Known as *i Ciompi*.

13

THUS the men of the plebs, those placed under the Wool Guild as well as those under the other guilds, were, for the causes mentioned, full of indignation. To these was added fear because of the arson and robbery they had done; and they often met by night to discuss events that had occurred and to point out to each other the dangers in which they found themselves. There, one of the most daring and more experienced spoke in this sense so as to inspire the others: "If we had to deliberate now whether to take up arms, to burn and rob the homes of the citizens, to despoil churches, I would be one of those who would judge it was a course to think over, and perhaps I would agree to put quiet poverty ahead of perilous gain. But because arms have been taken up and many evils have been done, it appears to me that one must reason that arms must not be put aside and that we must consider how we can secure ourselves from the evils that have been committed. Certainly I believe that if others do not teach us, necessity does. You see this whole city full of grievance and hatred against us: the citizens meet together; the Signoria is always on the side of the magistrates. You should believe that traps are being set for us and that new forces are being prepared against our strongholds.[1] We must therefore seek two things, and we must have two ends in our deliberations: one is to make it impossible for us to be punished for the things we have done in recent days, and the other is to be able to live with more freedom and more satisfaction than we have in the past. It is to our advantage, therefore, as it appears to me, if we wish that our old errors be forgiven us, to make new ones, redoubling the evils, multiplying the arson and robbery—and to contrive to have many companions in this, because when many err, no one is punished, and though small faults are punished, great and grave ones are rewarded; and when many suffer, few seek for revenge, because universal injuries are borne with greater patience than particular ones. Thus in multiplying evils, we will gain pardon more easily and will open the way for us to have the things we desire to have for our freedom. And it appears to me that we are on the way to a sure acquisition, because those who could hinder us are disunited and rich: their disunion will therefore give us victory, and their riches, when they have become ours, will maintain it for us. Do not let their antiquity of blood, with which they will reproach us, dismay you; for all men, having had the same beginning, are equally ancient and have been made by nature in one mode. Strip all of us naked, you will see that we are alike; dress us in their clothes and them in ours, and without a doubt we shall appear noble and they ignoble, for only poverty and riches make us

---

[1] Or heads.

unequal. It pains me much when I hear that out of conscience many of you repent the deeds that have been done and that you wish to abstain from new deeds; and certainly, if this is true, you are not the men I believed you to be, for neither conscience nor infamy should dismay you, because those who win, in whatever mode they win, never receive shame from it. And we ought not to take conscience into account, for where there is, as with us, fear of hunger and prison, there cannot and should not be fear of hell. But if you will take note of the mode of proceeding of men, you will see that all those who come to great riches and great power have obtained them either by fraud or by force; and afterwards, to hide the ugliness of acquisition, they make it decent by applying the false title of earnings to things they have usurped by deceit or by violence. And those who, out of either little prudence or too much foolishness, shun these modes always suffocate in servitude or poverty. For faithful servants are always servants and good men are always poor; nor do they ever rise out of servitude unless they are unfaithful and bold, nor out of poverty unless they are rapacious and fraudulent. For God and nature have put all the fortunes of men in their midst, where they are exposed more to rapine than to industry and more to wicked than to good arts, from which it arises that men devour one another and that those who can do less are always the worst off. Therefore, one should use force whenever the occasion for it is given to us; nor can a greater occasion be offered us by fortune than this one, when citizens are still disunited, the Signoria irresolute, and the magistrates dismayed so that they can easily be crushed before they unite and steady their spirits. As a result, either we shall be left princes of all the city, or we shall have so large a part of it that not only will our past errors be pardoned but we shall even have authority enabling us to threaten them with new injuries. I confess this course is bold and dangerous, but when necessity presses, boldness is judged prudence; and spirited men never take account of the danger in great things, for those enterprises that are begun with danger always end with reward, and one never escapes a danger without danger. Moreover, I believe that when one sees the prisons, tortures, and deaths being prepared, standing still is more to be feared than seeking to secure ourselves against them, for in the first case the evils are certain and in the other, doubtful. How many times have I heard you lament the avarice of your superiors and the injustice of your magistrates! Now is the time not only to free ourselves from them but to become so much their superiors that they will have more to lament and fear from you than you from them. The opportunity brought us by the occasion is fleeting, and when it has gone, it will be vain to try to recover it. You see the preparations of your adversaries. Let us be ahead of their thoughts; and whichever of us is first to take up arms again will without doubt be the conqueror, with ruin for the enemy and exaltation for himself. From this will come honor for many of us and security for all." These persuasions strongly inflamed spirits that were already hot for evil on their own, so that they decided to take up arms after they had secured more companions to do their will; and they swore an oath to help one another if it should happen that one of them were overwhelmed by the magistrates.

14

WHILE these men were preparing to seize the republic, their design came to the attention of the Signori; for they had in their hands one Simone dalla Piazza,[1] from whom they learned the whole conspiracy and how the conspirators meant to raise an uproar on the following day. Then, when the danger had been seen, they gathered the Collegi and those citizens who together with the syndics of the guilds negotiated over the union of the city (and before everyone was together, night had already come). By these men the Signori were advised that they should have the consuls of the guilds come, who then all advised that all the men at arms in Florence should come and that the Gonfaloniers of the people should be in the piazza in the morning with their armed companies. While Simone was being tortured and the citizens were gathering, the palace clock was being regulated by one Niccolò da San Friano. As Niccolò became aware of what was happening, he returned to his home and filled all his neighborhood with tumult so that in an instant more than a thousand armed men gathered in the Piazza Santo Spirito. This uproar reached the other conspirators, and San Piero Maggiore and San Lorenzo, the places designated by them, were filled with armed men.

Day had already come—it was the twenty-first of July—and in the piazza not more than eighty armed men in favor of the Signori had appeared; not one of the Gonfaloniers had come because, having heard that the whole city was filled with armed men, they feared to leave their homes. The first of the plebs to be in the piazza were those who had gathered at San Piero Maggiore, and at their arrival the armed men did not move. After these appeared another multitude, and, finding no opposition, with terrible cries they demanded their prisoners from the Signoria; and so as to have the prisoners by force since they had not been given up by threats, they burned the houses of Luigi Guicciardini: so the Signori gave them over for fear of worse. Having recovered the prisoners,

[1] "Simone dalla Piazza" is known as "Simoncino dalla Porta a S. Pietro Gattolini" by NM's source, and it is disputed whether "dalla Piazza" is intended as Simone's name (Carli) or to describe his usual haunt or plebeian origin (Fiorini).

they took the standard of justice from its executor, and under that banner they burned the houses of many citizens, hunting down those who were hated either for public or for private cause. And many citizens, to avenge their private injuries, led them to the houses of their enemies; for it was enough that a single voice shout out in the midst of the multitude, "to so-and-so's house," or that he who held the standard in his hands turn toward it. They also burned all the records of the Wool Guild. And that they might accompany the many evils they did with some praiseworthy work, they made Salvestro de' Medici and many other citizens knights. The number of all these reached sixty-four, among whom were Benedetto and Antonio degli Alberti, Tommaso Strozzi, and the like who were their confidants, notwithstanding that many of them were knighted forcibly. In this incident, it was more to be noted than anything else that many who saw their houses burned were soon after, on the same day, knighted by the same ones who burned their houses, so close was benefit to injury: this happened to Luigi Guicciardini, Gonfalonier of Justice. The Signori, seeing themselves abandoned in such tumults by the men-at-arms, by the heads of the guilds, and by their own Gonfaloniers, were bewildered, for no one came to their support in accordance with the order that had been given, and of the sixteen standards, only that of the Golden Lion and that of the Squirrel, under Giovenco della Stufa and Giovanni Cambi, appeared. And they lingered in the piazza only a short time, for when they saw they were not being followed by the others, they too departed. On the other hand, some citizens, seeing the fury of this unleashed multitude and the palace abandoned, stayed inside their homes, and some others followed the rabble of armed men so that by being among them they could better defend their houses and those of their friends. And so their power came to be rising and that of the Signori declining. This tumult lasted the whole day; and when night came, they stopped at the palace of Messer Stefano behind the Church of San Barnaba. They numbered more than six thousand; and before day came, with their threats they compelled the guilds to send them their ensigns. Then when morning came, with the Standard of Justice and with the ensigns of the guilds before them, they went to the palace of the Podestà; and as the Podestà refused to give them possession of it, they fought for it and won.

15

THE Signori, attempting to conciliate them since they saw no mode of stopping them by force, called upon four of their Collegi and sent them to the palace of the Podestà to learn what they had in mind. They found that the heads of the plebs, with the syndics of the guilds and certain citizens, had decided what they wanted to demand from the Signoria. So they returned to the Signoria with four men deputed from the plebs and with these demands: that the Wool Guild could no longer have a foreign judge; that three new guild corporations be formed, one for the carders and dyers, another for the barbers, doublet makers, tailors, and such mechanical arts, the third for the lesser people; and that from these three new guilds there would always be two Signori and from the fourteen lesser guilds three; that the Signoria should provide houses where these new guilds could meet; that no one placed under these guilds could be compelled, for two years, to pay a debt for a sum less than fifty ducats; that the *Monte*[1] suspend payment of interest and only repay capital; that those imprisoned and condemned be absolved; and that honors be restored to all the admonished. They demanded many other things besides these for the benefit of their particular supporters, and on the opposite side they wanted many of their enemies to be imprisoned and admonished. These demands, though dishonorable and grievous[2] for the republic, were, for fear of worse, immediately decided upon by the Signori, the Collegi, and the council of the people. But to have them brought to completion, it was necessary that they be passed also by the council of the commune, which, since the two councils could not meet on the same day, it was necessary to postpone until the next day. Nonetheless, it appeared that for the time being the guilds were left content and the plebs satisfied; and they promised that when the law was completed, all tumult would stop.

Then when morning came, while the council of the commune was deliberating, the impatient and fickle multitude came into the piazza under the usual ensigns with such loud and terrifying cries that they frightened the whole council and the Signori. On account of this, Guerrante Marignoli, one of the Signori, who was moved more by fear than by any other private passion, went downstairs under color of guarding the door below and fled to his home. As he came outside, he was unable to conceal himself so as not to be recognized by the mob; nor was any other injury done to him than that the multitude cried out as soon as they saw him that all the Signori should abandon the palace or else they would kill their children and burn down their houses. It was in the midst of this that the law was decided upon and the Signori were enclosed in their chambers; and the council went downstairs and, without going outside, remained in the loggia and the courtyard in despair for the safety of the city, seeing such

[1] Lit.: mountain, the public debt.
[2] Lit.: grave.

indecency in a multitude and such malignity or fear in those who could have checked or crushed it. The Signori too were confused and doubtful of the safety of their fatherland, as they saw themselves abandoned by one of them and supported by not one citizen with help or even with counsel. Being thus uncertain of what they could or should do, Messer Tommaso Strozzi and Messer Benedetto Alberti, either prompted by their own ambition to remain as Signori of the palace or because they really believed it to be good, persuaded them to yield to this popular impetus and to return to their homes as private individuals. Though others might yield to this advice, given by those who had been at the head of the tumult, Alamanno Acciaiuoli and Niccolò del Bene, two of the Signori, became indignant; and, a little vigor returning to them, they said that if the others wanted to leave, they could not remedy it, but they did not wish, before time required it, to relinquish their authority, lest they lose their lives with their authority. These differences redoubled the fears of the Signori and the indignation of the people, so that the Gonfalonier, preferring to end his magistracy with shame rather than danger, put himself in the care of Messer Tommaso Strozzi, who took him from the palace and conducted him to his houses. The other Signori left in a similar mode, one after the other, so that Alammano and Niccolò, so as not to be held more spirited than wise, seeing themselves the only ones remaining, also went; and the palace was left in the hands of the plebs and the Eight of War, who had not yet laid aside their magistracy.

16

WHEN the plebs entered the palace, one Michele di Lando, a wool carder, had in his hand the ensign of the Gonfalonier of Justice. This man, barefoot and scantily clothed, climbed up the stairs with the whole mob behind him, and as soon as he was in the audience chamber of the Signori, he stopped; and, turning around to the multitude, he said, "You see: this palace is yours and this city is in your hands. What do you think should be done now?" To which all replied that they wanted him to be Gonfalonier and lord, and to govern them and the city however seemed best to him. Michele accepted the lordship,[1] and because he was a sagacious and prudent man who owed more to nature than to fortune, he resolved to quiet the city and stop the tumults. And to keep the people busy and to give himself time to get in order, he commanded them to seek out one

[1] Lit.: the Signoria.

Ser Nuto who had been designated Bargello[2] by Messer Lapo da Casti-glionchio; the greater number of those around him went off on this errand. And so as to begin with justice the empire he had acquired by grace, he had it publicly commanded that no one burn or steal anything; and to frighten everyone, he had a gallows erected in the piazza. And to give a beginning to the reform of the city, he dismissed the syndics of the guilds and appointed new ones; he deprived the Signori and the Collegi of their magistracies; and he burned the bags of the offices. Meanwhile, Ser Nuto was carried by the multitude to the piazza and hung on the gallows by one foot; and as whoever was around tore off a piece from him, at a stroke there was nothing left of him but his foot. The Eight of War, on the other hand, believing themselves by the departure of the Signori to have been left princes of the city, had already designated new Signori. Anticipating this, Michele sent word to them to leave the palace at once, for he wanted to show everyone that he knew how to govern Florence without their advice. He then had the syndics of the guilds assemble, and he created the Signoria: four from the lesser plebs, two for the greater and two for the lesser guilds. Besides this, he made a new bagging and divided the state into three parts; he wanted one of these to go to the new guilds, another to the lesser, the third to the greater. He gave the income of the shops on the Ponte Vecchio to Messer Salvestro de' Medici and gave himself the podesteria of Empoli; and he gave many other benefits to many other citizens friendly to the plebs, not so much to compensate them for their deeds as that they might at all times defend him against envy.

17

IT appeared to the plebs that Michele in reforming the state had been too partisan toward the greater people, nor did it appear to them that they had as great a part in the government as was necessary to enable them to maintain and defend themselves in it; so, driven by their usual boldness, they took up arms again and under their ensigns came in tumult into the piazza, demanding that the Signori on the stairway come down to decide upon new measures relating to their security and good. Michele saw their arrogance and, in order not to make them more indignant and without learning otherwise what they wanted, censured the mode in which they made their demands and urged them to put down their arms; and then they would be conceded that which by force the Signoria could not con-cede with dignity. On account of this the multitude became indignant

---

[2] Sheriff or police chief.

with the palace and withdrew to Santa Maria Novella, where they ordered eight chiefs from among themselves, with ministers and other orders that gave them reputation and reverence. Thus the city had two seats and was governed by two different princes.

These chiefs decided among themselves that eight men, elected from the guild corporations, should always live in the palace with the Signori, and everything that was decided upon by the Signoria should be confirmed by them. They took from Messer Salvestro de' Medici and from Michele di Lando all that they had been conceded in their other decisions; they assigned offices and subsidies to many among themselves so that they could maintain their rank with dignity. When these decisions were taken, to validate them they sent two of their men to the Signoria to demand that they be confirmed by the councilors, with the purpose of getting what they wanted by force if they could not get it by accord. These two set forth their commission to the Signori with great boldness and greater presumption, and they reproached the Gonfalonier for behaving to them with so much ingratitude and so little respect after the dignity they had given him and the honor they had done him. And, when at the end of their speech they came to threats, Michele was unable to bear such arrogance; and, as he was mindful more of the rank he held than of his low condition, it appeared to him that he must check this extraordinary insolence with an extraordinary mode; and drawing the weapon he had at his waist, he first wounded them gravely and then had them bound and imprisoned. As soon as this thing became known, it inflamed the whole multitude with rage; and, believing that when armed they could attain what they had not obtained when disarmed, they took up their arms with fury and tumult and advanced to compel the Signori by their rage. Michele, on the other hand, was fearful of what might happen and decided to forestall it, thinking that it would be more to his glory to attack others than to wait for the enemy within the walls and to have to flee, as did his predecessors, with dishonor to the palace and with shame for himself. Thus he gathered a large number of citizens who already had begun to reflect on their error, mounted his horse, and, followed by many armed men, went to Santa Maria Novella to fight them. The plebs, as we said above, had made the same decision, and, almost at the same time that Michele advanced, it also left to go to the piazza; and chance had it that each took a different road so that they did not meet on the way. Thereupon Michele, having turned back, found that the piazza was taken and the palace was being attacked; and joining the fray against them, he conquered them; and part he drove out of the city, and part he compelled to leave their arms and hide. The campaign having succeeded, the tumults were settled solely by the virtue of the Gonfalonier. In spirit, prudence, and goodness he surpassed any citizen of his time, and he deserves to be numbered among the few who have benefited their fatherland, for had his spirit been either malign or ambitious, the republic would have lost its freedom altogether and fallen under a greater tyranny than that of the duke of Athens. But his goodness never allowed a thought to enter his mind that might be contrary to the universal good; his prudence led him to conduct things in such a mode that many yielded to his party and others he was able to subdue with arms. These things caused the plebs to lose heart and the better guildsmen to reflect and to consider what ignominy it was for those who had overcome the pride of the great to have to bear the stench of the plebs.

18

WHEN Michele gained his victory over the plebs, the new Signoria had already been drawn. In it were two men of such vile and infamous condition that a desire grew among men to free themselves from such infamy. Thus, on the first day of September, when the new Signori assumed the magistracy, the piazza was found to be full of armed men. As soon as the old Signori were out of the palace, a tumultuous shout came from the armed men that they did not want any of the lesser people to be Signori. So the Signoria, in order to satisfy them, deprived those two of their magistracy, of whom one was called *il Tria* and the other *Baroccio*,[1] and in their places elected Messer Giorgio Scali and Francesco di Michele. They also annulled the guild of the lesser people and deprived of their offices those subject to it, except for Michele di Lando, Lorenzo di Puccio, and some others of better quality; they divided the honors into two parts, assigning one to the greater and the other to the lesser guilds; they wanted that among the Signori there always be only five of the lesser guildsmen and four of the greater, and that the Gonfalonier should go to one member and the other in turn. The state having been so ordered, the city was put at rest for the time being; and although the republic had been taken out of the hands of the lesser plebs, the guildsmen of lesser quality remained more powerful than the popular nobles, for the latter, to satisfy the former, were compelled of necessity to yield so as to take away the favors of the guilds from the lesser people. This was favored also by those who desired the continued suppression of those who had offended so many citizens with so much violence under the name of the Guelf party. And because among those who favored this sort of government were Messer Giorgio Scali, Messer Benedetto Alberti, Messer Salvestro de'

[1] *Il Tria* was Giovanni di Domenico; *Baroccio* was Bartolo di Jacopo Costa.

Medici, and Messer Tommaso Strozzi, they were left almost as princes of the city. These things, carried on and managed as they were, confirmed the division already begun by the ambition of the Ricci and the Albizzi between the popular nobles and the lesser guildsmen, because of which very grave effects followed at various times; and since this will have to be mentioned many times, we shall call one of these the popular party and the other the plebeian. This state lasted for three years and was filled with exiles and deaths because those who governed lived with the greatest suspicion for the many malcontents inside and outside. The malcontents inside either tried or (it was believed) they might try new things every day, and those outside, having no respect to check them, sowed various scandals through this prince or that republic on this side and that.

19

IN these times Giannozzo da Salerno was in Bologna. He was the captain of Charles of Durazzo, who was descended from the kings of Naples and was planning to make a campaign on behalf of the Kingdom against Queen Giovanna. He kept this captain of his in Bologna because of the favors that had been done for him by Pope Urban, an enemy of the queen.[1] Also in Bologna were many Florentine exiles who had had very close dealings with Giannozzo and with Charles, which gave cause to those ruling in Florence to live in the greatest suspicion and to lend faith easily to calumnies against citizens who were suspected. It was revealed, then, to the magistracy, when their minds were in such suspense, that Giannozzo da Salerno was to appear in Florence with the exiles and that many inside the city were to take up arms and give the city over to him. On account of this report, many were accused; first named among them were Piero degli Albizzi and Carlo Strozzi, and after these Cipriano Mangioni, Messer Jacopo Sacchetti, Messer Donato Barbadori, Filippo Strozzi, and Giovanni Anselmi, all of whom, except Carlo Strozzi, who fled, were arrested. Lest any one dare to take up arms in their favor, the Signori deputed Messer Tommaso Strozzi and Messer Benedetto Alberti with many armed men to guard the city. The arrested citizens were examined, and, with regard to the accusation and the evidence, no fault was found in them; so, as the Captain was unwilling to condemn them, their enemies so excited the people and moved it to such rage against them that they were forcibly sentenced to death. The greatness of his house was no aid to Piero degli Albizzi, nor was his former reputation, since for a long time he had been honored and feared above any other citizen. Hence

[1] See *FH* I 33.

someone, whether a friend, so as to make him more humane in his greatness, or an enemy, so as to threaten him with the fickleness of fortune, sent him at a banquet he gave for many citizens a silver goblet filled with sweets, among which a nail was hidden. When it was uncovered and seen by all the guests, it was interpreted as a reminder to him that he should drive a nail into the wheel; since fortune had led him to the top, if it were to continue in its circle it could only drag him down to the bottom. This interpretation, which came before his ruin, was later verified by his death.

After this execution the city was left full of confusion because both the conquered and the conquerors were fearful, but the more malign effects arose from the fears of those who were governing because every slightest accident made them inflict new injuries on the Party[2] by condemning or admonishing or sending its citizens into exile. And they added to this new laws and new orders that were made often for the strengthening of the state. All of these things were carried out with injury to those who were suspect to their faction; and that is why they created forty-six men who together with the Signori were to purge the republic of those suspect to the state. These men admonished thirty-nine citizens and made many men of the people great and many of the great, men of the people. And so as to be able to oppose outside forces, they hired Sir John Hawkwood, English by birth and of very high reputation in arms, who for a long time had fought for the pope and for others in Italy. Suspicion of those outside arose from learning that many companies of armed men were being ordered by Charles of Durazzo to mount a campaign for the Kingdom, in which it was said there were many Florentine exiles with him. Against these dangers they provided sums of money as well as the forces they had ordered; for when Charles arrived at Arezzo, he received 40,000 ducats from the Florentines and promised not to molest them. Then he carried out his campaign and successfully occupied the kingdom of Naples, and Queen Giovanna was taken and sent to Hungary.[3] This victory again increased the suspicions of those who held the state in Florence, because they could not believe that their money could count for more in the mind of the king than that ancient friendship which his house had had with the Guelfs who were being oppressed by them with so much injury.

20

THUS, as suspicion grew, it made injuries grow, and these did not eliminate suspicion but increased it, so that the greater part of men lived very

---

[2] The Guelf party.

[3] In fact, Charles had her killed in 1382.

malcontent. Added to this was the insolence of Messer Giorgio Scali and of Messer Tommaso Strozzi, whose authority surpassed that of the magistrates, everyone fearing to be oppressed by them with the favor of the plebs. And not only to good men but even to the seditious the government appeared tyrannical and violent. But since the insolence of Messer Giorgio must at some time come to an end, it happened that someone familiar with him accused Giovanni di Cambio of having made plots against the state. He was found innocent by the Captain,[1] so that the judge wanted to punish the accuser with the penalty that the accused would have suffered had he been found guilty. Since Messer Giorgio could save him neither by his entreaties nor by any authority of his, he and Messer Tommaso Strozzi went with a multitude of armed men and freed him by force; and they sacked the palace of the Captain, who was compelled to hide if he wanted to save himself. This act filled the city with such hatred for Messer Giorgio that his enemies thought they could get rid of him and take the city not only out of his hands but out of the hands of the plebs, who by their arrogance had kept the city in subjection for three years.

In this the Captain also supplied a great opportunity. After the tumult was over, he went to the Signori and said that he had come voluntarily to the office to which the Signori had elected him because he thought he was to serve just men who would take up arms to favor and not to impede justice. But since he had seen and experienced the governors of the city and their mode of living, the dignity he had voluntarily taken up to acquire utility and honor he would voluntarily surrender to them to escape danger and harm. The Captain was consoled by the Signori, and they raised his spirits by promising him recompense for past harm and security for the future; and a part of them having consulted with some citizens whom they judged to be lovers of the common good and less suspect to the state, they concluded that a great opportunity had come to pluck the city from the power[2] of Messer Giorgio and the plebs, since the generality of people[3] had been alienated from him by this last insolence. Because of this, it appeared to them that they should use the opportunity before indignant spirits were reconciled, because they knew that the grace of the generality of people is gained and lost by every small accident; and they judged that if they wished to carry this thing through, it would be necessary to draw Benedetto Alberti to their wishes, without whose consent they judged the undertaking to be dangerous.

[1] The Captain of Justice.
[2] *Potestà*.
[3] Lit.: the universal. The same phrase is used in the following sentence.

Messer Benedetto was a very rich man, humane, severe, a lover of the liberty of his fatherland, a man to whom tyrannical modes were very displeasing, so that it was easy to pacify him and make him agree to the ruin of Messer Giorgio. For the cause that had made him an enemy to the popular nobles and to the sect of the Guelfs, as well as a friend to the plebs, had been the insolence of the former and their tyrannical modes. Then, when he saw afterwards that the heads of the plebs had become similar to the others, he had some time ago dissociated himself from them too, and the injuries that had been done to many citizens had been carried out altogether without his consent: thus, the causes that had made him take the side of the plebs were the same ones that made him leave them. Consequently, when Messer Benedetto and the heads of the guilds had been drawn to the will of the Signori and had provided themselves with arms, Messer Giorgio was arrested and Messer Tommaso fled. And on the next day Messer Giorgio was decapitated with so much terror on his part that no one moved; indeed, everyone competed for his ruin. So, as he saw himself coming to his death before that people which a short time before had adored him, he lamented his evil fate and the malignity of the citizens who, by injuring him wrongly, had constrained him to favor and honor a multitude in which there was neither any faith nor any gratitude. And recognizing Messer Benedetto Alberti among the armed men, he said to him: "And do you, Messer Benedetto, allow this injury to be done to me which, were I in your place, I would never have permitted to be done to you? But I announce to you that this day is the end of my evil and the beginning of yours." Then he lamented for himself that he had trusted too much in a people whom every voice, every act, every suspicion moves and corrupts.[4] And with these lamentations he died in the midst of his enemies, armed as they were and merry over his death. After him, many of his closest friends were killed and dragged about by the people.

21

THE death of this citizen made a commotion throughout the city because in its execution many had taken up arms in favor of the Signoria and the Captain of the People; many others also took up arms either out of their ambition or because they had been suspected themselves. And since the city was full of diverse humors, everyone had a different end, and all desired to accomplish them before arms were put down. The ancient no-

---

4 See *P* 9 for NM's comment on this lamentation.

bles, called "great," could not bear to be deprived of their public honors, and so they strove to recover them with all diligence; and for this they would have loved that authority be given back to the captains of the Party. The popular nobles and the greater guilds were not pleased with having to share the state with the lesser guilds and the lesser people; for their part, the lesser guilds wanted rather to increase than diminish their dignity; and the lesser people were afraid lest they lose their Collegi from their guilds. All these disputes made for many tumults in Florence in the space of a year: first the great took up arms, then the greater and then the lesser guilds and with them the lesser people; and many times in different parts of the city all were armed at a stroke. From this followed many engagements both among themselves and with the men of the palace, for the Signoria, now by yielding, now by fighting, tried to remedy such inconveniences as best it could. So, in the end, after two parliaments and several balìe were created to reform the city, after much damage, travail, and very grave dangers, a government was established by which all those who had been banished after Messer Salvestro de' Medici had been Gonfalonier were returned to their fatherland. The high positions and privileges were taken away from all those for whom they had been provided by the balìa of '78; honors were given back to the Guelf party; the two new guilds were deprived of their corporations and governors, and everyone who had been put under them was now reassigned to his former guild. The lesser guilds were deprived of their Gonfalonier of Justice and were reduced from a half to a third share of honors, and of these, the honors of greater quality were taken away. So it was that the party of the popular nobles and of the Guelfs regained the state, and the plebs lost it after having been prince of it from 1378 to '81, at which time these innovations occurred.

22

THIS state was neither less injurious toward its citizens nor less oppressive in its beginnings than that of the plebs had been; for many popular nobles who had been known defenders of the plebs were banished, together with a large number of the plebeian chiefs, among whom was Michele di Lando. Nor was he saved from the fury of the parties by the many goods of which his authority had been the cause when the unchecked multitude was licentiously ruining the city. So his fatherland was scarcely grateful to him for his good works, an error into which princes and republics fall many times—from which it results that men, dismayed by such examples, offend their princes before they can feel their ingratitude. These exiles and deaths displeased Messer Benedetto Alberti now as they had displeased him always, and he censured them publicly and privately. Thus the princes of the state feared him because they deemed him one of the first friends of the plebs, and they believed that he had agreed to the death of Messer Giorgio Scali not because Messer Giorgio's modes displeased him but so as to be alone in the government. His words and his modes, then, increased suspicion of him, which made the whole party that was prince turn its eyes on him so as to seize an opportunity to be able to crush him.

While men were living in these straits, things outside were not very grave; for anything that came from outside was more terrifying than harmful. For at this time Louis of Anjou came into Italy to restore the kingdom of Naples to Queen Giovanna and to drive out Charles of Durazzo. His passage frightened the Florentines very much because Charles, in accordance with the custom of old friends, sought help from them, and Louis, as does one who looks for new friends, asked that they remain in the middle. Thus the Florentines, so as to show that they were satisfying Louis and helping Charles, removed Sir John Hawkwood from their pay and had him captain for Pope Urban, who was a friend of Charles's. This ruse was easily discovered by Louis, and he felt himself very much hurt by the Florentines. And while the war between Louis and Charles was being waged in Apulia, new men came from France in support of Louis. When they reached Tuscany, they were led by exiles from Arezzo into Arezzo, and they expelled the party that was governing for Charles there. And while they were planning to change the state of Florence as they had changed that of Arezzo, the death of Louis occurred, and the order of things in Apulia and in Tuscany changed with fortune: for Charles was assured of the kingdom that he had almost lost, and the Florentines, who had doubted they could defend Florence, acquired Arezzo because they bought it from the men who were holding it for Louis. Charles, therefore, assured of Apulia, departed for the kingdom of Hungary, which had come to him by inheritance, and he left his wife in Apulia with Ladislas and Giovanna, his children, who were still small, as we explained in its place.[1] Charles acquired Hungary, but soon after, he was killed there.

23

FOR that acquisition, Florence made as joyous a celebration as any other city might have done for a proper victory. Both public and private mag-

[1] See *FH* I 33.

nificence were to be seen there because many families celebrated in competition with the public. But the one family that surpassed every other in pomp and magnificence was the Alberti; the displays and the tournaments held by them were not those of a private family but worthy of any prince. These things greatly increased envy for that family, which, added to the suspicion that the state had of Messer Benedetto, was the cause of his ruin. For those who were governing could not be content with him, since it appeared to them that at any hour it might arise that he, with the favor of the party, might regain his reputation and drive them from the city. And while they remained in doubt, it happened that while Benedetto was Gonfalonier of the companies, his son-in-law Filippo Magalotti was drawn as Gonfalonier of Justice. Such a thing redoubled the fear of the princes of the state, as they thought that too much force was being added to Messer Benedetto and too much danger to the state. And since they desired to remedy this without tumult, they inspired Bese Magalotti, his relative and enemy, to inform the Signori that Messer Filippo, lacking the age required for exercising that rank, neither could nor ought to have it. The case was examined among the Signori, and some out of hatred and some to avoid scandal judged Messer Filippo ineligible for that dignity. In his place Bardo Mancini was drawn, a man altogether opposed to the plebeian faction and very hostile to Messer Benedetto. So when he took up the magistracy, he created a balìa that, in taking over and reforming the state, banished Messer Benedetto Alberti and admonished the rest of his family except Messer Antonio.

Messer Benedetto, before his departure, called together all his relatives and, seeing them dejected and full of tears, said to them: "You see, my fathers and elders, how fortune has ruined me and threatened you. I do not marvel at this, nor ought you to marvel, because it always happens thus to those who wish to be good among the many wicked and who want to sustain that which most seek to ruin. Love of my fatherland made me join with Messer Salvestro de' Medici and then break with Messer Giorgio Scali. The same love made me hate the habits of those now governing, who, having no one to chastise them, also do not want anyone to rebuke them. And I am glad to free them by my exile from the fear that they have had, not only of me but of anyone they know who recognizes their tyrannical and criminal modes; and that is why by striking me they have threatened others. For myself, I do not sorrow, for the honors that my fatherland gave to me when it was free, it cannot take away when enslaved, and the memory of my past life will always give me greater pleasure than the unhappiness that will accompany me in my exile will give me displeasure. It does pain me much that my fatherland must remain the prey of a few and be subjected to their pride and avarice. I am pained for you because I fear that the evils that are ending for me today are beginning for you and will pursue you with greater harm than they have pursued me. I urge you therefore to steady your spirits against all misfortunes and to conduct yourselves in such a way that should any adversity come to you—for many will come—everyone will know that they came to you who were innocent and without blame." Afterwards, in order not to leave a lesser opinion of his goodness outside than he might have left in Florence, he went to the Sepulchre of Christ, and while returning from there, died in Rhodes. His bones were brought to Florence and were buried with the greatest honor by those who, when he was alive, had persecuted him with every calumny and injury.

24

NOT only the Alberti family was harmed in the travails of the city, but with it many citizens were admonished and banished, among whom were Piero Benini, Matteo Alderotti, Giovanni and Francesco del Bene, Giovanni Benci, Andrea Adimari, and with them a large number of lesser artisans. Among those admonished were the Covoni, the Benini, the Rinucci, the Formiconi, the Corbizzi, the Mannegli, and the Alderotti. It was the custom to create a balìa for a certain time; but those citizens, when they had done what they had been deputed for, used to resign for the sake of propriety, even though the time had not ended. When, therefore, it appeared to these men that they had satisfied the state, they wanted to resign according to the custom. Upon learning this, many ran armed to the palace, asking that before resigning they should banish and admonish many others. This was very displeasing to the Signori, and they entertained them with good promises until the Signori had made themselves strong, and then worked it so that fear would make them put down the arms that rage had made them take up. Nonetheless, so as to satisfy in part such an enraged humor and to take away more authority from the plebeian guildsmen, the Signori provided that, whereas they had had a third of the honors, they would now have a quarter; and so that there might always be two of them more faithful to the state among the Signori, they gave authority to the Gonfalonier of Justice and to four other citizens to make up a bag of selected names from which two would be drawn in every Signoria.

25

THE state that had been ordered in 1381 thus having been confirmed after six years, the city lived very quietly inside until '93. During this time,

Giovan Galeazzo Visconti, called Count of Virtue, captured Messer Bernabò, his uncle, and thereby became prince of all Lombardy.[1] He believed he could become king of Italy by force just as he had become duke of Milan by trickery; and in '90 he began a very great war against the Florentines.[2] And the managing of the war varied so that many times the duke was in greater danger of losing than the Florentines, who would have lost if he had not died. Nonetheless, the defense was spirited and admirable for a republic; and the end was much less evil than the war had been frightening, for when the duke had taken Bologna, Pisa, Perugia, and Siena and had had the crown prepared for his coronation in Florence as king of Italy, he died. His death did not allow him to taste his past victories, nor did it allow the Florentines to feel their actual losses.

While this war with the duke toiled on, Messer Maso degli Albizzi, whom the death of Piero had made an enemy to the Alberti, was made Gonfalonier of Justice. And because the humors of the parties were ever alert, Messer Maso thought that even though Messer Benedetto had died in exile, he would get his revenge from the rest of that family before his magistracy ended. He seized his opportunity from one who had been examined for certain dealings with the rebels, who named Alberto and Andrea degli Alberti. These men were quickly arrested, whereupon the whole city became excited; so the Signori provided themselves with arms, called the people to an assembly, and appointed men for a balìa by virtue of which they banished many citizens and made new baggings for offices. Among the banished were almost all the Alberti; also, many more guildsmen were admonished and killed. After so many injuries, the guilds and the lesser people rose up in arms, as it appeared to them that their honor and their lives might be taken from them. One part of them came into the piazza, and another ran to the house of Messer Veri de' Medici, who after the death of Messer Salvestro had been left head of the family. So as to beguile those who came to the piazza, the Signori gave them as heads, with the ensigns of the Guelf party and of the people in hand, Messer Rinaldo Gianfigliazzi and Messer Donato Acciaiuoli, who were men of the people accepted more by the plebs than any others. Those who ran to the house of Messer Veri begged[3] him to take over the state and free them from the tyranny of those citizens who were destroyers of the good and of the common welfare. All who have left any record of these times agree that if Messer Veri had been more ambitious than good, he could without any hindrance have made himself prince of the city; for the grave injuries that rightly or wrongly had been done to the

[1] See *FH* I 33.
[2] See *D* III 43.
[3] Or prayed.

guilds and to their friends had in a manner so inflamed their spirits toward revenge that to satisfy their appetites they lacked no more than a head to lead them. Nor did Messer Veri lack someone to remind him of what he could do, because Antonio de' Medici, who had had a particular enmity toward him for a long time, was trying to persuade him to seize dominion over the republic. Messer Veri said to him: "Your threats when you were my enemy did not frighten me, nor now that you are my friend will your advice bring me evil." And turning to the multitude, he urged them to be of good spirit, since he wanted to be their defender only if they would take advice from him. Going among them in the piazza and from there into the palace, he said before the Signori that he could not in any mode regret having lived in such a manner that the people of Florence loved him, but he regretted very much the judgment that had been made of him, which his past life did not deserve. Since he had never himself been an example of someone scandalous or ambitious, he did not know whence it arose that it should be believed he had been a supporter of scandals as a restless man or a seizer of the state as an ambitious one. He therefore begged the Signori that the ignorance of the multitude not be imputed to his sin because, as far as he was concerned, as soon as he could he had put himself in their power.[4] He reminded them that they should be content to use fortune modestly and to let it be enough for them to enjoy half a victory with the city in safety than, by wanting it all, to ruin it. Messer Veri was praised by the Signori and encouraged to have arms laid down; and then they would not fail to do what might be advised by him and the other citizens. After these words, Messer Veri returned to the piazza and joined his followers with those who had been led by Messer Rinaldo and Messer Donato. Then he told everyone that he had found in the Signori the best will toward them, and that many things had been spoken of; but because time was short and the magistrates were absent, they had not been settled. Therefore, he begged them to put down their arms and obey the Signori; and he pledged his faith that humanity rather than pride, prayers rather than threats, were about to move the Signori, and that they would not lack for rank and security if they let themselves be governed by him. And under his faith he made everyone return to his home.

26

WHEN arms had been laid down, the Signori first fortified the piazza, then conscripted two thousand citizens faithful to the state, divided

---

[4] Lit.: forces.

equally into companies with standards. They ordered them to be ready
to come to their rescue whenever they called them, and they prohibited
those not conscripted from arming themselves. When these preparations
were made, the Signori banished and killed many guildsmen who had
shown themselves to be fiercer than others in the tumults; and to give
more majesty and reputation to the Gonfalonier of Justice, they provided
that for the exercise of this office it was necessary to be forty-five years
old. In strengthening the state, they also made many provisions that were
unbearable to those against whom they were made and hateful to the
good citizens of their own party: for these did not judge a state good and
secure that would need to defend itself with such violence. And so much
violence was displeasing not only to those of the Alberti who remained
in the city and to the Medici, to whom it appeared the people had been
deceived, but also to many others. And the first who sought to oppose it
was Messer Donato di Jacopo Acciaiuoli. Although this man was
important[1] in the city and more a superior than a companion of Messer
Maso degli Albizzi, who because of the things done during his term as
Gonfalonier was almost a head of the republic,[2] he could not live well
content among so many malcontents; nor could he, as do most, secure
private advantage for himself from the common loss. Therefore, he
thought he would try if he could to restore their fatherland to the exiles
or at least their offices to the admonished. And he went about spreading
his opinion in the ear of this or that citizen, pointing out that the people
could not be quieted otherwise or the humors of the parties contained;
and he expected nothing else than to be of the Signori so as to carry his
desire into effect. And because delay in our actions brings tedium and
haste brings danger, to escape tedium he turned to danger. Among the
Signori were his relative Michele Acciaiuoli and his friend Niccolò Rico-
veri, whence it appeared to Messer Donato that an opportunity had been
given him that was not to be lost, and he asked that they propose a law to
the councilors that would include restitution for citizens.[3] These men,
persuaded by him, spoke of it to their companions, who answered that it
was no good to try new things when the acquisition was doubtful and the
danger certain. Thus, Messer Donato, having first tried all ways in vain
and overcome with anger, gave them to understand that as they did not
want the city to be ordered with the means at hand, it would be ordered
with arms. These words were so displeasing that when the thing had been
communicated to the princes of the government, Messer Donati was
cited; and when he appeared, he was convicted by the one to whom he

---

[1] Lit.: great.
[2] See *FH* III 25.
[3] The restitution of political rights.

had committed the embassy; so he was banished to Barletta. Also banished were Alamanno and Antonio de' Medici, with all those of the family who were descendants of Messer Alamanno, together with many lowly guildsmen who had credit with the plebs. These events took place two years after the state had been retaken by Messer Maso.

27

THUS stood the city with many malcontents inside and many exiles outside. Among the exiles in Bologna were Picchio Cavicciuli, Tommaso de' Ricci, Antonio de' Medici, Benedetto degli Spini, Antonio Girolami, Christofano di Carlone, with two others of vile condition, but all young, fierce, and disposed to try all fortune so as to return to their fatherland. They were shown in secret ways by Piggiello and Baroccio Cavicciuli, who were living admonished in Florence, that if they came secretly into the city, they would receive them at home. They could then go out to kill Messer Maso degli Albizzi and call the people to arms, for since the people were malcontent, they could easily be aroused, especially because they would be followed by the Ricci, Adimari, Medici, Mannegli, and many other families. Moved therefore by these hopes, on the fourth day in August in 1397 they came to Florence; and, having entered secretly where it had been ordered for them, they set up a watch on Messer Maso, for they intended to start a tumult by his death. Messer Maso left his house and stopped in at a nearby apothecary in San Piero Maggiore. The man who was to watch him ran to inform the conspirators, who took up arms and came to the place shown them but found that he had already left. Then, undismayed by the failure of their first design, they turned toward the Mercato Vecchio, where they killed one of the opposite party. And when they had raised an uproar by shouting "people, arms, liberty" and "death to the tyrants," they turned to the Mercato Nuovo, where at the end of Calimala they killed another; and as they continued on their way with the same cries, and yet no one took up arms, they withdrew to the loggia of the Nighittosa. Here they put themselves on a high place, with a great multitude around, which had run there more to see them than to favor them. With loud voices they urged the men to take up arms and escape the servitude they hated so much. They asserted that the grievances of the malcontents of the city, more than their own injuries, had moved them to want to free them, and that they had heard that many prayed God to give them an opportunity to get revenge—which they might do any time they had a head to move them. And now that the opportunity had come and they had heads to move them, they were looking at one another, stupidly waiting for the movers of their liberation to be killed and their own servitude to be aggravated. And they marveled that those who were used to taking up arms for the least injury were not moved for so many, and that they should want to tolerate the banishment of so many of their citizens and so many admonished; but now the choice was theirs to restore to the exiles their fatherland and the state to the admonished. These words, even though true, did not move the multitude in any way, either because of fear or because the killing of those two might have made the murderers hateful. So the movers of the tumult, seeing that neither their words nor their deeds had force to move anyone, perceiving too late how dangerous it is to want to free a people who want in every mode to be enslaved, despaired of their undertaking and retreated to the church of Santa Reparata, where they shut themselves in, not to save their lives but to postpone death. The Signori, alarmed by the first outcry, armed and locked the palace; but then when the case was known and it was learned who the movers of the scandals were and where they were shut in, they were reassured, and they commanded the Captain[1] to go with many armed men and take them. Thus, without much trouble the doors of the church were forced, and part of the exiles were killed defending themselves, part arrested. These were examined, and when none were found guilty besides them, except for Baroccio and Piggiello Cavicciuli, they were killed together with the others.

28

AFTER this accident, another one of greater importance arose from it. In these times the city, as we said before,[1] was at war with the duke of Milan. As he saw that open forces were not enough to crush it, he turned to hidden ones; and by means of Florentine exiles, with which Lombardy was filled, he ordered an accord, of which many inside were cognizant, by which it was concluded that on a certain day, from places very near Florence, a great party of exiles, fit for arms, would leave and enter the city by way of the river Arno. Together with their friends inside, they would rush to the houses of those first in the state, and when they had killed them, they would reform the republic according to their own will. Among the conspirators inside was one of the Ricci named Saminiato; and as it often happens in conspiracies that few are not enough and many expose them,[2] while Saminiato was seeking to gain companions, he

[1] The Captain of Justice.
[1] *FH* III 25.
[2] See *D* III 6.

found an accuser. He disclosed the affair to Salvestro Cavicciuli, whom the injuries to his relatives and himself ought to have made faithful; nonetheless, he valued the immediate fear more than the future hope, and he immediately exposed the whole treaty to the Signori, who had Saminiato taken and forced him to reveal the entire order of the conspiracy. But of those cognizant of it, none was taken except Tommaso Davizi, who was coming from Bologna and did not know what had happened in Florence, and was arrested before he arrived. All the others, after the capture of Saminiato, became frightened and fled. Saminiato and Tommaso therefore were punished for their failings, and a balìa was given to many citizens, who by their authority were to seek out the guilty and secure the state. These men declared as rebels six of the Ricci family, six of the Alberti, two of the Medici, three of the Scali, two of the Strozzi,[3] Bindo Altoviti, Bernardo Adimari, and many of the base; they also admonished all the Alberti family, the Ricci, and the Medici for ten years,[4] except for a few. Among the Alberti not admonished was Messer Antonio, considered a quiet and peaceful man. It happened that since suspicion of the conspiracy had not yet been eliminated, a monk was arrested who had been seen going from Bologna to Florence many times when the conspirators were plotting. He confessed to having carried letters many times to Messer Antonio, after which Antonio was immediately arrested; and although he denied everything from the beginning, he was proven guilty by the monk and thereupon fined and banished to three hundred miles from the city. And to keep the Alberti from putting the state in danger every day, they banished all in that family who were over fifteen years old.

29

THIS accident took place in 1400. Two years later Giovan Galeazzo, duke of Milan, died; and his death, as we said above,[1] put an end to the war that had lasted for twelve years. Since the government in that time had gained more authority, being without enemies outside or inside, an expedition was made to Pisa, and that city was won gloriously; and inside it was quiet from 1400 to '33.

Only in 1412, because the Alberti had breached their banishment, a new balìa was created against them that reinforced the state with new

---

[3] In fact, five Ricci, one Medici, three Strozzi.
[4] For twenty years.
[1] FH III 25.

provisions and harassed the Alberti with taxes. In this time the Florentines also made war with Ladislas, king of Naples, which ended with the
death of the king in 1414. And in the travail of that war the king, finding
himself inferior, yielded the city of Cortona, of which he was lord, to the
Florentines. But soon after, when he had regained his forces, he renewed
a war with them that was much more dangerous than the first; and if it
had not ended with his death, as the war with the duke of Milan had
already ended, he too would have brought Florence, as had the duke, into
peril of losing its liberty. Nor did this war end with less good luck than
the other, for when King Ladislas had taken Rome, Siena, the Marches,
and all of Romagna, and needed only Florence in order to enter Lombardy with all his power, he died. And thus death was always more
friendly to the Florentines than any other friend, and more powerful to
save them than their own virtue. After the death of this king, the city was
quiet outside and inside for eight years. At the end of that time, together
with the wars of Filippo, duke of Milan, the parties revived and did not
subside until the ruin of the state that had ruled from 1381 to 1434, which
had made so many wars with such glory and had acquired Arezzo, Pisa,
Cortona, Livorno, and Monte Pulciano for its empire. And greater things
would have been accomplished if the city had maintained itself united and
if the old humors had not been rekindled in it, as will be shown in particular in the following book.

BOOK IV

1

CITIES, and especially those not well ordered that are administered under the name of republic, frequently change their governments and their states not between liberty and servitude, as many believe, but between servitude and license. For only the name of freedom is extolled by the ministers of license, who are the men of the people, and by the ministers of servitude, who are the nobles, neither of them desiring to be subject either to the laws or to men. True, when it happens (and it happens rarely) that by the good fortune of a city there rises in it a wise, good, and powerful citizen by whom laws are ordered by which these humors of the nobles and the men of the people are quieted or restrained so that they cannot do evil, then that city can be called free and that state be judged stable and firm: for a city based on good laws and good orders has no necessity, as have others, for the virtue of a single man to maintain it. Many ancient republics endowed with such laws and orders had states with long lives; all those republics that have lacked and are lacking such orders and laws have frequently changed and are changing their governments from a tyrannical to a licentious state, and back again. In these, through the powerful enemies each of them has, there neither is nor can be any stability, because the one state displeases good men, the other displeases the wise; the one can do evil easily, the other can do good only with difficulty; in the one, insolent men have too much authority, in the other, fools. And both the one and the other must be maintained by the virtue and fortune of a single man who can either fail by death or become useless because of his travails.

2

I SAY, therefore, that the state that had its beginning in Florence with the death of Messer Giorgio Scali in 1381 was sustained first by the virtue of Messer Maso degli Albizzi, later by that of Niccolò da Uzzano. The city lived quietly from 1414 until '22,[1] since King Ladislas was dead and

[1] Cf. *FH* III 29.

146

the state of Lombardy was divided into many parts, so that neither from outside nor from within was there anything to make it fearful. Next to Niccolò da Uzzano, the citizens in authority were Bartolomeo Valori, Nerone di Nigi, Messer Rinaldo degli Albizzi, Neri di Gino, and Lapo Niccolini. The parties born out of the discord between the Albizzi and the Ricci, which were later revived by Messer Salvestro de' Medici with such scandal,[2] were never eliminated; and although the party more favored by the generality of people[3] ruled only three years and was conquered in 1381, nonetheless, because the humor of that party was shared by the greater part of the city, it could never be altogether eliminated. It is true that the frequent parliaments and continual persecutions committed against the heads of the party from '81 to 400 reduced it almost to nothing.

The first families persecuted as heads of the party were the Alberti, Ricci, and Medici, who were many times despoiled of men and riches, and if any of them remained in the city, their honors were taken from them. These blows brought their party low and almost wore it out. There remained nonetheless in many men a memory of injuries received and a desire to avenge them, which, finding support nowhere, remained hidden in their breasts. Those popular nobles, who governed the city peacefully, made two errors that were the ruin of their state: one was that they became insolent through unbroken dominion; the other was that through the envy they had of each other, and through long possession of the state, they did not take the care they should have for whoever could offend them.

3

THUS every day these men with their sinister modes were renewing the hatred of the generality of people;[1] and by not watching out for harmful things because they did not fear them or by nourishing them through their envy of one another, they made the Medici family regain authority. The first of that family to begin to rise again was Giovanni di Bicci. Having become very rich and being of a kindly and humane nature, he was brought to the highest magistracy by the concession of those who were governing. This made for such joy throughout the generality of people in the city, since to the multitude it appeared that it had gained a defender,

---

[2] *FH* III 29.
[3] Lit.: the universal.
[1] Lit.: the universal. The same phrase is used soon again in this chapter.

as was deservedly suspect to the wiser because all the ancient humors were seen beginning to reawaken. And Niccolò da Uzzano did not fail to alert the other citizens by pointing out how dangerous it was to foster one who had such reputation in the generality of people, and how easy it was to oppose disorders in their beginnings, but how difficult it was to remedy them when they were left alone to increase; and he recognized in Giovanni many parts superior to those of Messer Salvestro. Niccolò was not heeded by his peers because they were envious of his reputation and desired to have partners in defeating him. While they lived in Florence among these humors, which were secretly beginning to boil again, Filippo Visconti, second son of Giovanni Galeazzo, had by the death of his brother become lord of all Lombardy; and as it appeared to him that he could plan any enterprise whatsoever, he desired exceedingly to become lord of Genoa again, which at that time lived free under the doge Messer Tommaso da Campofregoso. But he was not confident of being able to succeed in this or any other enterprise if he did not first issue publicly a new accord with the Florentines, whose reputation, he judged, would be enough to enable him to satisfy his desires. He therefore sent his spokesmen to Florence to request it. Many citizens advised that it not be done, but that, instead of doing it, they should persevere in the peace that had been maintained with Genoa for many years; for they recognized the favor that making an accord would bring Filippo and the slight advantage the city would get from it. To many others it appeared right to make an accord and by virtue of it to impose terms on him that, if overstepped, would make everyone recognize his wicked intent and enable one to make war on him more justifiably if he should break the peace. And so, after the question had been much disputed, a peace was established in which Filippo promised not to meddle in affairs from the rivers Magra and Panaro to here.[2]

4

WHEN this accord had been made, Filippo seized Brescia and, soon after, Genoa, contrary to the opinion of those in Florence who had urged the peace because they believed that Brescia would be defended by the Venetians and that Genoa would defend itself. And because in the accord that Filippo had made with the doge of Genoa, Sarzana and the towns situated

---

[2] This treaty of 1420 established two spheres of influence: Lombardy and Genoa for the Visconti, Tuscany for the Florentines.

between here and the Magra had been left to him under the terms that, if he wished to give them away, he was obliged to give them to the Genoese, Filippo ended by violating the peace.[1] Furthermore, he had made an accord with the legate of Bologna. These things changed the minds of our citizens and brought them, fearing new evils, to think of new remedies. When these agitations came to the notice of Filippo, he, whether to justify himself or to test the spirits of the Florentines or to beguile them, sent ambassadors to Florence to point out that he marveled at their suspicions and to offer to renounce whatever he had done to generate any suspicion. These ambassadors produced no other effect than to divide the city, since one party and those who were more esteemed in the government judged that it would be well to arm and prepare to spoil the plans of the enemy; and if preparations were made and Filippo stayed quiet, there would be no war but cause for peace. Many others, either out of envy of those governing or out of fear of war, judged that one ought not suspect a friend lightly, that the things he had done were not worthy of such suspicion, but that they[2] knew well that to create the Ten[3] and to hire soldiers meant war, which, if taken up against such a prince, would result in sure ruin for the city and without being able to hope for anything useful from it, since we could not become the lords of anything we acquired because Romagna was in the middle, and we could not think of doing anything in the affairs of Romagna because of its affinity to the Church. Nonetheless, the authority of those who wished to prepare for war prevailed over that of those who wished to be ordered for peace, and they created the Ten, hired soldiers, and imposed new taxes. Since the taxes weighed more on the lesser citizens than the greater, they filled the city with complaints, and everyone condemned the ambition and greed of the powerful, accusing them of wishing to start an unnecessary war so as to indulge their appetites and to oppress the people so as to dominate them.

5

IT had not yet come to an open break with the duke, but everything was full of suspicion because Filippo, at the request of the legate of Bologna, who was afraid of Messer Antonio Bentivoglio, an exile staying at the Castel Bolognese, had sent men into that city; and as they were close to

---

[1] The treaty of 1420.
[2] The other party.
[3] The *Dieci di Balìa*, a committee appointed for management of war.

the domain of Florence, they kept its state suspicious of them. But what made everyone more fearful and gave ample cause for starting war was the campaign that the duke made to Forlì. The lord of Forlì was Giorgio Ordelaffi, who, as he was dying, left his son Tibaldo under the guardianship of Filippo; and since the guardian appeared suspect to Tibaldo's mother, she sent her son to her father, Ludovico Alidosi, who was lord of Imola. Nonetheless, she was forced by the people of Forlì to observe the will of his father and to put him back in the hands of the duke. Whereupon Filippo, to make himself less suspect and the better to conceal his intent, ordered the marquis of Ferrara to send Guido Torello as his deputy, with troops, to take the government of Forlì. Thus did that town come into the power[1] of Filippo. As soon as this thing was known in Florence, together with the news of the troops come to Bologna, it made the decision for war easier, despite the fact that much was said against it and that Giovanni de' Medici publicly discouraged it by showing that, however sure they might be of the evil mind of the duke, it was better to wait for him to attack you than to go against him with forces. For in this case, the war was as justified in the view of the princes of Italy on the side of the duke as on our side; nor could one ask for help as boldly as they could when the ambition of the duke was revealed; and they would defend their own things with a different spirit and with different forces than they would those of others. Others said that it was not good to wait for the enemy at home but to go find him; that fortune is more friendly to the one who attacks than to the one who defends; and that war is carried on in others' homes with less loss, even though at greater cost, than in one's own. So much did this opinion prevail that it was decided that the Ten should apply every remedy so that the city of Forlì might be taken out of the hands of the duke.

6

FILIPPO, seeing that the Florentines wanted to seize the things he had taken to defend, put scruples aside and sent Agnolo della Pergola with a large army to Imola so that its lord[1] would have to think about defending his own and would not think about the guardianship of his grandson. When Agnolo had, therefore, arrived near Imola—the troops of the Florentines being still at Modigliana, the cold being great and because of this the moats around the city being frozen—one night he furtively took the

[1] *Potestà.*
[1] Ludovico Alidosi; see *FH* IV 5.

town and sent Ludovico a prisoner to Milan. When the Florentines saw
that Imola was lost and that war had been opened, they sent their troops
to Forlì, where they laid siege to the city and tightened it from every side.
And so that the duke's troops could not unite to rescue it, they had hired
Count Alberigo,[2] who made raids from his own town of Zagonara every
day up to the gates of Imola. Agnolo della Pergola saw that he could not
relieve Forlì safely because of the strong position that our troops had
taken up; so he thought he would attempt the capture of Zagonara, judging that the Florentines were not about to let that place be lost; and by
wishing to save it, they would have to abandon their campaign at Forlì
and come to battle at a disadvantage. Thus the duke's troops compelled
Alberigo to ask for terms: they were conceded to him with his promise
that, if the Florentines had not relieved him in two weeks, he would surrender the town. When this disorder was perceived in the camp of the
Florentines and in the city, and as everyone desired that the enemy not
keep that victory, they made him gain even a greater one. For the army[3]
having left Forlì to rescue Zagonara, it was defeated as soon as it met with
the enemy, not so much by the virtue of its adversaries as by the malignity
of the weather. Our men, having walked several hours in very deep mud
and with the rain falling on their backs, found the enemy fresh and easily
able to conquer them. Nonetheless, in such a defeat, celebrated in all
Italy, no one died except Ludovico degli Obizzi, together with two of his
men who fell from their horses and drowned in the mud.[4]

7

AT the news of this defeat, the whole city of Florence grieved, but especially the great citizens who had advised the war, because they saw the
enemy vigorous and themselves disarmed, without friends, and the people against them. Through all the piazzas the people stung them with
abusive words, complaining of the taxes they had borne, of a war begun
without cause, and saying: "Now, did they create the Ten to bring terror
to the enemy? Now, have they rescued Forlì and taken it from the hands
of the duke? Look at how their advice has been exposed and to what end
they were moving: not to defend freedom, which is their enemy, but to
increase their own power, which God has justly diminished. They have
burdened the city not only with this campaign but with many, because

---

[2] Alberigo da Conio; see *FH* I 34 and *P* 12.
[3] Lit.: the camp.
[4] According to Ammirato, Florentine losses were 3,200 horse.

the one against King Ladislas was like this one.[1] To whom will they now turn for help? To Pope Martin, who was torn apart by them out of regard for[2] Braccio?[3] To Queen Giovanna, whom by abandoning they had made to throw herself into the lap[4] of the king of Aragon?" And besides this, they said all the things an angered people are wont to say. Therefore, to the Signori it appeared that they should assemble many citizens who would quiet the excited humors in the multitude with good words. So Messer Rinaldo degli Albizzi, who had been left as the eldest son of Messer Maso and who aspired to reach the highest rank of the city with his own virtues and with the memory of his father, spoke at length, pointing out that it was not prudent to judge things by their effects, because many times things well advised do not have a good outcome and things ill advised have a good one; and if wicked advice is praised for a good outcome, one does nothing but inspire men to err, which results in great harm to republics because bad advice is not always successful. So likewise it was an error to censure a wise course that might have an unhappy outcome, because it would take away from citizens the spirit to advise the city and to say what they mean. Then he showed why it had been necessary to take up that war and how if it had not been started in Romagna, it would have been fought in Tuscany. But, since God had willed the troops to be defeated, the loss would be that much more grave if others were abandoned; but if they faced fortune and applied what remedies they could, neither they would feel their loss nor the duke his victory. And they ought not to be dismayed by the expenses and the taxes to come, because it was reasonable to change the taxes, and the expenses would be much less than the last ones because less equipment is necessary for those who wish to defend than for those who seek to offend. He urged them finally to imitate their fathers, who by not having lost their spirit in any adverse situation had always defended themselves against any prince.

8

URGED thus on his authority, the citizens hired Count Oddo, son of Braccio, and gave him as governor Niccolò Piccinino, a student of Braccio's and more reputed than anyone else who had fought under his ensigns. They gave him in addition other condottieri, and they put back on

---

[1] See *FH* III 29.

[2] Lit.: in contemplation of.

[3] See *FH* I 38.

[4] See *FH* I 38 and *P* 12 for almost the same phrase applied to the unfortunate queen. But in *AW* I she is said to have jumped into the *arms* of the king of Aragon.

horse some who had been despoiled of them.[1] They created twenty citizens to levy a new tax, who, inspired by seeing the powerful citizens depressed by the last defeat, loaded them down without giving them any consideration. This tax hurt the great citizens very much, and at first, so as to appear more honorable, they did not complain of their own tax but criticized it as generally unjust and advised that it should be lightened. When this became known by many, it was blocked in the councils; hence, to make people feel by deeds the harshness of the tax and to make it hated by many, they arranged that the collectors should exact it with the utmost severity by giving them authority to be able to kill anyone who might defend himself against the public agents. From this arose many grievous accidents, with the death and wounding of citizens, from which it appeared that the parties would come to blood, and anyone who was prudent feared some future evil because the great men, accustomed to being respected, could not tolerate having hands laid on them, and the others wanted everyone to be burdened equally. Therefore, many of the first citizens gathered together and concluded that it was a necessity for them to take back the state, because their own lack of care had inspired men to take over public activities and had made bold those who were used to being the heads of the multitude. And having discussed these things many times among themselves, they decided they should all meet again together at a stroke, and more than seventy citizens assembled in the church of Santo Stefano with the permission of Messer Lorenzo Ridolfi and of Francesco Gianfigliazzi, who were then sitting as Signori. Giovanni de' Medici did not meet with them either because he was not called in, as being suspect, or because, being opposed to their opinion, he did not want to take part.

9

MESSER Rinaldo degli Albizzi spoke to all. He pointed out the condition of the city and how through their own negligence it had come again under the power[1] of the plebs, from which it had been extracted by their fathers in 1381. He reminded them of the iniquity of the state that had ruled from '78 to '81 and how, of all those present, this one's father and this one's grandfather had been killed by it; that they were returning to the same dangers and the city was falling again into the same disorders; for already the multitude had levied a tax to suit itself, and very soon, if it were not

[1] At the defeat of Zagonara.
[1] Potestà.

restrained by greater force or better order, it would create magistrates according to its own arbitrary will. If this should happen, it would seize their places and would wreck the state that had ruled with such glory for the city for forty-two years; Florence would then be governed either by chance under the arbitrary will of the multitude, in which one party would live in license and the other in danger, or under the empire of one who would make himself prince. Therefore, he declared, it was necessary for everyone who loved his fatherland and his own honor to come to his senses and remind himself of the virtue of Bardo Mancini,[2] who, with the ruin of the Alberti, had got the city out of the dangers it was in then; and that the cause of this audacity on the part of the multitude arose from the broad baggings[3] that had been made through their own negligence, and the palace had thus been filled with men who were new and vile. He concluded, therefore, that he saw only this mode by which to remedy it: restore the state to the great and take away authority from the lesser guilds by reducing them from fourteen to seven. This would make the plebs have less authority in the councils both because their number would be fewer and also because the great, having more authority there, would be unfavorable to them on account of old hostilities. He affirmed that it was prudence to know how to use men according to the times: for if their fathers had used the plebs to eliminate the insolence of the great, now that the great had become humble and the plebs insolent, it was well to check its insolence with their help. And as for carrying out these things, there was deceit or force to which they could easily have recourse, since some of them, as members of the Ten, could bring men secretly into the city. Messer Rinaldo was praised, and everyone approved his advice. And Niccolò da Uzzano, among others, said that all the things that had been said by Messer Rinaldo were true and the remedies good and sure if they could be accomplished without coming to an open division in the city. This would follow in any mode if they could not get Giovanni de' Medici to agree to their will, because if he concurred, the multitude, deprived of a head and of force, could not offend them, but if he did not concur, nothing could be done without arms; and with arms, he judged, there was danger either of not winning or of not being able to enjoy the victory. Then he modestly recalled to their memory his past advice and how they had not been willing to remedy these difficulties in times when they could easily have done so; but now there was no time to do it without fear of greater loss; and there was no other remedy than winning Giovanni de'

[2] Elected Gonfalonier in 1387; see *FH* III 23.
[3] That is, *squittini* with a too broad, or too democratic, set of names from which officials would be drawn; see *FH* II 28.

Medici over to them.[4] So the commission was given to Messer Rinaldo to go to Giovanni and see if he might attract him to their judgment.

10

THE knight executed his commission and in all the best terms he knew urged Giovanni to take up this enterprise with them and not to desire, by favoring a multitude, to make it bold with consequent ruin to the state and the city. To this Giovanni answered that he believed it the office of a wise and good citizen not to alter the accustomed orders of his city, there being nothing that offends men so much as changing these. For one must offend many, and where many are left malcontent, one can fear some nasty accident every day. And it appeared to him that their decision might do two very pernicious things: one, to give honors to those who, never having had them, esteem them less and, not having them, have less cause to complain; the other, to take them away from those who were accustomed to having them and who would never be quiet unless they were restored to them. And thus one would see that the injury done to one party would be much greater than the benefit to the other, so that whoever was author of this would acquire few friends and very many enemies; and the latter would be more fierce in injuring him than the former to defend him, since men are naturally more ready to avenge an injury than to be grateful for a benefit, as it appears to them that gratitude brings them loss while vengeance brings advantage and pleasure. Then he turned his talk to Messer Rinaldo and said, "And you, if you remember the things that have happened and by what deceits one proceeds in this city, you would be less warm for this decision, for whoever advises it, when he has taken authority from the people by means of your forces, will take it from you with the aid of the people who will have become your enemy for this injury. And it will happen to you as it did to Messer Benedetto Alberti, who consented, by the persuasion of those who did not love him, to the ruin of Messer Giorgio Scali and of Messer Tommaso Strozzi and soon after was sent into exile by the same men who had persuaded him." He urged him, therefore, to think more maturely about things and to wish to imitate his father, who, so as to get universal good will, lowered the price of salt, provided that anyone whose tax was less than half a florin might pay it or not as he saw fit, and that on the day the councils assembled, everyone might be safe from his creditors. In the end

---

[4] See *FH* IV 3.

he concluded that, as far as he was concerned, he was for leaving the city in its orders.

II

THESE things, so dealt with, were learned of outside and brought more reputation to Giovanni and hatred to the other citizens. He sought to detach himself from this so as to give less spirit to those who might plan new things under the cover of his favor; and in all his speech he gave everyone to understand that he was not for nourishing sects but for eliminating them and that, whatever anyone was expecting from him, he sought nothing but union in the city. Many of those who followed his part were malcontent at this because they would have liked him to show himself more active in things. Among these was Alamanno de' Medici, who was fierce by nature and did not cease inciting him to persecute his enemies and favor his friends, condemning him for his coldness and for his mode of proceeding slowly, which, he said, was the cause of his enemies' dealing against him without respect. These dealings would one day have their effect in the ruin of his house and his friends. Inspiring him also in the same way was his son Cosimo. Nonetheless, Giovanni, through something that might have been revealed or predicted to him, did not budge from his position; yet with all this, the party was already exposed, and the city was openly divided. In the palace there were two chancery clerks in the service of the Signori, Ser Martino and Ser Pagolo: the latter favored the party of da Uzzano, and the former that of the Medici. Messer Rinaldo, having seen that Giovanni did not wish to join them, thought it would be well to deprive Ser Martino of his office, judging that then he would always have the palace more favorable. As this was foreseen by his adversaries, not only was Ser Martino defended, but Ser Pagolo was deprived of his office with displeasure and injury to his party. This would have had nasty effects at once had it not been for the war threatening the city, which was frightened because of the defeat suffered at Zagonara; for while these things were toiling on in Florence, Agnolo della Pergola, with the troops of the duke, had taken all the towns in Romagna possessed by the Florentines, except for Castrocaro and Modigliana, partly because of the weakness of those places and partly by the fault of those who had watch over them. In the seizure of these towns two things happened to make one aware of how much the virtue of men is admitted even by the enemy and how much vileness and malignity are disliked.

12

THE castellan of the fortress of Monte Petroso was Biagio del Melano. As fire was set around him by the enemy and he saw no way of saving the fortress, he tossed out rags and straw on a side that was not yet burning and from above threw onto these his two small children while saying to the enemy, "Take for yourselves the goods that fortune has given me and that you can take from me; but those things I have of my spirit, wherein lie my glory and my honor, I will neither give you nor will you take from me." The enemy ran to save the children and brought ropes and ladders to him that he might save himself; but these he did not accept, for indeed he preferred to die in the flames than to be saved by the hands of the adversaries of his fatherland. An example truly worthy of much-praised antiquity!—and as much more wonderful than those as it is rarer. The enemy restored what things they could save to his children and sent them with utmost care to their relatives; the republic was not less kind to them, for as long as they lived they were supported at public expense. The contrary to this happened in Galatea, where Zanobi del Pino was the podestà. Without making any defense, he gave the fortress over to the enemy; and besides, he urged Agnolo to leave the mountains of Romagna to come to the hills of Tuscany, where he could make war with less danger and greater gain. Agnolo, unable to tolerate the vileness and wicked spirit of this man, gave him as prey to his servants, who, after much mockery, gave him paper painted as serpents to eat,[1] telling him that in this mode they wished to make him from Guelf into Ghibelline; and so starving, in a few days he died.

13

COUNT Oddo, meanwhile, together with Niccolò Piccinino, had entered Val di Lamona to see if they could bring the lord of Faenza[1] back to friendship with the Florentines or, at the least, to hinder Agnolo della Pergola from raiding Romagna so freely. But because the valley was very strong and its inhabitants bellicose, Count Oddo was killed there, and Niccolò Piccinino was sent from there to prison in Faenza. But fortune willed that the Florentines, by having lost, should get what perhaps they might not have gotten had they won; for Niccolò worked so well on the

---

[1] A serpent was the emblem of the Visconti.
[1] Guidantonio Manfredi.

lord of Faenza and his mother that he made them friends of the Florentines. In this accord Niccolò Piccinino was set free; but he himself did not take the advice that he gave to others, for while dealing with the city about his command, whether it was that the terms seemed poor to him or that he might find better ones elsewhere, he almost abruptly left Arezzo, where he had his quarters, and went to Lombardy, where he enlisted in the duke's pay. The Florentines, frightened by this unforeseen event and bewildered by their frequent losses, judged they could no longer support this war alone, and they sent spokesmen to the Venetians begging them to oppose, while it was easy for them, the greatness of one who, if they allowed him to rise, was ready to be as pernicious to them as he was to the Florentines. Urging them to the same undertaking was Francesco Carmignuola, a man held in those times to be very excellent in war. He had once been in the pay of the duke but had later rebelled against him. The Venetians hesitated in doubt, not knowing how much they could trust Carmignuola, fearing that the hostility between him and the duke might be feigned. And while they were in suspense, it happened that the duke, by means of a servant of Carmignuola's, had him poisoned; the poison was not potent enough to kill him, but it brought him to the limit. When the cause of his illness was discovered, the Venetians gave up their suspicion, and, as the Florentines were continuing to solicit them, they made a league with them. Each of the parties pledged itself to carry on the war at the common expense; acquisitions in Lombardy were to go to the Venetians, those in Romagna and Tuscany to the Florentines; Carmignuola was the captain general of the league. Thus, by this accord the war was confined to Lombardy, where it was conducted virtuously by Carmignuola. In a few months many towns were taken from the duke, together with the city of Brescia, a capture that in those times and for those wars was considered wonderful.

14

THIS war had lasted from '22 to '27, and the citizens of Florence were weary of the taxes imposed up to then; so they agreed to revise them. And that the taxes might be equal according to wealth, it was provided that they be imposed on goods and that he who had a hundred florins in value would have a tax of half a florin. Therefore, as it was for the law and not men to apportion the tax, it came to weigh very heavily on the powerful citizens; and before the law was decided upon, it was not favored by them. Only Giovanni de' Medici openly praised it, so much so that it passed. And because to apportion the tax each man's goods had to be listed, for which the Florentines say *accatastare*, the tax was called *catasto*. This mode placed a partial restraint on the tyranny of the powerful, because they could not strike at lesser persons and by threats make them keep silent in the councils as they were able to do before. Consequently, this tax was approved by the generality of people[1] but received with very great displeasure by the powerful. But as it happens that men are never satisfied and, having got one thing, do not content themselves with that but desire something else, the people, not content with the equality in taxation that arose from the law, demanded that they return to time past to see how much less the powerful had paid according to the *catasto* and to make them pay enough to be equal with those who, so as to pay what they did not owe, had sold their possessions. This demand, much more than the *catasto*, alarmed the great men, and in defending themselves from it, they condemned it ceaselessly, declaring that it was most unjust because it was imposed also on movable goods, which might be possessed today and lost tomorrow; and that beyond this, many persons had hidden money that the *catasto* could not find. To which they added that those who had left their businesses in order to govern the republic ought to be less burdened by it, as it ought to be enough that they had labored in person; and it was not just that the city should enjoy their belongings and their industry and only the money of others. Others who were pleased with the *catasto* answered that if movable goods vary, the taxes could also vary, and frequent variation of them could remedy that inconvenience. And as for those who had hidden money, it was not necessary to take account of it, as it is not reasonable to pay for money that bears no fruit; when it does bear fruit, it must be discovered; and if to take trouble for the republic did not please them, let them put it aside and not try themselves over it, because the republic would find more loving citizens to whom it would not appear difficult to help it with money and advice; and so many are the advantages and honors that go with governing that these ought to be enough for them without wishing not to share the burdens. But the ill was in what they did not say: for it pained them not to be able to carry on a war without loss to themselves, having to share in the expenses like others; and if this mode had been found earlier, the war with King Ladislas would not have been made, nor would this one with Duke Filippo; for these wars were made to fill up citizens and not out of necessity. These excited humors were quieted by Giovanni de' Medici, who pointed out that it was not good to go back over things past, but rather

---

[1] Lit.: the universal.

to provide for the future; and if the taxes had been unjust in the past, they should thank God that a mode had been found to make them just and should wish that this mode might serve to reunite, not divide, the city, as it would if past taxes were looked into and made to be equal with the present ones.[2] And he who is content with half a victory will always do better from it, since those who wish to do more than win often lose.[3] And with like words he quieted the humors and made them stop reasoning about equalization.

15

AS the war against the duke was continuing meanwhile, a peace was made in Ferrara through the mediation of a papal legate. As the duke did not at first observe its conditions, the league took up arms again and, having joined battle with his men, defeated him at Maclodio. After this defeat the duke started new discussions[1] for an accord, to which the Venetians and Florentines agreed: the Florentines because they had come to suspect the Venetians, as it appeared to them that they were spending a great deal to make others powerful, the Venetians because they saw Carmignuola, after the defeat dealt to the duke, going so slowly that it appeared to them they could no longer trust him. Thus a peace was concluded in 1428 by which the Florentines regained the towns they lost in Romagna, Brescia was left to the Venetians, and in addition the duke gave them Bergamo and its surrounding country. The Florentines spent three million five hundred thousand ducats in this war, from which the Venetians increased their state and greatness, and they, their poverty and disunion.

Peace having been achieved outside, war began again inside. Since the great citizens could not bear the *catasto* and saw no way of eliminating it, they thought up modes of making more enemies of it so as to have more companions in assailing it. Thus, they pointed out to the officials charged with applying it that the law compelled them to register the goods of those in [outlying] districts to see if among them there might be goods belonging to Florentines. Therefore, all subjects were summoned to present written lists of their goods within a certain time. Hence the Volterrans sent to the Signoria to complain about this thing, so that the officials became indignant and put eighteen of them in prison. This deed made the

---

[2] See *FH* III 3 and *D* I 37.
[3] See *D* II 27.
[1] Lit.: reasonings.

Volterrans very indignant; yet, out of regard for their prisoners, they did not move.

16

AT this time Giovanni de' Medici fell ill, and as he knew his illness was mortal, he called in his sons Cosimo and Lorenzo and said to them, "I believe I have lived out the time allotted to me by God and by nature at my birth. I die content because I leave you rich, healthy, and of quality such that if you will follow my footsteps, you will be able to live in Florence honored and in everyone's good graces. For no single thing makes me die so content as the recollection that I have never offended anyone; rather, I have benefited everyone insofar as I could. And so I urge you to do. In regard to the state, if you wish to live secure, accept from it as much as is given to you by laws and by men. This will bring you neither envy nor danger, since it is what a man takes himself, not what is given to a man, that makes us hate him; and always you will have more than they who, wanting others' share, lose their own, and before losing it live in continual unease. With these arts I have among so many enemies, among so many differences, not only maintained but increased my reputation in this city. Thus, if you will follow my footsteps, you will maintain and improve yourselves. But if you should do otherwise, do not think that your end will be any more prosperous than the ends of those who in our memory have ruined themselves and destroyed their houses." Shortly after, he died, and in the generality of people[1] in the city he left a very great longing for himself, as his excellent qualities deserved. Giovanni had been charitable, and not only did he give alms to whoever asked for them, but many times he supplied the needs of the poor without being asked. He loved everyone, praised the good, and had compassion for the wicked. He never asked for honors yet had them all. He never went into the palace unless he was called. He loved peace, he avoided war. He supported men in their adversity and aided their prosperity. He was averse to public plunder and an improver of the common good. Gracious in his magistracies, he had not much eloquence but very great prudence. In appearance he was melancholy, but then in his conversation he was pleasing and witty. He died very rich in treasure but even richer in good reputation and good will. This inheritance of fortune's goods as well as those of the spirit was not only maintained but increased by Cosimo.

[1] Lit.: the universal.

THE Volterrans were weary of being in prison[1] and to get free they promised to consent to what had been commanded to them. So, when they had been set free and had returned to Volterra, it was the time when their new priors were assuming their magistracies. Among these a certain Giusto was drawn, a plebeian man but with standing among the plebs, who was one of those who had been imprisoned in Florence. This man, himself inflamed with hatred for the public injury as well as his private one, was further incited against the Florentines by Giovanni di [Contugi],[2] a nobleman who sat in magistracy with him, to stir up the people, with the authority of the priors and with his grace, to take the town from the hands of the Florentines and make himself its prince. On his advice, Giusto took up arms, ran through town, seized the captain who was there for the Florentines, and, with the consent of the people, made himself its lord. This innovation in Volterra displeased the Florentines very much. Yet, as they had made a peace with the duke and the accords were still fresh, they judged they had time to reacquire it; and so as not to lose time, they immediately sent Messer Rinaldo degli Albizzi and Messer Palla Strozzi as commissioners for the undertaking. In the meantime, Giusto, thinking that the Florentines would attack him, asked the Sienese and the Lucchese for help. The Sienese refused it, saying that they were allied with the Florentines; and Pagolo Guinigi, who was lord of Lucca, in order to reacquire favor[3] with the people of Florence, which it appeared to him he had lost in the war with the duke when he showed himself to be Filippo's friend, not only refused help to Giusto but sent to prison in Florence the one who had come to ask it. The commissioners, meanwhile, so as to catch the Volterrans while still unprepared, gathered together all their men-at-arms, raised a very large infantry from below Valdarno and from the countryside of Pisa, and went off toward Volterra. But Giusto did not abandon himself even though he was abandoned by his neighbors and one could see that the Florentines were about to attack him; but trusting in the strength of the site and in the abundance of the city, he made ready for defense.

In Volterra there was a Messer Arcolano, brother of that Giovanni who had persuaded Giusto to take up the lordship and a man of account among the nobility. This man gathered certain of his confidants and pointed out to them that God had by this accident come to the aid of their city in its necessity: for if they were content to take up arms both to de-

---

[1] See *FH* IV 15.
[2] Apparently left blank by NM.
[3] Lit.: grace.

prive Giusto of lordship and yield the city back to the Florentines, it would follow that they would remain first in that town and would have preserved its ancient privileges for it. Having agreed on this, they went to the palace where the lord was; and as some of them stopped below, Messer Arcolano with three of them went upstairs to the hall; and when they found Giusto with some citizens, he drew him aside as if he wanted to reason with him about something important, and with one reason or another led him into the room where he and those who were with him attacked him with their swords. They were not so quick, however, as not to allow Giusto the advantage of putting his hand on his own weapon, and before they could kill him, he gravely wounded two of them; but in the end, unable to resist so many, he was killed and hurled to the ground from the palace. Those of Messer Arcolano's party took up arms and gave the city over to the Florentine commissioners who were standing nearby with their troops, and, without making any further terms, they entered it. This made conditions worse for Volterra because, among other things, they dismembered the greater part of its countryside and reduced it to a vicarate.

18

VOLTERRA having been thus lost and reacquired almost in a stroke, no cause for a new war would have been seen if the ambition of men had not set one in motion again. Niccolò Fortebraccio, born to a sister of Braccio da Perugia, had fought a long time for the city of Florence in the wars against the duke. Since peace had come, this man was dismissed by the Florentines; and when the case of Volterra came, he still quartered at Fucecchio, where the commissioners availed themselves of him and his troops in that campaign. There was an opinion that during the time Messer Rinaldo toiled in that war with Niccolò, he might have persuaded him to attack the Lucchese under cover of some fictitious quarrel, by showing him that if he did it, Rinaldo would work it out in Florence that a campaign against Lucca would be attempted and Niccolò would be made the head of it. Therefore, when Volterra had been acquired and Niccolò had returned to his quarters in Fucecchio, either by the persuasions of Messer Rinaldo or by his own will he seized Ruoti and Compito, fortified places of the Lucchese, in November of 1429, with three hundred horse and three hundred infantry. Then he descended into the plain and took a very great deal of booty. When the news of this attack was made public in Florence, all sorts of men gathered in groups throughout the city, and the greater number of them wanted the campaign against Lucca to be undertaken. Among the great citizens who favored it were those of the

Medici party, with whom Messer Rinaldo sided, moved to do so either because he judged the campaign useful to the republic or because of his own ambition, believing that he would have to be found at the head of that victory. Those who were not in favor of it were Niccolò da Uzzano and his party. And it appears a thing not to be believed that there should be such diverse judgments in the very same city over starting a war: for those citizens and that people who after ten years of peace had censured the war undertaken against Duke Filippo to defend their own city's freedom now, after so much expense incurred and with such distress in the city, were demanding that a war be started with every effective means to seize the freedom of others; and on the other hand, those who had wanted the earlier war now censured this one. So much do views vary with time and so much more ready is the multitude to seize what belongs to others than to watch out for its own; and men are moved so much more by the hope of acquiring than by the fear of losing, for loss is not believed in unless it is close, while acquisition, even though distant, is hoped for. And the people of Florence were filled with hope by the acquisitions that Niccolò Fortebraccio had made and was making and by letters from rectors near Lucca; for the vicars of Vico and Pescia wrote that permission should be given them to receive the fortified towns that were coming to surrender to them, so that soon the whole countryside around Lucca would be acquired. In addition to this, the lord of Lucca[1] sent an ambassador to Florence to complain about the attacks made by Niccolò and to beg the Signoria not to start a war against a neighbor and on a city that had always been friendly to it. The ambassador was called Messer Jacopo Viviani. A short time before, he had been held prisoner by Pagolo for having conspired against him, and although he had been found guilty, Pagolo had spared his life; and because he believed that Messer Jacopo had forgiven him the injury, Pagolo trusted him. But Messer Jacopo, more mindful of the danger than of the benefit, when in Florence secretly urged the citizens to take up the campaign. These urgings, added to the other hopes, made the Signoria assemble the council, where four hundred and ninety-eight citizens met; before them, the thing was debated by the principal men of the city.

19

AMONG the first who were for the campaign, as we said above, was Messer Rinaldo. He pointed out the profit to be gained from the acqui-

[1] Pagolo Giunigi.

sition; he pointed out the opportunity for the campaign, since Lucca had been left to them as booty by the Venetians and by the duke; and the pope, who was involved in the affairs of the Kingdom, could not hinder them. To this he added the ease of taking Lucca, since it was slave to one of its citizens and had lost that natural vigor and ancient zeal to defend its own freedom, so that it would be given up either by the people to chase out the tyrant or by the tyrant out of fear of the people. He recounted the injuries done by its lord against our republic and his ill will toward it, and how dangerous it was if either the pope or the duke should again start a war against the city;[1] and he concluded that no other campaign ever undertaken by the Florentine people was easier, more useful, or more just. Against this opinion Niccolò da Uzzano said that the city of Florence had never undertaken an enterprise more unjust, more dangerous, or one from which greater losses must arise. And first, they were going to hurt a Guelf city that had always been friendly to the Florentine people and that had many times taken to its bosom, and at peril to itself, Guelfs who could not stay in their fatherland. And in the record of our things it will never be found that a free Lucca had offended Florence, but if anyone who had made it a slave, like Castruccio before and now this one, had offended Florence, one could put the blame not on it but on the tyrant. And if one could make war on the tyrant without making it on the citizens, that would displease him less; but as this could not be, then he could not agree that a friendly citizenry should be despoiled of its goods. But since one lives today in such a way that just and unjust do not have to be of much account, he wished to leave out this point and think only of utility to the city. As to this, he believed that only those things could be called useful that could not easily bring loss: so he did not know how anyone could call that enterprise useful in which the losses were certain and the profits doubtful. The certain losses were the expenses that it would incur, which would be seen to be so great that they ought to make fearful a city at rest, let alone one wearied by a long and grave war as theirs had been. The profit they could gain was the acquisition of Lucca, which he confessed to be great; but he had also to consider the uncertainties that were in it, which to him appeared so many that he judged the acquisition impossible. And they should not believe that the Venetians and Filippo would be happy about this acquisition: for the Venetians would only appear to agree to it so as not to appear ungrateful, having shortly before got so much empire with Florentine money, and Filippo would dearly love them to be involved in a new war and in new expenses, so that, worn down and weary on every side, he could then attack them again. And he

[1] Against Florence.

would not lack a mode, in the midst of the campaign and with greater hope of victory, of helping the Lucchese either covertly with money or by dismissing his own troops and sending them to help the Lucchese as soldiers of fortune. He urged them therefore to refrain from the campaign and to live with the tyrant so that he would make as many enemies as possible within, because there was no more convenient way of subjugating it than to let it live under the tyrant and to let him afflict and weaken it. For if the thing was governed prudently, that city would reach the point where the tyrant could not hold it, and neither knowing how nor being able to govern itself, it would necessarily fall into their lap. But he saw that their humors were excited and that his words were not being heard. Even so, he wished to predict this to them: that they would make a war for which they would spend very much, would run into very many dangers, and, instead of seizing Lucca, they would free it from a tyrant; and out of a friendly city, subdued and weak, they would make a free city, hostile to them and in time an obstruction to the greatness of their republic.

20

WHEN they had spoken for and against the campaign, it was time, as was the custom, to find out secretly the will of the men; and of the whole number, only ninety-eight were against it. The decision having thus been made and the Ten created to handle the war, they hired soldiers for both foot and horse, deputed Astorre Gianni and Messer Rinaldo degli Albizzi as commissioners, and agreed with Niccolò Fortebraccio to receive from him all the towns he had taken and to have him continue with the campaign as our soldier. The commissioners arrived in the country around Lucca and divided the army; Astorre set out on the plain toward Camaiore and Pietrasanta, and Messer Rinaldo went toward the mountains, judging that if the city were despoiled of its countryside, it would be an easy thing to take it later. The campaigns of these men were unfortunate, not because they did not acquire many towns but because of the charges made against both of them in the management of the war. It is true that Astorre Gianni gave evident cause for his charges. There is a valley near Pietrasante called Seravezza, rich and filled with inhabitants. When they heard of the commissioner's arrival, they came before him and begged him to receive them as faithful servants of the Florentine people. Astorre pretended to accept these offers; then he had his troops seize all the passes and strongholds of the valley and had the men assemble in their principal church; and after he had taken them all prisoners, he had his troops sack and destroy the whole country, in a cruel and avaricious example, and sparing neither holy places nor women, whether virgin or married. As soon as these things happened, they were known in Florence and displeased not only the magistrates but the whole city.

21

SOME of the Seravezze who had escaped from the hands of the commissioner fled to Florence and recounted their miseries on every road and to every man, so that, urged by many who wanted the commissioner to be punished either as a wicked man or as contrary to their faction, they went to the Ten and asked to be heard. When they were introduced, one of them spoke in this sense: "We are sure, magnificent Signori, that our words will find faith and compassion in your Lordships when you learn the way in which your commissioner seized our country and in what manner we were treated afterwards by him. As the records of your ancient things can fully show, our valley was ever Guelf and has been many times a faithful shelter for those of your citizens who, persecuted by the Ghibellines, took refuge in it. And our ancestors and we have always revered the name of this illustrious republic because it was the head and prince of that party; and for as long as the Lucchese were Guelfs, we willingly submitted to their empire, but when they came under the tyrant who left his old friends to follow the party of the Ghibellines, we obeyed him because we were forced rather than voluntarily. And God knows how many times we prayed Him to give us an opportunity to show our spirit toward the old party. How blind are men in their desires! That which we desired for our safety[1] has been our ruin. For as soon as we heard that your ensigns were coming toward us, we went to meet your commissioner, not as enemies but as to our former lords, and we put the valley, our fortunes, and ourselves in his hands, and we commended ourselves to his faith, believing that he must have the spirit, if not of a Florentine, at least of a man. Your Lordships will forgive us, for not being able to endure worse than what we have endured inspires us to speak. This commissioner of yours has no more of a man than the appearance, nor of a Florentine more than the name: a death-dealing plague, a cruel beast, a hideous monster such as has never been imagined by any writer. For, having assembled us in our church under color of wanting to speak to us, he made us prisoners; ruined and burned the whole valley; seized, despoiled, sacked, beat, and killed its inhabitants and their property;

[1] Or salvation.

raped the women, deflowered the virgins, and, tearing them from the arms of their mothers, made them prey for his soldiers. If we had deserved so much evil by some injury done to the Florentine people or to him, or if we were armed and he had taken us in defending ourselves, we would complain less; indeed, we would accuse ourselves who either by our injuries or our arrogance would have deserved it. But as it was, we were unarmed, and we freely surrendered to him who then stole from us and despoiled us with such injury and ignominy that we are forced to complain. And as much as we could have filled Lombardy with complaints and spread throughout Italy the report of our injuries, with the blame on this city, we have not wanted to do it lest we befoul so decent and compassionate a republic with the indecency and cruelty of one wicked citizen. If we had recognized his avarice before our ruin, we would have forced ourselves to satisfy his greedy spirit, even though it has neither measure nor depth, and in that way we would have saved one part of our substance with the other. But since we are no longer in time, we have decided to come to you and pray you to relieve the distress of your subjects so that other men may not be frightened by our example of coming under your empire. And if our countless ills do not move you, may fear of the wrath of God move you, for He has seen His churches sacked and burned and our people betrayed in His bosom." And having said this, they threw themselves to the ground crying and praying that their property and their fatherland be returned to them and that they restore (since honor could not be) at least wives to their husbands and daughters to their fathers. The atrociousness of the thing, first learned and then understood from the living voices of those who had suffered it, touched the magistracy; and without delay Astorre was made to return and was then condemned and admonished.[2] They made a search for the goods belonging to the Seravezze, and those that could be found were restored; the others were in time satisfied by the city in various modes.

22

MESSER Rinaldo degli Albizzi, for his part, was defamed for carrying on the war not for the profit of the Florentine people but for his own. And it was said that after he became commissioner, any eagerness to take Lucca had flown from his mind because it was enough for him to sack the countryside and fill his estates with cattle and his houses with booty; and that since the booty his attendants gathered for his own use was not

---

[2] In fact, he was acquitted.

enough, he bought that of the soldiers—so that from being a commissioner he had become a merchant. When these slanders reached his ears,
they moved his sincere and haughty spirit more than was fitting for a
grave man; and so much did they perturb him that, indignant with the
magistracy and the citizens, and without waiting or asking for permission, he returned to Florence. Presenting himself before the Ten, he said
he knew very well how much difficulty and danger there was in serving
an unrestrained people and a divided city, because the one is filled up with
every rumor and the other persecutes wicked deeds, does not reward
good ones, and accuses doubtful ones. So if you are victorious, no one
praises you; if you err, everyone condemns you; and if you lose, everyone
slanders you: for the friendly party persecutes you out of envy, the hostile
party out of hatred. Nonetheless, he had never allowed himself, through
fear of an empty charge, to refrain from doing a deed that might bring a
sure profit to the city. It was true that the indecency of the present slanders had overcome his patience and made him change his nature. Therefore, he prayed that the magistracy wish to be more prompt in the future
to defend its citizens so that they might be still more prompt to act well
for their fatherland. And since it was not the custom in Florence to allow
citizens a triumph, it might at least be the custom to defend them from
false abuse; and they should remember that they too were citizens of that
city and that at any hour some charge could be brought against them,
from which they would learn how much offense false slanders may bring
to men of integrity. The Ten, as time permitted, strove to appease him,
and they asked Neri di Ginno and Alamanno Salviati to take charge of
the campaign. These men gave up raiding the countryside around Lucca
and brought their camp near the town; and because the season was still
cold, they placed themselves in Capannole, where it appeared to the commissioners they were wasting time. Although they wished to press closer
to the town, the soldiers did not comply because of the bad weather, despite the fact that the Ten urged the encampment and would accept no
excuse.

23

IN those times there was a most excellent architect in Florence, called
Filippo di ser Brunelleschi, of whose works our city is full. So great was
his merit that after his death his likeness in marble was placed in the principal church of Florence with an inscription on the pedestal that still gives
testimony of his virtues to whoever reads it. He showed how Lucca could
be flooded, considering the site of the city and the bed of the river Ser-

chio; and so much did he urge it that the Ten commissioned the experiment to be made. But nothing came of it other than disorder in our camp and security for the enemy, for the Lucchese raised the earth with a dike on the side where the Serchio was being made to come and then one night they broke the dike of the ditch through which the water was flowing. Thus, the water found the way toward Lucca blocked and the dike of the channel open, and it flooded the plain so that not only could the army not get near the town but it had to draw off.

24

THUS, as this enterprise did not succeed, the Ten who had newly assumed the magistracy sent Messer Giovanni Guicciardini as commissioner. As soon as he could, he encamped at the town. So the lord [of Lucca], seeing himself hard pressed, and at the urging of one Messer Antonio del Rosso, a Sienese who was with him in the name of the commune of Siena, sent Salvestro Trenta and Leonardo Buonvisi to the duke of Milan. They requested aid of the duke on behalf of the lord, and, finding him cold, they begged him secretly to give them troops, because they promised on behalf of the people to give their lord to him as a prisoner and afterwards to give him possession of the town. They warned him that if he did not take this course quickly the lord would give the town to the Florentines, who were importuning him with many promises. Thus, the duke's fear of this made him lay scruples aside, and he ordered his soldier Count Francesco Sforza to ask the lord publicly for permission to go to the Kingdom. Having obtained this, Sforza came to Lucca with his company, notwithstanding that the Florentines, knowing of this dealing and fearing what might come of it, sent to the count Boccacino Alamanni, his friend, to frustrate it. Therefore, when the count came to Lucca, the Florentines withdrew with their army to Ripafratta, and the count quickly encamped at Pescia, where the vicar was Pagolo da Diacceto. He, counseled by fear rather than by any better remedy, fled to Pistoia; and if the town had not been defended by Giovanni Malavolti, who was on guard there, it would have been lost. The count therefore, unable to take the city in the first assault, went to Borgo a Buggiano and took it; and he burned Stigliano, a fortified town next to it. When the Florentines saw this disaster, they had recourse to the remedies that had saved them many times, since they knew how, with mercenary soldiers, corruption would help where force was not enough; so they offered the count money not only to leave but to give them the town. Since it appeared to the count that he could extract no more money from Lucca, he turned readily to extract it from those who had it, and he agreed with the Florentines, not to give them Lucca, to which his decency would not allow him to consent, but to abandon it if he were given fifty thousand ducats. And having made this agreement, so that the people of Lucca might excuse him with the duke, he gave them a hand so that the Lucchese might drive out their lord.

25

MESSER Antonio del Rosso, the Sienese ambassador, was in Lucca, as we said above. By authority of the count, he plotted with the citizens for the ruin of Pagolo. The heads of the conspiracy were Piero Cennami and Giovanni da Chivizzano. The count was lodged outside the town on the Serchio, and with him was Lanzilao, son of the lord. From there the conspirators, forty in number, went armed at night to find Pagolo; at the noise they made, he went in utter astonishment to meet them and demanded the cause for their coming. To which Piero Cennami said that they had been governed by him for a long time and had been led to die by sword and hunger with enemies all about; and so they had decided they wanted to govern themselves in the future, and they demanded from him the keys of the city and its treasure. Pagolo answered them that the treasure was spent, that the keys and he were in their power;[1] he prayed them for this alone, that they be content, that as his lordship had begun and continued without blood, so it should end without blood. Pagolo and his son were taken to the duke by Count Francesco; later they died in prison.

The departure of the count had left Lucca free of its tyrant and the Florentines free of the fear of the count's troops; hence the Lucchese prepared themselves for defense while the Florentines returned to the offense. They elected as captain the Count of Urbino,[2] who, by pressing hard on the town, compelled the Lucchese to have recourse again to the duke. The duke sent Niccolò Piccinino to help them under the same color by which he had sent the count. As Niccolò was about to enter Lucca, our men met him at the Serchio, and in the crossing the battle was joined and they were defeated; the commissioner, with a few of our troops, saved himself in Pisa.

This defeat saddened all our city, and because the enterprise had been undertaken by the generality of people,[3] the people did not know whom to turn against. They slandered those who had administered it, since they

---

[1] *Podestà.*
[2] Guidantonio da Montefeltro.
[3] Lit.: the universal.

could not slander those who had decided it, and they revived the charges made against Messer Rinaldo. But more than anyone else, Giovanni Guicciardini was torn apart,[4] as they charged that he could have ended the war after the departure of Count Francesco but that he had been corrupted with money and that he had sent a sum of it home; and they accused the ones who had brought it and who had received it. And these rumors and accusations reached such a pitch that the Captain of the People, moved by these public voices and urged on by the opposing party, cited him. Messer Giovanni appeared, brimming with indignation; whereupon his relatives, for the sake of their honor, worked it out so that the Captain abandoned the undertaking.

After the victory, the Lucchese not only regained their own towns but seized all those in the district of Pisa except Bientina, Calcinaia, Livorno, and Ripafratta; and if a conspiracy made in Pisa had not been discovered, that city, too, would have been lost. The Florentines reordered their troops and made Micheletto, a pupil of Sforza's, their captain. For his part, the duke followed up the victory, and so as to be able to harass the Florentines with more forces, he made the Genoese, the Sienese, and the lord of Piombino league together for the defense of Lucca and hire Niccolò Piccinino for their captain—by which thing all was disclosed. Thereupon the Venetians and the Florentines renewed their league; and the war began to be waged openly in Lombardy and in Tuscany. And in both provinces different battles had varying fortune. So when everyone was weary, an accord was made among the parties in May of 1433,[5] by which the Florentines, Lucchese, and Sienese, who in the war had seized several fortified towns from one another, gave them all up, and each returned in possession of his own.

26

WHILE they were toiling in this war, all the malignant humors of the parties inside[1] were boiling up again. Cosimo de' Medici, after the death of his father Giovanni, conducted himself with greater spirit in public things and with greater zeal and more liberality toward his friends than his father had done; and as a result, those who were cheered by the death of Giovanni were saddened when they saw what sort Cosimo was. Cosimo was a very prudent man, of grave and pleasing appearance,

[4] See D 1 8.
[5] In fact, April 26, 1433.
[1] Inside Florence.

quite liberal, quite humane; he never attempted anything against either the Party or the state but took care to benefit everyone and with his liberality to make many citizens into his partisans. So his example increased the charge against those who were governing, and he himself judged that by this way he would either live in Florence as powerful and as safely as anyone else or, if because of the ambition of his adversaries it came to something extraordinary, he would be superior both in arms and in favor.

The great instruments for ordering his power were Averardo de' Medici and Puccio Pucci. Averardo with boldness, Puccio with prudence and sagacity, ministered to the favor and greatness he had. And so highly esteemed was the advice and the judgment of Puccio and so well known was he to everyone that Cosimo's party was named not for him but for Puccio. It was by this city, thus divided, that the campaign against Lucca was undertaken, in which the humors of the parties were excited rather than eliminated. And it happened that while Cosimo's party was the one that had favored the campaign, nonetheless many from the opposing party, as men of much reputation in the state, were sent to direct it. Since Averardo de' Medici and the others were unable to remedy this, they took care with every art and industry to slander them; and if any loss arose, and many did, it was not fortune or the force of the enemy that was accused, but want of prudence in the commissioner. This made them aggravate the sins of Gianni Astorre;[2] this was what made Messer Rinaldo degli Albizzi indignant and leave his commission without permission; this same thing made the Captain of the People recall Messer Giovanni Guicciardini; and from this arose all the other charges made against the magistrates and the commissioners, because the true ones were enlarged, the untrue were made up, and both the true and the untrue were believed by the people, who ordinarily hated them.

27

HOW these things were done and the extraordinary modes of proceeding were perfectly understood by Niccolò da Uzzano and the other heads of the Party. Together they had reasoned about remedies for it many times, but they found none because it appeared to them that to let the thing grow was dangerous and that to strike at it was difficult. And Niccolò da Uzzano was first among those to whom extraordinary ways were distasteful. So, while they were living with the war outside and these travails

[2] See *FH* IV 20–21.

within, Niccolò Barbadori, wishing to induce Niccolò da Uzzano to agree to the ruin of Cosimo, went to visit him at his home, where he was in his study absorbed in thought; and he encouraged him with all the best reasons he knew to induce him to want to unite with Messer Rinaldo to drive out Cosimo. To which Niccolò da Uzzano answered in this sense: "It would be better for you, for your house, and for our republic if you and the others who follow you in this opinion had beards of silver rather than gold, as they say you have;[1] for their counsels, coming from a grey head full of experience, would be wiser and more useful to everyone. It appears to me that those who think of driving Cosimo out of Florence must, before everything else, measure their forces and those of Cosimo. You[2] have baptized our side the party of the nobles and the opposing side that of the plebs. If truth were to correspond with the name, victory would be doubtful in any event, and we should rather fear than hope, moved by the example of the old nobility of this city who have been eliminated by the plebs. But we have much more to fear since our party is fragmented and that of our adversaries is whole. First of all, Neri di Gino and Nerone di Nigi, two of our first citizens, have never declared themselves in a mode that could allow it to be said that they are more our friends than theirs. There are many families here, indeed many houses, who are divided; for many out of envy of their brothers or relatives do not favor us and favor them. I want to remind you[3] of some of the more important of them; others you will think of for yourself. Of the sons of Messer Maso degli Albizzi, Luca, out of envy of Messer Rinaldo, has cast himself in their party; in the house of the Guicciardini, of the sons of Messer Luigi, Piero is an enemy of Messer Giovanni and favors our adversaries; Tommaso and Niccolò Soderini openly oppose their uncle Francesco out of the hate they bear for him. Consequently, if one considers well of what sort they are and of what sort we are, I do not know why our party deserves to be called the party of the nobles more than theirs. And if it is because they are followed by all the plebs, then we are in a worse position and they in a better one for this; all the more so, since, if it should come to arms or to divisions, we are not capable of resisting. And if we still have our dignity, it arises out of the ancient reputation of this state, which has been preserved for fifty years; but if it should come to a test in which our weakness was uncovered, we would lose it. And if you were to say that the just cause impelling us would add credit to us and take it from them, I answer you that this justice must be understood

---

[1] Barbadoro means "beard of gold."

[2] The speaker shifts from the familiar to the plural "you" (or plural of respect).

[3] Familiar "you."

and believed by others as by us. But it is quite the contrary, for the cause impelling us is altogether founded on the suspicion that a prince may be established in this city. If we have this suspicion, others do not; indeed, what is worse, they accuse us of what we accuse him. The deeds of Cosimo that make us suspect him are these: because he helps everyone with his money, and not only private individuals but the public, and not only Florentines but the condottieri; because he favors this or that citizen who has need of the magistrates; because by the good will that he has in the generality of people[4] he pulls this or that friend to higher ranks of honor. Thus one would have to allege as the causes for driving him out that he is merciful, helpful, liberal, and loved by everyone. So tell me: what law is it that forbids or that blames and condemns in men mercy, liberality, and love? And although these are all modes that send men flying to a princedom, nonetheless they are not believed to be so, nor are we adequate to the task of making them be so understood, because our modes have destroyed their faith in us, and the city, which is naturally partisan and, since it has always lived with parties, is corrupt, cannot give a hearing to such accusations. But let us suppose that you do succeed in driving him out, which could easily happen since the Signoria is favorable; how could you,[5] among so many of his friends who would remain here and would burn with desire for his return, ever prevent him from returning to us? This would be impossible because they are so many and he has universal good will, and you could never secure yourself against them; and as many of his first, open friends should you drive out, so many more enemies would you make for yourselves. Then after a while he would return here, and you would have gained this—you would have driven out a good man who would return to us a wicked one because his nature would be corrupted by those who recalled him, and, being obliged to them, he could not oppose them. And if you scheme to have him killed, you will never succeed by way of the magistrates because his money and your own corruptible minds will always save him. But let us suppose that he dies or does not return after he is expelled. I do not see what acquisition may be made for us inside our republic, for if it is freed from Cosimo, it becomes the slave of Messer Rinaldo; and as for myself, I am one of those who desire that no citizen surpass any other in power and authority, but if one of these two must prevail, I do not know what cause would make me love Messer Rinaldo more than Cosimo. Nor do I wish to say more to you[6] than this: may God keep this city that no one of its citizens becomes

---

[4] Lit.: the universal.
[5] Shift again to the plural "you."
[6] Shift back to the familiar "you."

prince of it, but even if our sins should deserve it, may He keep it from having to obey him. So do not wish to advise taking a course that is harmful in every way or believe that you, accompanied by a few, can oppose the will of many; for all these citizens, partly out of ignorance and partly out of malice, are prepared to sell this republic, and so much is fortune their friend that they have found a buyer. Be governed by my advice, therefore: take care to live modestly, and, as for liberty, you will have as much to suspect in our party as in the opposite one. And when any trial arises, by having lived neutrally you will be welcome to everyone, and thus you will help yourself and not hurt your fatherland."

28

THESE words checked the spirit of Barbadori somewhat, so that things remained quiet for as long as the war over Lucca lasted; but when peace came, and with it the death of Niccolò da Uzzano, the city was left without war and without a check. As a result, wicked humors grew without any hesitation, and as it appeared to Messer Rinaldo that he alone was left as prince of the Party, he did not cease begging and importuning all the citizens who he believed might become Gonfaloniers, that they arm themselves to liberate their fatherland from that man who of necessity, by the malignity of few and the ignorance of many, was leading it into slavery. The modes used by Messer Rinaldo and by those who favored the opposite party kept the city full of suspicion; and whenever a new magistracy was created, it was discussed publicly how many of one and how many of the other party were sitting in it; and in the drawing of the Signori, the whole city was stirred up. Every case that came before the magistrates, even the least, was reduced to a contest between them; secrets were published; the good as well as the bad was favored and not favored; good men as well as wicked were equally torn apart; and no magistrate did his duty.

Thus, while Florence remained in this confusion and Messer Rinaldo was intent on bringing low the power of Cosimo, he learned that Bernardo Guadagni could become a Gonfalonier, and he paid his taxes for him so that his public debt would not keep him from that rank. When it came to the drawing for the Signori, fortune, the friend of our discords, had Bernardo drawn as Gonfalonier to sit in September and October. Messer Rinaldo went at once to visit him and told him how much the party of the nobles and whoever desired to live well rejoiced in his having achieved this dignity, and that it was now up to him to act in such a mode that they should not have rejoiced in vain. Then he pointed out to him the dangers incurred in disunion and that there was no other way to bring about union than to eliminate Cosimo; for only Cosimo, through the favors that arose from his immoderate wealth, kept men unstable. Cosimo had been brought so high that, unless Bernardo saw to it, Cosimo would become prince; and it was the part of one good citizen to apply a remedy, to call the people into the piazza, and to take back the state so as to bring back freedom to the fatherland. He reminded him that Messer Salvestro de' Medici had been able to check unjustly the greatness of the Guelfs, to whom the government belonged because of the blood spent by their ancestors, and that what Salvestro had been able to do against so many unjustly, Bernardo could well do justly against one alone. He urged him not to be afraid, because friends with arms would be ready to help him; and he should not take account of the plebs who adored Cosimo, because Cosimo would get no more favors from it than Messer Giorgio Scali once had; nor should he be afraid of Cosimo's riches, because when he was in the power[1] of the Signori, his riches would be theirs; and he concluded to him that this deed would make the republic secure and united and himself glorious. To these words Bernardo answered briefly that he judged it was necessary to do all that Rinaldo had said and that, because it was time to act to eliminate Cosimo, he would take care to prepare forces so as to be ready, persuaded that he would have companions. When Bernardo assumed the magistracy, readied his companions, and made an agreement with Messer Rinaldo, he summoned Cosimo. Although Cosimo was discouraged from it by many friends, he presented himself, trusting more in his innocence than in the mercy of the Signori. As soon as Cosimo was in the palace and arrested, Messer Rinaldo came out of his house with many armed men, followed by the whole party, and they went to the piazza where the Signori had called the people and created two hundred men for a balìa to reform the state of the city. This balìa, as soon as it could, dealt with reform and with the life and death of Cosimo. Many wanted him to be sent into exile, many wanted him dead; many others were silent either out of compassion for him or out of fear of them. These differences did not permit anything to be concluded.

29

IN the tower of the palace, there is a place as large as the space of the tower allows, called the Alberghettino;[1] Cosimo was locked in there and

---

[1] *Podestà.*
[1] "The little inn."

placed under the watch of Federigo Malavolti. From this place Cosimo, hearing the assembly brought, the noise of arms that was made in the piazza, and the frequent sounding of the bell to the balìa, was in doubt of his life; but even more, he feared that his particular enemies might have him killed extraordinarily. Because of this he refused food, so that for four days he had eaten nothing but a little bread. When Federigo became aware of this, he said, "You are afraid, Cosimo, of being poisoned, and so you are making yourself die of hunger and doing me little honor by believing that I might want to have a hand in such wickedness. I do not believe that you are about to lose your life, so many friends do you have in the palace and outside. But even if you were to lose it, you may be sure that they will adopt other modes than using me as the minister for taking it from you because I do not wish to defile my hands with the blood of anyone, especially not yours, since you have never offended me. Therefore, be of good cheer, take your food and keep yourself alive for the sake of your friends and of your fatherland. And that you may do it with greater confidence, I will eat the same things with you." These words completely comforted Cosimo, and with tears in his eyes he embraced and kissed Federigo; and he thanked him with lively and effective words for such a merciful and kindly deed, promising to be most grateful to him if ever he were given the opportunity by fortune. So while Cosimo was somewhat comforted, and his case was being argued among the citizens, it happened that Federigo, so as to give him pleasure, brought to dine with him a friend of the Gonfalonier called Farganaccio, an amusing and witty man. And when they were almost finished dining, Cosimo, who thought he would take advantage of this man's coming because he knew him very well, nodded to Federigo that he should leave. As Federigo understood the cause, he pretended to go for something needed for the serving of dinner; and they being left alone, Cosimo, after some kindly words to Farganaccio, gave him a signed note and asked him to go to the overseer of Santa Maria Nuova for one thousand one hundred ducats: one hundred of these he should take for himself and one thousand take to the Gonfalonier and beg him to find a suitable occasion to come talk to him. Farganaccio accepted the commission; the money was paid; and Bernardo then became more humane. As a result, Cosimo was banished to Padua contrary to the will of Messer Rinaldo, who wanted him to be killed. Averardo and many others of the house of the Medici were also banished, and with them Puccio and Giovanni Pucci. And to frighten those who were malcontent at Cosimo's exile, they gave the balìa to the Eight of the Guard and to the Captain of the People.[2] After these decisions, Cosimo,

---

[2] See D I 49.

on the third day of October in 1433, came before the Signori and was sentenced to exile by them and warned to obey if he did not wish them to proceed more harshly against his goods as well as himself. Cosimo accepted banishment with a cheerful face, asserting that wherever that Signoria might wish to send him he was ready to stay voluntarily. He prayed, indeed, that, having spared his life, they would defend it for him, because he heard that in the piazza there were many who desired his blood. Then he offered himself and his property, in whatever place he might be, to the city, to the people, and to the Signori. He was comforted by the Gonfaloniers and kept in the palace until night came. Then the Gonfalonier took him to his home, had him dine with him, and then had him accompanied by many armed men to the borders. Wherever he passed, Cosimo was received with honor; and he was visited publicly by the Venetians, and not as an exile but honored as one placed in the highest rank.

30

FLORENCE having been left the widow of so great a citizen, so universally loved, everyone was frightened; those who had won and those who had been conquered were equally afraid. Hence, Messer Rinaldo, fearing future evil for himself, so as not to fail himself or the Party, gathered together many friendly citizens and told them that he saw their ruin prepared for them by having allowed themselves to be conquered by the prayers, tears, and money of their enemies. They were not aware that, soon after, they themselves would have to pray and weep and that their prayers would not be heard and that their tears would find no one with compassion for them. As for the money they had taken, they would have to restore the capital and pay usury with tortures, deaths, and exiles; and it would have been better for them to have let things be than to have left Cosimo alive and his friends in Florence, because great men must either not be touched or, if touched, be eliminated.[1] Nor did he see any other remedy for it now than to make themselves strong in the city so that when their enemies should be heard from again, and they would be heard from soon, they could be driven out by arms since it had not been possible to send them away by civil modes. And the remedy was the one that he, a long time before, had mentioned:[2] to gain back the great by giving back and conceding to them all the honors of the city and to make them-

---

[1] See *P* 3 and *D* III 6 for similar expressions.
[2] See *FH* IV 9.

selves strong with this party, since their adversaries had made themselves strong with the plebs. With this, their party would be more vigorous as it would have more life, more virtue, more spirit, and more credit; and he asserted that if this last and true remedy were not taken, he did not see by what other mode they could preserve a state among so many enemies, and he knew that the ruin of their party and of the city was imminent. Mariotto Bandovinetti, one of those assembled, opposed this by pointing out the pride of the great and their intolerable nature; he was not about to run back under certain tyranny by them so as to escape the doubtful dangers from the plebs. Hence Messer Rinaldo, seeing that his counsel was not listened to, lamented his misfortune and that of his party, imputing everything more to the heavens who wished it so than to the ignorance and blindness of men. And while the thing was left in this manner without making any necessary provision, a letter was found written by Messer Agnolo Acciaiuoli to Cosimo that described the disposition of the city toward him and urged him to have some kind of war set in motion and to make Neri di Gino his friend. For he judged that as the city would need money, no one would be found to provide it, and Cosimo's memory would come to be revived in the citizens as well as the desire to have him return. And if Neri should dissociate himself from Messer Rinaldo, that party would be so weakened that it would not be adequate to defend itself. When this letter came into the hands of the magistrates, it caused Messer Agnolo to be arrested, tortured, and sent into exile. Not even by such an example was the humor favoring Cosimo checked in any part.

Already nearly a year had gone by from the day that Cosimo had been driven out, and as the end of August 1434 came, Niccolò di Cocco was drawn to be one of the Gonfaloniers for the next two months, and with him eight Signori, all partisans of Cosimo. Such a Signoria terrified Messer Rinaldo and all his party. And since before the Signori assume the magistracy they remain private individuals for three days, Messer Rinaldo conferred again with the heads of his party; and he pointed out to them the certain and imminent danger and that the remedy was to take up arms and to get Donato Velluti, then sitting with the Gonfaloniers, to assemble the people in the piazza, make a new balìa, deprive the new Signori of the magistracy, and create new ones suitable to the state; and the bags should be burned and filled with new lists[3] of friends. This course was judged safe and necessary by many, by many others too violent and likely to carry too much blame with it. Among those who were displeased with it was Messer Palla Strozzi, who was a quiet man, gentle and humane, more suited to the study of letters than to restraining a party

[3] Lit.: *squittini*; see *FH* II 28.

and opposing civil discords. And so he said that courses of action, whether astute or bold, appear good in the beginning but then turn out to be difficult to deal with and harmful to finish. He believed that the fear of new wars from outside—the duke's troops being then in Romagna on our borders—would make the Signori think more about them than the discords inside. Also, if it was seen that they wanted to change (which they could not do without its being understood), there would always be time enough to take up arms and execute whatever appeared necessary for the common safety; and what they would be doing out of necessity would be attended with less wonder in the people and with less blame to themselves. It was concluded therefore that the new Signori should be allowed to enter their offices and that their movements should be watched; should anything be heard of against the party, everyone should take up arms and meet at the Piazza di Sant' Appollinare, a place near the palace, and from there they could go wherever it seemed necessary to them.

3 1

WHEN they had parted with this conclusion, the new Signori entered into the magistracy and the Gonfalonier, to give himself reputation and to frighten those who might scheme to oppose him, condemned his predecessor, Donato Velluti, to prison as a man who had profited from public money. After this, he sounded out his companions about having Cosimo return, and, having found them disposed to it, he spoke with those he judged to be the heads of the Medici party. Warmed by them, he summoned Messer Rinaldo, Ridolfo Peruzzi, and Niccolò Barbadori as the principals of the opposing party. After this summons Messer Rinaldo thought he should delay no longer, and he came out of his house with a great number of armed men and was quickly joined by Ridolfo Peruzzi and Niccolò Barbadoro. Among these were many other citizens and a great many soldiers who were then in Florence unhired; and all stopped, in accordance with the agreement they had made, at the Piazza di Sant' Apollinare. Messer Palla Strozzi, even though he had assembled many men, did not come out; the same with Messer Giovanni Giucciardini. Whereupon Messer Rinaldo sent to prompt them and to reproach them for their tardiness. Messer Giovanni answered that he was making enough war against the enemy party if by staying home he was keeping his brother Piero from going out to help the palace. Messer Palla, after many embassies had been sent to him, came to Sant' Apollinare on a horse with two men on foot, unarmed. At this, Messer Rinaldo confronted him and loudly reproached him for his negligence. Rinaldo said that his not coming with the others sprang from either lack of faith or lack of spirit; that a man ought to avoid both of these charges if he wished to be held as the sort he was held; and if he believed that by not doing his duty against the Party his enemies, if they won, would spare him either life or exile, he was deceived. As for what pertained to himself, should anything sinister happen, he would have the satisfaction of not having been wanting with advice before the danger and with force in the danger. But for Messer Palla and the others, regrets would be redoubled when they thought how they had betrayed their fatherland three times: once when they saved Cosimo, again when they did not take his advice, and now a third time when they did not rescue it with arms. To these words Messer Palla did not answer a thing that might be understood by the by-standers, but muttering he turned his horse around and went back to his home.

The Signori, hearing that Messer Rinaldo and his party had taken up arms and seeing themselves abandoned, had the palace locked up; de-prived of counsel, they did not know what to do. But since Messer Rinaldo delayed coming to the piazza in order to wait for forces that did not come, he deprived himself of the chance to win, gave the Signori spirit to provide for themselves and to many citizens to go to them and urge them to make terms so that arms might be put down. Thus, some who were less suspect went, on behalf of the Signori, to Messer Rinaldo and said that the Signoria did not know the cause for making these movements; that it had never thought of offending him; if it had reasoned about Cosimo, it had not thought of bringing him back; if this was the cause of suspicion, they would reassure him; and if they would be content to come to the palace, they would be well received and satisfied in their every de-mand. These words did not make Messer Rinaldo change his mind, but he said he wanted to secure himself by making them private individuals and then, for everyone's benefit, reorder the city. But it always happens that, where authorities are equal and opinions different, rarely is anything resolved for good. Ridolfo Peruzzi, moved by the words of these citizens, said that for himself he sought only that Cosimo not return; and since there was accord on this, it appeared victory enough to him. He did not want to fill his city with blood so as to have a greater one; therefore he was willing to obey the Signoria. And with his men he went into the palace, where he was gladly received. Thus Messer Rinaldo's stopping at Sant' Apollinare, the lack of spirit in Messer Palla, and the departure of Ridolfo had taken victory in the enterprise from Messer Rinaldo; and the spirits of the citizens who had followed him had begun to lose their first warmth. To this was added the authority of the pope.

32

POPE Eugene found himself in Florence, having been driven out of Rome by the people. Hearing of these tumults and feeling it his duty to quiet them, he sent the patriarch, Messer Giovanni Vitelleschi, very friendly to Messer Rinaldo, to him to pray him to come to the pope, for the pope would lack neither authority nor faith with the Signoria to make Rinaldo content and secure without blood and harm to the citizens. Persuaded, therefore, by his friend, Messer Rinaldo with all his armed followers went to Santa Maria Novella, where the pope was staying. Eugene informed him of the faith that the Signori had pledged to him, by which they had submitted all their differences to him. If Messer Rinaldo would lay down his arms, things would be ordered as appeared best to the pope. Since Messer Rinaldo had seen the coolness of Messer Palla and the flightiness of Ridolfo Peruzzi and had no better plan, he put himself in the arms of the pope, thinking surely that the authority of the pope would have to preserve him. Whereupon the pope had Niccolò Barbadori and the others who were waiting for Rinaldo outside instructed to go and put down their arms, because Messer Rinaldo was staying with the pontiff to negotiate an accord with the Signori. Upon this announcement, each made up his mind and disarmed.

33

THE Signori, seeing their adversaries disarmed, waited to negotiate the accord through the mediation of the pope; and on the other hand, they sent secretly to the mountains of Pistoia for infantry. They had this infantry, with all their men-at-arms, come by night into Florence; and when the strongholds in the city had been taken, the Signori called the people into the piazza and created a new balìa. As soon as the balìa assembled, it restored Cosimo to his fatherland as well as the others who had been banished with him; and from the enemy party it banished Messer Rinaldo degli Albizzi, Ridolfo Peruzzi, Niccolò Barbadori, and Messer Palla Strozzi, along with many citizens in such quantity that few towns in Italy were left to which they had not been sent in exile and many outside of Italy were filled with them. Thus Florence was deprived by the same accident not only of good men but of men of riches and industry. When the pope saw such ruin fall on those who had put down their arms at his prayers, he was very malcontent; and he lamented with Messer Rinaldo the injury done to him under his faith in him. He urged him to patience and to hope much from a change of fortune. To which Messer Rinaldo answered, "The little faith granted me by those who should have believed me and the too great faith that I placed in you have ruined me and my party; but I am sorry more for myself than anyone else, since I believed that you who had been driven from your own fatherland would be able to keep me in mine. As for the tricks of fortune, I have quite good experience; and as I had little confidence in prosperity, so adversity offends me less. I know that if it pleases fortune, she will be able to show me more joy; but if it should never please her, I shall always esteem it little to live in a city where the laws can do less than men. For that fatherland is desirable in which property and friends can be safely enjoyed, and not that in which property can easily be taken from you and friends, out of fear for their own, abandon you in your greatest necessities. And to wise and good men, it was always less grievous to hear about the evils of their fatherland than to see them, and they reputed it a more glorious thing to be an honorable rebel than a slave citizen." Then, full of indignation, he left the pope, and, often reproaching himself for both his own counsels and the coolness of his friends, he went off into exile. Cosimo, on the other hand, having been informed of his restitution, returned to Florence. And rarely does it happen that a citizen returning triumphant from a victory has been received by his fatherland by such a crowd of people and such a demonstration of good will as he received when he returned from exile. And he was greeted willingly by each as benefactor of the people and father of his fatherland.[1]

[1] Cf. NM's judgment on the government of the Ottimatti begun by Maso degli Albizzi and on its successor, managed by Cosimo de' Medici, in his *Discursus florentinarum rerum post mortem iunioris Laurentii Medices* (beg.).

BOOK V

I

USUALLY provinces go most of the time, in the changes they make, from order to disorder and then pass again from disorder to order, for worldly things are not allowed by nature to stand still. As soon as they reach their ultimate perfection, having no further to rise, they must descend; and similarly, once they have descended and through their disorders arrived at the ultimate depth, since they cannot descend further, of necessity they must rise. Thus they are always descending from good to bad and rising from bad to good.[1] For virtue gives birth to quiet, quiet to leisure, leisure to disorder, disorder to ruin; and similarly, from ruin, order is born; from order, virtue; and from virtue, glory and good fortune. Whence it has been observed by the prudent that letters come after arms and that, in provinces and cities, captains arise before philosophers. For, as good and ordered armies give birth to victories and victories to quiet, the strength of well-armed spirits cannot be corrupted by a more honorable leisure than that of letters, nor can leisure enter into well-instituted cities with a greater and more dangerous deceit than this one. This was best understood by Cato when the philosophers Diogenes and Carneades, sent by Athens as spokesmen to the Senate, came to Rome. When he saw how the Roman youth was beginning to follow them about with admiration, and since he recognized the evil that could result to his fatherland from this honorable leisure, he saw to it that no philosopher could be accepted in Rome. Thus, provinces come by these means to ruin; when they have arrived there and men have become wise from their afflictions, they return, as was said, to order unless they remain suffocated by an extraordinary force. These causes, first through the ancient Tuscans[2] and then the Romans, have made Italy sometimes happy, sometimes wretched. And it happened that afterwards, nothing was built upon the Roman ruins in a way that might have redeemed Italy from them, so that it might have been able to act gloriously under a virtuous principality.[3] Nonethe-

---

[1] See also *D* I 2, 39, II pr., 5, III 43, for NM's thoughts on the motion of worldly things.

[2] The Etruscans, whom NM likes to call Tuscans; see *D* II 4.

[3] Or principate. *Principato* can mean the ruling or dominating office as well as the realm of domination.

185

less, so much virtue emerged in some of the new cities and empires that arose among the Roman ruins that, even if one did not dominate the others, they were nonetheless harmonious and ordered together so that they freed Italy and defended it from the barbarians. Within these empires the Florentines, if they had less dominion, were not less in authority or power; indeed, because of their position in the middle of Italy, rich and ready for attack, either they successfully resisted a war begun against them or they gave victory to the one with whom they sided.

If from the virtue of these new principalities times did not arise that were quiet through a long peace, neither were they dangerous because of the harshness of war. For one cannot affirm it to be peace where principalities frequently attack one another with arms; yet they cannot be called wars in which men are not killed, cities are not sacked, principalities are not destroyed, for these wars came to such weakness that they were begun without fear, carried on without danger, and ended without loss. So that virtue which in other provinces used to be eliminated in a long peace was eliminated by vileness in the provinces of Italy, as can clearly be recognized in what will be described by us from 1434 to 1494. There it will be seen how in the end the way was opened anew for the barbarians and how Italy put itself again in slavery to them. And if the things done by our princes outside and at home may not be read, as are those of the ancients, with admiration for their virtue and greatness, they may perhaps be considered for other qualities with no less admiration when it is seen how so many very noble peoples were held in check by such weak and badly directed armies. And if in describing the things that happened in this devastated world one does not tell about either the strength of soldiers, or the virtue of the captain, or the love of the citizen for his fatherland, it will be seen with what deceits, with what guile and arts the princes, soldiers, and heads of republics conducted themselves so as to maintain the reputation they have not deserved. It may, perhaps, be no less useful to know these things than to know the ancient ones, because, if the latter excite liberal spirits to follow them, the former will excite such spirits to avoid and eliminate them.

2

ITALY had been brought by those who ruled it to such a term that when a peace arose by the concord of princes, it was upset soon after by those who kept arms[1] on hand: and so they did not acquire glory from war or quiet from peace. When peace was made, therefore, between the duke of

---

[1] *Armi*: arms or armies.

Milan and the league in the year 1433, the soldiers, wishing to live off war, turned against the Church. At that time there were two sects of arms in Italy: followers of Braccio and of Sforza. The head of the latter was Count Francesco, Sforza's son; of the other the prince was Niccolò Piccinino and Niccolò Fortebraccio;[2] to these sects nearly all the other Italian armies were connected. Of the two, Sforza's was in greater esteem both because of the virtue of the count and through the promise the duke of Milan had made of Madonna Bianca, his natural daughter, the expectation of which relationship brought him very great reputation.

Thus, after the peace of Lombardy, both sects of armed men, for different causes, attacked Pope Eugene. Niccolò Fortebraccio was moved by the ancient hostility Braccio had always had for the Church, and the count was moved by ambition; so Niccolò attacked Rome, and the count made himself lord of the Marches. Hence the Romans, not wanting to have war, drove Eugene out of Rome. Escaping with danger and difficulty, he came to Florence, where, having considered the danger he was in and seeing himself abandoned by the princes, who were unwilling for the sake of his cause to take up again the arms they had most eagerly put down, he came to accord with the count and conceded to him lordship over the Marches, even though the count added insult to the injury of having seized them. For in noting the place from which he was writing letters to his agents, he said, according to the Italian custom in Latin: "*Ex Girfalco nostro Firmano, invito Petro et Paulo.*"[3] Nor was he satisfied with the concession of towns; he wished also to be created gonfalonier of the Church. All was yielded to him, so much more did Eugene fear a dangerous war than a shameful peace. Having become a friend to the pope, therefore, the count pursued Niccolò Fortebraccio; and between them there occurred various unforeseen events in the towns of the Church for many months, all of which resulted in more loss to the pope and his subjects than to whoever was managing the war. Then, through the mediation of the duke of Milan, an accord was concluded between them by means of a truce, in which both remained as princes in the towns of the Church.

3

THIS war, though extinguished in Rome, was rekindled by Batista da Canneto in Romagna. He killed some of the Grifoni family in Bologna

---

[2] Two men named Niccolò, one prince.

[3] "From our Gerfalcon at Fermo, in spite of [or at the invitation of] Peter and Paul." Gerfalcon was the name of the count's castle.

and drove out of the city the governor for the pope with others of his enemies, and so as to hold the state by violence, he sent to Filippo for help; and the pope, so as to avenge the injury, asked for help from the Venetians and the Florentines. Both of them were supported, so that immediately there were two large armies in Romagna. Filippo's captain was Niccolò Piccinino; the Venetian and Florentine troops were commanded by Gattamelata and Niccolò da Tolentino; and the battle was joined near Imola. In it the Venetians and Florentines were defeated, and Niccolò da Tolentino was sent a prisoner to the duke; and in a few days, whether through fraud by the duke or from grief over the loss he had received, he died. After this victory, the duke, either because he was weak from the wars he had been through or because he believed that the league, having suffered this defeat, might pause, did not follow up his fortune further and thus gave the pope and his allies time to reunite. They chose Count Francesco[1] for their captain and undertook a campaign to drive Niccolò Fortebraccio out of the towns of the Church so as to see if they could end this war that they had begun in favor of the pope.

As soon as the Romans saw the pope so vigorous in the field, they sought an accord with him, and, having obtained it, accepted one of his commissioners. Niccolò Fortebraccio was holding, among other towns, Tivoli, Montefiasconi, Città di Castello, and Assisi. In this last Niccolò took refuge, since he was unable to stay in the open country, and there the count besieged him. As the siege went on for a long time because Niccolò was defending himself manfully, it appeared necessary to the duke either to prevent the league from a victory or, should it happen, to order himself to defend his own things. Wishing therefore to distract the count from the siege, the duke commanded Niccolò Piccinino to pass by way of Romagna into Tuscany so that the league, judging it more necessary to defend Tuscany than take Assisi, ordered the count to stop Niccolò, who was already with his army at Forlì, from passing through. The count, for his part, advanced with his troops and came to Cesena, having left to his brother Leone the war in the Marches and the care of his states.

And while Piccinino sought to pass through and the count to prevent him, Niccolò Fortebraccio attacked Leone, captured him, and plundered his troops with great glory to himself. Then, following up the victory, with the same thrust he seized many other towns of the Marches. This act afflicted the count very much because he thought all his states were lost; and leaving a part of his army to oppose Piccinino, he went with the rest toward Fortebraccio, fought him, and won. In this defeat Fortebraccio was taken prisoner and wounded, of which wound he died. This vic-

[1] Sforza.

tory restored to the pontiff all the towns that had been taken from him by Niccolò Fortebraccio and forced the duke of Milan to ask for peace, which was concluded through the mediation of Niccolò d'Este, marquis of Ferrara. In it the towns seized in Romagna by the duke were restored to the Church, and the duke's troops were returned to Lombardy; and, as happens to all those who maintain themselves in a state through the forces and virtue of others, when the duke's troops departed from Romagna, Batista da Canneto fled because his own forces and virtue were unable to keep him in Bologna. Messor Antonio Bentivoglio, head of the opposing party, returned there.

4

ALL these things happened in the time of Cosimo's exile.[1] After his return, those who had had him brought back and a great many injured citizens took thought, without any hesitation, about how to secure the state for themselves. And the Signoria that had acceded to the magistracy for November and December, not content with what had been done by its predecessors in favor of their party, extended and changed the exiles of many, and many others were exiled anew; and the citizens were hurt not so much by the humor of parties as by riches, relatives, and private enmities. If this proscription had been accompanied by blood, it would have been like that of Octavian and Sulla; and yet, it was tinged with blood in some part, for Antonio di Bernardo Guadagni was beheaded. And four other citizens, among whom were Zanobi de Belfrategli and Cosimo Barbadori, having passed beyond their confines, were found in Venice; and the Venetians, valuing the friendship of Cosimo more than their own honor, sent them to him as prisoners, where they were basely put to death. This affair gave great reputation to the party and very great fear to its enemies, when they considered that so powerful a republic would sell its liberty to the Florentines. It was believed that this was done not so much to benefit Cosimo as further to inflame the parties in Florence, and through bloodshed to make the division of our city more dangerous; for the Venetians saw no other opposition to their own greatness than its unity.

Thus, having stripped the city of enemies or suspects of the state, they turned to benefiting new men so as to invigorate their party. They restored to the fatherland the Alberti family and whoever else had been considered a rebel; they reduced all the great except for a very few to the

[1] See *FH* IV 28–29.

popular order; they divided the possessions of the rebels among themselves at a low price. Besides this, they strengthened themselves with laws and new orders, and they made new lists for the lot,[2] removing from the bags [the names of] their enemies and filling them with [the names of] their friends. And having been warned by the ruin of their adversaries, they judged that chosen lists might not be enough to hold the state firmly for themselves, and they decided that magistrates who have authority to shed blood should always be from the princes of their sect. They wished therefore that the couplers[3] in charge of filling the bags with new names should have authority together with the old Signoria to create the new one. They gave authority to shed blood to the Eight of the Guard; they provided that exiles who had finished their terms could not return unless thirty-four Signori and Collegi, who are thirty-seven in number, agreed to their return. They prohibited writing to exiles or receiving letters from them, and every word, every hint, every usage that might in any part be displeasing to those governing was very heavily punished. And if there remained in Florence any suspect who had not been reached by these inflictions,[4] he was hit with taxes that they ordered anew. In a short time, having driven out or impoverished all the enemy party, they secured the state for themselves. And so as not to be lacking help from outside and to rid themselves of those who might be planning to attack[5] them, they allied themselves with the pope, the Venetians, and the duke of Milan for the defense of their states.

5

WHILE things in Florence stood in this form, Giovanna, queen of Naples, died, and in her will left René of Anjou heir of the Kingdom. At the time, Alfonso, king of Aragon, was in Sicily, and he, through his friendship with many barons, was preparing to seize that kingdom. The Neapolitans and many barons favored René; the pope, for his part, wished neither René nor Alfonso to seize it but desired it to be administered by one of his own governors. Alfonso, however, came into the Kingdom and was received by the duke of Sessa; there he took into his pay some princes with the intent (since he had Capua, which the prince of Taranto was holding in the name of Alfonso) of compelling the Neapolitans to do his will; and he sent his fleet to attack Gaeta, which was being held for the

---

[2] *Squittini.*

[3] *Accoppiatori*, or matchmakers, who supervised or manipulated the lotteries for offices. See Nicolai Rubinstein, *The Government of Florence under the Medici 1434 to 1494*, chs. 1–2.

[4] Lit.: offenses.

[5] Lit.: offend.

Neapolitans. Because of this, the Neapolitans asked for aid from Filippo.[1] Filippo persuaded the Genoese to undertake this expedition, and they, not only to satisfy the duke, their prince, but to save the merchandise they had in Naples and Gaeta, armed a powerful fleet. Alfonso, for his part, when he heard of this, enlarged his own fleet and went in person to the encounter with the Genoese. The battle was joined near the island of Ponza; the Aragonese fleet was defeated, and Alfonso, together with many princes, was taken and given by the Genoese into the hands of Filippo. This victory frightened all the princes in Italy, who feared the power of Filippo because they judged he had a very great opportunity to make himself lord of it all. But he (so diverse are the opinions of men) took a course altogether contrary to this opinion. Alfonso was a prudent man, and as soon as he was able to talk to Filippo, he showed him how greatly he was deceived in favoring René and not favoring himself. For René, if he became king of Naples, would have to make every effort to have Milan belong to the king of France so that he would have assistance nearby and in time of need would not have to try to open a way for his rescuers; nor could he otherwise make himself secure in this except through Filippo's ruin, by making this state become French. But the contrary would come about if Alfonso should become prince, because, fearing no other enemy than the French, he would necessarily be compelled to love and embrace and—nothing less—obey whoever could open the way to his enemies. Therefore, the title of the Kingdom would come to Alfonso, but the authority and the power would be Filippo's. Thus it was much more Filippo's concern than Alfonso's to consider the dangers of the one course and the usefulness of the other, unless indeed he would rather satisfy an appetite of his than secure the state for himself. For in the one case he would be a prince and free, and in the other, being between two very powerful princes, either he would lose the state or he would live forever in suspicion and have to obey them both as a slave. These words had such power in the mind of the duke that he changed his plan, freed Alfonso, and sent him back honorably to Genoa and from thence into the Kingdom. Alfonso moved to Gaeta, which was seized by some lords who were his partisans as soon as they heard of his liberation.

6

WHEN the Genoese saw how the duke had liberated the king without any regard for them, and that he had been honored through their dangers and at their expense, that to him had gone gratitude for the liberation but to

---

[1] Filippo Maria Visconti, the duke of Milan.

them the injury of the capture and the defeat, they were all very indignant with him. In the city of Genoa, when it lives in liberty, a head is created by free suffrage whom they call doge, not to be an absolute prince or to decide alone, but as head in proposing what must be decided by the magistrates and their councils. That city has many noble families who are so powerful that they obey the rule[1] of the magistrates only with difficulty. Of all of them, the Fregosa and Adorni families are the most powerful. From these families arise the divisions of that city, and from them the civil orders are destroyed. For, as they fight among themselves over this principality, not civilly, but most of the time with arms, it always follows that one party is wounded and the other rules; and sometimes it happens that those who are deprived of their dignities resort to foreign arms, and they submit the fatherland they themselves are unable to govern to the empire of a foreigner. From this it arose and still arises that those who rule in Lombardy most of the time command Genoa; and so it was when Alfonso of Aragon was taken.

Among the first of the Genoese who had been the cause of submitting Genoa to Filippo had been Francesco Spinula, who, not long after he had made his fatherland a slave, as always happens in such cases, became suspect to the duke. He was so indignant at this that he had chosen to go almost as a voluntary exile to Gaeta, where he had been when the naval battle with Alfonso took place, and, having borne himself virtuously in the service of that campaign, it appeared to him that he had again enough merit with the duke that at the least, in reward for his merits, he might be able to stay safely in Genoa. But when he saw that the duke continued to be suspicious of him—for the duke could not believe that one who had not loved the liberty of his fatherland should love him—he decided to try his fortune again and with one stroke get back liberty for his fatherland and fame and security for himself, judging that there was no other remedy with his fellow citizens but to do a deed in which the medicine and cure would arise from what had been the wound. And when he saw the universal indignation engendered against the duke because of his liberation of the king, he judged that the time was right for putting his designs into effect, and he shared his counsel with as many as he knew were of the same opinion, and urged and disposed them to follow him.

7

THE festival day of Saint John the Baptist had come when Erasmo, the new governor sent by the duke, entered Genoa.[1] When he was already

---

[1] Lit.: empire.
[1] December 27, 1435; in fact, the festival of Saint John the Evangelist.

inside, accompanied by Opicino, the old governor, and by many Genoese, it appeared to Francesco Spinula that he must delay no longer. He came out of his house armed, together with those who were aware of his decisions, and as soon as he was on the piazza in front of his house, he cried out the name of liberty. It was a wonderful thing to see with what haste that people and those citizens ran to this name: so that anyone who for his own advantage or for any other cause might love the duke had not only no time to take up arms but hardly time to think of taking flight. Erasmo took refuge with some of the Genoese who were with him in the fortress that kept guard for the duke. Opicino, assuming that if he fled to the palace where he had two thousand armed men at his command he could either save himself or inspire his friends to defend him, turned in that direction; but before he could reach the piazza, he was killed, and his body, cut to pieces, was dragged all over Genoa. The Genoese, having returned their city to free magistrates, in a few days seized the castle and the other strongholds possessed by the duke and freed themselves altogether from the yoke of Duke Filippo.

8

THESE things being governed thus, whereas in the beginning they had frightened the princes of Italy, who feared that the duke might become too powerful, they gave those princes, when they saw the outcome, hope of being able to keep him in check. And despite the league newly made,[1] the Florentines and the Venetians came to an accord with the Genoese. Whereupon Messer Rinaldo degli Albizzi and the other heads of the exiled Florentines, seeing that things were upset and that the face of the world had changed, took hope of being able to induce the duke to undertake an open war against Florence. Having gone to Milan, Messer Rinaldo spoke to the duke in this sense: "If we, once your enemies, come confidently now to implore your help so that we may return to our fatherland, neither you[2] nor any other who considers how human things proceed and how changeable fortune is ought to marvel at it. Despite our past and present actions, we have manifest and reasonable excuses both with you, for what we have already done, and with our fatherland, for what we are now doing. No good man will ever reprove anyone who seeks to defend his fatherland in whatever mode he defends it. Nor was it ever our aim to injure you, but rather to guard our fatherland from injuries, of which it can be evidence to you that in the course of the great-

---

[1] The peace of August 1435.
[2] The familiar "you" throughout this speech.

est victories of our league, when we recognized that you had turned to a true peace, we were more desirous of it than you yourself. So we are not afraid of having ever done a thing to make us doubt that we could obtain any favor from you. Nor yet can our fatherland complain that we urge you now to take up those arms against it from which we defended it with such obstinacy, because that fatherland deserves to be loved by all its citizens that loves all its citizens equally, not one that, having overlooked all others, adores a very few. Nor may anyone condemn the use of arms against the fatherland in any mode whatever: for although cities are mixed bodies, they have a resemblance to simple bodies; and as in the latter many times infirmities arise that cannot be healed without fire and iron, so in the former often so many inconveniences arise that a pious and good citizen, even if iron should be necessary, would sin much more by letting them go uncured than by curing them. What therefore can be a greater disease in the body of a republic than slavery? What medicine is it more necessary to use than that which will relieve it from this infirmity? Only those wars are just that are necessary, and those arms pious where there is no hope outside them.[3] I do not know what necessity is greater than ours or what piety can exceed that which takes our fatherland out of slavery. It is very certain, therefore, that our cause is pious and just: this should be considered by us and you. Nor is justice lacking on your side, for the Florentines were not ashamed, after a peace celebrated with so much solemnity, to be allied with the Genoese, your rebels; so if our cause does not move you, let indignation move you. And so much more when you see the ease of the enterprise, for past examples ought not to dismay you wherein you have seen the power of that people and their obstinacy in defense, two things that should reasonably still make you fear if they were now of the same virtue as then. But now you will find quite the contrary: for what power do you expect in a city that has itself newly driven out the greater part of its riches and of its industry?[4] What obstinacy do you expect there to be in a people disunited by such varied and new hostilities? This disunion is the cause that even those riches which are left there cannot now be spent in the mode in which they could have been before, because men willingly consume their own patrimony when they see they consume it for the sake of glory, for honor, and their own state, hoping to reacquire easily in peace what war takes away from them; but not when they see themselves oppressed equally in war and peace, by having to bear the injury of their enemies in the one and the

---

[3] A quotation from Livy (IX.1.10), which is given as a quotation but without attribution by NM in *P* 26 and *D* III 12.

[4] See *FH* IV 33.

insolence of those who command them in the other. And the avarice of citizens is much more harmful to peoples than the rapacity of enemies, because one may hope that the latter will end sometime, but the former, never. Thus, in the past wars you bore arms against a whole city; now you bear them only against the smallest part of it. You came to take the state from many citizens and good ones; now you come to take it away from a few and mean ones. You came to take liberty from a city; now you come to give it back. And it is not reasonable that in such a disparity of causes equal effects will follow: indeed, a certain victory is to be hoped from it. How much the force of this may be for your state you can easily judge, since you will have Tuscany a friend and obliged for such and so great an obligation, from which you will get more value in your undertakings than from Milan. And whereas at another time that acquisition would have been judged ambitious and violent, at present it will be deemed just and pious. Therefore, do not let this occasion pass, and think that if your other expeditions against the city brought you, with difficulty, expense and infamy, this one must bring you, with ease, very great advantage and very honorable fame."

9

NOT many words were necessary to persuade the duke that he should start a war against the Florentines, for he was moved by a hereditary hatred and a blind ambition that demanded it of him; and he was spurred on all the more by the new injuries resulting from the accord made with the Genoese. Nonetheless, his past expenses, the dangers incurred, as well as the memory of his recent losses and the vain hopes of the exiles dismayed him. This duke, as soon as he had learned of the rebellion of Genoa, sent Niccolò Piccinino with all his men-at-arms and what infantrymen he could assemble from the countryside toward that city to make an effort to get it back before the citizens made up their minds and ordered the new government; for he had a great deal of confidence in the castle that was being held for him within Genoa. And although Niccolò had driven the Genoese out of the mountains and had taken the valley of Polcevera from them, where they had fortified themselves, and had pushed them back within the city walls, nonetheless he found such difficulty in advancing further, because of the obstinate spirits of the citizens in defending themselves, that he was compelled to withdraw. Hence the duke, at the persuasion of the Florentine exiles, commanded him to attack the coast on the east and, near the boundaries of Pisa, to make as much war as he could in the Genoese countryside, thinking that this campaign would have to show him, as time went on, what course he ought to take. So Niccolò attacked Sarzana and took it. Then, after much damage had been done, he came to Lucca, so as to make the Florentines grow suspicious, announcing that he wished to pass through so as to go to the Kingdom to help the king of Aragon. Pope Eugene, after these new accidents, left Florence and went to Bologna, where he discussed new accords between the duke and the league, pointing out to the duke that if he did not consent to the accord it would be necessary for the pope to yield to the league Count Francesco, who then, as his confederate, fought in his pay. And although the pontiff troubled himself much in this, nonetheless, all his troubles turned out to be vain, for the duke did not want to make an accord without Genoa, and the league wanted Genoa to remain free. And so each, not trusting in peace, prepared for war.

10

NICCOLÒ Piccinino having come to Lucca, therefore, the Florentines were afraid of new moves. So they had Neri di Gino ride with their own troops into the country around Pisa, obtained permission from the pontiff for Count Francesco to join with them, and with their army they came to a halt at Santa Gonda. Piccinino, who was in Lucca, asked for passage to go to the Kingdom, and when it was denied him, he threatened to take it by force. The armies were equal both in forces and in captains, and so, neither of them wanting to tempt fortune, since they were also held back by the cold season, as it was December, they lingered many days without attacking[1] one another. The first of them to move was Niccolò Piccinino, to whom it was shown that if he attacked Vico Pisano by night he would easily seize it. Niccolò undertook the enterprise, and though he did not succeed in seizing Vico, he sacked the countryside around it; he also plundered and burned the village of San Giovanni alla Vena.

Although this enterprise turned out in large part to be vain, it nonetheless inspired Niccolò to advance further, especially as he saw that the count and Neri had not moved; and so he attacked Santa Maria in Castello and Filetto, and won them. Not even for this did the Florentine troops move, not because the count was afraid, but because in Florence the war had not yet been decided upon by the magistrates out of reverence for the pope, who was negotiating peace. And what the Florentines did for the

[1] Lit.: offending.

sake of prudence their enemies believed they were doing out of fear; and it gave them more spirit for new undertakings. So they decided to storm Barga and appeared there with all their forces. This new assault made the Florentines, hesitations now set aside, decide not only to rescue Barga but to attack the country around Lucca. Therefore, the count went to meet Niccolò and, after the battle was joined below Barga, conquered him and, having nearly routed him, raised the siege. Meanwhile, as it appeared to the Venetians that the duke had broken the peace, they sent Giovan Francesco Gonzaga, their captain, to Ghiaradadda; and he, by greatly damaging the countryside of the duke's, compelled him to call back Niccolò Piccinino from Tuscany. This recall, together with the victory they had over Niccolò, inspired the Florentines to make a campaign against Lucca and to hope they could acquire it. In this they had neither fear nor hesitation, since they saw the duke, whom alone they feared, beaten by the Venetians, and that the Lucchese, who had received the enemies of Florence in their home and allowed them to attack it, could not in any way complain.

I I

IN April of 1437, then, the count moved his army; and as the Florentines, before attacking others, wanted to recover what was their own, they retook Santa Maria in Castello and every other place seized by Piccinino. Then, turning upon the country around Lucca, they attacked Camaiore, whose men, though faithful to their lords, surrendered—fear of the enemy nearby being more powerful with them than faith in a friend far away. With that same consideration, Massa and Sarzana were taken. When these things were done, around the end of May, the army turned toward Lucca and destroyed all the crops and grain, burned the houses, cut down the vines and trees, stole the cattle; nor did they neglect doing anything that one usually does and can do against enemies. The Lucchese, for their part, seeing themselves abandoned by the duke, despaired of defending their countryside and abandoned it. Then, with ramparts and every other opportune remedy, they strengthened the city, for which they did not fear, since they had it full of defenders and could defend it for a time. In this they placed their hope, moved by the example of other campaigns the Florentines had made against them. They feared only the inconstant spirits of the plebs, who, when tired of the siege, might value their own dangers more than the liberty of others and force them to some shameful and harmful accord. So to incite them to defense, they assembled them in the piazza, where one of the older and wiser men spoke in this sense: "You must always have understood that things done out of necessity neither should nor can merit praise or blame. Therefore, if you accuse us, believing that the war which the Florentines are waging here now is one we brought on ourselves because we received the duke's men in our home and allowed them to attack the Florentines, you would be deceiving yourselves very greatly. The ancient hostility of the Florentine people against you is well known to you. Neither your injuries nor their fear has caused it, but rather your weakness and their ambition; for the one gives them hope of being able to oppress you, and the other drives them to do it. Nor should you believe that any merit of yours can remove such a desire from them, nor that any offense of yours can inflame them any more to injure you. Therefore, they have to think of taking liberty away from you, you of defending it; and everyone can lament the things that they and we do to this end, but not marvel at them. Let us lament, therefore, that they attack us, that they take our towns, that they burn our houses and despoil our countryside; but who among us is so foolish as to marvel at it? For if we could, we would do the same or worse to them. And if they have started this war because of the coming of Niccolò, even if he had not come at all they would have started a war for another cause; and if this evil had been postponed, it would perhaps have been greater. So, his coming ought not to be blamed, but rather our bad luck and their ambitious nature. Besides, we could not refuse to receive the duke's troops; and once they had come, we could not keep them from making war. You know that without the help of someone powerful we cannot save ourselves, nor is there a power that can defend us with either more faith or more strength than the duke's. He has given back our liberty to us; it is reasonable that he will maintain it for us; he has always been very hostile to our perpetual enemies. Thus, if we had made the duke indignant so as not to injure the Florentines, we would have lost a friend and made the enemy more powerful and more ready to offend us. Consequently, it is much better to have this war with the love of the duke than peace with his hatred. And we must hope that he will get us out of those dangers in which he has put us, if only we do not abandon ourselves. You know with how much fury the Florentines have attacked us so many times and with how much glory we have defended ourselves from them; many times we have had no other hope than in God and in time, and these two have saved us. And if we defended ourselves then,[1] what cause is there that we ought not to defend ourselves now? Then all

---

[1] A reference to the victory of the Lucchese over the Florentines in 1429; see *FH* IV 24–25.

Italy had left us as prey,[2] now we have the duke for us, and we should
believe that the Venetians, as ones who are displeased that the power of
the Florentines is growing, will be slow to offend us. The other time, the
Florentines were more unconstrained, had more hope of help, and by
themselves were more powerful. We were weaker in every way because
then we were defending a tyrant, now we defend ourselves; then the glory
of defense was the others', now it is ours; then those who attacked us were
united, now disunited they attack us, for all Italy is full of rebels against
them. But had we not these hopes, there is an ultimate necessity that
ought to make us obstinate in defense. Every enemy must reasonably be
feared by you because all will wish for their glory and for your ruin; but
above all others, the Florentines must frighten us because our obedience
and our tribute, with empire over this city of ours, would not be enough
for them, but they would want our persons and our substance so as to be
able to satiate their cruelty with our blood and their avarice with our
property. So each one of whatever rank must fear them. And therefore,
let it not move you to see your fields destroyed, your homes burned, your
towns seized, because if we save this city, those will of necessity be saved;
if we lose it, they would be saved without any use to us, because by our
maintaining ourselves free, our enemy can possess them only with difficulty; if we lose our liberty, we will possess them in vain. Take up your
arms, therefore, and when you fight, remember that the reward of your
victory will be the salvation not only of your fatherland but of your
homes and your children." The last words of this man were received with
the greatest warmth of spirit by the people, and in unity each promised
to die before giving up or thinking of an accord that would in any way
stain their liberty. And they ordered among themselves all those things
necessary to the defense of a city.

1 2

THE army of the Florentines, in the meantime, was not losing time, and
after having done very much damage through the countryside, it took
Monte Carlo on terms. After this acquisition the army went to besiege
Nozzano so that the Lucchese, pressed on every side, could not hope for
help and, compelled by hunger, would surrender. The castle was very
strong and replete with a garrison, so that capturing it was not easy as
with the others. The Lucchese, as was reasonable, seeing themselves
pressed on all sides, went to the duke and with every expression both

---

[2] *FH* IV 19.

sweet and sour implored his favor; and in speaking, they pointed now to their own merits, now to the offenses of the Florentines; and they showed how much spirit it would give his other friends if he defended them, and how much terror if he left them undefended; and if they lost life with liberty, he lost honor with his friends and faith with all those who out of love for him would ever have to undergo any danger. To the words they added their tears, so that if obligation did not move him, compassion might. Thus the duke, having added to his ancient hatred of the Florentines a fresh obligation to the Lucchese, and above all desirous that the Florentines not grow by so great an acquisition, determined to send a huge army into Tuscany or to attack the Venetians with such fury that it would be necessary for the Florentines to leave their campaigns to relieve them.

I3

WHEN this decision was made, it was quickly learned in Florence that the duke was getting ready to send troops into Tuscany. This made the Florentines begin to lose hope in their campaign, and, to keep the duke busy in Lombardy, they urged the Venetians to press him with all their forces. But the Venetians too were afraid, because the marquis of Mantua[1] had abandoned them and gone over into the pay of the duke; and so, finding themselves disarmed as it were, they answered that not only could they not enlarge that war, but they could not maintain it unless Count Francesco were sent to them to be the head of their army, and with the condition that he be obliged to cross the Po in person. They were unwilling to hold to the old accords by which he was not obliged to cross, for they did not want to make war without a captain, nor could they put hope in anyone else but the count; and they could not make use of the count unless he was obliged to carry on the war everywhere. To the Florentines it appeared necessary that the war in Lombardy be waged vigorously; on the other hand, if left without the count, they saw their campaign in Lucca ruined; they also understood very well that this request had been made by the Venetians not so much out of the necessity that they had of the count as to interfere with their acquisition.[2] For his part, the count was ready to go into Lombardy whenever it pleased the league, but he

[1] Gian Francesco Gonzaga (1407–1444); see *FH* v 10.
[2] Of Lucca.

did not want to alter his obligation[3] as he did not desire to deprive himself of the hope of the marriage promised him by the duke.

Thus the Florentines were distracted by two diverse passions: by the wish to have Lucca and by the fear of war with the duke. Nonetheless, as always happens, fear won out; and they were content that the count, having won Nozzano, should go to Lombardy. There remained still another difficulty that, as it was not in the discretion of the Florentines to resolve, gave them more anxiety[4] and made them more fearful than the first: for the count did not want to cross the Po and the Venetians would not accept him otherwise. Since no mode was found to reconcile them so that one might freely yield to the other, the Florentines persuaded the count to oblige himself to cross the river by a letter he should write to the Signoria of Florence, pointing out to it that with this private promise he was not breaking his public pacts and that he could then carry on without crossing the river. The advantage following from this would be that the Venetians, who had incited the war, would be necessitated to continue it; from this would arise the diversion of the humor that they feared.[5] To the Venetians, on the other hand, they pointed out that his private letter was enough to obligate the count and so they should be content with it, for wherever they could save the count in his regard for his father-in-law, it was well to do it; nor was it useful to him or to them to reveal the obligation without manifest necessity. So in this way the passage of the count into Lombardy was decided; then, having taken Nozzano and built some bastions around Lucca to restrain the Lucchese, he left that war in the care of commissioners, crossed the mountains, and went to Reggio. There the Venetians, suspicious of his progress, so as to discover his intent before anything else, asked him to cross the Po and join their other troops. The count altogether refused to do this, and there were offensive words between him and Andrea Morosini, sent by the Venetians, each accusing the other of much pride and little faith; and after many protestations between them, the one that he was not obliged to serve, the other that he was not obliged to pay, the count returned to Tuscany and the other to Venice. The count was quartered in the territory of Pisa, and they hoped they could induce him to renew the war against the Lucchese. They did not find him disposed to do this: for when the duke learned that out of reverence for himself the count had not wanted to cross the Po, he thought that through the count he could yet save the Lucchese, and he begged him

---

[3] So as to be obliged to cross the river Po, the southern boundary of Lombardy.

[4] Lit.: passion.

[5] The duke of Milan's decision to attack the Florentines, or perhaps the Venetian propensity to make a separate peace.

to be content to make an accord between the Lucchese and the Florentines and to include the duke in it if he could, meanwhile giving him hope of marriage to his daughter when he wished. This marriage strongly moved the count, for through it he hoped, since the duke had no male children, to make himself lord of Milan. So he always kept breaking off the prosecution of the war for the Florentines and asserting that he was not about to move if the Venetians did not keep up their payment and their contract with him. Nor was payment alone sufficient, because if he wanted to live safely in his states, it was necessary for him to have other support than from the Florentines. Therefore, if he were abandoned by the Venetians, he was forced to look after his own affairs, and he cleverly threatened to come to an accord with the duke.

14

THESE dodges and deceits greatly displeased the Florentines, because they saw the campaign at Lucca lost, and besides, they feared for their own state any time the count and the duke were together. So, to compel the Venetians to maintain the contract with the count, Cosimo de' Medici went to Venice, believing that with his reputation he could move them. There, in their senate, he argued the matter at length, showing what straits the state of Italy was in, how great were the forces of the duke, where the reputation and the power of arms were; and he concluded that if the count joined with the duke, the Venetians would return to the sea and the Florentines to fighting for their liberty. To this the Venetians answered that they knew their own forces and those of the Italians, and they believed they could defend themselves in any mode, asserting that they were not used to paying soldiers to serve others. The Florentines should therefore expect to pay the count, since they were served by him; and it was more necessary for the Venetians, if they wished to enjoy their states securely, to put down the pride of the count than to pay him: for men have no limits to their ambition, and if now he were paid without serving, he would ask soon after for something more indecent and more dangerous. Therefore, it appeared to them necessary to put a check on his insolence in good time and not let it grow so much as to become incorrigible; and if the Florentines, either from fear or from some other desire, still wanted to keep him as a friend, they should pay him.

Cosimo returned thus with no other result. Nonetheless, the Florentines put pressure on the count to keep him from separating from the league, which he too would leave unwillingly; but his wish to conclude his marriage held him in doubt, so that even the least accident, as it happened, could have made him decide. The count had left Friulano, one of his best condottieri, to watch over his towns in the Marches. This man was instigated by the duke to renounce the pay of the count and come over to him—which made the count, all hesitation put aside, come to an accord with the duke out of fear for himself; and among the terms was that things in Romagna and Tuscany should not be meddled with. After this accord, the count insistently persuaded the Florentines that they should come to an accord with the Lucchese, and so pressed them that, seeing they had no other remedy, they made an accord in the month of April of the year 1438. By this accord the Lucchese were left with their liberty, the Florentines with Monte Carlo and some others of their fortified places. Thereafter, they filled all Italy with letters full of complaints, showing that since God and men had not wanted the Lucchese to come under their rule they had made peace with them. And rarely does it happen that anyone is so displeased at having lost his own things as were the Florentines for not having acquired those of others.

15

ALTHOUGH the Florentines in these times were busy with so great an campaign, they did not fail to think of their neighbors and to adorn their city. Niccolò Fortebraccio had died, as we have said;[1] he had been married to a daughter of the count of Poppi. At the death of Niccolò, the count held the Borgo San Sepolcro and the fortress of that town in his hands, and he had ruled them in the name of his son-in-law while he was living. Then, after Niccolò's death, he said that he owned it through his daughter's dowry and refused to yield it to the pope, who was demanding it as Church property. So the pope sent the patriarch[2] with his troops to gain possession of it. When the count saw he could not resist the attack, he offered that town to the Florentines; and they did not want it. But when the pope returned to Florence, they intervened between him and the count to bring them to accord; and as there were difficulties in the accord, the patriarch attacked the Casentino and took Prato Vecchio and Romena, which he likewise offered to the Florentines. They still did not want to accept them unless the pope would agree that they could hand them over to the count. After many arguments the pope agreed to this, but he wanted the Florentines to promise him to work it out that the count of Poppi restore the Borgo to him. Thus, when the pope's mind

---

[1] See *FH* v 3.
[2] Giovanni Vitelleschi, patriarch of Alexandria; see *FH* v 27.

had been set at rest in this way, it appeared to the Florentines that since the cathedral church of their city, called Santa Reparata (the construction of which had begun long before[3]), had come to a point where divine offices could be celebrated there, they would ask him if he would consecrate it personally. To this the pope agreed willingly, and for the greater magnificence of the city and of the church, and to honor the pope more, a ramp was made from Santa Maria Novella, where the pope was staying, to the church that was to be consecrated, four cubits wide and two high, and covered above and around with the richest draperies, over which only the pope and his court came, together with those magistrates of the city and citizens who had been deputed to accompany him. All the other citizenry and people waited along the way, by their houses and in the church, to see such a spectacle. And so all the ceremonies were done that are usually done in such consecrations, and the pope, to give a sign of greater love, honored Giuliano Davanzati with knighthood; he was then a Gonfalonier of Justice and at all times a citizen of the highest reputation. At this, the Signoria, so as not to appear less loving than the pope, granted him the captaincy of Pisa for one year.

16

IN these same times there were some differences between the Roman Church and the Greek such that they did not agree on divine worship in every regard. Since at the last council held in Basel there had been much discussion by the prelates of the Western Church on this matter, it was decided to use all diligence to get the emperor and the Greek prelates to meet in a council at Basel to see if they could come to an accord with the Roman Church. And although this decision was contrary to the majesty of the Greek Empire, and it might be displeasing to the pride of its prelates to yield to the Roman pontiff, nonetheless, as they were being oppressed by the Turks and judged they could not defend themselves alone, they decided to yield, so as to be able to ask for help from the others with more assurance. And so the emperor, together with the patriarch and other Greek prelates and barons, came to Venice so as to attend at Basel in accordance with the decision of the council; but, frightened by the plague, they decided to end their differences in the city of Florence. Thus the Roman and Greek prelates assembled together for many days in the cathedral church, and after many long disputations the Greeks yielded and came to accord with the Roman Church and pontiff.

[3] See *FH* II 31.

WHEN peace had been concluded between the Lucchese and the Florentines, and between the duke and the count,[1] it was believed that the arms of Italy, and especially those infesting Lombardy and Tuscany, could easily be laid down; for those that had been used in the kingdom of Naples between René of Anjou and Alfonso of Aragon must by the ruin of one of the two be laid down. And although the pope might remain malcontent for having lost so many of his towns, and although it was known how much ambition was in the duke and the Venetians, nonetheless it was assumed that the pope must come to a stop out of necessity and the others out of weariness. But the thing went otherwise because neither the duke nor the Venetians remained quiet; hence, the result was that arms were taken up again, and Lombardy and Tuscany were again filled with war. The lofty spirit of the duke could not bear that the Venetians should possess Bergamo and Brescia, much less when he saw them up in arms and every day plundering and harrying his country in many places; and he thought not only that he could hold them in check but that he could regain his towns whenever the Venetians might be abandoned by the pope, by the Florentines, and by the count. Therefore, he schemed to seize Romagna from the pontiff, judging that if he had it, the pope could not offend him; and the Florentines, seeing the fire close by, either would not move out of fear for themselves or, if they did move, could not attack him conveniently. The indignation of the Florentines against the Venetians over things at Lucca was also known to the duke, and because of it he judged them to be less ready to take up arms for the Venetians. As for Count Francesco, the duke believed that their new friendship, the hope of his marriage, would be enough to hold him fast; and so the duke, so as to avoid blame and to give less cause to anyone to move, especially since he could not attack Romagna because of the terms made with the count, ordered Niccolò Piccinino to enter upon that campaign as if he were doing it out of his own ambition.

When the accord between the duke and the count was made, Niccolò was in Romagna; and in accord with the duke, he pretended to be indignant because of the friendship established between him and the count, his everlasting enemy. He withdrew with his troops to Camurata, a place between Forlì and Ravenna, where he fortified himself as if he wished to stay there a long time until he took a new course. And the report of his indignation having been spread about everywhere, Niccolò let the pontiff understand how much he deserved from the duke and what his ingrati-

[1] See *FH* v 14.

tude had been; that the duke was letting it be understood that since he had almost all the arms of Italy under the two first captains, he was about to seize it. But if His Holiness wished, of the two captains that the duke was persuaded he had, Niccolò could make one hostile and the other useless: for if the pope provided him with money and maintained him in arms, he would attack the states of the count seized by him from the Church, so that the count, having to think about his own affairs, could not support the ambition of Filippo. The pope believed these words, as they appeared reasonable to him, and he sent five thousand ducats to Niccolò and filled him with promises, offering states to him and his children. And although the pope was warned by many of the deceit, he did not believe them, nor would he listen to anyone who said the contrary.

The city of Ravenna was governed by Ostasio da Polenta for the Church. As it appeared to Niccolò that there was no more time to delay his expedition, because his son Francesco had sacked Spoleto, to the ignominy of the pope, he decided to attack Ravenna, either because he judged the undertaking easier or because he had a secret understanding with Ostasio. And in a few days after he attacked, he took it by an accord. After this acquisition, Bologna, Imola, and Forlì were seized by him. And what was most marvelous is that of the twenty fortresses that were being guarded in those states on behalf of the pontiff, not one remained that did not come under the power[2] of Niccolò. Nor did it suffice him to have offended the pontiff with this injury; he also wished to ridicule him with words as he had with deeds; and he wrote that he had seized the cities deservedly since the pope had not been ashamed to want to break up a friendship such as that between the duke and himself and to fill Italy with letters that implied he had left the duke and taken the side of the Venetians.

18

HAVING seized Romagna, Niccolò left it under the guard of his son Francesco and went himself with the larger part of his troops into Lombardy. There he joined with the rest of the duke's troops, attacked the countryside of Brescia, and in a short time seized it; then he laid a siege on the city. The duke, who desired the Venetians to be left as his prey, excused himself to the pope, the Florentines, and the count by pointing out that the things done by Niccolò in Romagna, if contrary to the terms,[1] were

[2] *Potestà.*
[1] The terms of the pact with the count; see *FH* v 14.

also against his will, and by secret messengers he gave them to understand that he would make a clear example of this disobedience when time and opportunity allowed. The Florentines and the count did not put faith in him but did believe, as was the truth, that these arms had been set in motion to detain them, so that he could tame the Venetians. The Venetians, full of pride and believing they could resist the forces of the duke by themselves, did not deign to ask aid of anyone, but carried on the war with Gattamelata as their captain. Count Francesco wanted to go to the rescue of King René with the support of the Florentines, if unforeseen events in Romagna and Lombardy had not restrained him; and the Florentines too would have favored this willingly because of the ancient friendship their city had always maintained with the house of France. But the duke would have directed his favors toward Alfonso for the friendship he had contracted with him during his capture. But both of these, occupied in wars nearby, abstained from enterprises far away.

Thus, when the Florentines saw Romagna seized by the forces of the duke and the Venetians beaten, like those who from the ruin of others fear their own, they begged the count to come to Tuscany, where they could look into what might be done to oppose the forces of the duke, which were greater than they had ever been before. They asserted that if his insolence were not checked in some mode, everyone who held a state in Italy would, in a short time, suffer from it. The count recognized that the fear of the Florentines was reasonable; nonetheless, his wish that the marriage arranged with the duke should take place kept him in suspense, and the duke, who knew this desire of his, kept holding forth to him the greatest hopes if he would not move arms against him. And because the young girl was now of an age to celebrate the marriage, the duke brought the thing many times to the point where all the preparations necessary for it were made; then, with various dodges, everything would be canceled. And to make the count believe him better, he added deeds to the promises and sent him thirty thousand florins, which were due him according to the terms of the marriage.

19

NONETHELESS, the war in Lombardy was growing. Every day the Venetians were losing new towns; all the armed vessels they had put out on the rivers had been overcome by the ducal troops; the countryside around Verona and Brescia was completely occupied, and those two towns were so hard pressed that, in the common opinion, they could maintain themselves for only a short time. The marquis of Mantua, who for many years had been the condottiere of their republic, had, beyond all their belief, abandoned them and taken the side of the duke; so what pride did not permit them at the beginning of the war, fear made them do in the course of it. For, having recognized that they had no other remedy than the friendship of the Florentines and the count, they began to ask them for help, although ashamedly and full of suspicion, because they feared that the Florentines might give them the answer they had received from the Venetians in regard to the campaign of Lucca and in the affairs of the count.

But they found it easier than they had hoped and than their behavior deserved, so much more powerful in the Florentines was hatred for the ancient enemy than indignation over an old and customary friendship. And as they had recognized long before the necessity into which the Venetians must come, they had pointed out to the count that the ruin of the Venetians would be his own ruin, and he was deceiving himself if he believed that Duke Filippo would value him more in good fortune than in bad, and that fear of him was the cause of the duke's having promised him his daughter. And because those things that necessity makes one promise also make one observe, it was necessary that the duke be maintained in that necessity, which could not be done without the greatness of the Venetians. Therefore, he must remember that if the Venetians were compelled to abandon their state on land, he would lose not only the advantages he could get from them but also all those he could get from others out of fear of them. And if he considered the states of Italy well, he would see which were poor, which were his enemies; nor were the Florentines alone, as he had said many times, sufficient to maintain him; thus he would see it was to his advantage from every side to keep the Venetians powerful on land. These arguments, added to the hatred the count had conceived for the duke because it appeared to him that he had been made a fool of in the marriage alliance, made him consent to the accord; yet he was still not willing to oblige himself to cross the Po River. These accords were fixed in February 1438, by which the Venetians assumed two-thirds and the Florentines one-third of the expense; and each obligated itself, at its expense, to defend the states the count had in the Marches. Nor was the league content with these forces, for they added to them the lord of Faenza, the sons of Messer Pandolfo Malatesta da Rimini, and Pietro Gianpaolo Orsini; and although they tempted the marquis of Mantua with great promises, nonetheless they were unable to detach him from the friendship and pay of the duke; and the lord of Faenza, after the league had signed his contract, returned to the duke, having found better terms. This took away from the league any hope of being able to settle things quickly in Romagna.

LOMBARDY in these times was beset with travails: Brescia was besieged by the duke's troops such that it was feared that any day it might surrender out of hunger, and Verona was still so hard pressed that the same end was feared for it; and if one of these two cities was lost, all the other preparations for the war would be judged vain and the expense sustained until then lost. Nor was any other sure remedy seen than to make Count Francesco cross into Lombardy. There were three difficulties in this: first, to dispose the count to cross the Po and make war everywhere; second, that it appeared to the Florentines that without the count they would be left to the discretion of the duke (because the duke could easily retreat to his strongholds and keep the count at bay with part of his troops, and with the other part come into Tuscany with their rebels, of whom the state then ruling[1] was in very great terror); the third was what way the count and his troops should take that would lead him safely to the territory of Padua, where the other Venetian troops were. Of the three difficulties, the second pertaining to the Florentines was most to be feared; nonetheless, recognizing the need and the weariness of the Venetians, who demanded the count with every importunity, pointing out that without him they would give up, the Florentines put the necessity of others ahead of their own fears. There remained still the difficulty of the route; this, it was decided, should be secured by the Venetians. And because they had sent Neri di Gino Capponi to negotiate these agreements with the count and to dispose him to cross, it seemed to the Signoria that he should also go on to Venice in order to make this benefit more acceptable to that signoria[2] and to order the route and safe passage for the count.

21

SO Neri left Cesena and went by boat to Venice. And never was a prince received with as much honor by that signoria as he was, for they judged that on his coming and on what had to be decided and ordered through him depended the salvation of their empire. Then Neri, introduced to the senate, spoke in this sense: "My Signori, Most Serene Prince,[1] have always been of the opinion that the greatness of the duke would be the ruin

---

[1] The Medici and their party.

[2] The Venetian government. *Signoria* refers to a particular institution in Florence but not in Venice.

[1] The Venetian doge.

of this state and of their republic, and thus the salvation of both these states would be your greatness and ours. If the same thing had been believed by your lordships, we would find ourselves in a better condition, and your state would be safe from the dangers that now threaten it. But because in times when you should have, you lent us neither help nor faith, we have been unable to run quickly with remedies for your ill; nor could you have been ready to ask for them, since in your prosperity and in adversity you have little understood us and do not know that we are so made that whom we have once loved we always love, and whom we have once hated we always hate. The love that we have borne for your most serene signoria you yourselves know, who many times have seen Lombardy filled with our money and our soldiers so as to help you; the hatred we bear for Filippo and have always borne for his house the whole world knows; nor is it possible that an ancient love or an ancient hatred is easily canceled by new merits or new offenses. We have been and are certain that in this war we could have stayed in the middle with great gratitude from the duke and with not much fear for us: for although by your ruin he would have become lord of Lombardy, so much life would be left in Italy that we would not have to despair of our safety,[2] because with a growing power and state, enmities and envy also grow, from which war and injury then customarily arise. We knew also how much expense we would avoid by avoiding these present wars; how many impending dangers would have been avoided; and how, if we should move, this war, now in Lombardy, could be brought down into Tuscany. Nonetheless, all these doubts have been canceled by our ancient affection for this state, and we have decided to come to the aid of your state with the same promptness with which we would aid our own if it were attacked. That is why my Signori, judging that it was necessary before everything else to relieve Verona and Brescia, and judging that this could not be done without the count, sent me first to persuade him to cross into Lombardy and to make war everywhere (as you know he was not obliged to cross the Po). And I disposed him to do this by moving him with the same reasons that move us. And as it appears to him that he is invincible in arms, he also does not wish to be defeated in courtesy, and he wished to surpass the liberality that he sees us use toward you; for he knows well how much danger remains for Tuscany after his departure, and, seeing that we have deferred our dangers for your safety, he wished to defer his concerns for the same. I come therefore to offer you the count with seven thousand cavalry and two thousand infantry equipped to go and meet the enemy everywhere. I pray well, as do my Signori and the count pray you,

[2] Or salvation.

since the number of his men exceeds that with which he is obligated to serve, that you, too, will compensate him with your liberality so that he will not repent his having entered your service nor we repent our having encouraged him."

Neri's speech was heard by that senate with no less attention than would be paid to an oracle, and so inflamed were the listeners by his words that they would not suffer the prince to respond, as is the custom, but rising to their feet, with hands raised, the greater part of them weeping, they gave thanks to the Florentines for such a loving office and to him for having executed it with such care and speed; and they promised that never at any time, not only in their hearts but in those of their descendants, would it be forgotten and that their fatherland must always belong in common to the Florentines and themselves.[3]

22

WHEN this warmth had subsided, they reasoned over the way the count should take so that they could provide for the bridges, the level ground, and everything else. There were four ways. One was by Ravenna along the coast; since the greater part of it was constricted by the coast and by swamps, this one was not approved. Another was by the direct way: this way was blocked by a tower called the Uccellino, which was garrisoned for the duke; and to pass by, one needed to conquer it, which was difficult to do in so short a time as not to take away the opportunity for relief[1] that required speed and quickness. The third was through the forest of Lugo, but because the Po River had overflowed its banks, the passage through was made not only difficult but impossible. There remained the fourth way: through the open country of Bologna over the Puledrano bridge, by Cento and by Pieve, and between Finale and Bondeno, leading to Ferrara, and then by water and by land, they could get to the territory of Padua and join with the Venetian troops. Although this way had many difficulties and could be contended by the enemy at any place, it was chosen as the least bad. As soon as it was made known to the count, he departed with very great speed and on the 20th of June arrived in the territory of Padua.

The coming of this captain into Lombardy filled Venice and all its empire with good hope; and whereas at first the Venetians appeared desper-

---

[3] NM has greatly exaggerated the disposition of the Venetian senate to accept Neri's proposal.

[1] Relief of Brescia and Verona.

ate of their safety, they began to hope for new acquisitions. Before everything else, the count went to relieve Verona; to prevent this, Niccolò went with his army to Soave, a fortified place situated between the territory of Vicenza and that of Verona; and he encircled himself with a ditch that went from Soave to the swamps of the Adige. When the count saw that the way through the plain was blocked, he judged that he could go through the mountains and by that way approach Verona, thinking that Niccolò either would not believe he would take this route because it was rugged and mountainous or, if he did believe it, he would not have time to prevent him. He provided supplies for eight days, crossed the mountain with his troops, and arrived in the plain near Soave. And although some bastions had been built by Niccolò to block that way too to the count, nonetheless they were not sufficient to hold him. Thus Niccolò, seeing beyond all his own belief that the enemy had crossed, withdrew to the other side of the Adige so as not to come to battle at a disadvantage, and the count entered Verona without hindrance.

23

THE first task of freeing Verona from the siege thus having been successfully accomplished by the count, there remained the second, of relieving Brescia. This city is so close to Lake Garda that even if it were besieged by land, supplies could always be brought by way of the lake. This had been the cause for the duke's having made himself strong on the lake and for having seized at the beginning of his victories all the towns that could carry help to Brescia from the lake. The Venetians also had galleys there, but not enough of them to fight the duke's troops. Therefore, the count judged it necessary to support the Venetian fleet with troops on land, by which he hoped he could easily acquire the towns that were keeping Brescia famished. He placed his camp, therefore, at Bardolino, a fortified town situated on the lake, hoping that since he had this one, the others would surrender. Fortune was hostile to the count in this campaign, for a good part of his troops fell ill; so he dropped the campaign and went to Zevio, a Veronese fortified town, a place well supplied and healthful. Niccolò, having seen that the count had withdrawn, so as not to miss the opportunity, as it appeared to him, to gain mastery[1] of the lake, left his camp at Vegasio and went to the lake with some elite troops; and with a great thrust and greater fury, he attacked the Venetian fleet and took nearly all of it. Through this victory, few fortified towns on the lake were

---

[1] Or become lord of.

left that did not surrender to Niccolò. The Venetians, dismayed by this loss and fearing that because of it the Brescians might give up, urged the count with messengers and letters to relieve it. When the count saw that the hope of relieving it by way of the lake was lost, that it was impossible through the open country because of the ditches, bastions, and other obstacles ordered by Niccolò, and that to enter among them with a hostile army against him would lead to clear defeat, he decided that as the mountain way had let him save Verona, so might it also let him relieve Brescia. Thus, having made this scheme, the count left Zevio, went through the Val d'Affi to the Lake of Santo Andrea, and came to Torboli and Peneda on Lake Garda. From there he went to Tenno, where he set up his camp, because, if he wanted to pass through Brescia, it was necessary to seize this fortified place. Niccolò, when he understood the plans of the count, led his army to Peschiera, then, with the marquis of Mantua and some of his elite troops, went to meet the count; and when they came to battle, Niccolò was beaten and his troops scattered; some of them were taken, some fled to the army and some to the fleet. Niccolò withdrew to Tenno, and when night came, he thought that if he waited in this place for day to come, he could not escape falling into the hands of the enemy, and to escape a certain danger he tried a doubtful one. Of his many servants, Niccolò had with him only one, of German nationality, very strong in body, who had always been very faithful to him. Niccolò persuaded this man to put him in a sack, throw him over his shoulders, and take him to a safe place as if he were carrying baggage for his master. The army was all around Tenno, but because of the victory that day, it was without guards and without any order. So it was easy for the German to save his lord because, when he lifted him to his shoulders, dressed as a porter, he passed through the whole camp without any hindrance, and so brought him safe to his troops.

24

IF this victory, then, had been used with the success with which it had been gained, it would have brought greater relief to Brescia and greater success to the Venetians; but its being used badly made the cheer vanish quickly, and Brescia was left in the same difficulties. For when Niccolò returned to his troops, he thought it needful to cancel his loss with some new victory and to take from the Venetians their means of relieving Brescia. He knew the site of the citadel of Verona, and from the prisoners taken in that war he had learned that it was badly defended and the ease and the mode by which it might be acquired. It appeared to him, therefore, that fortune had put before him the matter for retrieving his honor and for causing the joy the enemy had had for its recent victory to change into pain for a more recent defeat. The city of Verona is located in Lombardy at the foot of the mountains that separate Italy from Germany so that it includes both mountains and plain. The river Adige issues from the valley of Trento and in entering Italy does not spread quickly through the open country but turns left along the mountains, finds the city, and passes through the middle of it, not, however, so that the parts are equal, because much more of it lies on the side of the plain than on the side of the mountains. On them are two fortresses, one named San Pietro, the other San Felice, which appear stronger for their site than for their walls and from a high place dominate the whole city. On the plain from here to the Adige, and astride the walls of the city, are two other fortresses, separated from each other by a thousand paces. One of these is named the old citadel, the other the new; from within one of them there is a wall that goes to join the other citadel and makes almost a string to the bow made by the ordinary walls of the city that go from one citadel to the other. All this space between one wall and the other is full of inhabitants and is called the Borgo of San Zeno. Niccolò Piccinino schemed to seize these citadels and the Borgo, thinking that he would easily succeed, both because of the negligent guard usually kept there and because he believed that with the recent victory the negligence would be greater, and because he knew that in war no enterprise is as likely to succeed as the one the enemy does not believe you can make. So, with a selection of his troops, he went together with the marquis of Mantua at night to Verona and, without being heard, scaled the walls and took the new citadel. From there his troops descended into the town and broke open the gate of San Antonio, through which all the cavalry passed. Those on guard for the Venetians at the old citadel, having first heard the sound when the guards of the new citadel were killed, and later, when the gate was broken, realizing that the enemy was there, began to shout and call the people to arms. Then when the citizens were awakened, all confused, those who had more spirit took up arms and ran to the piazza of the rectors. Meanwhile, Niccolò's troops had sacked the Borgo of San Zeno, and as they were advancing, the citizens, recognizing that the duke's troops were within and seeing no mode of defending themselves, urged the Venetian rectors to flee to the fortresses to save their persons and the town; they pointed out to them that it was better for them to keep themselves alive and the city rich for a better fortune than to want to die themselves and impoverish the city so as to avoid the present fortune. And so the rectors and anyone of a Venetian name fled to the fortress of San Felice. After this, some of the first citizens came out to meet Niccolò and the marquis of Mantua, begging them to take the city when rich, with honor to them, rather than to possess it poor, to their shame, especially since the Veronese had deserved neither gratitude from their first masters nor hatred from them for having defended themselves. These men were comforted by Niccolò and the marquis, and as much as they could in such military license, they defended it from the sack. And because they were almost sure that the count would come to recover the city, they strove with all their industry to have the strongholds in their hands; and those they could not get, they separated from the town with ditches and barricades so that it would be difficult for the enemy to get inside.

25

COUNT Francesco was at Tenno with his troops, and when he heard the news, he at first judged it baseless; but then, when he learned the truth from more certain information, he wanted to make up for his earlier negligence with haste. And though all the heads of his army advised him that, having dropped the campaign in Verona and Brescia, he should go to Vicenza so as not, by lingering there, to be besieged by the enemy, he would not agree to this but wanted to try his fortune in recapturing the city. And turning in the midst of these uncertainties of mind to his Venetian suppliers and to Bernardetto de' Medici, who was with him as commissioner for the Florentines, he promised them certain recapture of the city if one of the fortresses should await him. Thus putting his troops in order, he went toward Verona with maximum speed. At the sight of him, Niccolò believed that the count, as he had been advised by his own men, was going to Vicenza; but when he saw him turning his troops toward the town and leading them toward the fortress of San Felice, he wanted to put himself in order for defense. But he was not in time, because the barricades to the fortresses had not been made; the soldiers were scattered out of avarice for the booty and the ransoms; and he could not unite them quickly enough to prevent the count's troops from approaching the fortress and from descending by it into the city. They recaptured the city successfully, with shame to Niccolò and loss to his men. Together with the marquis of Mantua, he fled first to the citadel and then through the open country to Mantua. There, having assembled the remnants of their troops who had been saved, they joined with the others who were at the siege of Brescia. Thus, within four days Verona had been acquired and lost by the ducal army. After this victory, the count, since it was already winter and the cold was great, and after he had sent supplies to Brescia with much difficulty, went into quarters in Verona, and he ordered some galleys to be built over the winter in Torboli so that in the spring he could be strong enough by land and by water to be able to free Brescia completely.

26

WHEN the duke saw the war stopped for a time and the hope he had had of seizing Verona and Brescia cut short, that the cause of it all was the money and the advice of the Florentines, and that neither had they been alienated from their friendship for the Venetians by the injury they had received from them nor had he by the promises he had made to them been able to win them over, he decided, so that they might feel the fruits of their seeds nearer to them, to attack Tuscany. He was encouraged in this by the Florentine exiles and by Niccolò. What moved Niccolò was the desire to acquire the states of Braccio and to drive the count out of the Marches; the others were impelled by their desire to return to their fatherland: and each had moved the duke with reasons appropriate and conformable to his desire. Niccolò showed him how he could send him into Tuscany and keep Brescia besieged, since he was lord of the lake, had strongholds on land well fortified, and there remained captains and troops to oppose the count if he should wish to make another campaign (but it was not reasonable that the count should do this without freeing Brescia, and to free it was impossible); so he might come to make war in Tuscany and yet not leave off the campaign in Lombardy. He also showed him that it would be necessary for the Florentines, as soon as they saw him in Tuscany, to recall the count or lose; and whichever of these things happened, victory would result. The exiles asserted that it was impossible, if Niccolò approached Florence with an army, that the people, wearied by taxes and by the insolence of the powerful, would not take up arms against them. They showed him that it was easy to approach Florence, promising him that the way would be open through the Casentino because of the friendship that Messer Rinaldo had with that count,[1] so that the duke, already turning that way on his own, was confirmed in making this campaign all the more by their arguments. The Venetians, on the other side, for all that the winter was harsh, did not fail to beg the count to rescue Brescia with the whole army. This the count denied could be done in this weather, but it must wait for the new season. In the meantime, they must put the fleet in order, and then he would relieve it by water and by land. Hence the Venetians were in a bad mood and were

[1] The count of Poppi; see *FH* v 15.

slow in every provision, so that their army was very much in want of troops.

27

WHEN assured of all these things, the Florentines were terrified as they saw that the war was coming upon them and that in Lombardy there had not been much profit. Nor did the suspicions they had of the troops of the Church give them less worry, not because the pope was their enemy but because they saw his armies more obedient to the patriarch, who was very hostile to them, than to the pope. Giovanni Vitelleschi, of Corneto, was first an apostolic notary, then bishop of Recanati, and next patriarch of Alexandria; but having finally become a cardinal, he was named cardinal of Florence. He was spirited and astute and therefore knew how to work it out so that he was greatly loved by the pope and put in charge of the Church's armies by him; and of all the campaigns that the pope undertook in Tuscany, in Romagna, in the Kingdom, and in Rome, he was captain. Hence, he had achieved so much authority with the troops and with the pope that the pope was afraid to command him and the troops obeyed him only and no others. Since this cardinal, therefore, was in Rome with his troops when the news came that Niccolò wanted to pass through into Tuscany, the fear of the Florentines was redoubled. For after Messer Rinaldo had been driven out, the cardinal had always been hostile to that state, in view of the fact that the accords made between the parties through his mediation had not been observed but had, indeed, been managed with prejudice to Messer Rinaldo, since they had been the cause that he put down his arms and gave to his enemies the means to drive him out.[1] So, to the princes of the government it appeared that the time might have come for Messer Rinaldo to restore his losses if he took the side of Niccolò when he came into Tuscany. And they were all the more fearful as it appeared to them that the departure of Niccolò from Lombardy was inopportune, since he was leaving a campaign almost won so as to enter into one altogether doubtful, which they did not believe he would do without new intelligence or hidden deceit. They had warned the pope of this suspicion of theirs, but he had already recognized his error in giving others too much authority. But while the Florentines remained in suspense, fortune showed them the way to secure themselves against the patriarch.

That republic had careful inspectors everywhere among those who car-

[1] See *FH* IV 32.

ried letters so as to discover if anyone might be ordering anything against their state. It happened that at Montepulciano letters were seized that the patriarch was writing without the consent of the pontiff to Niccolò Piccinino, which the magistrate in charge of the war immediately presented to the pope. Although they were written in unusual characters and the sense was so complicated that one could not draw any particular meaning from them, nonetheless this obscurity, and the dealing with an enemy, so much aroused the suspicions of the pontiff that he determined to secure himself against him. He put in charge of this enterprise Antonio Rida da Padova, who had been posted as guard of the castle in Rome. As soon as this man received the commission, he was prepared to obey when the occasion he was awaiting should come. The patriarch had decided to come to Tuscany, and as he wished to leave Rome the following day, he notified the castellan to be on the castle bridge in the morning because, while passing over, he wished to reason with him about something. It appeared to Antonio that the occasion had come, and he ordered his men as to what they must do. At the appointed time he waited for the patriarch on the bridge next to the fortress, which for security could be raised or lowered as necessary. As soon as the patriarch was on it, and he had stopped him first for the reasoning, he signaled his men to raise the bridge, so that the patriarch found himself, from being the commander of armies, at a stroke the prisoner of a castellan. The troops with him at first made an uproar; afterwards, when they learned of the pope's will, they quieted down. But while the castellan comforted the patriarch with humane words, giving him hope that he would fare well, he answered that great men are not taken so as to be let go and that those who deserved to be taken did not deserve to be let go. And so, shortly after, he died in prison, and the pope placed at the head of his men Ludovico, patriarch of Aquileia. And while Ludovico in the past had never wanted to be involved in the wars of the league and the duke, he was content to take part now, and he promised to be ready for the defense of Tuscany with four thousand cavalry and two thousand infantry.

28

THE Florentines, freed from this fear, were left with their fear of Niccolò and of the confusion of things in Lombardy because of the differences between the Venetians and the count.[1] To understand these better, they sent Neri di Gino Capponi and Messer Giuliano Davanzati to Venice and

[1] See *FH* v 26 (end).

charged them to find out how the war would have to be managed the next year. They instructed Neri that after he learned the opinion of the Venetians he should go to the count in order to learn his opinion and to persuade him to do those things necessary for the safety of the league. These ambassadors were not yet in Ferrara when they learned that Niccolò Piccinino had crossed the Po with six thousand cavalry, which made them hurry their journey. When they reached Venice, they found its signoria all wanting that Brescia should be relieved without waiting for better weather, because that city could not wait for relief until the next season or for a fleet to be built, but if it saw no other aid, it would surrender to the enemy; this would make the duke entirely victorious and make them lose all their state on land. On this account Neri went to Verona to hear out the count and what he had to argue to the contrary. The count pointed out with many reasons why rushing toward Brescia in that weather was useless now and damaging to a future campaign, for, considering the weather and the site of Brescia, it would bear no fruit but would only disorder and exhaust his troops, so that when the season suitable for activity came, it would be necessary for him to return with the army to Verona to provide for things consumed during the winter and necessary for the next season: so all the time suitable for war would be spent in going and returning. With the count in Verona, having been sent to negotiate these things, were Messer Orsatto Giustiniani and Messer Giovanni Pisani. After many disputes, it was concluded with them that the Venetians should give the count eighty thousand ducats for the new year and to the others of his troops forty ducats for each lancer, and that he should be urged to go forth with the whole army to attack the duke so that fear for his own affairs would make Niccolò return to Lombardy. After this conclusion, they returned to Venice. Because the sum of money was large, the Venetians provided sluggishly in everything.

29

NICCOLÒ Piccinino, meanwhile, continued his journey and, once he had reached Romagna, worked with the sons of Messer Pandolfo Malatesta[1] so that they left the Venetians and sided with the duke. This thing displeased Venice, but Florence much more, because they believed that this was the way they could hold out against Niccolò; but when they saw that the Malatesti had revolted, they were frightened, especially because they feared that Pietro Gianpaolo Orsini, their captain, then in the towns of

[1] See *FH* v 19.

the Malatesti, might have everything taken from him, leaving them disarmed. This news frightened the count as well, because he was afraid of
losing the Marches if Niccolò crossed into Tuscany; and being disposed
to go to the relief of his own house, he came to Venice. When he was
brought before the prince,[2] he pointed out that his going to Tuscany was
useful to the league, for war had to be made where the army and the
captain of the enemy were, not where their towns and garrisons were,
because an army conquered is a war won, but if towns are conquered
while the army is left whole, the war often becomes more active. He
asserted that the Marches and Tuscany would be lost unless there was
vigorous opposition to Niccolò; if these were lost, there would be no
remedy for Lombardy; but even if there were a remedy, he did not intend
to abandon his subjects and his friends. He had come to Lombardy a lord
and he did not mean to depart a condottiere. To this the prince replied
that it was manifest to him that if the count not only left Lombardy but
recrossed the Po with his whole army, all their state on land would be
lost. And they were not about to spend anything more to defend it, for
he is not wise who tries to defend a thing he will have to lose in any mode;
and it is less infamy, and less loss, to lose states alone than states and
money. And if the loss of their things should occur, one would then see
how much the reputation of the Venetians mattered in the holding of
Tuscany and Romagna. So they were altogether contrary to his opinion,
because they believed that whoever won in Lombardy would win everywhere else; and winning was easy, since by the departure of Niccolò the
state of the duke was so weak that he could be ruined before he could
either recall Niccolò or provide himself with other remedies. Also,
whoever examined each thing wisely would see that the duke had not sent
Niccolò to Tuscany for anything else than to remove the count from these
campaigns and to carry on elsewhere the war that he had at home. So if
the count were to go after him, before an extreme necessity was visible,
one would see the duke's schemes fulfilled and see him succeed in his
intention; but if the troops were maintained in Lombardy, and in Tuscany
one provided as one could, the duke would become aware of his wicked
course too late, in time to have lost in Lombardy without remedy and not
to have won in Tuscany.

Thus, each having stated and repeated his opinion, it was concluded
that they should wait a few days to see what might come out of the accord
of the Malatesti with Niccolò, if the Florentines could make use of Pietro
Gianpaolo, and if the pope was keeping in step with the league as he had
promised. This conclusion reached, a few days later they were assured

---

[2] The doge.

that the Malatesti had made their accord with him more out of fear than for any cause of ill will, that Pietro Gianpaolo had gone with his troops toward Tuscany, and that the pope was more willing to help the league than before. This information put the count's mind at rest, and he was content to remain in Lombardy and that Neri Capponi return to Florence with a thousand of his cavalry and with five hundred others; and if things in Tuscany should proceed so that the count's activity was necessary there, they would write, and then the count would leave without any hesitation. Neri arrived in Florence, therefore, in April with these men, and on the same day Gianpaolo joined him.

30

NICCOLÒ Piccinino, meanwhile, since things were at a stop in Romagna, was scheming to descend on Tuscany. Though he wanted to cross over the mountain at San Benedetto and through the valley of Montone, he found those places so well guarded by the virtue of Niccolò da Pisa that he judged all his effort in that direction would be vain. And because the Florentines were ill provided with both soldiers and heads for this sudden attack, they had sent many of their citizens to guard these passes in the mountains with a hastily assembled infantry, among whom was Messer Bartolomeo Orlandini, a knight to whom the defense of the castle of Marradi and the pass over that mountain had been assigned. Thus, when Niccolò Piccinino judged he could not get through the pass at San Benedetto by the virtue of the one defending it, he judged he could overcome the pass at Marradi through the vileness of the one who had it to defend. Marradi is a fortified place situated at the foot of the mountains that divide Tuscany from Romagna, but on the side that looks toward Romagna, where the Val di Lamona begins; and although it is without walls, nonetheless the river, the mountains, and the inhabitants make it strong, because the men are warlike and faithful, and the river has eroded the earth and raised the banks so that to come from across the valley is impossible whenever the small bridge over the river is defended; and from the mountain side the banks are so rugged that they make the site very secure. Nonetheless, the vileness of Messer Bartolomeo made these men vile and the site very weak; for no sooner had he heard the sound of the enemy troops than he abandoned everything and fled with all his men; nor did he stop until he reached Borgo San Lorenzo. When Niccolò entered the places that had been abandoned, he was full of amazement that they had not been defended and full of joy at having acquired them; and he descended to the Mugello, where he seized some fortified places. He halted his army at Montepulciano and from there raided the whole countryside as far as the mountains of Fiesole. And he was so daring as to cross the Arno, and he plundered and destroyed everything up to three miles from Florence.

3 I

THE Florentines, for their part, were not dismayed, and before anything else they gave attention to keeping their government steady. Of this they could have little doubt because of the good will that Cosimo enjoyed among the people and because they had restricted their chief magistracies to a few powerful men, who held firm with their severity, if indeed there should be anyone malcontent or desirous of new things. Also they knew, from the accords reached in Lombardy, what forces Neri was returning with, and they were expecting troops from the pope, the hope of which kept them going until the return of Neri. When Neri found the city in these disorders and fears, he decided to go into the field to check Niccolò in part from sacking the countryside freely; and having put together more infantry, all from the people, with what cavalry was to be found there, he went forth and retook Remole, which the enemy was holding. Camping there, he prevented Niccolò from raiding and raised hope in the citizens of lifting the enemy encirclement. When Niccolò saw that the Florentines, when bereft of troops, had not made any move and understood with what assurance they lived in that city, it appeared to him that he was using up time in vain, and he decided to make other campaigns so that the Florentines would have cause to send troops after him and give him an opportunity to join battle, after which, if he won, he thought everything else would turn out well for him. In Niccolò's army there was Count Francesco di Poppi, who, since the enemy was in the Mugello, had rebelled against the Florentines with whom he was in league. Although at first the Florentines had been doubtful of him, in order to make him their friend with benefits, they increased his subsidy and made him commissioner over all their towns bordering his. Nonetheless (so great is the love of party in men), neither any benefit nor any fear could make him forget the affection he bore for Messer Rinaldo and the others governing in the former state. So as soon as he learned that Niccolò was near, he sided with him and urged him with every persuasion to get away from the city and go to the Casentino, pointing out to him the strength of the country and with how much security he could keep the enemy hemmed in from there. Niccolò therefore took this advice and, having reached the Casentino, seized Romena and Bibbiena; then he put his camp at Castel

San Niccolò. This fortified place is situated at the foot of the mountains that divide the Casentino from Valdarno, and as it is in a very elevated place and amply garrisoned from within, taking it was difficult, even though Niccolò attacked it continuously with catapults and similar artillery. This siege had lasted more than twenty days, in which time the Florentines had gathered their troops; already three thousand cavalry had assembled under many condottieri at Figline, commanded by Pietro Gianpaolo as captain and by Neri Capponi and Bernardo de' Medici as commissioners. To them came four men sent from Castel San Niccolò to beg them to give aid. The commissioners, having examined the site, saw that they could not help except by going through the mountains above Valdarno, the summit of which could be seized sooner by the enemy than by themselves because the enemy had a shorter route and the Florentines could not hide their approach. Thus it would be going to try a thing that could not succeed and that could result in the ruin of their troops. Hence the commissioners praised the faith of these men and authorized them to surrender when they could no longer defend themselves.

Thus Niccolò took this fortified place thirty-two days after setting up camp there, and the loss of so much time for so little acquired was in good part the cause of the ruin of his enterprise; for if he had stayed with his troops around Florence, he would have made whoever governed that city unable except with hesitation to press the citizens for more money, and they would gather troops and make every other provision only with much difficulty while the enemy was on their backs instead of far away; and many would have been of a mind to move toward some accord to secure themselves from Niccolò with peace when they saw that the war might be lasting. But Count Poppi's wish to avenge himself against the people of Castel San Niccolò, who had long been his enemies, made him give Niccolò that advice; and Niccolò, to satisfy him, took it, which was the ruin of both: it rarely happens that the passions of individuals are not harmful to the general[1] advantage. Niccolò, following this victory, took Rassina and Chiusi. The count of Poppi tried to persuade him to stay in these regions, pointing out to him that he could spread his men among Chiusi, Caprese, and Pieve, that he would have mastery[2] of the mountains and would be able to descend from his position upon the Casentino, Valdarno, Valdichiana, and Val di Tevere and would be ready for any move his enemies might make.

But Niccolò, having considered the roughness of the terrain, told him that his horses did not eat stones, and he went to Borgo San Sepolcro,

[1] Lit.: universal.
[2] Or be lord.

where he was amiably received. From that place he tested the intent of those in Città di Castello, who as friends of the Florentines did not listen to him. And desiring to have the Perugians devoted to him, he went to Perugia with forty cavalry and, being a citizen there, was lovingly received. But in a few days he became suspect there, and he tried many things with the legate and the Perugians but succeeded in none of them; so, having received 8,000 ducats from them, he returned to his army. From there he undertook negotiations in Cortona so as to take it from the Florentines, and since this thing was discovered ahead of time, his schemes were in vain. Among the first citizens of that city was Bartolommeo di Senso. As he was on his way one evening, by order of the captain, to stand watch at a gate, he was met by a friend of his from the country who gave him to understand that he should not go there if he did not want to be killed. Bartolommeo wanted to get to the bottom of this thing, and he found out the order in the dealing they had with Niccolò. This Bartolommeo revealed in turn[3] to the captain, who assured himself of the heads of the conspiracy, doubled the watch at the gates, and waited for Niccolò to come according to the order given. He came at night at the time ordered and, finding himself discovered, returned to his quarters.

32

WHILE things toiled on in Tuscany in this manner with little acquired for the duke's troops, in Lombardy things were not quiet but brought loss and damage to him. For as soon as the weather permitted, Count Francesco went into the field with his army, and because the Venetians had installed their fleet on the lake,[1] the count wanted before everything else to become lord of the water and to drive the duke from the lake, judging that when he had done this, other things would be easy for him. Therefore, with the Venetians' fleet he attacked the duke's and destroyed it, and with his troops on land he took the fortified places that obeyed the duke. So when others of the duke's troops who were then pressing Brescia by land learned of that disaster, they rushed away; and thus Brescia, after being besieged for three years, was freed from the siege. After this victory the count went to meet the enemy, who had assembled at Soncino, a fortified place situated on the river Oglio, and he dislodged them and made them retreat to Cremona, where the duke made a stand and de-

[3] Lit.: in order.
[1] See *FH* v 25 (end).

fended his states from that side. But as the count pressed him harder day by day, the duke, since he feared that he would lose either all or a large part of his states, realized the wickedness of the course he had adopted of sending Niccolò to Tuscany; and to correct the error, he wrote to Niccolò of the straits he was in and where his enterprises had led. Therefore, as soon as he could, Niccolò should leave Tuscany and return to Lombardy. Meanwhile, the Florentines, under their commissioners, had assembled their troops with those of the pope and had halted at Anghiari, a fortified place located at the foot of the mountains that divide Val di Tevere from Valdichiana, four miles away from Borgo San Sepolcro, with a level road and fields suitable for horses and for waging war. And because the Florentines had news of the count's victories and of Niccolò's recall, they judged they had won that war with swords sheathed and without raising dust; and because of this, they wrote to the commissioners to abstain from battle, since Niccolò could not remain for many days in Tuscany. This commission came to the notice of Niccolò; and though seeing the necessity of leaving, he decided to come to battle so as not to leave anything untried, thinking he would find his enemy unprovided and with thoughts far from battle. He was encouraged in this by Messer Rinaldo, by the count of Poppi, and by the other Florentine exiles, who realized their ruin was clear if Niccolò should leave; but if they came to battle, they believed they would either win the campaign or lose it honorably. Having made this decision, he moved the army from where it was between Città di Castello and the Borgo,[2] and, coming to Borgo without the enemy's being aware of it, he drew two thousand men from that town, who followed him, trusting in the virtue of the captain and in his promises and desirous of plunder.

33

SO Niccolò headed toward Anghiari with his ranks drawn for battle and was already closer than two miles to them when a great cloud of dust was seen by Micheletto Attenduli; and as he realized it was the enemy, he gave the cry to arms. The tumult in the Florentine camp was great because, though such armies ordinarily camp without any discipline, here negligence was added, since it appeared to them that the enemy was far away and more disposed to flight than to battle; so everyone was disarmed, far from his quarters and wherever he had been attracted by his wish either to escape the heat, which was great, or to follow some pleasure of his.

[2] Borgo San Sepolcro.

Yet such was the diligence of the commissioners and the captain that before the enemy had arrived, they were mounted and in order so that they could resist his thrust. As Micheletto was the first to discover the enemy, so was he first to arm and meet him, and he ran with his troops over the bridge that crosses the road not very far from Anghiari. And since Pietro Gianpaolo, before the coming of the enemy, had had the ditches that edged the road between the bridge and Anghiari leveled, Micheletto was posted facing the bridge; Simoncino, condottiere for the Church, with his legate, were put on the right-hand side; and on the left were the Florentine commissioners with Pietro Gianpaolo, their captain; and the infantry were placed on each side on the bank of the river. There was no other way left open, therefore, for the enemy to go and meet his adversary than straight over the bridge. Nor did the Florentines have anywhere to fight but the bridge, except that they had so ordered their infantry that if the enemy infantry left the road to reach the flanks of their men-at-arms, they would attack them with crossbows so that the enemy could not strike at the flanks of the Florentine cavalry crossing the bridge. Thus the first troops that appeared were not only vigorously resisted by Micheletto but repulsed by him; but when Astorre and Francesco Piccinino came with their elite troops, they struck Micheletto with such a thrust that they took the bridge from him and pushed him back to the beginning of the slope that rises to the village of Anghiari; then they were repulsed and pushed back off the bridge by Florentines attacking them on their flanks. This battle lasted two hours, during which first Niccolò and then the Florentine troops were masters[1] of the bridge. And although the battle for the bridge was even, nonetheless on either side of the bridge the fighting was to Niccolò's great disadvantage. For when Niccolò s troops crossed the bridge, they found the enemy strong, as they could maneuver on the ground that had been leveled and those who were tired could be relieved by fresh men; but when the Florentine troops crossed the bridge, Niccolò could not conveniently relieve his men because he was constrained by the ditches and banks that bounded the road. So it happened: for Niccolò's troops won the bridge many times, and always they were repelled by the fresh troops of his adversaries. But when the bridge was won by the Florentines, so that their troops gained the road, Niccolò did not have time, because of the fury of those who came and the inconvenience of the site, to relieve his men; those in front were mixed with those behind so that one disordered the other, and the whole army was compelled to turn around and everyone fled toward Borgo[2] without any hesitation. The

[1] Or lords.
[2] Borgo San Sepolcro.

Florentine soldiers attended to the spoil, which was very great in prisoners, harnesses, and horses, for only a thousand cavalry escaped with Niccolò. The inhabitants of Borgo who had followed Niccolò in order to plunder, from plunderers became plunder, and they were all taken and held for ransom; the ensigns and baggage wagons were captured. The victory was much more useful for Tuscany than harmful to the duke: for if the Florentines had lost the day, Tuscany was his; but having lost it himself, he lost nothing more than the arms and horses of his army, which he could replace with not much money. Nor were there ever times when war waged in the countries of others was less dangerous for whoever waged it than these. In such a defeat and in so long a battle that lasted from twenty to twenty-four hours, only one man died, and he not from wounds or any other virtuous blow, but, falling off his horse, he was trampled on and expired.[3] With such security did men fight then: for they were all on horse and covered with armor, and being secure from death whenever they surrendered, there was no cause that they should die. They were defended by arms while fighting, and when they could no longer fight, they surrendered.

34

THIS battle, for the things that happened during the fighting and after, is a great example of the lack of success of these wars. For when the enemy had been conquered and Niccolò had withdrawn to Borgo, the commissioners wanted to follow him and besiege him there so as to have a complete victory. But not one condottiere or soldier was willing to obey them, as they said that they wanted to store their booty and treat their wounds. And what is more noteworthy was that the next day, at noon, without permission or regard for commissioner or captain, they went to Arezzo and, having left their booty there, returned to Anghiari—a thing so contrary to every praiseworthy order and military discipline that any remnant of an army, however ordered, could easily and deservedly have taken from them the victory that they had so undeservedly gained.[1] Besides this, when the commissioners wanted the men of arms who had been taken to be held, so as to deprive the enemy of the opportunity of reforming itself, they freed them despite the will of the commissioners. All things to be marveled at: that in an army so made there was so much

---

[3] NM here departs from his source, Biondo, from whom it appears at least 70 died in the battle of Anghiari.

[1] Lit.: acquired.

virtue that it could win, and that in the enemy there was so much vileness that it could be conquered by such disorderly troops. Thus, in the going and coming of the Florentine troops to Arezzo, Niccolò had time to leave Borgo with his troops, and he went off toward Romagna; with him the Florentine rebels also fled. Having seen every hope of returning to Florence lost, they dispersed in many parts in and out of Italy, as suited each.

Of these, Messer Rinaldo chose to dwell in Ancona; and so as to earn a celestial fatherland for himself, since he had lost his earthly one, he went to the Sepulchre of Christ, whence he returned for the marriage of one of his daughters and while at the table suddenly died. Fortune favored him in this, that on the least unprosperous day of his exile, it had him die. He was a man truly honored in all fortune, but he would have been still more so if nature had had him born in a united city, because many of his qualities hurt[2] him in a divided city that would have rewarded him in a united city. So the commissioners, when their troops had returned from Arezzo and Niccolò had left, presented themselves at Borgo. The inhabitants of Borgo wanted to give themselves up to the Florentines, and the Florentines refused to accept them; and in the dealing for these accords, the legate of the pontiff became suspicious that the commissioners did not want that town to be seized for the Church, so that they came to exchange injurious words. There would have been disorder between the Florentine and ecclesiastical troops if the negotiations had gone on much longer, but because they ended with what the legate wanted, everything was pacified.

35

WHILE things in Borgo toiled on, it was learned that Niccolò Piccinino was on his way toward Rome, and other information said toward the Marches. So to the legate and to Sforza's troops it appeared that they should go toward Perugia to relieve either the Marches or Rome, wherever Niccolò might have gone; with them should go Bernardo de' Medici, and Neri with the Florentine troops should go to acquire the Casentino. This decision made, Neri went to camp at Rassina and took it and with the same thrust took Bibbiena, Prato Vecchio, and Romena; and from there he placed his camp at Poppi and enclosed it from two sides, one on the plain of Certomondo, the other on the hill on the road to Fronzoli. The count of Poppi, seeing himself abandoned by God and by men, had shut himself up in Poppi, not because he had hope of being able to get any help, but to make a less damaging accord if he could. There-

---

[2] Lit.: offended.

fore, as Neri pressed him, he asked for terms and found them as much as he could hope for at that time: to save himself, his children, and the things he could carry, but to yield his town and his state to the Florentines. And when they had stipulated the terms, he came down over the bridge at the Arno, which flows below the town, and all sorrowful and grieving, he said to Neri, "If I had measured well my fortune and your power, I would be coming now as a friend to rejoice with you in your victory, not as an enemy to beg you that my ruin be less grievous. The result now, as it is magnificent and happy for you, is painful and wretched for me. I had horses, arms, subjects, state, and wealth: Is it a marvel that I leave them unwillingly? But if you wish to command all Tuscany, and can do so, we others must obey you of necessity. And if I had not made this error, my fortune would not have been known and your liberality could not be known; for, if you preserve me, you will give to the world an eternal example of your clemency. Therefore, let your pity conquer my misdeed and leave at least this one house to the descendant of those from whom your fathers have received innumerable benefits." To which Neri replied that his having hoped too much in those who could do little had made him so err against the republic of Florence that, adding up present conditions, it was necessary for him to yield all his things and to abandon all those places as an enemy to the Florentines which he had not been willing to hold as their friend. For he had made such an example of himself that he could not be nourished where at every change of fortune he could harm that republic. For not he but his states were feared; but if he could be a prince in Germany, their city would desire it and would support him out of love of those ancestors of his whom he was mentioning. To this the count, quite indignant, answered that he would wish to see the Florentines much farther away. And so, dropping all loving reasoning, the count, seeing no other remedy, yielded the city and all his rights[1] to the Florentines, and with all his property, together with his wife and children, he departed, weeping, lamenting the loss of a state that his fathers had possessed for nine hundred years. As soon as all these victories were learned of in Florence, they were received by the princes of the government and by the people with marvelous joy. And because Bernardetto de' Medici found it to be false that Niccolò had gone toward the Marches or to Rome, he returned with his troops to where Neri was; and together they returned to Florence, where all the greatest honors that according to the order of the city could be decreed for them as victorious citizens were decreed. They were received by the Signori, by the captains of the Party, and then by the whole city in the custom of men triumphant.

¹ Lit.: reasons.

BOOK VI

I

IT has always been the end of those who start a war—and it is reasonable that it should be so—to enrich themselves and impoverish the enemy. For no other cause is victory sought, nor for anyone else are acquisitions desired than to make oneself powerful and the adversary weak. Hence, it follows that whenever your victory impoverishes you[1] or acquisition weakens you, you must forgo it or you will not arrive at the result for which wars are made. A prince or a republic that eliminates enemies and takes possession of booty and ransom is enriched by victories in wars. He who in conquest cannot eliminate enemies is impoverished by victories, and the booty and ransom belong not to him but to his soldiers. Such a one is unprosperous in his losses and very unprosperous in his victories, for in losing he suffers the injuries done him by enemies and in winning, suffers injuries done him by friends. Injuries done by friends, being less reasonable, are less endurable, especially when he sees that it is necessary for him to burden his subjects further with taxes and new offenses. And if he has any humanity himself, he cannot entirely rejoice at a victory by which all his subjects are afflicted. Ancient and well-ordered republics were accustomed to fill their treasuries with gold and silver from their victories, to distribute gifts among the people, to forgive the payment of tribute by their subjects, and to entertain them with games and solemn festivals. But victories in the times we are describing first emptied the treasury, then impoverished the people, and still did not secure you from your enemies. All of this arose out of the disorder with which these wars were conducted; for when conquered enemies were despoiled but then neither detained nor killed, they deferred attacking the conqueror only until whoever led them refurbished them with arms and horses. Since the ransom and booty also belonged to the soldiers, the conquering princes could not make use of them to pay for the new expenses of new enlistments, but tore such expenses from the vitals of their own peoples. Nor did victory bring any other benefit to peoples than to make the prince more eager and less hesitant to tax them. And these soldiers had brought war to such a point that new money was needed equally by the conqueror

[1] The familiar "you."

and the conquered if they wanted to be able to command their own troops. The latter needed money to equip men anew, the former to reward them; and just as those not put back on horse could not fight, the others were unwilling to fight without new rewards. From this it arose that the one enjoyed victory little and the other felt loss little, because the conquered had time to restore himself and the victorious had no time to follow up his victory.

2

THIS disorder and perverse mode in the military made it possible for Niccolò Piccinino to be back on horse before his ruin[1] was known throughout Italy, and he made more war on the enemy after his loss than before. This enabled him to seize Verona after his defeat at Tenna; it enabled him to come into Tuscany with a large army after he had been stripped of his troops at Verona. It enabled him, after being defeated at Anghiari, before coming to Romagna, to be more powerful in the field than before; and he could fill the duke of Milan with hope of being able to defend Lombardy, which, because of Niccolò's absence, appeared to him to have been nearly lost. For while Niccolò filled Tuscany with tumults, the duke was reduced to a strait in which he was afraid for his own state. He judged that his own ruin might come before Niccolò Piccinino, whom he had recalled, could arrive to rescue him. To check the thrust of the count and to temporize with industry the fortune he was unable to sustain with force, he had recourse to remedies that in similar straits had often helped him: he sent Niccolò d'Este, prince of Ferrara, to Peschiera, where the count was. The prince, for his part, urged the count to peace and pointed out to him that this war was not to his advantage, for if the duke so weakened himself that he could not maintain his reputation, the count would be the first to suffer from it because he would no longer be valued by the Venetians and the Florentines. And as proof that the duke desired peace, he offered the count fulfillment of the marriage. The duke would send his daughter to Ferrara, and he promised that when peace was secured, he would give her into his hands. The count answered that if the duke truly sought peace he could find it easily, as it was something desired by the Florentines and the Venetians. The truth was that the duke could hardly be believed because it was known he had never made peace except out of necessity; and when necessity disappeared, the will for war would return to him. Nor could the count put faith in his marriage, since he had been

---

[1] The defeat at Anghiari, *FH* v 33–34.

fooled so many times. Nonetheless, if a peace was concluded, he would then do whatever his friends counseled him about the marriage.

3

THE Venetians, who were suspicious of their soldiers[1] even in things that were unreasonable, were with reason greatly suspicious of these dealings. The count, wishing to dispel that suspicion, continued the war vigorously. Nonetheless, the spirit he had from ambition and the Venetians had from suspicion cooled down, so that for the rest of the summer they made few campaigns. Thus, when Niccolò Piccinino returned to Lombardy and winter had already begun, all the armies had gone to their quarters: the count to Verona, the duke to Cremona, the Florentine troops to Tuscany, and those of the pope to Romagna. After the pope's troops had won at Anghiari, they attacked Forlì and Bologna so as to take them from the hands of Francesco Piccinino, who governed them in the name of his father; but they did not succeed because the cities were vigorously defended by Francesco. Nonetheless, their coming gave the inhabitants of Ravenna such a fright of returning under the empire of the Church that by agreement with Ostasio da Polenta, their lord, they put themselves in the power[2] of the Venetians. The Venetians, as a reward for the town they had received—so that at no time could Ostasio take back from them by force that which with little prudence he had given them— sent him together with one of his sons to die in Candia. Notwithstanding the victory of Anghiari, the pope lacked money for these campaigns, and he sold the castle at Borgo San Sepolcro to the Florentines for twenty-five thousand ducats.[3] While things remained on these terms and it appeared to each that he was safe from war since it was winter, no one thought any more of peace, and especially not the duke, since he had been reassured by Niccolò Piccinino and by the season. He had therefore broken off all reasoning about an accord with the count, and with great diligence he put Niccolò back on horse and made whatever other provision that a future war might require. When the count was informed of this, he went to Venice to consult with its senate about how they should conduct themselves for the coming year. Niccolò, for his part, finding himself in order and seeing his enemy in disorder, did not wait for spring to come; and in the coldest part of winter he crossed the Adda River, entered Bre-

---

[1] The soldiers they hired.
[2] *Potestà.*
[3] See *FH* v 34.

scia, and seized the whole territory except for Asolo and Orzi. There he plundered and captured more than two thousand of Sforza's cavalry who were not expecting the attack. But what displeased the count more and frightened the Venetians more was that Ciarpellone, one of the leading captains of the count, rebelled against him. With this news, the count left Venice immediately and, when he arrived at Brescia, found that Niccolò, having done his damage, had returned to his quarters. Thus, since the count found the war eliminated, he did not think it worthwhile to rekindle it; but since the weather and the enemy had given him opportunity for reordering himself, he wanted to use it so that he could get revenge for the old offenses in the new season. So he had the Venetians recall their troops who were in Tuscany serving the Florentines, and in place of Gattamelata, who was dead, he asked Micheletto Attenduli to lead them.

4

THUS, when spring came, Niccolò Piccinino was the first to take the field, and he besieged Cignano, a fortified place twelve miles away from Brescia. To its aid came the count; and the war was managed between these two captains according to their custom. And since the count feared for Bergamo, he took up camp at Martinengo, a fortified town located in a place from which, once it was taken, he could easily relieve Bergamo. This city had been gravely harmed[1] by Niccolò; and because he had foreseen he could be impeded by his enemy only by way of Martinengo, he had had that town furnished with every defense, so that it was necessary for the count to go with all his forces to take it. Then Niccolò with his whole army placed himself where he cut off supplies to the count; and he had fortified himself with breastworks and bastions so that the count could not attack him except with manifest danger to himself. The thing came to such a strait that the besieger was in greater danger than those in Martinengo who were besieged. Hence, the count could no longer continue the siege because of hunger or get away because of the danger, and a clear victory for the duke was seen and a definite ruin for the Venetians and the count. But fortune, who never lacks a mode to help its friends and disfavor its enemies, made such ambition and insolence grow in Niccolò Piccinino through hope of this victory that, having no respect for the duke or himself, he sent to the duke to say that since he had fought under the duke's ensigns a long time and had not yet acquired enough land to be able to bury himself, he wished to know from him what prizes

---

[1] Lit.: offended.

he might have to reward him for his troubles. For it was in his power[2] to make the duke lord of Lombardy and to put all his enemies into his hands; and since it appeared to him that from a sure victory must arise a sure reward, he desired the duke to give him the city of Piacenza, so that, when wearied of so long in the military, he could find repose there at some time. Nor was he ashamed, in the end, to threaten the duke with dropping the campaign if he did not consent to this demand of his. This injurious and insolent mode of demanding offended the duke so much, and he took such umbrage at it, that he decided he would rather lose the campaign than yield to him. And the duke, whom so many perils and so many threats from his enemies had not subdued, was subdued by the insolent modes of his friends, and he decided to come to an accord with the count. He sent Antonio Guidobono da Tortona to the count and through him offered his daughter and conditions of peace, which were eagerly accepted by the count and all his allies. And with the pacts secretly concluded between them, the duke sent a command to Niccolò to make a truce for one year with the count, pointing out that he was so troubled by expenses that he could not give up a sure peace for a dubious victory. Niccolò was left in wonder at this decision, as he could not understand what cause would move the duke to abandon so glorious a victory, nor could Niccolò believe that, because the duke did not want to reward his friends, he would want to save his enemies. Therefore he opposed this decision in whatever mode appeared best to him, so that the duke was compelled to quiet him by threatening that if he did not consent, he would give him in prey to his soldiers and to his enemies. So Niccolò obeyed with no other spirit than does one who is forced to abandon his friends and fatherland, lamenting his wicked fate, since now fortune, now the duke, were taking victory over his enemies from him. When the truce was made, the marriage of Madonna Bianca and the count was celebrated, and for her dowry the duke consigned the city of Cremona to him. This done, peace was concluded in November of 1441, which Francesco Barbadico and Paolo Trono signed for the Venetians, and Messer Agnolo Acciaiuoli for the Florentines. In it the Venetians gained Peschiera, Asolo, and Lonato, fortified towns of the marquis of Mantua.

5

ALTHOUGH the war in Lombardy had ceased, there remained the armies of the Kingdom; and since they were unable to remain quiet, they were

[2] *Potestà.*

the cause that arms were again taken up in Lombardy. King René had been despoiled of all his realm except Naples by Alfonso of Aragon while the war in Lombardy was toiling on. Thus, as it appeared to Alfonso that he had victory in his hands, he decided while besieging Naples to take from the count Benevento and others of his states that he possessed in the environs; for he judged he could succeed in doing this without danger to himself, as the count was occupied in the wars of Lombardy. This enterprise, therefore, succeeded easily for Alfonso, and with little trouble he seized all those towns. But when the news of peace in Lombardy came, Alfonso feared that the count might come back for the sake of his towns in support of René, and René hoped for him for the same causes. So René sent to plead to the count, begging him to come to rescue a friend and get revenge on an enemy. On the other side, Alfonso begged Filippo that, for the friendship he had for Alfonso, he should give the count so many worries that the count would be occupied in greater enterprises and would necessarily have to let this one go. Filippo accepted this request without thinking that he was disturbing the peace he had made shortly before with so much disadvantage to himself. He therefore let Pope Eugene know that now was the time to get back those towns of the Church that the count was holding; and to do this he offered him Niccolò Piccinino with pay while the war lasted. Niccolò was staying with his troops in Romagna after the peace had been made. Eugene accepted this advice avidly because of his hatred for the count and his desire to get back his own; and if another time he had been deceived by Niccolò with the same hope, he believed that now, since the duke was involved, he could have no fear of deceit; and putting his men beside those of Niccolò, he attacked the Marches. The count, struck by so unexpected an attack, gathered his troops and went against the enemy. Meanwhile, King Alfonso seized Naples; thus all that kingdom except Castelnuovo came into his power.[1] So René, having left Castelnuovo well guarded, departed, and when he came to Florence was received most honorably; he stayed there a few days and, when he saw he could make no more war, left for Marseilles. In the meantime, Alfonso had taken Castelnuovo; and in the Marches, the count found himself inferior to the pope and to Niccolò. So he turned again to the Venetians and Florentines for assistance of men and money, pointing out that if they did not think about checking the pope and the king now, while he was still full of life, they would soon afterward have to think about their own safety, because the pope and the king would side with Filippo and divide Italy among themselves.

The Florentines and the Venetians stayed undecided for some time,

[1] *Potestà.*

235

either because they were judging whether it was good to make enemies of the pope and the king or because they were occupied with things of the Bolognese. Annibale Bentivoglio had driven Francesco Piccinino out of that city, and, to be able to defend himself from the duke, who favored Francesco, Annibale had asked the Venetians and the Florentines for help, and they had not denied it to him. Thus, occupied in these undertakings, they could not resolve whether to help the count. But as it happened that Annibale defeated Francesco Piccinino, and since those things appeared to be settled, the Florentines decided to help the count; but first, to secure themselves with the duke, they renewed their league with him. The duke did not draw back from this, as it was he who had agreed war should be made against the count while King René was in arms; but when he saw René exhausted and deprived of the whole Kingdom, he was not pleased that the count should be despoiled of his states; so he not only agreed to aid the count, but he wrote to Alfonso that he should be content to return to the Kingdom and not make any more war. And although Alfonso did this unwillingly, nonetheless, because of the obligations he had to the duke, he decided to satisfy him and retreated with his troops to the other side of the Tronto.

6

WHILE in Romagna things were toiling on in this way, the Florentines did not remain quiet among themselves. Among the citizens of repute in the government in Florence was Neri di Gino Capponi. Cosimo de' Medici feared his reputation more than any other's because to the great credit he had in the city was added that which he had with the soldiers; for having been at the head of the Florentine armies many times, he had earned it with his virtue and his merits. Besides this, the memory of the victories credited to him and to his father Gino (Gino having taken Pisa[1] and Neri having defeated Niccolò Piccinino at Anghiari[2]) made him loved by many and feared by those who desired not to have him as partner in the government. Among many other heads of the Florentine army was Baldaccio of Anghiari, a very excellent man at war, for in those times there was no one in Italy who surpassed him in virtue of body and spirit. He had so much reputation among the infantry, since he had always been the head of it, that every man considered they should agree with him in every undertaking and every wish of his. Baldaccio was very friendly to

[1] *FH* III 29.
[2] *FH* V 33–34.

Neri, just as Neri loved him for the virtues of which he had always been witness—which was the source of very great suspicion among other citizens. And judging it dangerous to let Baldaccio go and very dangerous to keep him, they decided to eliminate him. Fortune was favorable to this thought of theirs. The Gonfalonier of Justice was Messer Bartolomeo Orlandini. It was he who had been sent to guard Marradi when, as we said above, Niccolò Piccinino came into Tuscany, and it was he who vilely ran away from there and abandoned a pass that was almost defended by its nature.[3] Such vileness displeased Baldaccio, and with injurious words and in letters he made known the mean spirit of this man. Messer Bartolomeo was ashamed of this and greatly displeased, and he was highly desirous of avenging himself, because he thought that by the death of his accuser he could cancel the infamy of his own faults.

7

THIS desire of Messer Bartolomeo's was known to other citizens; so without much trouble they persuaded him he ought to eliminate Baldaccio and with one stroke avenge himself for the injury and free the state from a man whom one needed either to nourish with danger or to dismiss with harm. Therefore, Bartolomeo, having made the decision to kill him, closeted many armed youths in his room, and when Baldaccio came into the piazza where he came every day to deal with the magistrates about his contract, the Gonfalonier sent for him, and Baldaccio obeyed without any suspicion. The Gonfalonier met him and walked with him two or three times up and down the passageway along the chambers of the Signori, while discussing the contract. Then, when the time appeared to him to be right, as they had come close to the room where he had hidden the armed men, he gave them a signal. They jumped out and, finding Baldaccio alone and unarmed, killed him; and once he was dead, they threw him out of the window facing the palace of the Dogana;[1] and from there they carried him into the piazza and cut off his head, and for a whole day made a spectacle of it for all the people. Baldaccio left only one son whom his wife Annalena had borne a few years earlier and who did not live long. Annalena, left deprived of her son and husband, did not wish to be with another man; and, having made a convent of her houses, she shut herself inside with many noblewomen who joined her, where she died and lived in holiness. Her memory, through the convent created and named by her,

[3] *FH* v 30.
[1] The customhouse.

as it lives now, so will it live always. This deed decreased in part the power of Neri and took reputation and friends from him. Nor was this enough for the citizens in the state: because ten years had already passed since the beginning of their state and the authority of the balìa was over, and because many were more spirited in speeches and deeds than was required, the heads of the state, who did not want to lose it, judged it necessary to take it up again by giving new authority to their friends and beating down their enemies. And because of this, in 1444 they created a new balìa through the council that reformed the offices; gave authority to a few, empowering them to create the Signoria; renewed the Chancellery with reforms, depriving Ser Filippo Peruzzi of it, and proposed for it one who would conduct himself according to the views of the powerful; lengthened the term of banishment for the banished; put Giovanni di Simone Vespucci in prison; deprived of their offices couplers[2] of the enemy state, and with them the sons of Piero Baroncelli, all the Serragli, Bartolomeo Fortini, Messer Francesco Castellani, and many others. And by these modes they gave themselves authority and reputation, and took away the confidence of enemies and suspects.

8

WHEN they had thus settled and retaken the state, they turned to things outside. Niccolò Piccinino, as we said above,[1] had been abandoned by King Alfonso, and the count had become powerful with the help he had had from the Florentines. Hence, the count attacked Niccolò near Fermo and defeated him, so that Niccolò, deprived of nearly all his troops, took refuge with a few of them in Montecchio. There he fortified and defended himself so well that in a brief time all his troops returned to him, and in such number that he was easily able to defend himself from the count, especially as winter had already come and both captains were compelled to send their troops to quarters. Niccolò spent the whole winter enlarging his army and was helped by the pope and by King Alfonso; so when spring came, both captains took to the field, where Niccolò, now superior, brought the count to extreme necessity, and he would have been conquered if Niccolò's designs had not been defeated by the duke. Filippo had sent to Niccolò to beg him to come quickly to him because he had to speak to him directly about some very important things. Thus Niccolò, eager to hear him, abandoned a certain victory for an uncertain good; he

---

[2] For "couplers," see *FH* V 4.
[1] *FH* VI 5.

left his son Francesco at the head of the army and went himself to Milan. When the count heard this, he did not lose the opportunity to fight while Niccolò was absent, and when battle was joined near the fortified town of Monte Loro, he defeated Niccolò's troops and captured Francesco. Having arrived in Milan, Niccolò saw he had been taken in by Filippo, and when he learned of the defeat and capture of his son, he died from grief in the year 1445 at the age of sixty-four. He had been a more virtuous than prosperous captain. Surviving him were Francesco and Jacopo, who had less virtue and worse fortune than their father, so that the arms of the Bracci were almost eliminated, and the arms of the Sforza, aided always by fortune, became more glorious. The pope, seeing Niccolò's army defeated and Niccolò dead, and not hoping for much assistance from Aragon, sought peace with the count; and it was concluded through the intervention of the Florentines. Osimo, Fabrino, and Ricanati, among the towns of the Marches, were restored to the pope; all the rest were left under the empire of the count.

9

WHEN peace came in the Marches, all Italy would have been pacified if it had not been disturbed by the Bolognese. In Bologna were two very powerful families, the Canneschi and the Bentivogli; Annibale was head of the latter and Battista of the former.[1] So as to trust each other better, they had contracted marriages between themselves; but among men who aspire to the same greatness, it is easy to make a marriage but not a friendship. Bologna was in a league with the Florentines and Venetians, which had been brought about by Annibale Bentivoglio after the Bolognese had driven out Francesco Piccinino;[2] and as Battista knew how much the duke desired to have that city favorable to him, Battista conferred with him about killing Annibale and bringing the city under the duke's ensigns. Having agreed on the means, on the 24th day of June, in 1445, Battista with his men attacked Annibale and killed him. Then he ran through the town shouting the name of the duke. The Venetian and Florentine commissioners were in Bologna, and at the first clamor they retired to their houses; but when they saw that the people did not favor the killers, that instead, assembled in great number with arms in the piazza, they lamented the death of Annibale, the commissioners raised their spirits, and, finding themselves with these men, they joined them. When they were

[1] Cf. *P* 19.
[2] *FH* VI 5.

set, they attacked the Canneschi men and conquered them in a short time; some they killed, some they drove out of the city. Battista, not having had time to flee, nor his enemies time to kill him, hid inside his own house in a cellar made for storing grain. And while his enemies looked for him all day, since they knew he had not left the city, they so frightened his servants that one of his boys out of fear pointed him out to them. Then pulled from that place still clad in arms, he was first killed and then dragged through the town and burned. Thus the duke's authority was sufficient to get Battista to make the attempt, and his power was not in time to rescue him.

10

THOUGH the tumults were put to rest by the death of Battista and the flight of the Canneschi, the Bolognese remained in very great confusion as there was no one in the house of the Bentivogli fit to govern, since Annibale had left only one son called Giovanni, six years old. So it was feared that division would arise among the friends of the Bentivogli, which might let the Canneschi return, to the ruin of their fatherland and their party. And while they were in this uncertainty of mind, Francesco, who had been the count of Poppi,[1] stopping in Bologna, gave the first men of the city to understand that if they wanted to be governed by one descended from the blood of Annibale, he could instruct them. And he told how, about twenty years ago, Ercole, a cousin of Annibale's, was in Poppi, and Francesco knew that he had known a girl of that fortified town of whom a son called Santi was born from this, whom Ercole had affirmed many times to be his own. Nor did it appear he could deny it, because anyone who knew Ercole and now knew the youth saw a very great likeness between them. These citizens put faith in the words of this man, and they did not delay a moment to send citizens to Florence to identify the youth and to arrange with Cosimo and with Neri that he be given to them. The man reputed to be father of Santi was dead; so the youth was living in the custody of an uncle called Antonio da Cascese. Antonio was rich and childless and a friend of Neri's. Therefore, when Neri understood what this was about, he judged it better neither to despise it nor to accept it rashly; and he asked Santi to talk, in the presence of Cosimo, with those who had been sent from Bologna. They all met together, and Santi was not only honored by the Bolognese but almost worshipped, so powerful in their spirits was love of parties. Nothing was

[1] See *FH* v 35.

yet concluded when Cosimo called Santi aside and said to him: "No one can counsel you better in this case than you yourself, because you have to take that part toward which your spirit inclines you. For if you are going to be the son of Ercole Bentivoglio, you will turn to undertakings worthy of that house and your father; but if you are to be the son of Agnolo da Cascese, you will stay in Florence to waste your life vilely in the wool trade." These words moved the youth, and where at first he had almost declined to take such a course, he said he would be guided in everything by what Cosimo and Neri should decide. So, as they were in accord with the Bolognese who had been sent, Santi was adorned with clothes, horses, and servants, and shortly afterward, accompanied by many, he was taken to Bologna, where he was made governor of Annibale's son[2] and of the city. He conducted himself with so much prudence that in the place where his ancestors had all been killed by their enemies, he lived peacefully and died most honorably.

II

AFTER the death of Niccolò Piccinino and the ensuing peace in the Marches, Filippo desired to have a captain to command his armies and held secret talks with Ciarpellone, one of Count Francesco's head men. When an accord between them had been settled, Ciarpellone asked the count for permission to go to Milan to take possession of some fortified places that had been given to him by Filippo in the recent wars. The count feared what was; so, to prevent the duke from making use of Ciarpellone against his own designs, he had Ciarpellone first arrested and shortly afterward killed, alleging to have found him in a fraud against himself. Filippo was very greatly displeased and indignant at this—which pleased the Florentines and Venetians, for they feared very much lest the arms of the count and the power of Filippo become friendly. This indignation, therefore, was the cause of inciting a new war in the Marches. The lord of Rimini, Sigismondo Malatesta, being the count's son-in-law, was hoping for the lordship of Pesaro; but when the count seized it, he gave it to his brother Alessandro—at which Sigismondo became strongly indignant. To this indignation was added the fact that Federico da Montefeltro, his enemy, had seized the lordship of Urbino through the support of the count. This made Sigismondo come over to the duke and urge the pope and the king to make war on the count. The count, to make Sigismondo feel the first fruits of the war he desired, decided to anticipate him and, in

[2] Giovanni.

one stroke, attacked him. Thereafter Romagna and the Marches were quickly filled again with tumults, because Filippo, the king, and the pope sent much aid to Sigismondo, and the Florentines and Venetians provided the count with money if not troops. Nor was the war in Romagna enough for Filippo, but he schemed also to take Cremona and Pontremoli from the count; but Pontremoli was defended by the Florentines and Cremona by the Venetians. As a result, the war was renewed in Lombardy, where after some travails in the territory of Cremona, Francesco Piccinino, the duke's captain, was defeated at Casale by Micheletto and by troops of the Venetians. Through this victory the Venetians hoped to be able to take the duke's state from him, and they sent a commissioner of theirs to Cremona; they attacked Ghiaradadda and seized all of it except for Crema; after that, crossing the Adda, they raided as far as Milan. So the duke appealed to Alfonso and begged Alfonso to rescue him, pointing out the dangers to the Kingdom if Lombardy were in the hands of the Venetians. Alfonso promised to send him help—which, without the count's consent, could get through only with difficulty.

12

THEREFORE, Filippo appealed to the count with prayers that he must not abandon his father-in-law, already old and blind. The count felt himself offended by the duke for having begun war against him; on the other hand, the greatness of the Venetians did not please him; already he lacked money, and the league was providing it sparingly because the Florentines had lost the fear of the duke that had made them value the count; and the Venetians desired his ruin because they judged that the state of Lombardy could not be taken from them except by the count. Nonetheless, while Filippo was seeking to draw the count into his pay and was offering him the principate of all his troops on condition that he leave the Venetians and restore the Marches to the pope, the Venetians were also sending ambassadors to him promising him Milan, should they take it, and the permanent captaincy of their troops on condition that he pursue the war in the Marches and prevent aid from Alfonso from coming into Lombardy. Thus, the promises of the Venetians were great and their deserts very great, for they had made war to save Cremona for the count; on the other hand, the duke's injuries were fresh, and his promises untrustworthy and weak. Even so, the count was in doubt as to which side he should choose: for on one side his obligation to the league, the faith he had pledged, their recent deserts, and the promise of future things moved him. On the other side were the prayers of his father-in-law, and above all the poison that he feared might be hidden under the grand promises of the Venetians, for he judged that as to both promises and state he would have to remain at their discretion from whatever time they conquered—to which no prudent prince would, except out of necessity, ever deliver himself. The count's difficulties in deciding were removed by the ambition of the Venetians. Having hope of seizing Cremona through certain understandings they had within the city, they had their soldiers move close to the city under another color. But the thing was discovered by those on guard for the count so that the scheme proved vain. Because of this, they did not acquire Cremona and they lost the count, who, setting aside all hesitations, took the side of the duke.

13

POPE Eugene had died, and Nicholas V had been created as his successor. The count already had his whole army at Cotignola ready to move into Lombardy when news reached him that Filippo had died, which happened at the end of August, in the year 1447. This news filled the count with anxieties because it appeared to him his men would not be in order since they had not had their full pay; he feared the Venetians, who were in arms and were his enemies, as he had so recently left them to join the duke; he feared his perpetual enemy Alfonso; he had hope in neither the pope nor the Florentines: not in the Florentines, for being allied with the Venetians, and not in the pope, as he possessed some towns of the Church. Yet he decided to show his face to fortune and to take counsel according to its accidents, because many times when one acts, plans reveal themselves that, to one standing still, would always be hidden. He put great hope in the belief that if the Milanese wanted to defend themselves from the ambitions of the Venetians, they could not turn to any other arms but his. And so in good spirit, he advanced into the territory of Bologna, and when he had passed Modena and Reggio, he halted with his men by the Enza; and he sent an offer of himself to Milan.

When the duke died, some of the Milanese wanted to live free, some under a prince. Of those who loved the prince, one part wanted the count, the other King Alfonso. Therefore, since those who loved liberty were more united, they prevailed over the others and ordered a republic to suit themselves. It was not obeyed by many cities in the dukedom, since they judged they too could enjoy their liberty as did Milan; and those cities that did not aspire to liberty did not want the lordship of the Milanese. So Lodi and Piacenza gave themselves to the Venetians; Pavia and Parma made themselves free. When the count heard of these confusions, he went to Cremona, where his spokesmen met together with those of the Milanese, with the conclusion that the count would be captain of the Milanese under terms that had last been made with Duke Filippo. To these terms they added that Brescia should belong to the count, and if he acquired Verona, it should be his and Brescia given back.

14

BEFORE the duke died, Pope Nicholas, after his assumption of the pontificate, sought to create peace among the Italian princes. For this he arranged, with the spokesmen that the Florentines had sent him at his creation, for a diet to be held in Ferrara to negotiate either a long truce or a firm peace. Thus the pope's legate, the Venetian, ducal, and Florentine spokesmen met in that city; those of King Alfonso did not attend. Alfonso was in Tivoli with many troops on foot and on horse, and from there he supported the duke; and it was believed that since the king and the duke had drawn the count to their side, they meant to attack the Florentines and the Venetians openly, and that they would maintain the peace negotiations at Ferrara only for as long as the count's troops delayed coming to Lombardy. The king sent no one there, asserting that he would ratify whatever was agreed to by the duke. The peace was negotiated for many days, and after many arguments a peace forever or a truce for five years was concluded, whichever of the two should please the duke; but when the ducal spokesmen went to Milan to learn the duke's will, they found him dead. The Milanese wanted to carry out the accord notwithstanding his death, but the Venetians did not, for they had taken up very great hopes of seizing that state, especially when they saw that Lodi and Piacenza, immediately after the death of the duke, had surrendered to them. So they hoped to be able by either force or accord to strip Milan in a short time of all its state and then to overpower it so that it would surrender before anyone could help; and they were all the more persuaded of this when they saw the Florentines involved in war with King Alfonso.

15

THAT king was in Tivoli, and he wanted to pursue the campaign in Tuscany according to what he had decided upon with Filippo. As it appeared to him that the war that had already begun in Lombardy would give him time and opportunity, he desired to put a foot in the Florentine state before he moved openly. So he made a deal in the fortress of Cennina in upper Valdarno, and seized it. The Florentines, shaken by this unexpected accident and seeing the king had moved to come and harm them, hired soldiers, created the Ten, and according to their custom prepared for war. Already the king had arrived with his army near the territory of Siena and was making every effort to win that city to his wishes. Those citizens, however, remained firm in their friendship with the Florentines and did not receive the king in Siena or in any of their towns; they did provide him with supplies, for which their impotence and the strength of the enemy excused them. To the king it did not appear good to enter by way of Valdarno, as he had schemed at first, both because he had lost Cennina and because the Florentines were already provided with troops in some places; and he set out toward Volterra and seized many fortified towns around Volterra. From there he went to the territory of Pisa and, through favors done him by Arrigo and Fazio, counts of the Gherardesca family, he took some fortified towns and from these attacked Campiglia, which he was unable to capture because it was defended by the Florentines and by winter. Then the king left a guard to defend the towns he had taken and to be able to raid the countryside, and with the rest of his army withdrew to quarters in the country around Siena.

The Florentines, meanwhile, aided by the season, with all zeal provided themselves with troops, at whose head were Federico, the lord of Urbino, and Sigismondo Malatesta of Rimini. Although there was discord between them, yet by the prudence of the commissioners, Neri di Gino and Bernardetto de' Medici, they were kept united so that they went into the field though it was still deep in winter, and they retook the towns lost around Pisa and Pomarance in the territory of Volterra; and the king's soldiers who before had plundered the Maremma were checked so that they could hardly keep the towns given them to be guarded. But when spring came, the commissioners brought all their troops to halt at Spedaletto, in number five thousand cavalry and two thousand infantry; and the king came with his men, numbering fifteen thousand, to within three miles of Campiglia. And when it was assumed that he would turn to besiege that town, he threw himself upon Piombino, hoping to take it easily because that town was ill provided and because he judged that that acquisition would be very useful to him and very destructive to the Florentines—since from that place he could wear out the Florentines with a long war by getting provisions by sea and agitating all the country around Pisa. This attack displeased the Florentines, therefore, and, consulting with each other about what to do, they judged that if they could stay with the army in the thickets of Campiglia, the king would be forced to depart either defeated or disgraced. And for this they armed four galleys they had at Livorno and with them posted three hundred infantry in Piombino, and because they judged it dangerous to camp in the thickets of the plain, they stationed them at Caldana, a place where it would be difficult to attack them.

16

THE Florentine army was getting its provisions from the surrounding towns, which, as they were few and thinly populated, provided them with difficulty. The army was suffering, especially from the lack of wine, for since they were not getting it there and could not get it elsewhere, it was not possible for everyone to have some. But the king, even though closely confined by the Florentine troops, had plenty of everything except fodder because all was brought in by sea. Therefore, the Florentines wanted to try whether their troops could also be supplied by sea, and they loaded four of their galleys with supplies and had them come. They were met by seven of the king's galleys, and two of them were taken and two chased away. This loss made the Florentine troops lose hope of fresh supplies, whereupon two hundred or more foragers fled to the camp of the king, especially for lack of wine; and the other troops grumbled, asserting that they were not about to stay in very hot places where there was no wine and the water was bad. So the commissioners decided to abandon that place and turned to the recapture of certain fortified towns that still remained in the hands of the king. The king, for his part, even though he did not suffer for want of supplies and was superior in troops, also saw himself in need because his army was full of diseases that marshy places by the sea produce in that season. The diseases were of such power that many died from them and almost all were ill. Hence negotiations toward an accord were begun, in which the king demanded fifty thousand florins and that Piombino be left to his discretion. When this thing was debated in Florence, many desirous of peace accepted it, asserting that they did not know how they could hope to win a war when so many expenses were necessary to sustain it. But Neri Capponi, who had gone to Florence,[1] so discouraged this proposal with his reasons that all the citizens with one accord agreed not to accept it; and they received the lord of Piombino[2] under their protection and promised to help him in time of peace and war on condition that he not surrender and that he want to defend himself as he had until now. When the king learned of this decision and saw that because of the illness in his army he could not acquire the

---

[1] In fact, he remained with the Florentine army near Piombino.
[2] Rinaldo Orsini.

town, he got out almost as if he had been routed from his camp. He left more than two thousand dead there; and with the remainder of his sick army he retired to the country around Siena and from there into the Kingdom, full of indignation against the Florentines and menacing them with another war in another season.

17

WHILE things were toiling on in a like mode in Tuscany, in Lombardy Count Francesco, who had become captain of the Milanese,[1] before everything else made himself the friend of Francesco Piccinino, who was fighting for the Milanese, so that he would support the count in his enterprises or be more hesitant to injure him. Thus the count gathered his army in the field, so that people in Pavia judged they could not defend themselves against his forces; and since they did not want on the other hand to submit to the Milanese, they offered the town to him with this condition, that he not put them under the empire of Milan. The count desired to take possession of that city, for it appeared to him a bold beginning, enabling him to color over his designs; nor was he restrained by fear or shame in breaking his faith, for great men call it shame to lose, not to acquire by deceit. But he was afraid that by taking it he might so anger the Milanese that they would give themselves to the Venetians; and if he did not take it, he feared the duke of Savoy, to whom many citizens wanted to give themselves;[2] and in either case it appeared he would be deprived of empire over Lombardy. Nonetheless, thinking the danger of taking that city might be less than that of letting it be taken by someone else, he decided to accept it, persuading himself that he could calm the Milanese. He made them understand the dangers that would be incurred if he had not accepted Pavia, for those citizens would have given themselves to either the Venetians or the duke, and in either case their state was lost. And they ought to be content to have him nearby as a friend rather than a power[3] such as either of those and hostile. The Milanese were very much disturbed by this case, since it appeared to them that they had discovered the count's ambition and the end toward which he was heading; but they judged they could not reveal themselves because they did not see, if they broke off with the count, where to turn other than to the Venetians, whose pride and harsh conditions they feared. Because of this,

---

[1] See *FH* VI 12, 13.

[2] Ludovico of Savoy, son of Amedeo VIII; he was also a brother-in-law of the deceased Filippo Maria Visconti.

[3] Lit.: a powerful one.

they decided not to break with the count and for the time being to remedy through him the evils that hung over them, while hoping that, once freed from those, they would also be able to free themselves from him, because they were being attacked not only by the Venetians but also by the Genoese and the duke of Savoy, in the name of Charles of Orleans, born of a sister of Filippo.[4] This attack the count suppressed with little trouble. Thus there remained as enemies only the Venetians, who with a powerful army wanted to seize that state and were holding Lodi and Piacenza. The count laid a siege on Piacenza and after much trouble took it and sacked it. Then, because winter had come, he returned his men to their quarters and then went himself to Cremona, where all winter he rested with his wife.

18

BUT when spring came, the Venetian and Milanese armies went into the field. The Milanese desired to acquire Lodi and then to make an accord with the Venetians, because the expenses of the war were becoming burdensome to them and the faith of their captain[1] was suspect to them; so they were exceedingly desirous of peace so as to gain rest and secure themselves against the count. They decided, therefore, that their army should go to acquire Caravaggio, as they hoped that Lodi would surrender when that fortified town was taken from the hands of the enemy. The count obeyed the Milanese, even though his desire[2] would have been to cross the Adda and attack the territory of Brescia. Thus, having left a siege at Caravaggio, he fortified himself with ditches and other defenses, so that if the Venetians wanted to make him lift the siege, they would have to attack him at their disadvantage. The Venetians on the other side came with their army, under their captain Micheletto, within two bowshots of the count's camp; there they lingered for several days and had many skirmishes. Nonetheless, the count kept squeezing the fortified town and brought it to the point where it had to surrender. This was distressing to the Venetians, since it appeared to them that with the loss of that town they had lost the campaign. Among their captains, therefore, a very great dispute arose about the mode of relieving it, and they saw no other way except to penetrate the defenses to find the enemy, where the disadvantage was very great; but they so valued the loss of that fortified town that

[4] Charles of Orleans was the son of Louis of Orleans and Valentina Visconti, sister of Filippo Maria.
[1] Francesco Sforza, captain of the Milanese, is probably meant; Micheletto Attendolo was captain for the Venetians (see below).
[2] *Animo*: his intent if possible.

the Venetian senate, naturally timid and far removed from any dubious and dangerous policy, preferred to put everything in danger so as not to lose that town rather than with the loss of it to lose the campaign. So they made a decision to attack the count in any mode whatever, and, rising early one morning armed, they attacked him on the side that was less guarded, and in the first thrust, as happens in attacks that are not expected, they upset the whole of Sforza's army. But so quickly was all the disorder repaired by the count that his enemies, after having made many efforts to get over the embankments, were not only thrown back but so routed and broken that of the whole army, in which there had been more than twelve thousand cavalry, not one thousand were saved, and all their articles and wagons were plundered: never before that day had greater and more frightening ruin been dealt to the Venetians. And among the booty and men taken was found a Venetian quartermaster,[3] completely dejected, who before the battle and in managing the war had spoken abusively of the count, calling him bastard and vile; so, finding himself a prisoner after the defeat and remembering his faults and fearing to be rewarded in accordance with his deserts, he arrived before the count, all timid and frightened according to the nature of proud and vile men, which is to be insolent in prosperity and abject and humble in adversities, threw himself down on his knees, weeping, and asked to be forgiven for the injuries he had done against him. The count raised him up and, taking him by the arm, gave him good spirit and urged him to hope for the good. Then he told him that he marveled that one who wanted to be considered a man of prudence and gravity should have fallen into so great an error as to speak basely about those who did not deserve it. And as to those things for which he had been reproached, he did not know what Sforza, his father, might have done with Madonna Lucia, his mother, because he was not there and could not have provided them the modes of their union, so that, as for what they had done, he did not believe he could get either blame or praise from it; but he knew well that, of what he himself had had to do, he had conducted himself so that no one could reproach him: of this he and his senate could provide fresh and true testimony. He urged him in the future to be more modest in speaking of others and more cautious in his undertakings.

19

AFTER this victory the count came with his victorious army into the territory of Brescia and seized the whole countryside; and then he placed his

---

[3] NM left the name blank in manuscript.

camp two miles from Brescia. After receiving the defeat, the Venetians, for their part, feared, as did happen, that Brescia would be the first blow, and they had provided it with as good a guard as quickly as could be found. Then with all diligence they gathered forces and brought them together with the remnants they could get from their army; and they asked the Florentines for help by virtue of their league. Because the Florentines were free of the war with King Alfonso, they sent a thousand infantry and two thousand cavalry in aid of the Venetians. With these forces, the Venetians had time to think about accords. It was at one time something almost fated to the Venetian republic to lose in war and to win in accords; and those things that they lost in the war, peace later gave back to them many times doubled.

The Venetians knew that the Milanese feared the count, that the count desired to be not captain but lord of the Milanese, and that the choice was theirs to make peace with one of the two—the one desiring peace out of ambition and the other out of fear; and they elected to make peace with the count and to offer him help in the acquisition of Milan. And they were persuaded that as soon as the Milanese saw they had been deceived by the count, in their indignation they would be willing to subject themselves to anyone rather than to him, and when they had brought themselves to such a strait that they could neither defend themselves nor trust the count any longer, they would be forced, having nowhere to throw themselves, to fall into the lap of the Venetians. Having adopted this plan, they tried the intent of the count and found him very much disposed to peace, since what he desired was that the victory at Caravaggio should be his and not for the Milanese. Thereupon they made an accord in which the Venetians obligated themselves to pay the count, for as long as it took him to acquire Milan, thirteen thousand florins per month, and also to help him with four thousand cavalry and two thousand infantry during the war. The count, for his part, obligated himself to restore to the Venetians their towns, prisoners, and anything else that had been seized by him in that war, and to be content himself with only those towns that Duke Filippo possessed at his death.

20

AS soon as this accord became known in Milan, the city was saddened much more than it had been gladdened by the victory of Caravaggio. The princes lamented, the popular men grieved, women and children wept, and all together called the count traitor and disloyal. And even though they did not believe that they could recall him from his ungrateful resolve with either prayers or promises, they sent ambassadors to him to see with what face and what words he would accompany his wickedness. When they came before the count, therefore, one of them spoke in this sense: "Usually those who desire to obtain something from someone assail him with prayers, rewards, or threats, so that he will condescend to do whatever they desire of him, moved by mercy, or profit, or fear. But with men who are cruel, very avaricious, and, in their own opinion, powerful, these three modes have no place, for those who believe that they will humble such men with prayer, or win them with rewards, or frighten them with threats trouble themselves in vain. As we therefore recognize your cruelty, ambition, and pride now—though late—we come to you[1] not because we wish to entreat you for anything, nor in the belief that we would obtain it if indeed we asked for it, but to remind you of the benefits you have received from the people of Milan and to show you with how much ingratitude you have repaid them, so that, at least among so many ills we feel, we may taste some pleasure by rebuking you. You ought to remember very well what your situation was after the death of Duke Filippo: you were an enemy of the pope and the king; you had deserted the Florentines and the Venetians, to whom you had become almost an enemy because of their just and fresh indignation and because they had no more need of you; you were weary of the war you were carrying on with the Church, with few troops, without friends, without money, and deprived of all hope of being able to hold your states and your former reputation. Because of these things, you would easily have fallen if it had not been for our simplicity; for we alone received you at home, moved by the reverence we had for the prosperous memory of our duke, with whom you had a marriage of alliance and a new friendship. We believed your love would pass to his heirs,[2] and if to his benefits ours should be joined, the friendship ought to be not only firm but inseparable. That is why we added Verona or Brescia to the old agreements.[3] What more could we have given you and promised you? And you, what more could you—I do not say get, but even desire—I do not say from us, but in those times, from anyone? You received from us, therefore, an unhoped-for good, and we in return received from you an unhoped-for evil. Nor have you delayed until now to show us your wicked intent, because no sooner were you prince of our armies than you accepted Pavia against all justice;[4] this ought to have warned us what must have been the aim of this friendship of yours. We bore this injury thinking that the greatness of this acquisition must fulfill your ambition. Alas! To those who desire the whole, a part cannot be satisfying. You promised that from then on we would

---

[1] The familiar "you" throughout this speech.
[2] Apparently to the Milanese.
[3] See *FH* vi 13 (end).
[4] *FH* vi 17.

enjoy the acquisitions made by you, because you well knew that what you gave us at many times you could take back from us at a stroke: thus it was after the victory of Caravaggio. That victory, prepared first with our blood and with our money, was then followed by our ruin. Oh, how unprosperous are those cities that have to defend their liberty against the ambition of one who wants to oppress them! But much more unprosperous are those who must of necessity defend themselves with mercenary and faithless arms like yours! At least may this example profit posterity, since that of Thebes and Philip of Macedon was of no value to us. Philip, after the victory over their enemies, from their captain became first their enemy and then their prince.⁵ We cannot therefore be accused of any other fault than of having trusted very much in one in whom we should have trusted little; for your past life, your vast spirit, never content with any rank or state, should have warned us. Nor should we have put hope in one who had betrayed the lord of Lucca, levied ransom on the Florentines and the Venetians, lightly esteemed the duke, insulted a king, and above all persecuted God and His Church with so many injuries; nor should we ever have believed that so many princes would have less authority in the breast of Francesco Sforza than the Milanese, and that he would have to observe that faith with us which he had violated many times with others. Nonetheless, this imprudence that accuses us does not excuse your perfidy or purge the infamy that our just quarrels will bring upon you throughout the whole world. Nor will it keep the just pricking of your conscience from tormenting you when the arms that were prepared by us to injure and frighten others will come to wound and injure us, because you yourself will judge yourself worthy of the punishment parricides have deserved. And even if ambition blinds you, the whole world as witness to your wickedness will open your eyes; God will open them for you, if perjuries, if violated faith and betrayals displease Him, and if He does not always wish to be the friend of wicked men, as up to now He has done for some hidden good. So do not promise yourself sure victory, for that will be kept from you by the just wrath of God; and we are ready to lose our liberty with death; if ever we cannot defend it, we will submit to any other prince rather than you. And even if our sins have yet been such that we have fallen into your hands against every wish of ours, have firm faith that the kingdom you have begun with deceit and infamy will come to an end for you or your sons with disgrace and harm."⁶

⁵ Cf. *P* 12; *D* II 13.

⁶ On the acquiring and maintaining of Milan by Sforza, see *P* 1, 7, 12, 14, 20; *D* II 24; *AW* I.

ALTHOUGH the count felt stung on every side by the Milanese, he answered, without showing any extraordinary change with either words or gestures, that he was content to attribute the grave injury of their unwise words to their irate spirits. He would answer in detail if he were before someone who ought to be judge of their differences, because one would see he had not injured the Milanese but had provided for himself that they could not injure him. For they well knew how they had conducted themselves after the victory at Caravaggio: instead of rewarding him with Verona or Brescia, they had sought to make peace with the Venetians so that the burdens of the Venetians' hostility were left to him alone and the fruits of the victory, with the credit of peace and all the profit that had been gained from the war, were left to them. So they could not complain if he had made the accord that they had tried to make first; if he had delayed the least bit in taking that course, he would now have to reproach them for the same ingratitude with which they now reproached him. Whether this was true or not, that God upon whom they called to avenge their injuries would demonstrate at the end of the war; through Him they will see which of them is more His friend and which has fought with greater justice. When the ambassadors had departed, the count ordered himself so as to be able to assault the Milanese, and they prepared for defense. They thought that with Francesco and Jacopo Piccinino, who had been faithful to the Milanese because of the ancient hatred of the Bracci for the Sforza, they would defend their liberty at least until they could detach the Venetians from the count, for the Milanese did not believe that the Venetians meant to be either faithful or friendly for long. For his part, the count, who recognized this same thing, thought it would be a wise course to keep the Venetians firm with a reward, since he judged that obligation would not be enough. Therefore, in assigning the campaigns of the war he was content to have the Venetians attack Crema, and he, with the other troops, would attack the rest of the state. This meal set before the Venetians was the cause that their friendship with the count lasted until the count had seized the whole dominion of the Milanese and had so restricted them to their town that they could not provide themselves with any necessary thing. So despairing were they of all other help that they sent spokesmen to the Venetians to beg them to have compassion in their regard and to be content, in accordance with what ought to be the custom of republics, to favor their liberty and not a tyrant whom, if he should succeed in becoming lord of their city, the Venetians would not be able to restrain at will. Nor should the Venetians believe that the count would be content with the boundaries set down on paper, for he would want to restore the former boundaries of the Milanese state. The Venetians had not yet become lord of Crema, and as they wanted to become its lord before they showed a change of face, they answered publicly that they could not help the Milanese because of their accord with the count; but in private they dealt with the Milanese so that the Milanese, hoping for an accord, could give their signori a firm hope in it.

22

THE count with his men was already so close to Milan that he was fighting in the outskirts when to the Venetians, who had taken Crema, it appeared that they should no longer postpone making an alliance with the Milanese. They came to an accord with the Milanese, and, among the chief articles, the Venetians promised to do their utmost for the defense of their liberty. When the accord was made, the Venetians directed the troops they had with the count to leave his camps and withdraw into Venetian territory. They also informed the count of the peace they had made with the Milanese and gave him twenty days' time to accept it. The count did not marvel at the course taken by the Venetians because he had foreseen it a long time before and feared it might happen any day. Nonetheless, now that it had happened, he could not help lamenting it and feeling the same distress the Milanese had felt when he abandoned them. He took two days to respond to the ambassadors who had been sent by Venice to tell him of the accord—during which time he decided to divert the Venetians and not abandon his enterprise. And therefore he said publicly that he wanted to accept the peace, and he sent his ambassadors to Venice with full mandate to ratify it, but aside he charged them that in no mode should they ratify it but that they should postpone concluding it with various contrivances and dodges. And to make the Venetians more ready to believe that he told the truth, he made a truce with the Milanese for one month, withdrew from Milan, and distributed his troops to quarters in places they had seized in the vicinity. This course was the cause of his victory and of the ruin of the Milanese; for the Venetians, trusting in the peace, were slower in providing for a war, and the Milanese, seeing the truce made, the enemy moving away, and the Venetians friendly, wholly believed that the count was about to abandon his enterprise. This opinion harmed them in two modes: one was that they neglected orders for their own defense; the other was that in country free of the enemy, since it was the time for sowing, they had sown much grain—hence, the result was that the count could starve them more quickly. To the count on the other hand, all those things were advantageous that injured his enemies; and furthermore, that time gave him opportunity to be able to catch his breath and provide himself with assistance.

23

IN this war in Lombardy, the Florentines had not declared themselves for either side. They had not given any favor to the count, neither when he was defending the Milanese nor afterward, because the count had no need then and had not sought aid with any urgency. They had sent aid only to the Venetians, after the defeat at Caravaggio, by virtue of their obligations to the league.[1] But when Count Francesco was left alone and had no recourse anywhere, it became necessary for him to request aid urgently from the Florentines, both publicly from the state and privately from friends—especially from Cosimo de' Medici, with whom he had always maintained a constant friendship and by whom he had always been faithfully counseled and handsomely assisted in every enterprise. Nor in this great necessity did Cosimo abandon him, but as a private citizen he helped him abundantly and encouraged him to pursue his enterprise. He also desired the city to help him publicly; but here was difficulty. In Florence, Neri di Gino Capponi was very powerful. To him it did not appear a benefit to the city that the count should seize Milan, and he believed it would be more for the safety of Italy that the count ratify the peace[2] rather than continue the war. First, he feared that the Milanese, out of indignation against the count, might give themselves entirely to the Venetians—which would be the ruin of everyone. Then, if indeed the count should succeed in seizing Milan, it appeared to him that so many arms joined with such a state would be formidable, and if as count he was unbearable, he judged that as a duke he would be most unbearable. Therefore, he asserted that it would be better for the republic of Florence and for Italy that the count rest content with his reputation for arms and that Lombardy be divided into two republics, which would never unite to offend the others, while each would be unable to offend by itself. And to do this, he saw no better remedy than not to support the count and to maintain the old league with the Venetians. These reasons were not accepted by Cosimo's friends because they believed Neri was moved to this conclusion not because he believed that this was for the good of the republic but because he did not want the count, a friend of Cosimo's, to become duke,

[1] See *FH* VI 19.
[2] See *FH* VI 22.

since it appeared to him that by this Cosimo would become too powerful. And Cosimo also used reasons to show that helping the count was very useful to the republic and to Italy, because to him it was hardly a wise opinion to believe that the Milanese could keep themselves free. For the qualities of their citizenry, their mode of living, and the ancient sects in that city were contrary to every form of civil government, so that it was necessary that either the count become their duke or the Venetians their lords; and in such a case no one was so foolish as to doubt which would be better, to have a powerful friend close by or a very powerful enemy. Nor did he believe it was to be feared that the Milanese, by having a war with the count, would submit themselves to the Venetians, for the count had a party in Milan and the Venetians did not; therefore, whenever they could not defend themselves as free men, they would always sooner submit to the count than to the Venetians. These differences of opinion kept the city in great suspense; and in the end they decided that ambassadors should be sent to the count to deal with the mode of an accord; and if they should find the count strong enough to enable them to hope he would win, they should conclude one, but if not, they should make difficulties and postpone it.

24

THESE ambassadors were in Reggio when they learned that the count had become lord of Milan. For when the period of the truce was over, the count returned with his troops to that city, hoping to seize it in a short time despite the Venetians, because they could not relieve it except from the direction of the Adda, a passage he could easily close off. Since it was winter, he did not fear that the Venetians would encamp near him, and he hoped to have victory before the winter should end, especially as Francesco Piccinino had died and his brother Jacopo was left alone as head of the Milanese. The Venetians had sent one of their spokesmen to Milan to urge its citizens to be ready to defend themselves, promising them great and speedy assistance. Thus, during the winter, some light skirmishes continued between the Venetians and the count, but as the weather became milder, the Venetians under Pandolfo Malatesta[1] came to a halt with their army on the Adda. In resolving there whether, to rescue Milan, they ought to attack the count and try their fortune in battle, Pandolfo, their captain, decided he was not about to make this experiment, as he knew the virtue of the count and of his army. And he believed that he could

---

[1] Sigismondo Pandolfo Malatesta; see *FH* VI 11.

win for sure without fighting, because the count would be driven away by want of fodder and grain. He advised, therefore, that they remain in that encampment to give the Milanese hope of rescue so that they would not surrender in despair to the count. This course was approved by the Venetians because they judged it sound and also because they had hope that by keeping the Milanese in that necessity they would be forced to put themselves again under the Venetian empire; they had persuaded themselves that the Milanese would never give themselves to the count, considering the injuries they had received from him. Meanwhile, the Milanese had been brought almost to extreme misery; and as that city naturally abounded with poor, they were dying of hunger in the streets; hence, uproar and complaints arose in different places in the city. The magistrates were greatly afraid of this and made every effort to keep people from gathering together. The whole multitude is slow enough to turn to evil, but when so inclined, every little accident moves it. Thus, while two men of not much consequence were discussing near the Porta Nuova the calamity of the city and their own misery and what modes there might be for safety, others began to join them, so that they became a goodly number—whence rumors spread throughout Milan that those at the Porta Nuova were in arms against the magistrates. Because of this, the whole multitude, which was only waiting to be moved, took up arms; they made Gaspare da Vimercate their head and went to the place where the magistrates were assembled. So violent were they against the magistrates that they killed all those who could not flee; among them was Leonardo Venero, the Venetian ambassador, whom they killed as the cause of their hunger and for taking cheer from their misery. And thus, having become almost princes of the city, they consulted among themselves about what had to be done if they wished to escape from so many afflictions and at some time enjoy rest. And everyone judged that since liberty could not be preserved, it was necessary to take refuge under a prince who would defend them; and some wanted to call upon King Alfonso, some upon the duke of Savoy, and some upon the king of France to be their lord. No one reasoned for the count, so powerful still was the indignation they had for him. Nonetheless, when they did not agree on others, Gaspare da Vimercate was the first to name the count. He showed amply that, if they wanted to lift the war from their backs, there was no other mode than to call him; for the people of Milan had need of a sure and immediate peace, not of a distant hope of future support. With his words he excused the enterprises of the count, accused the Venetians, and accused all the other princes of Italy, who, one out of ambition, another out of avarice, had not wanted the Milanese to live free. And furthermore, if their liberty had to be given away, it should be to one who knew them and could defend them, so that at least peace might arise out of slavery and not greater harm and a more dangerous war. This man was listened to with wonderful attention, and when he had finished speaking, they all shouted for the count to be called; and they made Gaspare their ambassador to call upon him. By command of the people, Gaspare went to find the count and brought him the joyous and prosperous news. The count accepted it joyfully, and, entering Milan as prince the twenty-sixth of February in 1450, he was received with utmost and marvelous joy by those who not long before had defamed him with so much hatred.

25

WHEN the news of this acquisition reached Florence, the Florentine spokesmen, who were already on the road, were ordered that, instead of going to negotiate an accord with the count, they should congratulate the duke[1] on his victory. These spokesmen were honorably received by the duke and honored profusely, for he well knew that against the power of the Venetians he could have neither more faithful nor more vigorous friends in Italy than the Florentines. The Florentines having put aside their fear of the house of Visconti, it was seen that they had to combat the forces of the Aragonese and the Venetians, because the Aragonese kings of Naples were their enemies through the friendship they knew that the Florentine people had always had for the house of France; and the Venetians recognized that the old fear of the Visconti had become a new fear of themselves and, since they knew with how much zeal the Florentines had persecuted the Visconti, that the Florentines, fearing the same persecutions, would seek the ruin of the Venetians. These things were the cause that the new duke readily drew close to the Florentines and that the Venetians and King Alfonso came to an accord against their common enemies. The Venetians and the king bound themselves to move their armies at the same time, the king to attack the Florentines and the Venetians the duke. Because the duke was new in his state, they believed he could not sustain it with either his own forces or the help of others. But because the league between the Florentines and the Venetians continued, and the king had made peace with the Florentines after the war of Piombino,[2] they did not think they could break the peace unless war were justified under some color. Therefore, each one sent ambassadors to Florence, who on behalf of their lords made it understood that the league had

[1] Francesco Sforza, no longer count, now duke of Milan.
[2] FH vi 16.

been made not for offending anyone but for defending their states. Then the Venetian complained that the Florentines had given passage through Lunigiana to Alessandro, brother of the duke,[3] so that he had come into Lombardy with his troops; and furthermore, they had been the aiders and advisers of the accord made between the duke and the marquis of Mantua. All these things they asserted to be opposed to their state and to the friendship they had together; and therefore they reminded them lovingly that he who wrongfully offends gives cause to others, with reason, to feel offended, and he who breaks the peace may expect war. Cosimo was commissioned by the Signoria to respond. In a long and wise speech, he went over all the benefits done by his city for the Venetian republic; he showed how much empire it had acquired with money, troops, and advice from the Florentines; and he reminded them that, since the cause of friendship had come from the Florentines, the cause for enmity would never come from them. Having always been lovers of peace, they praised very much the accord between the Venetians and the king if it were made for peace and not for war. It was true that they marveled greatly at the quarrels raised when they saw that so great a republic took so much account of a thing so slight and vain; but even if it were worthy of being considered, they let everyone understand that they wanted their country to be free and open to anyone and that the duke was a person of such quality that to make an alliance with Mantua he had need of neither their favors nor their advice. And therefore, he feared that these quarrels might be concealing some other poison that they were not revealing; should this be so, they would easily make everyone know that, just as much as the friendship of the Florentines was useful, so much was their enmity harmful.

26

FOR the time being the thing passed off lightly, and it appeared that the spokesmen went away satisfied. Nonetheless, the league was established, and the modes of the Venetians and the king made the Florentines and the duke fear a new war rather than hope for a firm peace. Therefore, the Florentines allied themselves with the duke; and meanwhile, the evil intent of the Venetians was revealed. For they made an alliance with the Sienese and drove out all Florentines and their subjects from their city and empire. And shortly afterwards, Alfonso did the same without paying any attention to the peace made the year before and without having, not

---

[3] Alessandro Sforza, lord of Pesaro; see *FH* VI 11.

a just, but even a colorable cause. The Venetians sought to acquire the Bolognese for themselves, and, having strengthened the exiles, sent them with many troops at night through the sewers of Bologna; nor did anyone learn of their entrance before they themselves raised the alarm. Santi Bentivoglio, awakened by this, realized that the whole city was occupied by rebels, and although he was advised by many to save his life by flight since by staying he could not save his state, nonetheless he wished to show his face to fortune. He took up arms, gave his men spirit, and, having gathered some friends, attacked part of the rebels; and when these were defeated, he killed many of them and drove the rest out of the city. Whereupon he was judged by everyone to have given very true proof of belonging to the house of the Bentivogli. These deeds and revelations confirmed in Florence belief in a future war, and so the Florentines turned to their ancient and customary defense; they created the magistracy of the Ten, hired new condottieri, sent spokesmen to Rome, Naples, Venice, Milan, and Siena to seek help from their friends, to clear up suspicions, win over the doubters, and discover the plans of the enemies. From the pope they drew nothing but general words, a good disposition, and encouragement to peace; from the king, empty excuses for having sent away the Florentines, putting himself forward as desiring to give safe conduct to anyone who should ask it. And although he strained to the utmost to hide the plans for the new war, nonetheless the ambassadors recognized his evil intent and discovered his many preparations for coming to harm their republic. With the duke they again strengthened their league with various pledges, and through his mediation fashioned a friendship with the Genoese; and the ancient differences over reprisals and many other quarrels were settled, notwithstanding that the Venetians sought in every mode to disturb such a settlement. Nor did the Venetians fail to beseech the emperor of Constantinople to drive those of Florentine birth[1] from his country. With such hatred did they take up this war and so powerful in them was the desire to rule that they wanted to destroy without any hesitation those who had been the cause of their greatness; but they were not listened to by the emperor. The Florentine spokesmen were forbidden entrance into the state of that republic by the Venetian senate, which alleged that, since they were in alliance with the king, they could not listen to the Florentines without his participation. The Sienese received the ambassadors with kind words, fearing lest they be undone before the league could defend them; and for this it appeared to them better to lull the arms that they could not resist. The Venetians and the king wanted, as was then conjectured, to send spokesmen to Florence so as to

---

[1] Lit.: the Florentine nation.

justify the war; but the Venetian did not want to intrude into the Florentine dominion, and since the king's did not wish to do that office alone, the mission remained unaccomplished. And through this the Venetians realized that they were esteemed less by the same Florentines they had esteemed little not many months before.

27

AMIDST the fear raised by these movements, Emperor Frederick III came to Italy to be crowned. On the thirtieth day of January 1451, he entered Florence with fifteen hundred cavalry and was most honorably received by the Signoria, and he remained in the city until the sixth day of February, when he departed to go to Rome for his coronation. There he was solemnly crowned, and, having celebrated his marriage with the empress, who had come to Rome by sea, he returned to Germany; and in May he again came through Florence, where the same honors were accorded him as at his coming. And since he had been benefited by the marquis of Ferrara, while returning he gave the marquis Modena and Reggio to compensate him. At this same time the Florentines did not fail to prepare for imminent war; and to give reputation to themselves and terror to the enemy, they and the duke made an alliance with the king of France for the defense of both[1] states, which they announced publicly with great magnificence and joy throughout Italy. The month of May of the year 1452 had come when it appeared to the Venetians that they should no longer defer making war on the duke; and with sixteen thousand cavalry and six thousand infantry, they attacked him on the side of Lodi; and at the same time, the marquis of Monferrat, either for his own ambition or urged by the Venetians, also attacked him on the side of Alessandria. The duke, for his part, had put together eighteen thousand cavalry and three thousand infantry, and, having provided Alessandria and Lodi with troops and similarly fortified all the places where the enemy might be able to harm[2] him, with his troops he attacked the territory of Brescia, where he did very great damage to the Venetians; and on every side the country was looted and the weak villages sacked. Then, after the marquis of Monferrat was defeated at Alessandria by the duke's troops, the duke was able to oppose the Venetians with greater forces and to attack their country.

[1] Lit.: common.
[2] Lit.: offend.

28

WHILE the war in Lombardy was toiling on with various but feeble accidents little worth remembering, in Tuscany at the same time war arose between King Alfonso and the Florentines, and it was managed with neither great virtue nor greater danger than the one that was being managed in Lombardy. Ferdinand, an illegitimate son of Alfonso's, came into Tuscany with twelve thousand soldiers captained by Federico, lord of Urbino. Their first campaign was to attack Foiano in Valdichiana, because, having the Sienese as friends, they entered into the Florentine empire from that side. The fortified town had a feeble wall; it was small and therefore not filled with many men, but, in accordance with those times, they were reputed to be fierce and faithful. In the fortified town were two hundred soldiers sent by the Signoria to guard it. At this fortified town thus strengthened, Ferdinand encamped, and either the virtue of those within was so great or his was so little that not before thirty-six days was he able to become lord of it. This time gave the city[1] opportunity to provision other places of greater importance, to assemble their troops, and to order themselves for defense better than they had been. When the enemy had taken this fortified town, they passed into Chianti, where they were unable to capture two little villages owned by private citizens. So leaving these, they went to encamp at Castellina, a nearby fortified town situated at the border of Chianti, about ten miles from Siena, weak by art and very weak in its site; yet these two weaknesses could not surpass the weakness of the army that attacked it, for after the forty-four days that they stayed to fight for it, they departed in shame. So formidable were these armies and so dangerous those wars that towns that today are abandoned as places impossible to defend were defended then as things impossible to take. And while Ferdinand remained in camp at Chianti, he made many plundering incursions into Florentine territory and raided as close as six miles from the city, bringing fear and great losses for the subjects of the Florentines. The Florentines in these times brought their troops, in number eight thousand soldiers under Astorre da Faenza[2] and Sigismondo Malatesta, toward the fortified town of Colle and kept them at a distance from the enemy, fearing that they might be forced of necessity to join battle; for they judged that if they did not lose the battle, they could not lose the war, because small fortified towns, if lost, are recovered when peace is made, and they were sure of the large towns, since they knew the enemy was not about to attack those. The king still had a fleet

[1] Florence.
[2] Astorre Manfredi, lord of Faenza.

of about twenty vessels, including galleys and foists, in the waters of Pisa; and while Castellina was being fought for on land, he directed this fleet against the fortress of Vada, which he seized because of the carelessness of the castellan. Because of this, the enemy then harassed all the surrounding countryside, but their harassment was easily stopped by some soldiers whom the Florentines sent to Campiglia, who kept the enemy close to the shore.

29

THE pontiff did not become involved in these wars except insofar as he believed he could bring about an accord between the parties; and although he abstained from the war outside, he was to find one more dangerous at home. Living at that time was a Messer Stefano Porcari, a Roman citizen, noble by blood and by learning, but much more so by the excellence of his spirit.[1] This man desired, according to the custom of men who relish glory, to do or at least to try something worthy of memory; and he judged he could do nothing else than try to see if he could take his fatherland from the hands of prelates and restore it to its ancient way of life, hoping by this, should he succeed, to be called the new founder and second father of that city. What made him hope for a prosperous end to his undertaking were the evil customs of the prelates and the discontent of the barons and the Roman people, but above all, what gave him hope were those lines of Petrarch in the canzone that begins "Gentle spirit[2] that rules those limbs," where he says:

> Atop Mount Tarpeio, Oh! canzone, you will see
> a knight whom all Italy honors
> more thoughtful of others than of himself.[3]

Messer Stefano knew that many times poets are filled with divine and prophetic spirit;[4] so he judged that in any mode the thing Petrarch had prophesied in that canzone must come, and that it was he who ought to be the executor of so glorious an undertaking, since it appeared to him that he was superior to every other Roman in eloquence, learning, grace, and friends. Thus, having fallen upon this thought, he was unable to con-

---

[1] *Animo.*

[2] *Spirito.* Cf. the "higher and greater spirit" of describing in *FH*, Letter dedicatory; and "an Italian spirit" in *P* 26.

[3] Petrarch, *Rime* LIII, 99–101.

[4] *Spirito.*

duct himself in a mode cautious enough not to reveal himself by his words, his habits, and his mode of living. So he became suspect to the pontiff, who, to take away his opportunity to do evil, banished him to Bologna and commissioned the governor of that city to check on him every day. Messer Stefano was not dismayed by this first obstacle; indeed, he pursued his undertaking with greater zeal, and by more cautious means he was able to hold meetings with his friends. Many times he went to Rome and returned with such speed that he was in time to present himself to the governor within the required limits.[5] But then, when it appeared to him that he had attracted enough men to his will, he decided not to postpone attempting the thing. He commissioned his friends who were in Rome to order a splendid dinner at a fixed time, to which all the conspirators should be called with orders that each should have with him his most trusted friends; and he promised to be with them before the dinner was finished. All was ordered according to his plan, and Messer Stefano had already arrived at the house where they were dining, so that as soon as the dinner was over, he, dressed in cloth of gold, with necklaces and other ornaments that gave him majesty and reputation, appeared among the guests; and, having embraced them, he urged them with a long speech to steady their spirits[6] and be ready for so glorious an under-taking. Then he revealed the mode; and he ordered that on the following morning one part of them should seize the palace of the pontiff and the other should call the people to arms throughout Rome. The thing came to the notice of the pontiff that night: some say it was because of faith-lessness among the conspirators; others, that it became known Messer Stefano was in Rome. However it was, on the same night the dinner had taken place, the pope had Messer Stefano arrested, with the greater part of his partners, and then, according to what their faults deserved, had them killed. Such was the end of this design of his. And truly, the inten-tion of this man could be praised by anyone, but his judgment will always be blamed by everyone because such undertakings, if there is some shadow of glory in thinking of them, have almost always very certain loss in their execution.

30

THE war in Tuscany had already lasted almost a year, and the time had come in 1453 for the armies to return to the field, when Signor Alessan-

---

[5] The journey is of course much too long for a day.
[6] *Animo.*

dro Sforza, brother of the duke, came with two thousand cavalry to the support of the Florentines. And because of this, since the army of the Florentines had increased and the king's diminished, it appeared to the Florentines that they should go to recover things lost; and with little trouble they recovered some towns. Then they encamped at Foiano, which because of the carelessness of the commissioners had been sacked, so that the inhabitants, who were dispersed, went back to live there with great difficulty; but with exemptions and other rewards they were brought back. The fortress of Vada was also reacquired because, when the enemy saw they could not keep it, they abandoned and burned it. And while these things were being done by the Florentine army, the Aragonese army, not having the boldness to approach the army of the enemy, assembled near Siena and many times raided Florentine territory, where they carried out robberies, started tumults, and raised very great fear. Nor did the king fail to see if he could attack his enemies by some other way and divide their forces, and weaken them by new travails and assaults. The lord of Val di Bagno was Gherardo Gambocorti; either for friendship or out of obligation, he, together with his predecessors, had always been paid or protected by the Florentines. King Alfonso dealt with this man so that he would give the king that state and in exchange the king would give him another state of the Kingdom in recompense. This dealing was revealed in Florence, and, to discover Gherardo's intent, the Florentines sent him an ambassador to remind him of the obligations of his predecessors and his own and to urge him to continue in his faith to the republic. Gherardo pretended to be astonished and with solemn oaths affirmed that never had such a villainous thought entered his mind and that he would come in person to Florence as a pledge of his faith, but that, as he was indisposed, that which he could not do he would have his son do, whom he turned over to the ambassador as a hostage to take with him to Florence. These words and this demonstration made the Florentines believe that Gherardo was telling the truth and that his accuser was a liar and worthless; and so they rested on this thought. But Gherardo pursued his dealing with the king with greater urgency; as soon as it was concluded, the king sent Frate Puccio, a knight of Jerusalem, to Val di Bagno with many troops to take possession of Gherardo's fortresses and lands. But the peoples of Bagno, who had become fond of the Florentine republic, promised obedience to the king's commissioners with dislike. Frate Puccio had already taken possession of almost the whole state; he failed only to become lord of the fortress of Corvano. With Gherardo, among the men around him while he was making this delivery, was Antonio Gualandi of Pisa, young and bold, to whom Gherardo's betrayal was displeasing; he considered the site of the fortress and the men there to guard it, and in their faces and gestures he discerned their discontent. And when Gherardo stood at the gate to let in the Aragonese, Antonio circled around toward the inside of the fortress and with both hands pushed Gherardo outside and commanded the guards to lock the gates of that fortress in the face of so villainous a man and save it for the Florentine republic. As soon as this uproar was heard in Bagno and in other nearby places, each of those peoples took up arms against the Aragonese and, having raised the banners of Florence, chased them out. As soon as this thing was learned of in Florence, the Florentines imprisoned the son of Gherardo given them as hostage and sent troops to Bagno to defend that country for their republic, and they made that state, which had been governing itself by a prince, into a vicarate. But Gherardo, traitor to his lord and to his son, was barely able to flee, and he left his wife and family with all his property in the power[1] of his enemies. This accident was much appreciated in Florence, because if the king had succeeded in making himself lord of the country, he could have raided the Val di Tevere and the Casentino with little expense and at his pleasure. There he would have given the republic so much annoyance that the Florentines would not have been able to oppose all their forces to the Aragonese army that was in Siena.

3 1

BESIDES making preparations in Italy to check the forces of the hostile league, the Florentines had sent Messer Agnolo Acciaiuoli as their spokesman to the king of France to negotiate with him so that he would give King René of Anjou the means to come to Italy in favor of the duke and themselves. Thus would he come to defend his friends, and then, once in Italy, he could think about acquiring the kingdom of Naples: and to this effect they promised him aid in men and money. And so, while the war in Lombardy and Tuscany, as we have narrated, was toiling on, the ambassador concluded an accord with King René: he should come to Italy for all June with two thousand four hundred cavalry; and upon his arrival in Alessandria, the league should give him thirty thousand florins and then, during the war, ten thousand for each month. But when, by virtue of the accord, the king wanted to come into Italy, he was held back by the duke of Savoy and the marquis of Monferrat, who, as friends of the Venetians, would not allow him passage. Hence, the king was urged by the Florentine ambassador that to give reputation to his friends he should return to Provence and come down into Italy by sea with some of

[1] *Potestà.*

his men; and on the other side he should bring pressure on the king of France to work on the duke so that his troops could pass through Savoy. And just as he was advised, it happened; for René came into Italy by sea, and his troops were received in Savoy out of regard for the king. King René was welcomed by Duke Francesco very honorably; and when the Italian and French troops were placed together, they attacked the Venetians, bringing so much terror that in a short time they recovered all the lands the Venetians had taken in the territory of Cremona; and not content with this, they seized nearly all the territory of Brescia; and the Venetian army, no longer feeling safe in the field, withdrew close to the walls of Brescia. But since winter had come, it appeared to the duke time to retire his troops into quarters, and he assigned lodgings in Piacenza to King René. And so, the winter of 1453 having passed without any campaign, when summer came and it seemed time for the duke to go into the field and strip the Venetians of their state on land, King René informed the duke that it had become necessary for him to return to France. This decision was new and unexpected by the duke, and he was therefore very greatly displeased; and although he immediately went to the king to dissuade him from departing, he could move him neither with prayers nor with promises. René promised only to leave some of his troops and to send his son Jean to serve the league in his own place. The Florentines were not displeased with his departure, for since they had recovered their own fortified towns, they no longer feared the king;[1] but on the other hand they did not want the duke[2] to get back any more than his towns in Lombardy. So René left and sent his son, as he had promised, into Italy. His son did not stop in Lombardy but came to Florence, where he was received most honorably.

32

THE departure of the king made the duke turn willingly to peace; the Venetians, Alfonso, and the Florentines also desired it, for they were all weary. The pope too had given every appearance of desiring it and still desired it; for this same year Mahomet the Grand Turk had taken Constantinople and made himself lord of all Greece. This conquest frightened all Christians, and more than anyone else the Venetians and the pope, as it appeared to each of these that already they felt his armies in Italy.

The pope therefore begged the Italian powers to send spokesmen to him with authority to establish a universal peace. They all obeyed; but

[1] The king of Naples, Alfonso of Aragon.
[2] The duke of Milan, Francesco Sforza.

when they were together and came to the merits of the thing, great difficulty was found in negotiating it: the king wanted the Florentines to repay him for his expenses in that war, and the Florentines wanted satisfaction from it themselves; the Venetians demanded Cremona from the duke, the duke demanded Bergamo, Brescia, and Crema from them; so it appeared that these difficulties were impossible to resolve. Nonetheless, that which in Rome appeared difficult to do among many was done in Milan and Venice very easily between two; for while the negotiations for peace were being held in Rome, the duke and the Venetians concluded it on the ninth day of April in 1454. By virtue of the peace, each returned to the towns held before the war, and the duke was allowed to recover the towns that the princes of Monferrat and Savoy had seized from him; and the other Italian princes were allowed one month to ratify it. The pope, the Florentines, and, with them, the Sienese and other lesser powers ratified it in time; and not content with this, the Florentines, the duke, and the Venetians established a peace for twenty-five years. Only King Alfonso, of the princes of Italy, showed he was malcontent with this peace, as it appeared to him to have been made with little regard for him, since he was to be accepted in it not as a principal but as an accessory, and therefore he remained uncertain for a long time without letting anyone know his intention. Yet, after many solemn embassies had been sent to him by the pope and other princes, he let himself be persuaded by them, and especially by the pontiff, and he entered this league with his son for thirty years. The king and the duke together made a double kinship and a double marriage, each giving and taking a daughter from the other for their sons. Nonetheless, so that the seeds of war might remain in Italy, the king did not consent to make peace unless he was first given permission by the allies enabling him, without injury to them, to make war on the Genoese, on Sigismondo Malatesta, and on Astorre, prince of Faenza. And when this accord had been made, Ferdinand, his son, who was in Siena, returned to the Kingdom, having acquired nothing in empire and lost a great many of his troops by his coming into Tuscany.

33

THIS universal peace thus accomplished, the only fear was that King Alfonso might disturb it through his enmity toward the Genoese; but the fact went otherwise, because peace was disturbed not openly by the king but, as had always happened before, by the ambition of mercenary soldiers. The Venetians, as is customary when peace is made, had dismissed from their hire Jacopo Piccinino, their condottiere. Joined by some other condottieri without employment, he came into Romagna and from there into the territory of Siena, where Jacopo stopped to make war, and he seized some towns from the Sienese. At the beginning of these movements at the start of the year 1455, Pope Nicholas died, and his successor, Calixtus III, was elected. So as to suppress the new war nearby, this pontiff immediately gathered as many troops as he could under his captain Giovanni Ventimiglia and, with the troops of the Florentines and of the duke, who also contributed to suppress these movements, sent them against Jacopo. And when they came to battle near Bolsena, although Ventimiglia ended a prisoner, Jacopo remained the loser, and he withdrew defeated to Castiglione della Pescaia. If he had not been subsidized with money by Alfonso, he would have been completely undone. This thing made everyone believe that the action of Jacopo was undertaken by order of the king; so when it appeared to Alfonso that he was found out, so as to redeem himself with his allies of the peace, whom he had almost alienated by this feeble war, he arranged that Jacopo restore to the Sienese the towns he had seized, and they were to give him twenty thousand florins. When the accord was made, the king received Jacopo and his troops in the Kingdom.

Even while the pope was thinking in these times of checking Jacopo Piccinino, nonetheless he did not fail to prepare himself to support Christendom, which, it was seen, was about to be oppressed by the Turks; and so he sent spokesmen and preachers throughout the Christian provinces to persuade princes and peoples to arm themselves on behalf of their religion and to support an undertaking against the common enemy with their money and their persons. Consequently, in Florence many offerings were made, and also many marked themselves with a red cross as being ready to carry on that war in person; also, solemn processions were made; nor did they fail in public or in private to show that they wished to be among the first Christians with advice, money, and men for such an undertaking. But this warmth for the crusade was cooled somewhat when the news came that the Turk, with his army around Belgrade to assault it—a fortified town located in Hungary on the Danube River—had been defeated by the Hungarians and wounded. So, as the fear that the pontiff and the Christians had conceived at the loss of Constantinople ceased, they proceeded with their preparations for the war more tepidly; and likewise in Hungary, after the death of John Waywode, captain in that victory, they cooled down.

34

BUT turning to things in Italy, I say how the year 1456 went, when the tumults stirred by Jacopo Piccinino ended. Thereupon, when arms had been put away by men, it appeared that God wished to take them up Himself: so great was a wind storm that then occurred, which in Tuscany had effects unheard of in the past and for whoever learns of it in the future will have marvelous and memorable effects. Starting on the 24th of August, an hour before daybreak, from the regions of the Upper Sea[1] toward Ancona and crossing through Italy, it entered the Lower Sea[2] below Pisa, a whirlwind of a cloud, huge and dense, which reached almost two miles wide throughout its course. This whirlwind, driven by superior forces, whether they were natural or supernatural, broke on itself and fought within itself; and the shattered clouds, now rising toward the sky, now descending toward the earth, crashed together; and then they moved in circles with very great velocity and stirred up ahead of them a wind violent beyond all measure;[3] and in the battling between them appeared frequent blazes and the most brilliant flares. From these clouds, so broken and confused, from such furious winds and frequent flashes, arose a noise never before heard from any earthquake or thunder of any kind or greatness; from it arose such fear that anyone who heard it judged that the end of the world had come and that earth, water, and the rest of the sky and the world would return mixed together to its ancient chaos. This terrifying whirlwind, wherever it passed, had unheard-of and marvelous effects; but more remarkable than those anywhere else were the ones that occurred around the fortified town of San Casciano. This fortified town is located eight miles from Florence, on a hill that separates the valleys of the Pesa and the Greve. Thus, between this town and the village of Sant' Andrea, situated on the same hill, passed this furious storm, not reaching Sant' Andrea and grazing San Casciano so that only some battlements and the chimneys of some houses were broken off; but outside, in the space between the places mentioned, many houses were destroyed to the level of the ground. The roofs of the churches of San Martino Bagnolo and Santa Maria della Pace were carried entire, just as they had been on the churches, more than a mile away. A wagoner, together with his mules, was found dead far from the road in the nearby valley. All the largest oaks, all the strongest trees that would not yield to such fury, were not only torn away but carried very far from where they had had their roots. When the storm passed and day came, men were left altogether stupefied. They saw the country desolate and broken, they saw the ruin of the houses and churches, they heard the laments of those who saw their possessions destroyed and had left under the ruins their animals and relatives,

[1] The Adriatic.
[2] The Tyrrhenian.
[3] Lit.: mode.

dead. It was a thing that brought the greatest compassion and fright to anyone who saw and heard it. Without doubt, God wanted to warn rather than punish Tuscany; for, if such a storm had entered into a city among many and crowded houses and inhabitants, as it did enter among few and scattered oaks and trees and houses, without doubt it would have made ruin and torment greater than that which the mind can conjecture. But God meant for then that this small example should be enough to refresh among men the memory of His power.

35

TO return, then, to where I left off, King Alfonso, as we said above, was ill content with the peace. Since the war that he had had Jacopo Piccinino start[1] against the Sienese without any reasonable cause gave rise to no important effect, he wanted to see what effect would come from the one he could start in accordance with the agreements of the league. And so in the year 1456 he made war on the Genoese, by sea and by land, as he was desirous of giving over that state to the Adorni and of depriving the Fregosi of it, who were governing then; and from the other side he had Jacopo Piccinino cross the Tronto against Sigismondo Malatesta. This man, because he had equipped his own towns well, had little regard for Jacopo's attack, so that on this side the king's undertaking had no effect; but the war in Genoa brought forth for him and his Kingdom more war than he would have wished.

Pietro Fregoso was then duke of Genoa. Fearing he could not sustain the thrust of the king, he decided that what he could not hold he would at least give to someone who would defend it from his enemies and who at some time could give him just reward for such a benefit. Therefore, he sent spokesmen to Charles VII, king of France, and offered him empire over Genoa. Charles accepted the offer, and to take possession of that city he sent Jean of Anjou, son of King René, who a short time before had left Florence and returned to France. And Charles persuaded himself that Jean, who had taken on so many Italian customs, could govern that city better than anyone else, and partly he judged that from there he could think about an expedition against Naples, the kingdom of which Alfonso had despoiled his father René. Therefore, Jean went to Genoa, where he was received as prince, and the fortresses of the city and of the state were given into his power.[2]

[1] Cf. *FH* VI 33 (beg.).
[2] *Potestate.*

THIS unforeseen event displeased Alfonso, as it appeared to him that he had pulled down too important an enemy on his back. Nonetheless, unfrightened by this, he pursued his enterprise with a frank spirit; and he had already led his fleet to Villa Marina at Portofino when, taken by a sudden illness, he died. By this death Jean and the Genoese were freed from the war, and Ferdinand, who succeeded to the kingdom of Alfonso, his father, was full of suspicion, having an enemy of such reputation in Italy and doubting the faith of many of his barons, who, desiring new things, might join the French. He also feared the pope, whose ambition he recognized and who, because Ferdinand was new in the Kingdom, might scheme to despoil him of it. Ferdinand had hope only in the duke of Milan, who was not less anxious about affairs of the Kingdom than was Ferdinand, because he feared that if the French became lords of the Kingdom they might scheme to seize his state as well, which he knew they believed they could demand as something belonging to them.[1] Therefore, the duke, immediately after the death of Alfonso, sent letters and troops to Ferdinand—the troops to give him aid and reputation and the letters to urge him to be of good spirit, indicating that he was not about to abandon him in his necessity.

The pontiff, after the death of Alfonso, schemed to give the kingdom of Naples to his nephew Pietro Ludovico Borgia; and to make this enterprise seem decent and to get more agreement with the other princes of Italy, he announced that he wanted to bring that kingdom under the empire of the Roman Church. Therefore, he persuaded the duke that he ought not to give any favor to Ferdinand, while offering the duke towns the duke already possessed in that kingdom. But in the midst of these thoughts and new trials, Calixtus died, and to the pontificate succeeded Pius II, of Sienese birth, of the family Piccolomini, named Aeneas. This pontiff, thinking only of benefiting Christians and honoring the Church, and putting aside all his private passion, crowned Ferdinand in the Kingdom at the urging[2] of the duke of Milan, as he judged that he could more quickly put Italian arms to rest by supporting whoever possessed the crown than if he either favored the French in seizing that kingdom or schemed, as did Calixtus, to take it for himself. Nonetheless, for this benefit Ferdinand made Antonio, a nephew of the pope, prince of Amalfi

---

[1] The French might claim Milan through the marriage of Valentina Visconti, sister of Duke Filippo Maria, to Louis of Orleans. Their son was Charles of Orleans; see *FH* VI 17.

[2] Or prayers.

and gave him in marriage an illegitimate daughter of his. He also restored
Benevento and Terracina to the Church.

37

IT appeared, therefore, that arms had been laid down in Italy. The pontiff
was ordering himself to move Christendom against the Turks in accordance with what had already been begun by Calixtus when dissension
arose between the Fregosi and Jean, lord of Genoa, which rekindled wars
greater and more important than those past. Petrino Fregoso was in a
fortified town of his on the Riviera. To him it appeared he had not been
rewarded by Jean of Anjou according to his merits and those of his house,
since they had been the cause of making Jean prince in that city;[1] so they
came to open hostility. This thing pleased Ferdinand as the single remedy
and the only way to his own safety; he supported Petrino with men and
money and judged that by means of him he could drive Jean from that
state. As Jean recognized this, he sent to France for aid, with which he
confronted Petrino, who, through much support[2] that had been sent him,
was very strong; so Jean withdrew to guard the city. Petrino, having entered the city one night, took some places in it, but when day came, he
was attacked and killed by Jean's troops, and all his troops were either
killed or taken.

This victory inspired Jean to undertake a campaign into the Kingdom,
and in October of 1459 he left Genoa in that direction with a powerful
fleet, stopped at Baia, and from there went to Sessa, where he was received by its duke. The prince of Taranto, the Aquilanians, and many
other cities and princes sided with Jean, so that the Kingdom was nearly
all in ruin. When Ferdinand saw this, he turned to the pope and the duke
for help, and, so as to have fewer enemies, he made an agreement with
Sigismondo Malatesta. This so disturbed Jacopo Piccinino, since Sigismondo was his natural enemy, that he left the hire of Ferdinand and sided
with Jean. Ferdinand also sent money to Federico, lord of Urbino, and as
soon as he could, he gathered together a good army, for those times, and
confronted his enemies on the Sarni River. When the battle was joined,
King Ferdinand was defeated and many of his most important captains
taken. After this disaster, the city of Naples, along with some few princes
and towns, remained faithful to Ferdinand; the greater part surrendered
to Jean. Jacopo Piccinino wanted Jean, upon this victory, to go to Naples

---

[1] Genoa.
[2] Lit.: many favors.

and to make himself lord of the capital[3] of the Kingdom; but Jean was unwilling, saying that he wanted first to despoil Ferdinand of his whole dominion and then to attack him, thinking that when Ferdinand was deprived of his towns the conquest of Naples would be easier. To the contrary, the course he took snatched victory in that enterprise away from him, for he did not realize how much more easily the limbs follow the head than the head the limbs.

38

AFTER his defeat, Ferdinand had taken refuge in Naples, and there he received those who had been driven out of his states; and in the most humane modes he could, he collected money and gathered a small army. Again he sent for help to the pope and the duke and was supported by each of them with greater speed and more abundantly than before, for they lived now in great fear that he might lose the Kingdom. King Ferdinand, having thus become strong, went out of Naples, and, beginning to reacquire his reputation, he reacquired some of the towns lost. And while the war in the Kingdom was toiling on, an accident arose that entirely deprived Jean of Anjou of his reputation and the opportunity of winning that campaign.

The Genoese had become impatient with the greed and pride of the French, so much so that they took up arms against the royal governor and forced him to take refuge in the Castelletto. In this enterprise the Fregosi and the Adorni were agreed, and they were aided by the duke of Milan with money and troops as much in acquiring the state as in keeping it. So King René, who then came with a fleet in support of his son, hoping to reacquire Genoa by virtue of the Castelletto, was defeated while bringing his troops on land, with the result that he was forced to return in shame to Provence. As soon as this news was received in the kingdom of Naples, it greatly frightened Jean of Anjou; nonetheless, he did not abandon the campaign but kept the war going longer, helped by barons who, because of their rebellion, did not believe they could find any place with Ferdinand. Yet in the end, after many unforeseen events had occurred, the two royal armies were joined in battle at which Jean was defeated in Troia in the year 1463. The defeat did not hurt[1] him as much as the desertion of Jacopo Piccinino, who went over to Ferdinand; and so, stripped of forces, Jean retired to Ischia, from whence he later returned

---

[3] Lit.: head; see the end of the chapter.
[1] Lit.: offend.

to France. This war lasted four years, and he lost it through his own negligence although he had won it many times through the virtue of his soldiers. In this war the Florentines were not involved in any mode that was apparent: it is true that they had been requested by King John of Aragon, newly become king in that kingdom by the death of Alfonso, through his embassy, to provide support in his nephew Ferdinand's things as they had been obliged to do by the league recently made with his father, Alfonso. To this, it was replied on behalf of the Florentines that they had no obligation to him and that they were not about to help his son in a war that his father had started with his arms; and since the war had been begun without their advice or knowledge, so he must deal with it and end it without their aid. Then the spokesmen on behalf of their king protested the weight of the obligation and the Florentines' share in the damage, and, indignant at that city, they departed. The Florentines, therefore, remained at peace during this war, as to things outside, but they were indeed not in repose within, as will be shown in detail in the following book.

BOOK VII

I

PERHAPS it will appear to those who have read the preceding book that a writer on Florentine things may have strayed too far in telling about things that happened in Lombardy and the Kingdom. Nonetheless, I have not avoided, nor in the future shall I avoid, such narrations, for although I may never have promised to write about things of Italy, it does not appear to me that therefore I should omit telling about things that are notable in that province. For by not narrating them, our history would be less understood and less pleasing, especially since the wars in which the Florentines were compelled of necessity to intervene arose most times from the actions of other Italian peoples and princes: thus, from the war of Jean of Anjou and King Ferdinand arose the hatreds and grave enmities that later ensued between Ferdinand and the Florentines, and particularly with the Medici family. For the king complained that in that war not only was he not assisted but favor was granted to his enemy; his indignation was the cause of very great evils, as our narration will show. And because I have reached as far as 1463 in writing about things outside, it is necessary for me now, as I wish to tell about the travails inside, to go back many years.

But first, I want to say something, reasoning in accordance with our custom, about how those who hope that a republic can be united are very much deceived in this hope. It is true that some divisions are harmful to republics and some are helpful. Those are harmful that are accompanied by sects and partisans; those are helpful that are maintained without sects and partisans. Thus, since a founder of a republic cannot provide that there be no enmities in it, he has to provide at least that there not be sects. And therefore it is to be known that citizens in cities acquire reputation in two modes: either by public ways or by private modes. One acquires it publicly by winning a battle, acquiring a town, carrying out a mission with care and prudence, advising the republic wisely and prosperously. One acquires it in private modes by benefiting this or that other citizen, defending him from the magistrates, helping him with money, getting him unmerited honors, and ingratiating oneself with the plebs with games and public gifts. From this latter mode of proceeding, sects and partisans arise, and the reputation thus earned offends as much as reputation helps when it is not mixed with sects, because that reputation is founded on a common good, not on a private good. And although even among citizens so made[1] one cannot provide by any mode that there will not be very great hatreds, nonetheless, having no partisans who follow them for their own utility, they cannot harm the republic; on the contrary, they must help it, because to pass their tests it is necessary for them to attempt to exalt the republic and to watch each other particularly so that civil bounds are not transgressed. The enmities in Florence were always accompanied by sects and therefore always harmful; never did a winning sect remain united except when the hostile sect was active, but as soon as the one conquered was eliminated, the ruling one, no longer having fear to restrain it or order within itself to check it, would become divided again. The party of Cosimo de' Medici was left on top in 1434, but because the beaten party was large and full of very powerful men, Cosimo's party maintained itself united and humane for a time through fear, as long as they made no error among themselves and did not make the people hate them through any sinister mode of theirs. So at any time that the state had need of the people to regain its authority, it always found the people disposed to cede to its heads every balìa and power that they desired. And thus, from 1434 to '55, which are twenty-one years, they reassumed the authority of the balìa six times ordinarily through the councils.

2

IN Florence, as we have said many times, there were two very powerful citizens, Cosimo de' Medici and Neri Capponi. Neri was one of those who had acquired his reputation by public ways, so that he had many friends and few partisans. Cosimo, on the other hand, who had had the private and public way open to his power, had many friends and partisans. Since these two were united while they both lived, they were always able to get what they wanted from the people without any difficulty, because grace was mixed with their power. But when the year 1455 came, with Neri dead[1] and the enemy party eliminated, the state found difficulty in reassuming its authority, and Cosimo's own friends, very powerful in the state, were the cause of it, because they no longer feared the adverse party that had been eliminated, and they were glad to diminish Cosimo's power. This humor gave a beginning to the division that came later,[2] in 1466, so that those to whom the state belonged advised in the

---

[1] By reputation founded on a common good.
[1] In fact, Neri Capponi died in 1457.
[2] See FH VII 10.

councils where the administration of the public was reasoned about publicly that it was well not to use the power[3] of the balìa again and that the bags should be locked up and the magistrates should be drawn by lot with a view to the advantages of past lists.[4] To check this humor, Cosimo had one of two remedies: either regain the state by force with the partisans who remained to him and oppose all the others, or let the thing go and in time have his friends learn that they were taking state and reputation not from him but from themselves. Of these two remedies, he chose the latter because he knew well that in this mode of governing, since the bags were filled with his friends, he ran no risk and could retake his state at his ease. Since the city had been brought back to creating magistrates by lot,[5] it appeared to the generality[6] of citizens that they had their liberty again and that the magistrates were judging in accordance not with the will of the powerful but with their own judgment, so that sometimes a friend of someone powerful and sometimes a friend of another was punished. And so, those who were used to seeing their houses full of well-wishers and gifts saw them empty of possessions and men. They also saw that they had become the equals of those whom they were long accustomed to consider inferior, and they saw those superior who used to be their equals. They were neither respected nor honored; indeed, many times they were made fun of and derided, and they and the republic were reasoned about both in the streets and in the piazza without any consideration, such that they soon knew that not Cosimo but they themselves had lost the state. Cosimo pretended not to know about these things, and when some deliberation arose that might please the people, he was the first to favor it. But what frightened the great more and gave Cosimo greater opportunity to make them recognize their mistake was the revival of the mode of the *catasto* of 1427,[7] whereby the taxes were assessed not by men but by law.

3

WHEN this law had been won and the magistracy that was to execute it had already been installed, it made all the great draw together and go to Cosimo to beg him that he be so kind as to be willing to rescue them and himself from the hands of the plebs and to restore to the state the same

[3] *Potestà.*

[4] That is, no new names should be added to the lists of those eligible to be chosen for office by lot.

[5] Since February 23, 1454.

[6] Lit.: the universality.

[7] See *FH* IV 14.

reputation that had made him powerful and themselves honored. To them Cosimo answered that he was willing but that he wanted the law to be made in the ordinary way, with the will of the people and not by force, about which he would not reason with them in any mode. A law to make a new balìa was attempted in the councils and was not enacted, whereupon the great citizens turned to Cosimo and with every mark of humility prayed him to be willing to consent to a parliament; this Cosimo refused altogether, as he wanted to reduce them to a strait in which they would fully recognize their error. And because Donato Cocchi, who was Gonfalonier of Justice, wished to hold a parliament without his consent, Cosimo had him so ridiculed by the Signori who were sitting with him that he went mad and was sent back as a fool to his houses.

Nonetheless, since it is not well to let things go so far that they cannot be brought back later at one's ease, when Luca Pitti, a spirited and bold man, became the Gonfalonier of Justice, to Cosimo it appeared time to let him govern the thing, so that if that enterprise should incur any blame, it would be imputed to Luca and not to himself. Luca, therefore, in the beginning of his magistracy proposed to the people many times to renew the balìa, and, not succeeding, he threatened those who sat in the councils with abusive words full of pride. To these words he soon after added deeds; for in August of 1458, on the eve of San Lorenzo,[1] having filled the palace with armed men, he called the people into the piazza and by force and with arms made them consent to that which they had not consented to voluntarily before. Thereupon the state was reassumed; a balìa and then the first magistrates were created in accordance with the views of the few; and to give a beginning of terror to this government that they had begun with force, they banished Messer Girolamo Machiavelli with some others, and they also deprived many others of honors. This Messer Girolamo was declared a rebel for not having observed the confines of his banishment, and while he circulated around Italy stirring up princes against his fatherland, he was arrested in Lunigiana through the faithlessness of one of those lords; and after he was brought to Florence, he was put to death in prison.

4

THIS was the quality of government, unbearable and violent for the eight years it lasted; for since Cosimo, now old and weary, made feeble by the ill condition of his body, was unable to be present at public affairs in the mode he used to be, a few citizens plundered the city. Luca Pitti was made

---

[1] In fact, two days later, on August 11.

a knight as a reward for the work he had done for the benefit of the republic, and so as not to be less grateful to the republic than it had been to him, he wanted those formerly called Priors of the Guilds to be called Priors of Liberty so that they could at least retain the title of the possession lost.[1] Also, whereas before the Gonfalonier used to sit above the rectors on the right, he wanted him in future to sit in their midst. And so that God himself might appear to take part in their enterprise, they held public processions and solemn offices to thank Him for the honors they assumed. Messer Luca was richly bestowed with presents by the Signoria and by Cosimo, and the whole city vied with them; the opinion was that the presents added up to the sum of twenty thousand ducats. Thus he rose to such reputation that not Cosimo but Messer Luca governed the city. He gained such confidence from this that he began two buildings, one in Florence, the other in Rusciano, a place nearly one mile from the city—both splendid and royal, but the one in the city was altogether greater than any other that had been built by a private citizen until that day. To bring these buildings to completion, he did not spare any extraordinary mode, for not only did citizens and individual men make him presents and help him with the things necessary for the building, but the communes and whole peoples provided assistance. Besides this, all the banished and anyone else who had committed murder or theft or any other thing for which he might fear public punishment,[2] provided he was a person useful to the building, took refuge safely within those buildings. The other citizens, if they did not build as he did, were not less violent or less rapacious than he: thus if Florence did not have war from outside to destroy it, the city was destroyed by its own citizens.

During this time, as we have said, the wars of the Kingdom took place; and some the pontiff carried on in Romagna against the Malatesti because he desired to despoil them of Rimini and of Cesena, which they possessed. So, between these enterprises and his thoughts of making a campaign against the Turk, Pope Pius spent his pontificate.

5

BUT Florence continued in its disunions and travails. Disunion began in Cosimo's party in '55 for the causes given, which through his prudence, as we have narrated, were arrested for the time being. But when the year '64 came, Cosimo's illness became so serious again that he passed from this life. His friends and enemies lamented his death, because those who

[1] See *FH* II 11.
[2] Lit.: penance.

for cause of state did not love him saw what had been the rapacity of citizens, while he was living, whose reverence for him made them less unbearable; they feared that without him, they would be altogether ru- ined and destroyed. And they did not have much confidence in his son Piero, for notwithstanding that he was a good man, nonetheless, they judged that because he too was infirm and new in the state, it would be necessary for him to respect those men, so that without a bit in their mouths they could be more excessive in their rapacity. Therefore, Cos- imo left a very great regret[1] for himself in everyone.

Cosimo was the most reputed and renowned citizen, as an unarmed man, of whom not only Florence but any other city had ever had mem- ory. For he surpassed every other man of his times not only in authority and riches but also in liberality and prudence, because among all the other qualities that made him prince in his fatherland was that, above all other men, he was liberal and magnificent. His liberality appeared very much more after his death, when his son Piero set about to realize his posses- sions: for there was no other citizen who had any quality in that city to whom Cosimo had not lent a large sum of money; many times without being asked, when he learned of the necessity of a noble man, he helped him. His magnificence appeared in the abundance of buildings built by him; for in Florence, the cloisters and churches of San Marco and San Lorenzo and the monastery of Santa Verdiana, and on the hills of Fiesole, San Girolamo, and the Badia, and in the Mugello, a church of the Minor Friars—he not only initiated but built anew from the foundations. Be- sides all this, in Santa Croce, in the Servi, in the Angioli, and in San Miniato he had very splendid altars and chapels built. Besides building these churches and chapels, he filled them with raiments and everything necessary to the adornment of divine service. In addition to these sacred buildings were his private houses, which are: one in the city of a sort befitting so great a citizen; four outside, in Careggi, Fiesole, Cafaggiuolo, and Trebbio—all palaces not of private citizens but of kings. And because it was not enough for him to be known for the magnificence of his build- ings in Italy, he also built in Jerusalem a hospital for poor and sick pil- grims. In these buildings he spent a very great amount of money. And although these dwellings and all his other works and actions were kingly, and he alone in Florence was prince, nonetheless, so tempered was he by his prudence that he never overstepped civil modesty. For in his conver- sations, in his servants, in riding on horse, in his whole mode of living, and in his marriage alliances, he was always like any modest citizen. For he knew how extraordinary things that are seen and appear every hour make men much more envied than those that are done with the deed and

---

[1] Lit.: desire.

are covered over with decency. Therefore, when he had to give wives to his sons, he did not look for alliances with princes but united Cornelia degli Alessandri with Giovanni and Lucrezia de' Tornabuoni with Piero; and of his grandchildren born to Piero, he married Bianca to Guglielmo de' Pazzi and Nannina to Bernardo Rucellai. No one in his time was equal to him in his understanding of the states of princes and civil governments; hence, it arose that in such variety of fortune and in so various a city and so changeable a citizenry, he held one state for thirty-one years. For, being very prudent, he recognized evils at a distance and therefore was in time either not to let them grow or to be prepared so that, if they did grow, they would not offend him. Hence not only did he conquer domestic and civil ambition, but he overcame that of many princes with such prosperity and prudence that whoever allied with him and with his fatherland would come out either equal or superior to the enemy, and whoever opposed him would lose his time and money or state. Of this, the Venetians can give good testimony, who were always superior against Duke Filippo when they were with him and when they were disunited from him were always conquered and beaten, first by Filippo and then by Francesco; and when they allied with Alfonso against the republic of Florence, Cosimo with his own credit emptied Naples and Venice of money, so that they were constrained to accept the peace that he was willing to concede to them. So of the difficulties that Cosimo had inside the city and outside, the outcome was glorious for him and harmful for his enemies; and thus civil discords always increased his state in Florence, and wars outside increased his power and reputation, in consequence of which he added Borgo San Sepolcro, Montedoglio, the Casentino, and Val di Bagno to the empire of his republic. And thus his virtue and fortune eliminated all his enemies and exalted his friends.

6

HE was born in 1389, the day of St. Cosimo and St. Damiano. His early life was full of trials, as his exile, arrest, and dangers of death demonstrate; and from the Council of Constance, where he had gone with Pope John,[1] he had to flee in disguise after that pope's ruin to save his life. But after forty years of his life had passed, he lived very prosperously, so that not only those who sided with him in his public undertakings but also those who managed his treasure throughout Europe shared in his prosperity. From this arose much excessive wealth in many families of Florence, such as came to the families of the Tornabuoni, Benci, Portinari,

---

[1] Pope John XXIII, the antipope deposed at the Council of Constance in 1415.

and Sassetti. After these, all those who depended on his advice and fortune became rich, such that, although in the building of churches and in charities he spent continually, he complained sometimes to his friends that he had never been able to spend as much in honor of God as he found in His books that he was a debtor. He was of common size, olive complexion, and venerable presence. He was without learning but very eloquent and full of a natural prudence and was thus kindly to his friends, merciful to the poor, useful in conversations, cautious in advice, quick in executions, and in his sayings and replies he was keen and grave. Messer Rinaldo degli Albizzi sent to tell him early in his exile that the hen was brooding, to which Cosimo answered, she could brood but poorly outside the nest. And to other rebels who let him know they were not sleeping, he said that he believed it, since it was he who had taken sleep from them. He said of Pope Pius when he was summoning princes to a campaign against the Turk that he was old and was carrying on a campaign for the young. To the Venetian spokesmen who came to Florence together with those of King Alfonso to complain of the republic, he appeared with his head bared and asked them what color it was, to which they responded, "White"; and he then rejoined, "It won't be long before your senators will have heads as white as I have." When his wife asked him a few hours before his death why he kept his eyes closed, he answered, "To get them used to it." When some citizens told him after his return from exile that the city was being spoiled and that it was acting against God to send away from it so many men of means, he answered that a city spoiled was better than one lost, that two lengths of rose cloth made a man of means,[2] and that states were not held with paternosters in hand— which sayings gave matter to his enemies to slander him as a man who loved himself more than his fatherland and this world more than the other. One could repeat many other sayings of his, which will be omitted as unnecessary. Cosimo was also a lover and exalter of literary men; he therefore brought Argyropoulos to Florence, a man of Greek birth and very learned for those times, so that Florentine youth might learn from him the Greek language and other teachings of his. He took into his home Marsilio Ficino, second father of Platonic philosophy, whom he loved extremely; and that Ficino might pursue his studies of letters more comfortably and that he might be able to use him more conveniently, Cosimo gave him a property near his own in Careggi. Then his prudence, his riches, mode of living, and fortune made him feared and loved in Florence by citizens and marvelously esteemed by princes not only in Italy but in all Europe. Hence, he left such a foundation to his descendants that with virtue they could equal him and with fortune surpass him by a long

---

[2] The amount needed to make the coat of a Florentine Prior.

way, and the authority Cosimo had in Florence they could have not only in that city but in all Christendom. Nonetheless, in the last years of his life, he felt very grave sorrow because of the two sons he had, Piero and Giovanni. The latter, in whom he had more confidence, died; the other was ill and, because of the weakness of his body, hardly fit for public or private affairs. So, as he had himself carried through the house after his son's death, he said, sighing, "This is too big a house for so small a family." It distressed the greatness of his spirit that it did not appear to him that he had increased the Florentine empire by an honorable acquisition, and he grieved all the more as it appeared to him that he had been deceived by Francesco Sforza, who while he was count had promised him that as soon as he had become lord of Milan he would make a campaign against Lucca on behalf of the Florentines. This did not happen because the count changed his mind with his fortune and, when he became a duke, wanted to enjoy that state in the peace that he had acquired with war; therefore, he did not try to satisfy either Cosimo or anyone else by any campaign. Nor, after he became duke, did he wage any wars other than those necessary to defend himself. This was cause for very great annoyance to Cosimo, for it appeared to him that he had endured trouble and expense to make an ungrateful and unfaithful man great. It appeared to him, besides this, that, because of the infirmity of his body, he could not bring his former diligence to public or private affairs, so that he saw both being ruined because the city was being destroyed by the citizens and his substance by his agents and his sons. All these things made him pass the last years of his life in disquiet. Nonetheless, he died full of glory and with a very great name in the city and outside. All the citizens and all the Christian princes mourned his death with his son Piero, and he was accompanied to his tomb with very great pomp by all citizens and was buried in the Church of San Lorenzo; and by public decree, on his tombstone he was named Father of his Fatherland. If I, in writing about the things done by Cosimo, have imitated those who write the lives of princes, not those who write universal histories, one should not wonder at it, because, he being a man rare in our city, I was compelled of necessity to praise him in an extraordinary mode.

7

IN these times, while Florence and Italy were in the condition that has been described, Louis, king of France,[1] was assailed by a very grave war,

[1] Louis XI (1461–1483).

which was begun against him by his barons with the help of Francis, duke of Brittany, and Charles, duke of Burgundy. The war was of such moment that he could not think of assisting Jean of Anjou in the campaigns against Genoa and the Kingdom, and yet, as he judged that Jean needed help from someone, since the city of Savona had remained in the power[2] of the French, he made Francesco, duke of Milan, lord of it and let him understand that, if he wanted, he could make the campaign against Genoa with his grace. This was accepted by Francesco, and with the reputation that his friendship with the king gave him and through the favors granted him by the Adorni, he made himself lord of Genoa; and so as not to show himself ungrateful toward the king for benefits received, he sent as support to the king in France fifteen hundred cavalry captained by Galeazzo, his oldest son.

Here, therefore, were Ferdinand of Aragon and Francesco Sforza, one duke of Lombardy and prince of Genoa, the other king of the whole kingdom of Naples. Having made a marriage alliance together, they were thinking of how they could establish their states so that they could enjoy them securely while they lived and leave them freely to their heirs when they died. And for this they judged it was necessary for the king to secure himself against those barons who had offended him in Jean of Anjou's war[3] and for the duke to work to eliminate the arms of the Bracci, natural enemies of his bloodline. They had risen to very great reputation under Jacopo Piccinino, because he now remained the first captain in Italy. Since Jacopo had no state, whoever did have a state had to fear him, and especially the duke, to whom, moved by his own example, it did not appear that he could either hold his state or leave it secure for his children so long as Jacopo was living. Therefore, the king with all his industry sought an agreement with his barons and used every art to secure them. This succeeded prosperously for him, because those princes saw that if they continued at war with the king, their own ruin was manifest; and if they made an agreement and trusted in him, they stood in doubt. And because men always flee more willingly from the evil that is certain, it follows that princes can easily deceive lesser powers: those princes believed in the peace of the king when they saw the manifest dangers of war, and when they had put themselves into his arms in various modes and for various causes, they were eliminated by him. This frightened Jacopo Piccinino, who was at Sulmona with his men; and so as to deprive the king of the opportunity to suppress him, he held negotiations with Duke Francesco, through the mediation of his friends, to reconcile himself with the duke.

[2] *Potestà.*
[3] See *FH* vi 36–37.

And when the duke had made him the best offer he could, Jacopo decided to put himself into his arms, and he set off, accompanied by a hundred cavalry, to meet him in Milan.

8

JACOPO had fought for a long time under his father and with his brother, first for Duke Filippo and then for the people of Milan. Thus, through his long association he had many friends and universal good will in Milan, which present conditions had increased because the prosperous fortune and present power of the Sforzas had given birth to envy, while for Jacopo things adverse and his long absence had generated pity in that people and a very great desire to see him. All these things became apparent on his coming, because few of the nobility remained who would not meet him, and the streets where he passed were overflowing with those who desired to see him. The name of his family was shouted out everywhere. These honors hastened his ruin, because the desire of the duke to eliminate him grew with mistrust; and so as to do it more covertly, he wanted the marriage of Drusiana, his natural daughter, whom he had betrothed to Jacopo long ago, to be celebrated. Then he arranged with Ferdinand that Ferdinand hire him with the title of captain of his men and a hundred thousand florins for provisions. After this was concluded, Jacopo, together with a ducal ambassador and his wife, Drusiana, went to Naples, where he was joyously and honorably received and entertained for many days with every kind of festivity. But when he asked for permission to go to Sulmona, where his troops were, he was invited by the king to a banquet in the castle, and after the banquet he, together with his son, Francesco, was imprisoned and after a short time put to death. So much did our Italian princes fear in others the virtue that was not in themselves, and they eliminated it, so that, since no one remained who had it, they exposed this province to the ruin that not long after wasted and afflicted it.[1]

9

POPE Pius, in these times, had settled things in Romagna, and so he thought it time, seeing the universal peace that followed, to move Christians against the Turk; and he resumed all those orders that had been

[1] Cf. *P* 24.

made by his predecessors. All the princes promised either money or men, and in particular, Matthias, king of Hungary, and Charles, duke of Burgundy,[1] promised to be with him in person, the pope having made them captains of the enterprise. And the pontiff went so far with his hope that he left Rome and went to Ancona, where the whole army had been ordered to assemble; the Venetians had promised ships to take it into Slavonia. After the arrival of the pontiff, so many people assembled in that city that in a few days all the food that was in the city and that could be brought there from nearby places ran out, so that everyone was overcome by hunger. Furthermore, there was no money to provide those who had need of it, nor arms to furnish those who lacked them; and Matthias and Charles did not appear, and the Venetians sent one of their captains with several galleys more to show off their pomp and to show that they had observed their faith than to enable the armies to cross. Hence the pope, being old and ill, died in the midst of these trials and disorders; after his death, everyone returned to his home. The pope died in year 1465, and Paul II, of Venetian birth, was elected to the pontificate. And so that almost all the principates of Italy would change government, in the following year Francesco Sforza, duke of Milan, also died, sixteen years after having seized the dukedom, and his son Galeazzo was declared duke.

10

THE death of this prince caused divisions in Florence to become stronger and to produce their effects more quickly. After Cosimo died, his son Piero, left heir to the property[1] and state of his father, called to himself Messer Dietisalvi Neroni, a man of great authority, very highly reputed by other citizens, in whom Cosimo had had so much confidence that, as he was dying, he charged Piero to conduct himself in regard to his property and state according to that man's advice. So Piero made known to Messer Dietisalvi the faith that Cosimo had had in him, and, because he wanted to obey his father after his death as he had obeyed him in life, he desired to consult with him regarding his patrimony and the government of the city. And to begin with his own property, he would have all the calculations of his accounts[2] brought together and put into Messer Dietisalvi's hands so that he could learn their order and disorder and, having learned that, advise him in accordance with his prudence. Messer Dieti-

---

[1] In fact, Philip the Good.
[1] Lit.: substances.
[2] Lit.: reasons.

salvi promised to use diligence and faith in everything; but when the accounts came and he had examined them well, he discovered that in every part there was much disorder. Since his own ambition was more compelling to him than his love for Piero or the old benefits received from Cosimo, he thought it would be easy to take Piero's reputation from him and deprive him of the state that his father had left him as hereditary. Therefore, Messer Dietisalvi came to Piero with advice that appeared altogether decent and reasonable but under which his ruin was hidden. He pointed out to Piero the disorder of his things and how much money it was necessary for him to provide if he did not want to lose with his credit the reputation of his property and his state. And for this he told him that he could not remedy his disorders with greater decency than by seeking to collect the sums of money that were owed to his father by many, foreigners as well as citizens. For Cosimo, in order to gain partisans in Florence and friends outside, had been very liberal in sharing his property with everyone, so that for those causes he was creditor of a sum neither small nor of slight importance. To Piero, the advice appeared good and decent, as he wanted to remedy his disorders with what was his own; but as soon as he ordered that the money be demanded, the citizens, as if he wanted to take away from them their own rather than demand what was his, became resentful; and without respect they spoke ill of him and slandered him as ungrateful and avaricious.

I I

THEN, when Messer Dietisalvi saw the common and popular disgrace that Piero had incurred through his advice, he drew close to Messer Luca Pitti, Messer Agnolo Acciaiuoli, and Niccolò Soderini, and they determined to take reputation and state from Piero. These men were moved by diverse causes: Messer Luca desired to succeed to Cosimo's place because he had become so great that he was indignant at having to defer to Piero; Messer Dietisalvi, who knew that Messer Luca was not fit to be the head of government, thought that, with Piero out of the way, of necessity all reputation would in a brief time fall to himself; Niccolò Soderini liked to have the city live more freely and be governed by the will of the magistrates. Messer Agnolo held a particular hatred for the Medici for these causes: his son Raffaello had some time earlier taken Alessandra de' Bardi as his wife, with a very great dowry. Either because of her shortcomings or through the defects of others, she was ill treated by her father-in-law and her husband; whereupon Lorenzo di Larione, her relative, was moved by pity for the girl, and, accompanied one night by many

armed men, he took her from the house of Messer Agnolo. The Acciaiuoli complained of the injury done them by the Bardi. The cause was
taken to Cosimo, who judged that the Acciaiuoli must restore Alessandra's dowry to her and that afterward the girl's return to her husband
should be left to her own will. It did not appear to Messer Agnolo that in
this judgment Cosimo had treated him as a friend, and since he could not
avenge himself against Cosimo, he determined to do so against his son.
With such diversity of humors, these conspirators nonetheless announced
publicly one identical cause, asserting that they wanted the city to be governed by the magistrates and not by the advice of a few. Besides this, the
hatreds toward Piero and the causes for abusing him grew, as many merchants failed at this time; for this, Piero was publicly blamed, since by
desiring against all expectation to recover his money, to the disgrace and
harm of the city, he had made them fail. Added to this was his negotiating
to have Clarice degli Orsini given as wife to Lorenzo, his eldest son—
which gave everyone even more matter for slandering him, as they said it
was plain to see that, since he refused a Florentine marriage for his son,
the city no longer included him as a citizen and that therefore he was
preparing to seize a principate: for he who does not want citizens as relatives wants them as slaves, and therefore it is reasonable that he not have
them for friends. To the heads of this sedition it appeared that they had
victory in hand, because the greater part of the citizens, deceived by the
name of liberty that these men had taken as their ensign to give their
enterprise the appearance of decency, were following them.

12

THUS, while these humors were boiling again in the city, it appeared to
some[1] of those who disliked civil discords that one should see if they
could be checked with some new merriment, because most of the time
idle peoples are an instrument for whoever wants to make a change.
Thus, to be rid of this idleness and to give men something to think about
that would lift their thoughts from the state, as a year had already passed
since Cosimo's death, they took the opportunity for doing something
that would cheer up the city, and they ordered two festivals, very sump-
tuous by comparison to others held in that city. One represented the
Three Kings coming from the Orient following the star that indicated the
birth of Christ, which was of such pomp and so magnificent that the

---

[1] Or someone.

ordering and making of it kept the whole city busy many months. The other was a tournament (so they called a spectacle that represents a battle of men on horseback), where the first youths of the city were to take part together with the most renowned knights of Italy. And among the young Florentines, the most highly reputed was Lorenzo, oldest son of Piero, who not by favor but by his own worth carried off the first prize.

After these spectacles had been celebrated, the same thoughts returned to the citizens, and each one followed his own opinion with more zeal than ever. Great disputes and travails resulted from this that were greatly increased by two accidents: one was that the authority of the balìa had ended;[2] the other was the death of Francesco, duke of Milan. Hence Galeazzo, the new duke, sent ambassadors to Florence to confirm the terms that his father, Francesco, had kept with the city, in which, among other things, it was provided that every year a certain sum of money was to be paid to the duke. Thereupon those princes contrary to the Medici took up the occasion of this demand, and in the councils they opposed this decision publicly, pointing out that the alliance had been made not with Galeazzo but with Francesco; so with Francesco dead, the obligation was dead. Nor was there cause to revive it, because the virtue that had been in Francesco was not in Galeazzo, and consequently, they ought not and could not hope for the same profit from it; and if they had had little from Francesco, they would have less from this one; and if some citizen wanted to hire him for his own power, that was something against civil life and the liberty of the city. Piero, on the contrary, pointed out that it was not good to lose so necessary an alliance out of avarice and that there was nothing so salutary to the republic and to all Italy as to be leagued with the duke, so that the Venetians, seeing them united, might not hope through either false friendship or open war to crush the duke. For as soon as the Venetians felt the Florentines to be alienated from the duke, they would have arms in hand against him, and, finding him young, new in his state, and without friends, they could easily win him over either by deceit or by force—and in either case one would see the ruin of the republic.

13

THESE reasons were not accepted, and enmities began to be shown openly; each of the parties met at night in different companies, for the

---

[2] The balìa (see *FH* VII 3) was supposed to last until the end of September 1465 but was dissolved early on September 16.

friends of the Medici gathered at the Crocetta and their adversaries at the Pietà. The latter, intent on Piero's ruin, had had many citizens enlisted as favorable to their enterprise. On one night among the times when they were together, they held a particular consultation about their mode of proceeding. To diminish the power of the Medici was pleasing to each, but there were differences over the mode. One party, which was the most temperate and modest, wanted to take care that after the authority of the balìa was ended, its resumption should be blocked. If this were done, it would accord with everyone's intention, because the councils and the magistrates would govern the city, and in a short time Piero's authority would be eliminated. With the loss of the reputation of his state would come the loss of his credit in trade, because his property was in such a strait that if he were strongly held back from being able to make use of public money, he would of necessity be ruined. Were it carried out in this way, there would be no more danger from him, and they would succeed in having recovered their liberty without exiles and without bloodshed, which every good citizen ought to desire. But if one sought to use force, one could bring on very many dangers, because people will let fall one who falls of himself, but if he is pushed by others, they sustain him. Besides this, if nothing extraordinary were ordered against him, he would not have cause to arm himself and look for friends; and if he should do this, he would be so much blamed and would generate so much suspicion in every man that he would make his ruin more easily by himself and would give others greater opportunity to crush him. To many others of those assembled, this length of time was not pleasing, since they asserted that time was in his favor and not theirs; for if they showed themselves content with ordinary things, Piero bore no risk and they ran many risks, because the magistrates, his enemies, would let him enjoy the city, and his friends would make him prince, with ruin to them, as happened in '58. And if the advice that had been given[1] was from good men, this was by wise men; and therefore, he must be eliminated while men were inflamed against him. The mode was to arm themselves inside the city and outside to hire the marquis of Ferrara so as not to be unarmed; and when the lot gave them a friendly Signoria, they would be prepared to secure themselves against him. So they came to this decision: that they should wait for the new Signoria and govern themselves accordingly. Among these conspirators was Ser Niccolò Fedini, who served them as secretary. Attracted by a more certain hope, he revealed all the negotiations held by Piero's enemies to him and brought him the list of conspirators and their subscribers. Piero was dismayed when he saw the number and quality of

[1] The first advice.

the citizens who were against him, and after consulting with his friends, he decided that he too would make a list of his friends. And having given the care of this enterprise to some of his most trusted men, he found such variety and instability in the minds of the citizens that many of those listed as against him were also listed in his favor.

14

WHILE things were toiling on in this manner, it came time to renew the supreme magistracy; and Niccolò Soderini was appointed as Gonfalonier of Justice. It was a marvelous thing to see how great a crowd not only of honored citizens but of all people accompanied him to the palace, and on the route a wreath of olive was placed on his head to show that on him both the safety and the liberty of his fatherland must depend. One sees by this and many other experiences that it is not desirable to take on either a magistracy or a principate with an extraordinary expectation, because if one cannot match it with one's deeds—since men desire more than they can attain—in time it brings you dishonor and infamy. Messer Tommaso Soderini and Niccolò were brothers: Niccolò was the more fierce and spirited, Messer Tommaso more wise. The latter, because he was very friendly to Piero and understood his brother's humor—that Niccolò desired only the freedom of the city and that the state be made firm without offense to anyone—urged him to make a new list by which the bags would be filled with the names of citizens who loved free life. If this were done, the state would come to be confirmed and secured without tumult and without injury to anyone, in accordance with his wish. Niccolò readily trusted the advice of his brother and set about to waste the time of his magistracy in these vain thoughts; and he was allowed to waste it by the heads of the conspirators, his friends, since they out of envy did not want the state to be renewed by the authority of Niccolò, and they always believed that they had time to work this out with another Gonfalonier. Therefore, the end of Niccolò's magistracy came, and as he had begun many things and not finished any, he left it with much more dishonor than the honor with which he had taken it.

15

THIS example made Piero's party bolder; his friends were more confirmed in their hope, and those who had been neutral joined Piero; so things being balanced, they temporized for months without further tumult. Nonetheless, Piero's party was gathering ever more force, so that his enemies became aroused and met together again; and that which they had not known or wanted to do easily by means of the magistrates they thought to do by force. They decided to have Piero, who was ill at Careggi, killed and, to effect this, to have the marquis of Ferrara come with his troops toward the city and, when Piero was dead, to come armed into the piazza and make the Signoria establish a state in accordance with their will, because even if all of it was not friendly, they hoped that they could make the part that was opposed yield through fear. Messer Dietisalvi, in order to better conceal his intent, visited Piero often, reasoned with him about the unity of the city, and advised him. All these dealings had been revealed to Piero; and furthermore, Messer Domenico Martelli let Piero know that Francesco Neroni, brother of Messer Dietisalvi, had asked him to be with them, pointing out to him certain victory and the winning side. Then Piero determined to be the first to take up arms, and he took the dealings of his adversaries with the marquis of Ferrara as his occasion. He pretended, therefore, to have received a letter from Messer Giovanni Bentivoglio, the prince in Bologna, which informed him that the marquis of Ferrara was on the river Albo with troops and that they were saying publicly that they were coming to Florence. And so, with this information, Piero took up arms and, in the midst of a great multitude of armed men, came to Florence. After this, all those who followed his party armed themselves, and the adverse party did the same; but Piero's party was in better order, as his had been prepared, and the others were not yet in the order of their scheme. Messer Dietisalvi, because he had his houses near Piero's, did not feel safe in them but kept going first to the palace to urge the Signoria to make Piero put down his arms, then to find Messer Luca to keep him solidly in their party. But of all, Niccolò Soderini showed himself more lively than anyone; he took up his arms and was followed by almost all the plebs of his quarter, and he went to the houses of Messer Luca and begged him to mount his horse and come to the piazza in support of the Signoria, which was for them—where without a doubt there would be certain victory—and not stay in his house to be either overcome vilely by armed enemies or shamefully deceived by the unarmed. And he would soon repent not having done what he would be in time to do; and if he wanted the ruin of Piero by war, he could have it easily; if he wanted peace, it was much better to be in a position to give, not receive, the conditions of peace. These words did not move Messer Luca, for he had already put aside his intent and had been brought around by Piero with promises of new alliances and new conditions; for they had joined in marriage one of his nieces with Giovanni Tornabuoni. So he urged Niccolò to put down his arms and go home, because it ought to be enough for him that the city be governed by the magistrates; and so it would happen, and every man would put down his arms; and the Signori, where they[1] had a larger party, would know how to be judges of their differences. Thus, as Niccolò was unable to persuade him otherwise, he went home, but first said to him, "I cannot do good alone for my city, but I can well foretell evil for it; this course that you are taking will make our fatherland lose its liberty, you your state and property, and me and the others our fatherland."

16

THE Signoria had closed the palace during this tumult and had shut itself in with its magistrates, not showing favor to any of the parties. When the citizens, especially those who had followed the party of Messer Luca, saw Piero armed and his adversaries unarmed, they began to think not about how they must offend Piero but about how they must become his friends. Hence, the first citizens, heads of the factions, met at the palace in the presence of the Signoria, where they reasoned over many things relating to the state of the city and many relating to a reconciliation in it. And as Piero could not be present, due to the weakness of his body, all in accord determined to go to his houses to find him, except Niccolò Soderini, who, having first entrusted his children and his things to Messer Tommaso, went out to his villa to await there the outcome of the thing, which he expected to be unprosperous for himself and damaging to his fatherland. When the other citizens then arrived at Piero's, one of them who had been commissioned to speak complained of the tumults that had arisen in the city, pointing out that those were more to blame who had first taken up arms; and as they did not know what Piero wanted, who had been the first to take them up, they had come to learn his will, and if it conformed to the good of the city, they were ready to follow it. To these words, Piero answered that he who first takes up arms is not the cause of scandals but rather the one who is first to give cause for their being taken up. If they thought more about what their modes had been toward him, they would marvel less at what he had done to save himself; for they would see that nocturnal meetings, enlistments, and dealings to take the city and his life from him had made him arm himself. Since he had not moved these arms from his houses, they were a clear sign of his intent of having taken them up to defend himself, not to offend others.

[1] The conspirators opposed to the Medici.

Nor did he want anything or desire anything but his own safety or quiet;
nor had he ever given a sign that he desired anything else for himself,
because, when the authority of the balìa had ended, he never thought of
any extraordinary mode of turning it over to himself, and he was very
content that the magistrates govern the city, if they were content with
that. And they should remember that Cosimo and his sons knew how to
live honored in Florence with the balìa as well as without the balìa; and in
'58 it was not his house but theirs that had reassumed it; and if now they
did not want it, he too did not want it; but this was not enough for them,
because he had seen that they did not believe they could remain in Florence if he were there. Truly, this was a thing he would not only never
have believed but not even thought: that his friends and his father's friends
should not believe they could live in Florence with him, since he had
never given any sign himself but that of a quiet and peaceful man. Then
he turned to speak to Messer Dietisalvi and his brothers, who were present, and he rebuked them with grave words full of indignation for the
benefits they had received from Cosimo, the faith he had had in them,
and their great ingratitude. And his words were so forceful that some of
those present were so moved that, if Piero had not held them back, they
would have handled them with arms. Finally, Piero declared that he was
ready to approve all that they and the Signoria decided and that he would
ask for nothing other than to live quietly and safely. Many things were
said about this but nothing decided then, except that generally it was necessary to reform the city and give new order to the state.

17

SITTING as the Gonfalonier of Justice in those times was Bernardo Lotti,
a man not trusted by Piero. So to Piero it appeared that, while that man
was in his magistracy, he should not attempt anything; he judged that it
was not very important, since his magistracy was near its end. But when
the election came of the Signori who were to sit in September and October of the year 1466, Roberto Lioni was elected to the highest magistracy.
As soon as he had taken up his magistracy, all other things being prepared, he called the people to the piazza and made up a new balìa entirely
from Piero's party, which soon after created magistrates according to the
will of the new state. These things frightened the heads of the enemy
faction, and Messer Agnolo Acciaiuoli fled to Naples, and Messer Dietisalvi Neroni and Niccolò Soderini to Venice; Messer Luca Pitti remained
in Florence, trusting in the promises made to him by Piero and in their

new marriage alliance.[1] Those who had fled were declared rebels, and all of the Neroni family were scattered; Messer Giovanni di Neroni, then archbishop of Florence, chose voluntary exile for himself in Rome so as to escape greater evil. Many other citizens who left immediately were banished to various places. Nor was this enough, for a procession was ordered to thank God for having preserved the state and reunited the city, during which solemnity some citizens were arrested and tortured; and then some were killed and some sent into exile. Nor in this change of things was there so noteworthy an example as that of Messer Luca Pitti, for he learned immediately what the difference is between victory and defeat, between dishonor and honor. In his house one saw very great solitude, where before it was frequented by very many citizens; in the streets his friends and relatives feared not only to accompany him but even to greet him, because from some of them honors had been taken away and from others property, and all were equally threatened. The splendid buildings that he had begun were abandoned by the builders, the benefits that had been done him before were converted into injuries, the honors into insults; hence, many of those who had given him something of great worth by their grace were asking to have it returned as something loaned, and others who used to praise him to the sky blamed him as an ungrateful and violent man. So he repented late for not having believed Niccolò Soderini and for not having sought to die honored with arms in hand rather than to live dishonored among his victorious enemies.

18

THOSE who found themselves driven out began to think among themselves of various modes of reacquiring the city that they had not been able to preserve. Nonetheless, Messer Agnolo Acciaiuoli, being in Naples, before thinking of any innovation, wanted to test Piero's intent to see if he could hope to be reconciled with him, and he wrote a letter in this sense: "I am laughing at the games of fortune and at how it makes friends become enemies and enemies become friends as it suits it. You[1] can remember when in your father's exile I considered his injury more than my own dangers, I lost my fatherland and nearly lost my life; nor, while I lived under Cosimo, did I ever fail to honor and support your house;[2] nor after his death had I any intent of offending you. It is true that your bad

---

[1] See *FH* VII 15.
[1] The familiar "you" is used in these letters except where noted.
[2] The plural "your."

constitution and the tender age of your children dismayed me, so that I judged it better to give such a form to the state that after your death our fatherland would not be ruined. From this arose things that were done, not against you but for the benefit of my fatherland—which, even if it was an error, deserves to be canceled because of my meaning well and my past deeds. Nor can I believe, since your house[3] found such faith in me for so long a time, that I cannot now find compassion in you and that my many merits will be destroyed by one single mistake." Having received this letter, Piero answered it thus: "Your laughing over there is the cause that I do not weep, because if you were laughing in Florence, I would be weeping in Naples. I confess that you wished my father well, and you will confess that you received well from him; so much more was your obligation than ours, as deeds must be valued higher than words. Thus, since you have been well recompensed for your good, you ought not now to marvel if your evil brings you just rewards. Nor does love of the fatherland excuse you, because there will never be anyone who will believe that this city has been loved and increased less by the Medici than by the Acciaiuoli. So live there in dishonor, since you did not know how to live here in honor."

19

IN despair, therefore, of being able to obtain pardon, Messer Agnolo came to Rome and joined with the archbishop and other exiles; and within the most active limits, they exerted themselves to destroy the credit of the account of the Medici that was carried on in Rome. Piero provided against this with difficulty; yet, as he was helped by his friends, their scheme failed. Messer Dietisalvi, for his part, and Niccolò Soderini sought with all diligence to move the Venetian senate against their fatherland, for they judged that if the Florentines were attacked in a new war, they could not resist it, because their state was new and hated. In Ferrara at that time lived Giovan Francesco, son of Messer Palla Strozzi, who had been driven out of Florence with his father in the changeover of '34. This man had great credit and, according to other merchants, was considered to be very rich. These new rebels pointed out to Giovan Francesco the ease with which they could be repatriated if the Venetians should make an undertaking of it. And they easily believed that the Venetians would do it if some contribution could be made toward the expense; otherwise, the exiles were doubtful of it. Giovan Francesco, who desired to avenge

[3] The familiar "your."

himself for the injuries he had received, believed easily in the advice of
these men and promised that he would be glad to assist this undertaking
with all his means. Hence, the exiles went to the doge and complained to
him of their exile, which they said they suffered for no other error than
having wished that their fatherland live by its laws and that the magistrates, and not a few citizens, be honored—for which error Piero de'
Medici with his followers, who were accustomed to living tyrannically,
had by deceit taken up arms, by deceit made them put theirs down, and
then by deceit had them driven out of their fatherland. Nor were they
content with this, but they used God as a means to oppress many others
who remained in the city under the faith that had been given; and so that
God be a participant in their treacheries, they had had many citizens imprisoned and killed in the midst of public and sacred ceremonies and solemn prayers—an act of impious and wicked example.[1] To avenge this,
they did not know where they could go for recourse with more hope than
to this senate, which, as it had always been free, ought to have compassion for those who had lost their liberty. Thus, they were stirring up free
men against tyrants, pious against impious; and the Venetians should remember how the Medici family had taken from them empire over Lombardy when Cosimo, quite apart from the wish of other citizens, favored
and helped Francesco against this senate:[2] so if the Florentines' own just
cause did not move them, a just hatred and a just desire to avenge themselves ought to move them.

20

THESE last words stirred the whole senate, and they decided that their
captain, Bartolomeo Colleoni, should attack the Florentine dominion.
And as soon as it was possible, the army was assembled and was joined
by Ercole d'Este, who had been sent by Borso, marquis of Ferrara. In
their first attack, the Florentines being not yet in order, they burned the
village of Dovadola and did other damage in the countryside around it.
But the Florentines, when the party hostile to Piero had been driven out,
made a new league with Galeazzo, duke of Milan, and with King Ferdinand, and for their captain hired Federico, count of Urbino; thus finding
themselves in order with friends, they thought less of their enemies. For
Ferdinand sent Alfonso, his oldest son, and Galeazzo came in person—
each with suitable forces; they all gathered at Castracaro, a fortified place

[1] See *FH* VII 17.
[2] *FH* VI 23.

the Florentines located at the foot of the mountains where they descend from Tuscany into Romagna. The enemy, in the meantime, had withdrawn toward Imola, and so between one army and the other light skirmishes took place, according to the customs of those times. Neither one nor the other attacked or besieged towns or gave the enemy opportunity to join battle; but each remaining in its tents, each conducted itself with marvelous vileness. This thing was displeasing to Florence, because it saw itself oppressed by a war in which it was spending much and from which it could hope for little; and the magistrates complained of it to those citizens whom they had deputed as commissioners of the undertaking. The commissioners answered that the cause of it all was Duke Galeazzo, who had much authority and little experience and did not know how to take useful courses, nor did he put faith in those who did know; and it was impossible for them to do anything virtuous or useful while he stayed with the army. Therefore, the Florentines let the duke know that it was convenient and very useful to them for him to come in person to their aid, because his reputation alone was apt to frighten the enemy; nonetheless, they valued much more his safety and his state than their own convenience, because with that safe, they hoped every other thing would be prosperous, but if it suffered, they feared every sort of adversity. Therefore, they did not judge it very secure that he should stay absent from Milan a long time, he being new in that state and having powerful and suspicious neighbors, so that anyone who wanted to plot against him could do it easily. Hence, they urged him to return to his state and to leave part of his men for their defense. Galeazzo was pleased with this advice and without another thought returned to Milan. Thus the captains of the Florentines, left without this impediment, pressed the enemy, more so as to demonstrate that the cause of proceeding slowly that they had cited was the true one: so they came to an ordered battle that lasted half a day without either side's yielding. Nonetheless, no one was killed; only some horses were wounded and a few prisoners taken on each side. Winter had already come, the time when the armies were accustomed to withdraw to their quarters; therefore, Messer Bartolomeo retreated toward Ravenna, the Florentine troops into Tuscany, and those of the king and the duke each withdrew to the states of their lords. But since no movement was felt in Florence from this attack such as the Florentine rebels had promised, and as money was lacking for the soldiers, a truce was discussed, and after not much negotiation it was concluded. Thereupon, the Florentine rebels, deprived of all hope, departed for various places. Messer Dietisalvi withdrew to Ferrara, where he was received and sheltered by Marquis Borso; Niccolò Soderini went to Ravenna, where on a small pension received from the Venetians he grew old and died. He had been considered a just and spirited man, but hesitant and slow in making up his mind—which made him as Gonfalonier of Justice lose the opportunity of winning what later, as a private individual, he wished to reacquire and could not.

21

PEACE having come, to those citizens who had been left on top in Florence it did not appear that they had won unless they afflicted with every injury not only their enemies but those suspect to their party. They worked with Bardo Altoviti, who was sitting as Gonfalonier of Justice, once again to take away honors from many citizens and the city from many others. This increased power for themselves and terror to the others; they exercised this power without any hesitation and so conducted themselves that it appeared that God and fortune had given them that city in prey. Of these things, Piero understood little, and he could do little to remedy them because he was oppressed by his infirmity; for he was so stiffened that he could make use only of his tongue. Nor could he apply other remedies than to warn those citizens and pray them to live civilly and enjoy their fatherland safe rather than destroyed.

And to cheer up the city, he decided to celebrate with magnificence the marriage of his son, Lorenzo, to whom Clarice, born of the Orsini house, had been engaged. The wedding was held with the splendor of ornaments and every other magnificence that such a man required; many days were spent in new kinds[1] of balls, banquets, and ancient dramas.[2] Besides these things, there were two military spectacles to show further the greatness of the house of Medici and its state: one was done by men on horseback, in which a combat in the field was represented; the other showed the capture of a town. These things were done with order and executed with virtue that could not have been greater.

22

WHILE things proceeded in this manner in Florence, the rest of Italy lived quietly but with great suspicion of the power of the Turk. The Turk, with his campaigns, continued fighting the Christians and had captured Negropont with great disgrace and harm to the Christian name. Borso, mar-

---

[1] Lit.: orders.
[2] Lit.: representations.

quis of Ferrara, died in those times, and he was succeeded by his brother Ercole. Sigismondo of Rimini, a perpetual enemy to the Church, died and left as heir to his state Roberto, his natural son, who was later most excellent in war among the captains of Italy. Pope Paul died, and elected to succeed him was Sixtus IV, previously called Francesco da Savona, a man of very base and vile condition;[1] but by his virtues he had become general in the order of Saint Francis and then cardinal. This pontiff was the first who began to show how much a pontiff could do and how many things formerly called errors could be hidden under pontifical authority. He had in his household Piero and Girolamo, who, according to what everyone believed, were his sons; nonetheless, he cloaked them under other, more decent names. Piero, because he was a friar, he elevated to the dignity of the cardinalate with the title of San Sisto; to Girolamo he gave the city of Forlì and took it away from Antonio Ordelaffi, whose ancestors had for a long time been the princes of that city. This ambitious mode of proceeding made him more esteemed by the princes of Italy, and each tried to make him his friend; and this was why the duke of Milan gave Caterina, his natural daughter, to Girolamo and, for her dowry, the city of Imola, which he had taken in spoil from Taddeo degli Alidosi. Also, between this duke and King Ferdinand a new marriage was contracted, for Elisabella, born to Alfonso, the king's eldest son, was betrothed to Gian Galeazzo, oldest son of the duke.

23

LIFE in Italy, therefore, went very quietly, and the greatest care of these princes was to observe one another and to secure themselves against one another with marriages, new friendships, and leagues. Nonetheless, in such peace Florence was greatly afflicted by its citizens, and Piero, hindered by illness, was unable to oppose their ambition. Nonetheless, to unburden his conscience and to see if he could shame them, he called them all to his house and spoke to them in this sense: "I would never have believed that the time could come when the modes and customs of my friends would make me bitter and desire enemies, and victory make me desire defeat; for I thought I had in my company men who had some limit or measure to their cupidity and for whom it would be enough to live safe and honored in their fatherland and, besides that, to have had revenge on their enemies. But I know now how greatly I have deceived myself as one who knew little of the natural ambition of all men and less of yours.

[1] "A spirited pope," according to *P* 11.

For it is not enough for you to be princes in such a city and for you few to have these honors, dignities, and advantages with which previously many citizens were wont to be honored; it is not enough for you to have divided among yourselves the goods of your enemies; it is not enough for you to be able to afflict all others with public burdens and for yourselves, free from those, to have all the public profits; nor for you to afflict everyone with every sort of injury. You despoil your neighbor of his goods, you sell justice, you escape civil judgments, you oppress peaceful men and exalt the insolent. Nor do I believe that in all Italy are there so many examples of violence and avarice as in this city. Then did this fatherland of ours give us life so that we might take life from it? Make us victorious so that we might destroy it? Honor us so that we might insult it? I promise you, by the faith that ought to be given and received by good men, that if you continue to carry on in a mode that makes me repent having won, I too shall carry on in a manner that will make you repent having ill used the victory." Those citizens answered accommodatingly in keeping with the time and place; nonetheless, they did not withdraw from their sinister deeds. So Piero had Messer Agnolo Acciaiuoli come secretly to Cafaggiuolo and talked with him at length about the condition of the city; nor can there be any doubt at all that if he had not been interrupted by death he would have had all the exiles restored to their fatherland to check the rapacity of those within. But these very decent thoughts of his were thwarted by death; for, overburdened by the ills of his body and the anxieties of his spirit, he died in his fifty-third year. His fatherland could not entirely know his virtue and goodness, because he had been accompanied almost to the end of his life by his father Cosimo and because those few years that he survived him were consumed in civil dissensions and by illness. Piero was buried in the church of San Lorenzo next to his father; and his funeral was conducted with the pomp that so great a citizen deserved. Two sons were left by him, Lorenzo and Giuliano; although they gave everyone hope of being men who ought to be very useful to the republic, nonetheless their youth frightened everyone.

24

AMONG the first citizens of the government in Florence and by far superior to the others was Messer Tommaso Soderini, whose prudence and authority were known not only in Florence but among all the princes of Italy. After the death of Piero, he was attended to by the whole city; many citizens visited him in his houses as the head of the city, many princes wrote to him. But as he was prudent and best understood his fortune and that of his house, he did not answer the letters of princes and gave the citizens to understand that they should visit not his houses but those of the Medici. And to show effectively what he had demonstrated in his arguments, he gathered all the first men of the noble families in the Convent of San Antonio, where he had Lorenzo and Giuliano de' Medici come also, and there, in a long and grave oration, he discussed the condition of the city, that of Italy, and the humors of its princes. He concluded that if they wanted those in Florence to live united in peace and safe from division within and from wars outside, it was necessary to follow[1] those young men and to maintain the reputation of their house. For men never complain of doing the things they are used to doing; as quickly as new things are taken up, they are dropped; and it has always been easier to maintain a power that by length of time has eliminated envy than to raise up a new one that for very many causes could easily be eliminated. Following after Messer Tommaso, Lorenzo, although he was young, spoke with such gravity and modesty that he gave everyone hope of being that which he later did become. And before they left that place, these citizens swore they would accept the youths as sons and they, the citizens as fathers. As they had thus come to this conclusion, Lorenzo and Giuliano were honored as princes of the state; and the citizens did not deviate from the advice of Messer Tommaso.

25

AND while life went on very quietly inside and outside, since there was no war to disturb the common quiet, an unexpected tumult arose that was like a presage of future harm. Among the families that were ruined with the party of Messer Luca Pitti was that of the Nardi, for Salvestro and his brothers, heads of that family, were first sent into exile, and then later, because of the war begun by Bartolomeo Colleoni, they were declared rebels. Among them was Bernardo, brother of Salvestro, a ready and spirited young man. Unable to bear exile because of his poverty and seeing no mode for his return because of the peace that had been made, he determined to try something that could give cause for a new war. For many times a weak beginning gives birth to mighty effects, since it may be that men will be more ready to pursue a thing in motion than to move it. Bernardo was well acquainted in Prato, very well acquainted in the country around Pistoia, and especially among the Palandra, a family that, although still rural, abounded in men who, like other Pistolese, were

[1] Lit.: observe.

brought up in arms and blood. He knew how malcontent they were for having been maltreated by the Florentine magistrates because of their hostility. Besides this, he was acquainted with the humors of the Pratese and how it appeared to them that they had been proudly and greedily governed; and he knew of the ill intent of some against the state. So all these things gave him hope of kindling a fire in Tuscany by making Prato rebel, where so many would then come together to keep it going that those who wanted to put it out would not be enough. He imparted this thought of his to Messer Dietisalvi and asked him, if he should succeed in seizing Prato, how much help he could hope for through him from the princes. The enterprise appeared very dangerous to Messer Dietisalvi and almost impossible of success; nonetheless, seeing that he could try his own fortune again through dangers to others, he urged Bernardo to the deed and promised very certain assistance from Bologna and Ferrara if Bernardo managed to hold and defend Prato for at least fifteen days. Thus Bernardo, overflowing with prosperous hope from this promise, took himself secretly to Prato, and he communicated the thing to others he found very well disposed there. That same spirit and willingness he also found among the Palandra; and, having agreed together on the time and the mode, Bernardo had Messer Dietisalvi informed of everything.

26

THE podestà of Prato for the people of Florence was Cesare Petrucci. Such governors of towns are accustomed to keep the keys of the gates with them, and sometimes, especially in time of no suspicion, someone in the town asks for them to go out or enter the city at night, and they give them to him. Bernardo knew of this practice, and close to the day agreed upon, together with the Palandra and around a hundred armed men, he appeared at the gate that looks toward Pistoia. Those inside who knew of the plot also armed themselves; one of them asked the podestà for the keys, pretending he was asking for them for someone who wished to enter. The podestà, who could have feared nothing from such an accident, sent his servant with the keys; and as soon as he was some distance from the palace, they were taken from him by the conspirators, the gate opened, and Bernardo let in with his armed men. When they had gathered together, they divided into two parts: one of them, guided by Salvestro Pratese, seized the citadel, the other, together with Bernardo, took the palace, and they gave Cesare with all his family in charge to some of them. Then they raised an alarm and went through the city shouting the name of "Liberty!" Day had already come, and at the alarm many men of the people ran into the piazza; and when they learned that the fortress and the palace had been seized and the podestà arrested with his men, they stood wondering how this accident could have arisen. The Eight Citizens, who in that town held the highest rank in their palace, met to consult about what they should do. But Bernardo and his men had run through the town once and had seen that they had been pursued by no one. After he heard that the Eight were together, he went to them and told them that the cause of his enterprise was his wish to free them and his fatherland from slavery, and how much glory would be theirs if they would take up arms and accompany him in this glorious enterprise, from which they would acquire perpetual quiet and eternal fame. He reminded them of their ancient liberty and present condition, and showed them that aid was certain if they were willing to oppose for a very few days such forces as the Florentines could put together; he asserted that he had support[1] in Florence, which would show itself as soon as it was learned that their town had united to follow him. The Eight were not moved by these words, and they answered that they did not know whether in Florence people lived free or slave, as it was a thing they were not waiting to learn, but they knew well that for themselves they had no desire for any other liberty than to serve the magistrates that governed Florence, from whom they had never received such an injury as would require their taking up arms against them. Therefore, they urged Bernardo to leave the podestà at his liberty and the town free of his troops and to retrieve himself quickly from the danger he had entered into with little prudence. Bernardo was not dismayed at these words, but he decided to see if fear would move the Pratese, since prayers did not; so to frighten them, he thought he would have Cesare killed. After taking him out of prison, he commanded that he be hanged at the palace windows. Cesare was already near the windows with the noose around his neck when he saw Bernardo urging his death. Turning to him he said, "Bernardo, you are having me killed believing that the Pratese will then follow you, but it will turn out the contrary for you, because the reverence this people has for the rectors that the people of Florence send here is so great that as soon as this injury done to me is seen, so much hate will be stirred up against you as will bring your ruin. So not my death but my life can be the cause of your victory, for if I command them as pleases you, they will obey me more readily than you, and if I follow your orders, you will secure your purpose." Since Bernardo was short of plans, this advice appeared good to him; and he commanded Cesare, who had come to a balcony overlooking

---

[1] Lit.: understanding.

the piazza, to command the people to obey Bernardo. When this had been done, Cesare was put back in prison.

27

THE weakness of the conspirators was already uncovered, and many Florentines who lived in the town met together, among them Messer Giorgio Ginori, a knight of Rhodes. This man was the first to take up arms against the conspirators, and he attacked Bernardo, who was going through the piazza discoursing, now begging, now threatening if he was not followed and obeyed; and when the rush was made against him by many who followed Messer Giorgio, Bernardo was wounded and taken. This done, it was an easy thing to free the podestà and to overcome the others. Because they were few and divided in several parts, they were almost all taken or killed. Meanwhile, the report of this unforeseen event had come to Florence, but of something much greater than what had happened, since it was understood that Prato was taken, the podestà and his family killed, and the city filled with enemies, and that Pistoia was in arms and many of its citizens were in the conspiracy. So the palace was immediately filled with citizens who had come to consult with the Signoria. Roberto da San Severino, a captain of very high repute in war,[1] was then in Florence; so it was decided to send him to Prato with as many troops as could be brought together, and he was commissioned to approach the town and report details of the thing and to apply such remedies as should occur to his prudence. Roberto had just passed the town of Campi when he was met by someone sent by Cesare, who informed him that Bernardo had been taken, his companions put to flight and killed, and all tumult put to rest. Thus Roberto returned to Florence, and soon after, Bernardo was brought there. When he was asked by the magistracy about the truth of his enterprise and they found it weak, he said that he had done it because he had decided to die in Florence rather than live in exile, and he wanted his death to be accompanied at least by some memorable deed.

28

AFTER this tumult had arisen and been suppressed almost at a stroke, the citizens returned to their accustomed mode of living, thinking to enjoy without any hesitation the state they had established and made firm.

[1] Cf. *P* 12.

Hence arose those evils in the city that are customarily generated most often in peace, because the young men, more unrestrained than usual, were spending beyond bounds[1] on dress, banquets, and other similar abandonments; and being at leisure, they consumed time and substance in games and women; they studied to appear splendid in their dress and to be clever and smart in their speech, and he who was more deft at biting the others was wiser and more esteemed. These customs, having been so made, were intensified by the courtiers of the duke of Milan, who, together with his wife and the whole ducal court, to satisfy, as was said, a vow, came to Florence, where he was received with the pomp befitting such a prince and such a friend of the city. At that time was seen a thing never before seen in our city: this being the season of Lent, in which the Church commands that one fast by not eating meat, his court, without respect to Church or God, all fed on meat. And because many spectacles were held to honor him, among which was represented the giving of the Holy Spirit to the Apostles in the church of Santo Spirito, and because that church burned down as a result of the many fires that are made in such solemnities, it was believed by many that God, angered against us, had wished to show that sign of his wrath. Thus, if the duke found the city of Florence full of courtly delicacies and customs, contrary to all well-ordered civility, he left it much more so. Therefore, the good citizens thought it necessary to apply a brake, and with a new law they set a limit on clothing, burials, and banquets.

29

IN the midst of so much peace, a new and unexpected tumult arose in Tuscany. An alum mine was found in the countryside around Volterra by some of the citizens. As they realized its value, they approached some Florentine citizens so as to have someone with money to help them and with authority to defend them, and they made these Florentines sharers in the profit that would be derived from it. In the beginning, as happens most often in new enterprises, this was valued little by the people of Volterra, but with time they recognized its value and wanted then to remedy late and without profit what they could have remedied easily in good time. They began to agitate the thing in the councils, asserting that it was not proper that an industry found on public land be converted to private use. They sent spokesmen on this to Florence: the cause was put to some citizens, who, either because they had been corrupted by a party or because they judged it well so, submitted that the people of Volterra was

---

[1] Lit.: mode.

not seeking justice in desiring to deprive its citizens of their labors and industry, and that therefore the alum mines belonged to the private individuals and not to the people. But it would be very proper for them to pay a certain quantity of money each year as a sign that they recognized the people as superior. This answer did not diminish but increased the tumults and hatred in Volterra, and nothing else was agitated, not only in their councils but outside through the whole city: the generality of people[1] demanding what appeared to have been taken from them, and particular individuals wanting to preserve what they had first acquired and then had been confirmed as theirs by the judgment of the Florentines. So much were these disputes agitated that a citizen of high reputation in that city, called Il Pecorino, was killed and after him many others who took sides with him; and their houses were sacked and burned. Those moved by this same impulse barely refrained from killing the rectors who were there on behalf of the Florentine people.

30

AFTER this first insult, they decided before all else to send spokesmen to Florence, who gave the Signori to understand that if the Signori wanted to keep the old agreements, the Volterrans too would keep their city in its old subjection. The response was much discussed. Messer Tommaso Soderini advised that the Volterrans ought to be received in whatever mode they wanted to return, as it did not appear to him the right time to fan a flame so close that could burn down our house. For he feared the nature of the pope and the power of the king and had confidence neither in the friendship of the Venetians nor in that of the duke, as he did not know how much faith there was in one or virtue in the other. He recalled that trite judgment, "Better a lean truce than a fat victory." On the other side, Lorenzo de' Medici, who thought it an occasion to demonstrate how much his advice and prudence were worth, especially as he was being encouraged by those who were envious of the authority of Messer Tommaso, decided to undertake a campaign and punish with arms the arrogance of the Volterrans. He asserted that if they were not set right by a memorable example, others without any reverence or fear would not hesitate to do the same thing for any light cause. This campaign decided upon, the response given to the Volterrans was that they could not ask observance of those agreements that they themselves had broken; and therefore either they must submit to the will of the Signoria or they must expect war. When the Volterrans returned with this response, they pre-

[1] Lit.: the universal.

pared to defend themselves by fortifying the town and sending a summons for help to all the Italian princes. They were heard by few, for only
the Sienese and the lord of Piombino gave them any hope of support. The
Florentines, on the other side, thinking that the importance of victory to
them was in speed, put together ten thousand infantry and two thousand
cavalry, who, under the command of Federico, lord of Urbino, appeared
in the countryside around Volterra and seized it all easily. Then they set a
camp before the city, which was situated in a high place and cut off from
almost every side; it could not be attacked except from the side where the
church of San Alessandro stood. The Volterrans had hired around a thousand soldiers for their defense; and these soldiers, seeing the mighty siege
the Florentines were laying down and losing confidence that they could
defend it, were slow in defense and very prompt in the injuries they inflicted every day on the Volterrans. Thus were those poor citizens attacked from outside by enemies and oppressed inside by friends, so that,
despairing of their safety, they began to think about an accord; and not
finding anything better, they put themselves in the arms of the commissioners.[1] The commissioners had the gates opened, and when they had
let in the greater part of the army, they went to the palace where their
priors were and commanded them to return to their houses. On the way,
one of the priors was plundered, in contempt, by a soldier. From this
beginning, as men are more ready for evil than good, arose the destruction and sacking of the city. For a whole day it was robbed and overrun;
neither women nor holy places were spared, and the soldiers—both those
who had defended it badly and those who had fought against it—stripped
it of its property. The news of this victory was received with very great
joy by the Florentines, and because it had been altogether Lorenzo's campaign, he rose to very great reputation from it. Whence one of Messer
Tommaso Soderini's most intimate friends reproached him for his advice,
saying to him: "What say you now that Volterra has been acquired?" To
which Messer Tommaso replied, "To me it appears lost; for if you had
received it by accord, you would have had advantage and security from
it; but since you have to hold it by force, in adverse times it will bring
you weakness and trouble and in peaceful times, loss and expense."

31

IN these times the pope, avid to keep the towns of the Church in their
obedience, had Spoleto sacked, since it had rebelled through its internal
factions. Then, because Città di Castello was in the same defiance, he had

---

[1] The Florentine commissioners inside Volterra.

it besieged. The prince in that town was Niccolò Vitelli.[1] He kept up a great friendship with Lorenzo de' Medici, from whom he did not fail to get assistance that was not as much as would defend Niccolò, yet quite enough to sow the first seeds of enmity between Sixtus and the Medici that shortly after produced very evil fruits. Nor would these have delayed their appearance very long if the death of Frate Piero, cardinal of San Sisto,[2] had not occurred; for as this cardinal had made a circuit of Italy and gone to Venice and Milan under color of paying his respects to the marriage of Ercole, marquis of Ferrara, he went about sounding out the intents of those princes to see how they were disposed toward the Florentines. But when he returned to Rome, he died, not without suspicion of having been poisoned by the Venetians, since they feared the power of Sixtus so long as he could make use of the spirit and work of Frate Piero. For notwithstanding that he was by nature of mean birth and then meanly brought up within the bounds of a monastery, as soon as he reached the cardinalate there appeared in him such pride and such ambition that not only the cardinalate but even the papacy could not contain him; for he did not hesitate to give a banquet in Rome that would have been judged extraordinary for any king, for which he spent more than twenty thousand florins. Thus Sixtus, deprived of this minister, carried out his schemes more slowly. Nonetheless, since the Florentines, the duke, and the Venetians had renewed their league and left places for the pope and the king to enter into it, Sixtus and the king also leagued together, leaving places for other princes so they could enter. And so Italy saw itself divided into two factions, because every day things arose that generated hatred between these two leagues. This happened with the island of Cyprus, to which King Ferdinand aspired and which the Venetians seized: so the pope and the king came to be bound together more. In Italy then, Federico, prince of Urbino, was held most excellent in arms; he had fought for the Florentine people for a long time. The king and the pope decided, therefore, to win Federico over to themselves so as to deprive the enemy league of this head; the pope advised him, and the king begged him to come to visit him in Naples. Federico accepted, to the amazement and displeasure of the Florentines, who believed that what had happened to Jacopo Piccinino would happen to him.[3] Nonetheless, the contrary resulted, for Federico returned from Naples and from Rome highly honored and captain of their league. The king and the pope also did not neglect to sound out the intents of the lords of Romagna and of the Sienese, so as to make them

[1] See *P* 20 and *D* II 24.
[2] See *FH* VII 22.
[3] See *FH* VII 8.

friends and through them offend the Florentines. When the Florentines became aware of this, they armed themselves with every remedy at hand against such ambition, and since they had lost Federico of Urbino, they hired Roberto da Rimini.[4] They renewed their league with the Perugians and leagued themselves with the lord of Faenza. The pope and the king alleged that the cause of their hatred of the Florentines was that they desired the Florentines to dissociate themselves from the Venetians and become leagued with them, because the pope judged that the Church could not maintain its reputation, nor could Count Girolamo keep the states of Romagna, if the Florentines and Venetians were united. On the other side, the Florentines feared that the pope and the king wanted the Florentines to be enemies of the Venetians not to make the Florentines their friends but to be able to injure them more easily; so Italy lived in these suspicions and diverse humors for two years before any tumult arose. But the first one to arise, although small, was in Tuscany.

32

BRACCIO of Perugia, a man, as we have shown many times, very much reputed in war, left two sons: Oddo and Carlo. Carlo was of tender age, and Oddo was killed by the men of Val di Lamona, as we have shown above;[1] but when Carlo reached military age, he was received by the Venetians into the condottieri of that republic for the sake of the memory of his father and the hope they had in him. The end of his contract had come in these times, and he did not then want to be rehired by the senate; instead, he decided to see if with his name and the reputation of his father he could recover his states in Perugia. The Venetians easily consented to this, since they were accustomed always to increase their empire by innovations in things. Carlo therefore came to Tuscany and found that things in Perugia were difficult because of its league with the Florentines. Yet, since he wanted this move of his to bring forth something worthy of memory, he attacked the Sienese, alleging that they were debtors to him for services they had received from his father in the affairs of that republic, for which he wanted satisfaction from them. And he attacked with such fury that he turned almost their whole dominion upside down. Seeing such an attack, the citizens persuaded themselves—since it was easy for them to believe ill of the Florentines—that all had been executed with their consent, and they heaped complaints on the pope and the king.

[4] Roberto Malatesta; see *FH* VII 22.
[1] See *FH* IV 13.

They also sent spokesmen to Florence to complain of so great an injury, and they skillfully pointed out that, without having been helped, Carlo could not have injured them with such security. The Florentines excused themselves, asserting they were ready to do everything to make Carlo stop offending them, and, in just the mode that the spokesmen wished, they commanded Carlo to refrain from attacking the Sienese. Of this Carlo complained, pointing out that because the Florentines had not helped him they had deprived themselves of a great acquisition and had deprived him of great glory, since he promised them possession of that town in a short time, such vileness had he found in it and so few orders for defense. Thus Carlo left and returned to the usual stipends of the Venetians; and the Sienese, although they had been liberated from so much harm by the Florentines, remained nonetheless full of indignation against them, because it did not appear to them that they had any obligation to those who had liberated them from an evil of which they had first been the cause.

33

WHILE these things between the king and the pope and in Tuscany were toiling on in the modes narrated above, an unforeseen event of greater moment, which was the presage of greater evils, took place in Lombardy. In Milan, Cola Montano,[1] a lettered and ambitious man, taught the Latin language to the leading youths of that city. This man, whether because he loathed the life and customs of the duke or because some other cause moved him, in all his reasonings execrated life under a prince who was not good, calling those glorious and happy whom nature and fortune had allowed to be born and live in a republic. He pointed out that all famous men had been nourished in republics and not under princes: for republics nourish virtuous men, princes eliminate them; the one profits from the virtue of others, the other fears it. The young men with whom he had had the greatest familiarity were Giovannandrea Lampognano, Carlo Visconti, and Girolamo Olgiato. Many times he reasoned with them about the most wicked nature of the prince, about the unhappiness of anyone governed by him; and he came to have such confidence in the spirit and will of those youths that he had them swear that, as soon as they were of an age when they could, they would free their fatherland

---

[1] Niccolò Capponi di Gaggio Montano. On the following conspiracy, see *D* III 6, where it is used as a cautionary example of not completing the execution of a conspiracy.

from the tyranny of that prince. Thus, since the youths were overflowing with this desire, which kept growing with their years, the customs and modes of the duke, and still more the particular injuries done to themselves, hastened them toward putting their desire into effect. Galeazzo was lecherous and cruel; frequent examples of these two things made him very much hated, because not only was it not enough for him to corrupt noble women, but he also took pleasure in making this public. Neither was he content to have men put to death unless he killed them in some cruel mode. Nor did he escape the infamy of having killed his mother, because it did not appear to him that he was prince so long as she was there. He behaved toward her in such a mode that she came to want to retire to her own dower residence in Cremona, on the journey to which she was suddenly taken ill and died—whereupon many judged that her son had had her killed. This duke had dishonored Carlo and Girolamo by way of women, and he had refused to give Giovannandrea possession of the abbey of Miramondo, since it had been assigned by the pontiff to a close relative of his. These private injuries increased the desire of the youths to liberate their fatherland from so many evils—with revenge for themselves—in the hope that whenever they should succeed in killing him, they would be followed not only by many of the nobles but by the whole people. Having thus determined on this undertaking, they were often together—which because of their old familiarity was no wonder. They always reasoned about this thing, and to strengthen their spirits for the deed, they struck one another on the sides and breasts with the sheaths of the knives they had destined for the work. They reasoned about the time and place: in the castle did not appear safe to them; on the hunt, uncertain and dangerous; at times when the duke strolled about the city, difficult and not likely to succeed; and at banquets, doubtful. Therefore, they decided to overpower him at some ceremony and public spectacle to which they were certain he would come, where they could assemble their friends under various colors. They also concluded that if any of them were for some cause held by the court, the others must, with sword and amidst armed enemies, kill the duke.

34

THE year was 1476 and the festival of Christ's birth was near. Because on the day of San Stefano the prince was accustomed to visit with great pomp the church of that martyr, the conspirators decided that this would be the convenient place and time to execute their thought. Thus, when the morning of that saint's day came,[1] they had some of their most trusted friends and servants armed, saying that they wanted to go to the aid of Giovannandrea, who wanted to put an aqueduct through to his possessions against the wish of some of his rivals. They led those armed men to the church, alleging that before departing they wanted to get permission from the prince. They also had gathered at that place, under various colors, many others of their friends and relatives, hoping that when the thing was done, everyone would follow them in the rest of the enterprise. It was their intent, when the prince was dead, to join together with the armed men and go around that part of the town where they believed they could more easily rouse the plebs, and to have it arm against the duchess and the princes of the state. And they supposed that the people, whose hunger had been aggravated, ought easily to follow them, because they designed to give them the houses of Messers Cecco Simonetta, Giovanni Botti, and Francesco Lucani, all princes in the government, to plunder and in that way secure themselves and bring liberty to the people. This scheme made and their minds hardened to its execution, Giovannandrea, with the others, was at the church early; they heard Mass together, and, having heard it, Giovannandrea turned to a statue of Saint Ambrose and said: "O, patron of our city, you know our intention and the end for which we are willing to put ourselves in so many dangers. Be favorable to our enterprise and show by favoring justice that injustice displeases you." To the duke, on the other hand, who was to come to church, came many signs of his future death: for when day came, he dressed, as he was often accustomed to do, in a cuirass, which he immediately took off as if it offended him either in comfort or in appearance.[2] He wanted to hear Mass in the castle but found that his chaplain had gone to San Stefano with all his chapel accoutrements; he wanted the bishop of Como to celebrate the Mass in place of the chaplain, and the bishop brought up some reasonable objections. So almost by necessity, he decided to go to the church; but first he had his sons Gian Galeazzo and Ermes come to him, and he embraced and kissed them many times—it appeared he could not separate himself from them. Finally, however, having decided on going, he went out of the castle, and, placing himself between the spokesmen from Ferrara and Mantua, he went to the church. The conspirators, meanwhile, so as to make themselves less suspicious and to escape the cold, which was very great, had retired to the chamber of the archbishop of the church, who was their friend, intending to come into the church as soon as the duke came. Both Giovannandrea and Girolamo placed them-

[1] On December 26, 1476.
[2] Lit.: in presence or in person.

314

selves on the right side of the entrance of the church, and Carlo on the left. Those preceding the duke were already entering the church; then he entered, surrounded by a great multitude as was proper on that solemn occasion to a ducal procession. The first to move were Lampognano and Girolamo. Pretending to open a way for the prince, they got close to him and grasped their weapons, short and sharp, which they had hidden in their sleeves, and attacked him. Lampognano gave him two wounds, one in the belly, one in the throat; Girolamo also struck him in the throat and the breast. Because Carlo Visconti was positioned nearer to the door and the duke had already passed by him, he could not wound the duke in front when he was attacked by his companions, but with two blows pierced his back and his shoulder. These six wounds were so quick and so sudden that the duke was on the ground almost before anyone was aware of the deed; nor could he do or say anything except, as he fell, to call once only the name of Our Lady to his aid. The duke having fallen to the ground, a great alarm was raised. Many swords were drawn, and, as happens in cases not foreseen, some fled from the church and some ran toward the tumult without having any assurance or knowing the cause of the affair. Nonetheless, those who were nearest to the duke and had seen the duke slain, and recognized the killers, pursued them. And of the conspirators, Giovannandrea, seeking to get out of the church, came upon the women, who were many and sitting on the ground according to their custom. Caught and held by their clothes, he was overtaken by a Moor, a groom of the duke's, and killed. Carlo too was killed by bystanders. But Girolamo Olgiato, having got out among the people and the churchmen, seeing his companions dead, and not knowing where else to escape, went to his home, where he was received by neither his father nor his brothers. Only his mother, having compassion for her son, entrusted him to a priest, an old friend of the family, who dressed him in his clothes and took him to his home, where he stayed two days, not without hope that in Milan some kind of tumult would arise to save him. This did not happen, and, fearing that he might be found in that place, he turned to flee unrecognized. But he was recognized and brought to the Podestà of Justice,[3] where he revealed the whole plan of the conspiracy. Girolamo was twenty-three years old; nor was he less spirited in dying than he had been in action; for finding himself naked and with the executioner before him, knife in hand to quarter him, he said these words in Latin, for he was lettered: "Death is bitter, fame perpetual; the memory of this deed will long endure."

[3] The Casella text has *potestà*, not *podestà, della giustizia*, hence: "brought under the power of justice."

The undertaking of these unhappy youths was planned secretly and executed spiritedly; and then they were ruined when those they had hoped would have to follow and defend them neither defended nor followed them. Therefore, may princes learn to live in a manner and act in a mode that will make them revered and loved, so that no one can hope, by killing him, to save himself; and may others know how vain is the thought that makes one trust too much that a multitude, even though malcontent, will either follow you or accompany you in your dangers. This accident frightened all Italy; but much more so did those accidents that followed a short while afterward in Florence, which broke the peace that had lasted for twelve years in Italy, as will be shown by us in the following book, which, if it has a sad and lamentable end, will have a bloody and terrifying beginning.

BOOK VIII

I

SINCE the beginning of this eighth book lies in the middle of two conspiracies—one already narrated and taking place in Milan, the other yet to be narrated and occurring in Florence—it would appear the proper thing, if we want to follow our custom, to reason on the qualities of conspiracies and their importance. This would be done willingly if I had not spoken of it in another place[1] or if it were matter that could be passed over with brevity. But, as something that requires much consideration and has already been told in another place, we shall leave it out; and passing to another matter, we shall tell about the state of the Medici after it had conquered all the enmities that had come against it openly. If that house wanted to take sole authority in the city and to stand out from the others by living civilly, it was necessary that it also overcome those that schemed secretly against it. For although the Medici fought with some other families as equals in authority and reputation, citizens who were envious of their power could openly oppose them without fear of being suppressed in the beginnings of their enmities; for since the magistrates had become free, none of the parties had cause to fear except after defeat. But after the victory of '66,[2] the whole state had been so restricted to the Medici, who took so much authority, that it was required for those who were malcontent at it either to endure that mode of living with patience or, if indeed they wanted to eliminate it, attempt to do so by way of conspiracy and secretly. Such ways, because they succeed only with difficulty, most often bring ruin to whoever moves them and greatness to the one against whom they are moved. Hence, almost always a prince of a city, attacked by such conspiracies, if he is not killed as was the duke of Milan—which happens rarely—rises to greater power and many times from being a good man, becomes bad. For conspiracies by their example give him cause to fear; and in fearing, to secure himself; and securing himself, to injure; hence arise hatreds later, and often his ruin. And so these conspiracies immediately crush whoever moves them and in time offend in every mode the one against whom they are moved.

[1] *D* III 6; also *P* 19.
[2] See *FH* VII 16.

317

2

ITALY, as we have shown above,[1] was divided into two factions: pope and king on one side; Venetians, duke, and Florentines on the other. And although war had not yet been ignited between them, nonetheless every day gave them new causes for igniting one; and the pontiff, especially, in whatever his enterprise, strove to offend the state of Florence. Thus, when Messer Filippo de' Medici, archbishop of Pisa, died, the pope, against the will of the Signoria of Florence, invested Francesco Salviati with that archbishopric, one he knew was hostile to the Medici family. Then, as the Signoria was unwilling to give possession of it to him, there followed new offenses between the pope and the Signoria in the management of this thing. Besides this, in Rome he did very great favors for the Pazzi family and in every action disfavored the Medici.

At that time in Florence the Pazzi were the most splendid in wealth and nobility of all Florentine families. The head of them was Messer Jacopo, who had been made a knight by the people for his wealth and nobility. He had no children other than a natural daughter; he had a good many relatives, born of his brothers Piero and Antonio. The first among them were Guglielmo, Francesco, Rinato, and Giovanni, and next to them Andrea, Niccolò, and Galeatto. Cosimo de' Medici, seeing their wealth and nobility, married his niece Bianca to Guglielmo, hoping that this alliance might make these families more united and take away the enmities and the hatreds that most times customarily arise from suspicion. Nonetheless, so uncertain and mistaken are our designs that the thing went otherwise: for whoever advised Lorenzo showed him how very dangerous it was to him and contrary to his authority to join wealth and state in citizens. In consequence, Messer Jacopo and his relatives were not granted those ranks of honor that it appeared to the other citizens they merited. From this arose in the Pazzi their first indignation and in the Medici their first fear; and as one of these grew, it gave matter for the other to grow upon. Hence, in every action in which other citizens might contest them, the Pazzi were not well regarded by the magistrates. And the magistracy of the Eight, when Francesco de' Pazzi was in Rome, without showing the respect that is usually accorded to great citizens, compelled him to come to Florence for a trivial cause. So the Pazzi complained everywhere with injurious words full of indignation, which increased suspicion in others and injuries to themselves. Giovanni de' Pazzi had for wife the daughter of Giovanni Buonromei, a very rich man, whose property, when he died, would go to his daughter, since he had no other children.

[1] See *FH* VII 31.

Nonetheless, Carlo, his nephew, seized a part of these goods; and when the thing was litigated, a law was passed by virtue of which the wife of Giovanni de' Pazzi was despoiled of the inheritance of her father and it was given to Carlo—an injury the Pazzi attributed entirely to the Medici. Giuliano de' Medici complained of this thing many times to his brother Lorenzo, saying that he feared that by wanting too many things, all of them might be lost.

3

NONETHELESS, Lorenzo, hot with youth and power, wanted to take thought for everything and wanted everyone to recognize everything as from him. So the Pazzi, with such nobility and wealth, could not bear such injuries, and they began to think how they might avenge themselves. The first to advance any reasoning against the Medici was Francesco. He was more spirited and more sensitive than any of the others; so he decided either to acquire what he lacked or to lose what he had. And because the governors of Florence were hateful to him, he lived almost always in Rome, where, according to the custom of the Florentine merchants, he worked with a large treasure. And since he was very friendly with Count Girolamo,[1] they often complained to one another of the Medici; so after many complaints they came to the reasoning that it was necessary, if one of them was to live in his states and the other in his city securely, to change the state of Florence—which they thought could not be done without the deaths of Giuliano and Lorenzo. They judged that the pope and the king would easily approve if it could be shown to each of them how easy the thing was. Thus, having slipped into this thought, they communicated the whole of it to Francesco Salviati, archbishop of Pisa, who, as he was ambitious and shortly before had been offended by the Medici, agreed willingly. And considering among themselves what was to be done, they decided, so that the thing might proceed more easily, to attract Messer Jacopo de' Pazzi to their will, without whom they did not believe they could do anything. Thus, it appeared opportune that Francesco de' Pazzi should go to Florence to this effect, and the archbishop and the count should remain in Rome to be with the pope when the time appeared right to tell him about it. Francesco found Messer Jacopo more hesitant and more difficult than he would have liked; and when he made this known in Rome, it was thought that a greater authority was required to dispose him toward it; consequently, the archbishop

---

[1] Count Girolamo Riario (1443–1488), married to Caterina Sforza; see *FH* VII 22.

and the count communicated everything to Giovan Battista da Monte-secco, the pope's condottiere. Battista was highly esteemed in war and obligated to both the count and the pope. Nonetheless, he showed the thing to be difficult and dangerous. The archbishop strove to eliminate these dangers and difficulties, pointing out the aid that the pope and the king would supply to their enterprise and, in addition, the hatreds that the citizens of Florence bore toward the Medici, the relatives that the Sal-viati and the Pazzi had behind them, the ease of killing the Medici because they went about the city without company and without suspicion, and later, when they were dead, the ease of changing the state. These things Giovan Battista did not entirely believe, as he had heard many other Flor-entines speak otherwise.

4

WHILE they were engaged in these reasonings and thoughts, it happened that Signor Carlo di Faenza[1] became so ill that it was feared he was dying. It appeared therefore to the archbishop and the count that they had an occasion to send Giovan Battista to Florence and from there to Romagna under color of regaining certain towns that the lord of Faenza had seized from him. Therefore, the count commissioned Giovan Battista to speak with Lorenzo and to ask him on the count's behalf for advice on how things in Romagna ought to be governed; then he should speak with Francesco de' Pazzi and see if together they could dispose Messer Jacopo de' Pazzi to follow their will. And to enable them to move him with the authority of the pope, they wanted before his departure to speak to the pontiff, who made all the largest offers he could on behalf of the enter-prise. Therefore, when Giovan Battista arrived in Florence, he spoke with Lorenzo, by whom he was very humanely received, and, when he asked for advice, was advised wisely and affectionately, so that Giovan Battista was taken with admiration for Lorenzo, since it appeared to him he had found another man than the one that had been shown to him; he judged Lorenzo altogether humane, altogether wise, and very friendly to the count. Nonetheless, he wanted to speak with Francesco, and, not finding him there because he had gone to Lucca, he spoke with Messer Jacopo and found him in the beginning very adverse to the thing. Nonetheless, before he left, the authority of the pope moved Jacopo somewhat; and so he told Giovan Battista to go to Romagna and return, and that in the meantime Francesco would be in Florence, and then they would reason

[1] Carlo Manfredi, lord of Faenza, a city under the protection of Florence.

about the thing in more detail. Giovan Battista went and returned, and carried on his pretended reasoning with Lorenzo de' Medici about the count's things; afterward he withdrew with Messer Jacopo and Francesco de' Pazzi, and they worked on Messer Jacopo, so that he agreed to the enterprise. They reasoned about the mode. To Messer Jacopo, it did not appear it would succeed if both brothers[2] were in Florence; and therefore one should wait for Lorenzo to go to Rome, as it was reported he wanted to do, and then the thing would be executed. Francesco was pleased that Lorenzo would be in Rome; nonetheless, if indeed he did not go there, Francesco asserted that both brothers could be overcome[3] at a wedding or at a game or in church. As to aid from foreigners, it appeared to him that the pope could put together troops for a campaign against the forti-fied town of Montone, as he had just cause for seizing it from Count Carlo[4] because of the tumults already spoken of that he had raised around Siena and Perugia. Nonetheless, no other conclusion was reached except that Francesco de' Pazzi and Giovan Battista should go to Rome, and there everything should be concluded with the count and the pope. In Rome, they negotiated this matter again, and finally it was concluded that, since the campaign against Montone was resolved upon, Giovan Francesco da Tolentino, a soldier of the pope, should go on to Romagna and Messer Lorenzo da Castello[5] to his own district; and each of them should, with troops of the district, keep their companies in order, ready to do whatever they were ordered to do by Archbishop de' Salviati and Francesco de' Pazzi; and with Giovan Battista da Montesecco, they should come to Florence, where they should provide whatever was nec-essary for the execution of the enterprise, to which King Ferdinand, through his spokesman, had promised some help. Thereupon the arch-bishop and Francesco de' Pazzi came to Florence and drew Jacopo di Mes-ser Poggio[6] to their view; he was a literary youth, but ambitious and very desirous of new things. They attracted two Jacopo Salviatis, one a brother and the other a relative of the archbishop; they also brought in Bernardo Bandini and Napoleone Franzesi, ardent youths and very much obligated to the Pazzi family. Of the foreigners, besides those named be-fore, Messer Antonio da Volterra and one Stefano, a priest who lived in Messer Jacopo's houses to teach his daughter the Latin language, were included. Rinato de' Pazzi, a prudent and grave man who knew best the evils that arise from such enterprises, did not approve of the conspiracy;

---

[2] Both Medici brothers, Lorenzo and Giuliano.
[3] Lit.: oppressed.
[4] Son of Braccio da Montone; see *FH* VII 32.
[5] Lorenzo Giustini, vicar of the pope in Città del Castello.
[6] Giacomo, son of Poggio Bracciolini.

indeed, he detested it, and in whatever mode he could decently adopt, he frustrated it.

5

THE pope had been maintaining Raffaello de' Riario, nephew of Count Girolamo, at the University of Pisa to learn canon law;[1] and while he was in that place, the pope promoted him to the dignity of the cardinalate. It appeared therefore to the conspirators that they should bring this cardinal to Florence so that his coming would cover up the conspiracy, as it would enable them to hide the conspirators they needed among his retinue,[2] and from this they could take the opportunity[3] of executing it. So the cardinal came and was received by Messer Jacopo de' Pazzi at Montughi, his villa near Florence. The conspirators desired to bring Lorenzo and Giuliano together by means of the cardinal and, as soon as this happened, to kill them. Therefore, they arranged[4] for the Medici to hold a banquet for the cardinal at their villa in Fiesole, which either by chance or on purpose Giuliano did not attend. So, since this scheme turned out to be vain, they judged that if they invited him to a banquet in Florence the two would have to come of necessity. And so, the order having been given, they fixed this banquet for Sunday, the twenty-sixth of April, in the year 1478. Thus, as the conspirators were thinking how they could kill them in the middle of the banquet, they were together on Saturday night, when they planned all that they would have to execute the following morning. But when day came, Francesco was informed that Giuliano was not coming to the banquet. Therefore, the leaders of the conspiracy assembled again and concluded that carrying it into effect was not to be delayed, because it was impossible, since it was known to many, that it not be discovered. And thus they decided to kill the Medici in the cathedral church of Santa Reparata; since the cardinal would be there, the two brothers would attend in accordance with custom. They wanted Giovan Battista to assume the task of killing Lorenzo, and Francesco de' Pazzi and Bernardo Bandini to kill Giuliano. Giovan Battista refused to consider doing it, either because the familiarity he had had with Lorenzo had softened his spirit or because some other cause moved him; he said he would never have enough spirit to commit such an excess in church and accompany be-

---

[1] Lit.: pontifical letters; he was Raffaello Sansoni, son of a sister of Count Girolamo Riario.
[2] Lit.: family.
[3] Lit.: cause.
[4] Lit.: ordered.

trayal with sacrilege. This was the beginning of the ruin of their enterprise, because, since time was pressing, of necessity they had to give this task to Messer Antonio da Volterra and to the priest Stefano, two men who by practice and by nature were very inept for so great an undertaking. For if ever any deed requires a great and firm spirit made resolute in both life and death through much experience, it is necessary to have it in this, where it has been seen very many times that men skilled in arms and soaked in blood have lacked spirit.[5] The decision thus made, they determined that the signal for action should be the taking of communion by the priest who celebrated High Mass in the church; and in the meantime, Archbishop de' Salviati, together with his men and with Jacopo di Messer Poggio, were to seize the public palace so that the Signoria, either willingly or forced, following the deaths of the two youths, would be favorable to them.

6

THIS decision made, they went to the church, to which the cardinal had already come with Lorenzo de' Medici. The church was filled with people, and the divine office had begun, but Giuliano de' Medici was not yet in church. Hence, Francesco de' Pazzi, together with Bernardo appointed for Giuliano's death, went to his house to find him and with prayers and art led him to church. It is a thing truly worthy of memory that so much hatred, so much thought about such an excess, could be covered up with so much heart and so much obstinacy of spirit by Francesco and Bernardo; for, though they led him to church, both on the way and in the church they entertained him with jests and youthful banter.[1] Nor did Francesco, under color of caressing him, fail to press him with his hands and arms so as to see if he were provided with either a cuirass or other similar protection. Giuliano and Lorenzo knew of the bitter spirit of the Pazzi against themselves and how they desired to take the authority of the state from them; but they did not fear for their lives, since they believed that, even though the Pazzi might have to try something, they would have to do it civilly and not with such violence. And therefore, Lorenzo and Giuliano, taking no care for their own safety, also pretended to be their friends. Thus the murderers were prepared: some at the side of Lorenzo, where they could stand easily without suspicion because of the

[5] See *D* III 6, where NM blames the failure of the Pazzi conspiracy on the lack of time for the two substitutes to "harden their spirits."
[1] Lit.: reasonings.

multitude in the church, the others with Giuliano. The appointed hour came; Bernardo Bandini, with a short weapon prepared to this effect, pierced the breast of Giuliano, who after a few steps fell to the ground; Francesco de' Pazzi threw himself on him, filled him with wounds, and struck him with such zeal that, blinded by the fury that transported him, he wounded himself gravely in the leg. Messer Antonio and Stefano, for their part, attacked Lorenzo and, after aiming many blows at him, struck him with one light wound in the throat. For either their negligence or the spirit of Lorenzo, who, seeing himself attacked, defended himself with his arms, or the aid of whoever was with him made every effort of theirs vain. So, terrified, they fled and hid themselves; but when they were found later, they were killed and dragged through the whole city in shame. Lorenzo, for his part, bringing with himself those friends he had about him, shut himself in the sacristy of the church. Bernardo Bandini, upon seeing Giuliano dead, also killed Francesco Nori, a very good friend of the Medici, either because he hated him of old or because Francesco had striven to help Giuliano. And not content with these two homicides, he ran to find Lorenzo and to make up with his spirit and quickness for what the others by their sluggishness and weakness had failed to do, but, finding that Lorenzo had taken refuge in the sacristy, he could not do it. In the midst of these grave and tumultuous accidents, which were so terrible that it appeared the church must fall, the cardinal clung to the altar, where with effort he was kept safe by the priest until the Signoria, when the noise was over, could take him to his palace; there he remained in the greatest fear until his liberation.

7

IN Florence at this time were some Perugians driven from their homes because of parties, whom the Pazzi had drawn to their will by promising to restore their fatherland to them. Hence, Archbishop de' Salviati, who had gone to seize the palace, together with Jacopo di Messer Poggio and the Salviati and their friends,[1] had taken the Perugians with him. When he arrived at the palace, he left some of his men below with orders that as soon as they heard sounds they should seize the gate. Then, with the greater part of the Perugians, he went upstairs; he found that the Signoria was dining, because the hour was late, and after a while he was brought in by Cesare Petrucci,[2] Gonfalonier of Justice. So, having entered with a

---

[1] See *FH* VIII 5 (end).
[2] See *FH* VII 26.

few of his men, he left the others outside, the greater part of whom
locked themselves in the chancery by their own hand because the door
was fixed so that once shut it could not be opened either from inside or
from outside without the use of a key. The archbishop, meanwhile, who
had been allowed entrance by the Gonfalonier under color of wanting to
report some things to him on behalf of the pope, began to speak to him
with broken and hesitant words in such a mode that the alteration shown
in both his appearance and his words aroused such suspicion in the Gonfalonier that in an instant,[3] shouting, he hurled himself from the room
and, coming upon Jacopo di Messer Poggio, took him by the hair and
put him into the hands of his sergeants. When the alarm was raised
among the Signori, with whatever arms chance supplied them all those
who had come upstairs with the archbishop, some being locked up, some
cowed, were either killed immediately or thrown alive out of the palace
windows; among them, the archbishop, the two Jacopo Salviatis, and
Jacopo di Messer Poggio were hanged. Those who had been left below
in the palace had overcome the guard and seized the gate and the lower
parts, so that the citizens who had run to the palace at the alarm could
neither give help if armed nor, if unarmed, offer advice to the Signoria.

8

FRANCESCO de' Pazzi and Bernardo Bandini, meanwhile, seeing Lorenzo alive and one of their own, in whom all hope of the enterprise had
been placed, gravely wounded, had become frightened. Hence Bernardo,
thinking of his own safety with the frankness of spirit with which he had
thought to injure the Medici, when he saw the thing lost, fled unharmed.
Francesco, having returned home wounded, tried whether he could handle himself on horse, because the order had been to circle the town with
armed men and to call the people to liberty and arms. But he could not,
so deep was his wound and so much blood had he lost by it. Hence, un-
dressing, he threw himself naked upon his bed and begged Messer Jacopo
to do that which he could not do himself. Messer Jacopo, although old
and not practiced in such tumults, mounted on horse to make this last
trial of their fortune with perhaps a hundred armed men who had been
prepared for such an enterprise and went to the piazza of the palace, calling to his aid the people and liberty. But because the one had been made
deaf by the fortune and liberality of the Medici and the other was not
known in Florence, he had no response from anyone. Only the Signori,

---

[3] Lit.: at a stroke.

who were still masters of the upper part of the palace, greeted him with stones and threats to frighten him as much as they could. And while Messer Jacopo stood in doubt, he was met by Giovanni Serristori, his brother-in-law, who first reproved him for the scandals they had started, then urged him to go home, assuring him that the people and liberty were as much in the hearts of other citizens as in his own. Thus deprived of all hope, Messer Jacopo, seeing the palace hostile, Lorenzo alive, Francesco wounded, and no one following him, not knowing what else to do, decided to save his life if he could by flight; and with the company he had with him in the piazza, he left Florence to go to Romagna.

9

MEANWHILE, the whole city was in arms, and Lorenzo de' Medici, accompanied by many armed men, had withdrawn to his houses. The palace had been recovered by the people, and all those who had seized it were either captured or killed. Already throughout the city the name of the Medici was being shouted, and the limbs of the dead were seen fixed on the points of weapons or being dragged about the city, and everyone pursued the Pazzi with words full of anger and deeds full of cruelty. Already their houses were seized by the people, and Francesco, naked as he was, was dragged from his house, led to the palace, and hanged beside the archbishop and the others. Nor was it possible, by injury done him or spoken to him either on the way or later, to make him say anything; but staring fixedly at the others and otherwise without complaint, he sighed quietly. Guglielmo de' Pazzi, brother-in-law of Lorenzo, saved himself in Lorenzo's houses both by his innocence and by the help of his wife, Bianca. There was no citizen armed or unarmed who did not go to the houses of Lorenzo in that necessity, and each one offered himself and his property to him: so great was the fortune and the grace that had been acquired by this house through its prudence and liberality. Rinato de' Pazzi had retired to his villa when the event took place; then, when he learned of it, he wanted to flee in disguise. Nonetheless, he was recognized on the way, taken, and led to Florence. Messer Jacopo was also taken while crossing the mountains,[1] because the mountain people, having heard of the event in Florence and seeing him in flight, attacked him and led him back to Florence; nor, although he begged them many times, could he get them to kill him on the way. Messer Jacopo and Rinato were condemned to death four days after the event had taken place; and among

[1] The Apennines.

the many deaths inflicted in those days—so many that the streets were filled with the parts of men—no other was looked on with pity except that of Rinato, since he had always been held a wise and good man; nor was he noted for that pride of which the rest of that family had been accused. And that this event might not be lacking in any extraordinary example, Messer Jacopo was entombed first in the sepulchre of his ancestors, then dragged from there as excommunicated, and buried along the walls of the city; and from there dug up again, he was dragged naked through the whole city by the noose with which he had been hanged; then, since no place on land had been found for his tomb, he was thrown, by the same ones who had dragged him, into the Arno River, whose waters were then at their highest. Truly a very great example of fortune, to see a man of such wealth and from such a very prosperous state fall into such unprosperity with such ruin and such contempt! Some vices of his were talked of, among them games and blasphemies more than would be fitting for a lost man—vices that he compensated for by many charities, because he used to help generously many who were needy as well as holy places. Also, one can say this good of him, that on the Saturday before the Sunday appointed for so much homicide, so as not to make anyone else share in his adverse fortune, he paid all his debts, and all the merchandise that was in the customs or in his house and that belonged to somebody, he consigned with marvelous solicitude to their owners. Giovan Battista da Montesecco, after a long examination made of him, was beheaded; Napoleone Franzesi escaped punishment by flight; Guglielmo de' Pazzi was banished, and his cousins who remained alive were imprisoned in the fortress of Volterra. When all the tumults had ceased and the conspirators had been punished, funeral rites were celebrated for Giuliano. He was accompanied by all the citizens in tears, because there had been as much liberality and humanity in him as could be desired in anyone born in such fortune. He left one natural son, born a few months after his death and called Giulio,[2] who was filled with the virtue and fortune that in these present times all the world recognizes; and when we come to present things, if God gives life for it, they will be shown amply by us.[3] The troops who were under Messer Lorenzo da Castello in Val di Tevere, together with those who were under Giovan Francesco da Tolentino in Romagna, had started out to come to Florence to give support to the Pazzi, but then when they learned of the failure of the enterprise, they turned back.

[2] The future Pope Clement VII, to whom NM's *Florentine Histories* are dedicated.
[3] A promise, apparently not carried out, to bring this work to "present things."

IO

BUT since the change of state did not occur in Florence as the pope and the king desired, they decided that what they had not been able to do by conspiracy they would do by war. With the greatest speed, both put their men together to attack the state of Florence, while proclaiming that they wanted nothing other from the city than that it should rid itself of Lorenzo de' Medici, whom alone, of all the Florentines, they held for an enemy. The king's troops had already crossed the Tronto, and those of the pope were in Perugia; and so that the Florentines might feel spiritual wounds in addition to their temporal ones, the pope excommunicated and cursed them. Hence, the Florentines, seeing such great armies coming against them, prepared themselves with every care for defense. And before everything else, Lorenzo de' Medici, since by report the war was being made against him, wanted to assemble all qualified citizens, more than three hundred in number, in the palace with the Signoria. To them he spoke in this sense: "I do not know, exalted Signori, and you, magnificent citizens, whether I lament with you over the things that have occurred or whether I rejoice over them. And truly, when I think with how much fraud, with how much hatred I have been attacked and my brother killed, I cannot but grieve over it and lament it with all my heart and all my soul. When I consider, next, with what promptness, with what zeal, with what love, and with what united consent in the whole city my brother has been avenged and myself defended, it is fitting that I should not only rejoice in it but exult and glory in all of myself. And truly, if this experience has made me learn that I had more enemies in this city than I thought, it has shown me also that I had more fervent and ardent friends in it than I believed. Thus I am forced to lament with you the injuries of others and to rejoice in your merits, but I am indeed constrained to lament the injuries much more, as they are more rare, more without example, and less deserved by us. Consider, magnificent citizens, where evil fortune had led our house, that among friends, among relatives, in church, it was not secure. Those who fear death are accustomed to resort to their friends for aid, are accustomed to resort to their relatives,[1] and we found them armed for our destruction. All those who for public or private cause are persecuted are accustomed to take refuge in churches. Thus, by whomever others are defended, we are killed; where parricides, assassins are secure, the Medici find their killers. But God, who has never in the past abandoned our house, has again saved us and taken up the defense of our just cause. For what injury have we done to anyone that

---

[1] The Medici were related by marriage to the Pazzi; see *FH* VIII 2.

deserved such a desire for revenge? And truly, those who have shown themselves to be such great enemies we never offended privately, because if we had offended them, they would not have had opportunity to offend us. If they have attributed public injuries to us, should any have been done them—which I know not—they offend you more than us, more this palace and the majesty of this government than our house, by making it appear that for our cause you injured undeservedly your own citizens. This is altogether distant from any truth, because we, if we had ever been able to do it, and you, if we had wanted it, would not have done it; because whoever indeed seeks the truth will find that our house was always exalted by you with such agreement for no other cause than that it has striven with humanity, liberality, with benefits, to surpass everyone. Thus, if we have honored strangers, how would we have injured our relatives? If they were moved to this by a desire to dominate, as the seizing of the palace demonstrates, to come with armed men into the piazza reveals and condemns by itself how ugly, ambitious, and damnable this cause is. If they did it out of the hatred and envy they have of our authority, they offend you, not us, since it was you who gave it to us. And truly, those authorities deserve to be hated that men usurp, not those that men earn by liberality, humanity, and munificence. And you know that our house never rose to any rank of greatness to which it was not thrust by this palace and by your united consent. My grandfather Cosimo did not return from exile with arms and by violence but with your consent and union. My father, old and infirm, did not indeed himself defend the state against·so many enemies, but you with your authority and benevolence defended it; nor after the death of my father, since one could say I was still a boy, would I have maintained the rank of my house if it had not been for your advice and favors; my house could not have ruled and would not be able to rule this republic if you together with it had not ruled and did not rule now. Thus, I do not know what their cause of hatred against us could be, nor what just cause of envy. Let them bear hatred for their own ancestors, who with pride and avarice took from themselves the reputation that ours knew how to earn with efforts contrary to theirs. But let us concede that the injuries done them by us were great and that they deservedly desired our ruin: why come to offend this palace? Why make a league with the pope and the king against the liberty of this republic? Why break the long peace of Italy? For this they have no excuse, for they ought to offend whoever offends them and not confound their private enmities with public injuries. The result is that, although they are eliminated, our ill is more acute, since the pope and the king come armed to meet us on behalf of their causes—a war they claim to make against me and my house. Would to God it were true, because the remedies would be quick and certain; nor would I be so wicked a citizen that I would value my safety more than your perils; indeed, I would willingly put out your fire with my ruin. But because the powerful always disguise the injuries they do with some less indecent color, they have taken this way of hiding their indecent injury. But nonetheless, should you believe otherwise, I am in your hands: it is for you to rule or leave me; you are my fathers, you my defenders; and however much I am commissioned to do by you, I shall always do willingly; never shall I refuse, if it seems right to you, to end this war, begun with the blood of my brother, with mine." The citizens could not keep back their tears while Lorenzo was speaking, and with the same mercy with which they listened, he was answered by one of those whom the others had commissioned, who told him that the city recognized how great were his merits and those of his family, that he should be of good spirit, that with the same readiness with which they had avenged the death of his brother and saved his life they would save his reputation and state for him; nor would he lose that state before they lost their fatherland. And so that their deeds should match their words, they provided publicly a certain number of armed men for the protection of his body, to defend him from domestic plots.

II

AFTERWARD, the Florentines took up the mode for war, putting together troops and money in the greatest sum they could. They sent for help, by virtue of their alliance, to the duke of Milan and to the Venetians. And since the pope had shown himself to be a wolf and not a shepherd, so as not to be devoured as guilty, they justified their cause by every mode they could and filled all Italy with the treachery done against their state, showing the impiety of the pontiff and his injustice and that the pontificate that he had seized wickedly he exercised wickedly. For he had sent those whom he had elevated to the highest prelacies,[1] in the company of traitors and parricides, to commit such treachery in church, in the middle of the divine office, at the celebration of the sacrament; and afterward, because he had not succeeded in killing the citizens, changing the state of their city, and plundering it as he pleased, he interdicted it and threatened and offended it with pontifical maledictions. But if God was just, if acts of violence were displeasing to Him, then those of his vicar must have displeased Him, and He must be glad that offended men, finding no refuge

---

[1] Cardinal Sansoni and Archbishop Salviati.

in that place, would have recourse to Him. Therefore, not only did the Florentines not accept the interdict and obey it, but they forced the priests to celebrate the divine office, and they called a council in Florence of all the Tuscan prelates who were subject to their empire, in which they made an appeal against the injuries of the pontiff to the future council. Neither was the pope lacking in reasons to justify his cause; and so he declared that it belonged to the pontiff to eliminate tyranny, oppress the wicked, exalt the good—to which things he must apply remedies at every opportunity—but that it was indeed not the office of secular princes to arrest cardinals, to hang bishops, to kill, dismember, and drag around priests, and to slay the innocent and the guilty without any distinction.

12

NONETHELESS, amidst such quarrels and accusations, the Florentines returned the cardinal, whom they had in their hands, to the pontiff. This made the pope, without hesitation, attack them with all his forces and those of the king. When the two armies—under Alfonso, eldest son of Ferdinand and duke of Calabria, and in the command of Federico, count of Urbino[1]—entered Chianti by way of the Sienese, who were of hostile parties,[2] they seized Radda and many other fortified towns and plundered the whole region; then they went to camp at Castellina. As the Florentines saw these attacks, they were in great fear, since they were without troops and saw that help from their friends would be slow; for although the duke sent help, the Venetians had denied they were obligated to help Florentines in private causes. Since it was a war made for private individuals, they were not obligated to help them in it, because individual enmities do not have to be defended publicly. So the Florentines, so as to dispose the Venetians to a sounder opinion, sent Messer Tommaso Soderini as their spokesman to that senate; and in the meantime, they hired soldiers and made Ercole, marquis of Ferrara, captain of their armies. While these preparations were being made, the enemy army pressed Castellina so that the inhabitants, despairing of help, surrendered after they had withstood the siege for forty days. From here the enemy turned toward Arezzo and besieged Monte San Savino. The Florentine army was now in order, and, having gone to face the enemy, it had been posted three miles distant from it and was giving it such trouble that Federico of Urbino asked for a truce of several days. This was conceded to him with

[1] The pope's army.
[2] Hostile to the Florentines.

such disadvantage to the Florentines that those who had asked for it marveled that they got it; for if they had not obtained it, they would of necessity have had to depart in shame, but having had with those days opportunity to reorder themselves, when the time of the truce was over, they seized that fortified town right in front of our men. But winter had come now, and the enemy withdrew into Sienese territory to winter in comfortable places. The Florentine troops also withdrew to more comfortable quarters; and the marquis of Ferrara, having made little profit for himself and less for others, returned to his state.

13

IN these times Genoa rebelled against the state of Milan for the following causes. Since Galeazzo had died and left his son Gian Galeazzo of an age unfit to govern, dissension arose among Sforza, Ludovico, his uncles Ottaviano and Ascanio, and his mother Madonna Bona,[1] because each of these wanted to take charge of the little duke. In this contention Madonna Bona, the old duchess, through the advice of Messer Tommaso Soderini, then spokesman for the Florentines in that state, and of Messer Cecco Simonetta, who had been Galeazzo's secretary, came out on top. Whereupon the Sforzas fled from Milan, and, in crossing the Adda, Ottaviano was drowned; and the others were banished to different places, together with Signor Roberto da San Severino, who in those travails had left the duchess and joined them. When the tumults in Tuscany then took place, those princes, hoping through new accidents to be able to find new fortune, broke out of their banishments,[2] and each of them attempted something new so as to return to his state.

King Ferdinand saw that the Florentines (in their necessities) had been assisted only by the state of Milan. So as to take even that aid away from them, he ordered that the duchess be given so much to think about in her own state that she would not be able to provide aid to the Florentines. By means of Prospero Adorno, Signor Roberto, and the Sforza rebels, he made Genoa rebel from the duke. Only the Castelletto remained in the duke's power,[3] and, putting her hope in that, the duchess sent a great many men to recover the city; and they were defeated. Thus, when she saw the danger that could hang over the state of her son and herself if the war lasted—since Tuscany was upside down and the Florentines, in

---

[1] These are, respectively, Sforza Maria Sforza, Ludovico Sforza, Ottaviano Sforza, Ascanio Sforza, and Madonna Bona of Savoy, who assumed the regency on January 3, 1477.

[2] They left the places to which they had been banished.

[3] *Potestà*.

whom alone she had hope, were in distress—she decided that since she could not have Genoa as a subject she would have it as a friend. She agreed with Battista Fregoso, the enemy of Prospero Adorno, to give him the Castelletto and make him prince in Genoa, provided that he drive out Prospero and not favor the Sforza rebels. After this conclusion Battista, with the help of the castle and of his party, became lord of Genoa and, in accordance with their custom, made himself doge. Consequently, the Sforzas and Signor Roberto, driven from Genoa, came to Lunigiana with those troops who followed them. When the pope and the king saw how the travails of Lombardy had been settled, they took the opportunity offered by those driven out of Genoa to stir up Tuscany near Pisa, so that the Florentines, by dividing their forces, would be weakened; and for this they managed, winter now being over, that Signor Roberto should depart with his troops from Lunigiana and attack the territory of Pisa. So Signor Roberto made a very great tumult; he sacked and took many fortified towns in Pisan territory and overran it, plundering as far as the city of Pisa.

14

IN these times spokesmen from the emperor, from the king of France, and from the king of Hungary came to Florence, sent by their princes to the pontiff, who persuaded the Florentines to send spokesmen to the pope, promising to make every effort with the pope that this war might be ended with an excellent peace. So as to be excused afterwards by anyone, the Florentines did not refuse to try this experiment, as for their part they loved peace. So the spokesmen went and returned without any result. Whence the Florentines, to get honor themselves from the reputation of the king of France,[1] since they had been partly offended and partly abandoned by the Italians, sent as spokesman to the king Donato Acciaiuoli, a man very learned in Greek and Latin whose ancestors had always held great rank in the city. But on the way, when he reached Milan, he died; hence his fatherland, to remunerate those whom he left and to honor his memory, buried him with very great honor at public expense and gave exemptions to his sons and dowries to his daughters sufficient for them to marry. In his place as spokesman to the king, it sent Messer Guidantonio Vespucci, a man very expert in imperial and canon law.[2] The attack made by Signor Roberto on the countryside around Pisa very

---

[1] The Florentines got a "name rather than a defense"; *D* II 11.
[2] Lit.: imperial and pontifical letters.

much disturbed the Florentines, as do unexpected things, for since they were engaged in a very grave war on the side of Siena, they did not see how they could provide for places near Pisa; yet with conscripts and other such provisions, they relieved the city of Pisa. And to keep the Lucchese faithful, so that they would not aid the enemy with either money or food, they sent Piero di Gino di Neri Capponi to them as ambassador. He was received by them with so much suspicion on account of the hatred that city holds for the people of Florence, born from old injuries and constant fear, that he was many times in danger of being killed by the people; so his having gone there gave cause for new indignation rather than a new union. The Florentines recalled the marquis of Ferrara,[3] hired the marquis of Mantua,[4] and with great urgency requested from the Venetians Count Carlo, son of Braccio,[5] and Deifobo, son of Count Jacopo, who were finally, after much dodging, sent by the Venetians: for, having made a truce with the Turk and so having no excuse to cover them, they were ashamed not to keep faith with the league. Therefore, Count Carlo and Deifobo came with a good number of men at arms and together with them put all those men at arms who could be detached from the army that was fighting under the command of the marquis of Ferrara against troops of the duke of Calabria; then they went toward Pisa to meet Signor Roberto, who with his troops was near the river Serchio. And although Roberto had made it seem as if he wished to wait for our troops, nonetheless he did not wait but withdrew into Lunigiana to the quarters he had left when he entered the country around Pisa. After his departure, Count Carlo recovered all those towns in the countryside of Pisa that had been taken by the enemy.

15

ONCE the Florentines were freed of attacks from the direction of Pisa, they had all their troops assemble between Colle[1] and San Gimignano. But since, by the coming of Count Carlo, there were Sforza and Braccio followers in that army, the old enmities between them were immediately awakened;[2] and it was believed that if they had to be together for long they would come to arms. Consequently, to lessen this evil, it was decided to divide the troops and to send one part under Count Carlo into

---

[3] Ercole d'Este; cf. *FH* VIII 12.
[4] Federico Gonzaga.
[5] Carlo da Montone, son of Braccio Fortebraccio da Montone; see *FH* VII 32.
[1] Colle Val d'Elsa.
[2] See *FH* V 2.

the territory of Perugia and the other part to stop at Poggibonsi, where they would make an encampment strong enough to be able to keep the enemy from entering Florentine territory. They considered that by this course they would also force the enemy to divide their troops: for they believed that either Count Carlo would seize Perugia, where they thought he had many partisans, or the pope would be forced of necessity to send a large army there to defend it. Besides this, so as to lead the pope into greater necessity, they ordered Messer Niccolò Vitelli, an exile from Città di Castello, where the head was his enemy Messer Lorenzo,[3] to approach the town with his troops so as to provide force to drive out his adversary and remove the town from its obedience to the pope. In these beginnings it appeared that fortune wanted to favor Florentine things, because Count Carlo was seen to make great progress around Perugia; Messer Niccolò Vitelli, although he had not succeeded in entering Castello, was with his troops superior in the field, and he plundered around the city without any opposition. So also the troops who had remained in Poggibonsi made raids every day to the walls of Siena; nonetheless, in the end, all these hopes turned out to be vain. First, Count Carlo died amidst the hope of his victories. His death, however, bettered the condition of the Florentines, if they had known how to use the victory that arose from it: for as soon as the death of the count was known, immediately the troops of the Church who were already all together in Perugia took hope that they could crush the Florentine troops, and, going out into the field, they placed their camp on the lake[4] three miles from the enemy. On the other side, Jacopo Guicciardini, who was the commissioner of that army, on the advice of the magnificent Roberto da Rimini,[5] who when Count Carlo died was left as first and most reputed in that army, recognizing the cause of the enemy's pride, decided to await them. Thus, when they came to blows by the lake, where indeed Hannibal the Carthaginian dealt the Romans that memorable defeat, the men of the Church were defeated. This victory was received in Florence with praise for their heads and with pleasure by everyone; and it would have been an honorable and profitable enterprise if the disorders that arose in the army that was at Poggibonsi had not upset everything. And so the good that one army did was entirely destroyed by the other: for those troops had taken booty from around Siena, and in dividing it a difference came up between the marquis of Ferrara and the marquis of Mantua, so that they fell to arms and attacked each other with every kind of offense; and it was such that the Florentines,

---

[3] Lorenzo Giustini; see *FH* VIII 4.
[4] Lake Trasimene, scene of Hannibal's victory in 217 B.C.
[5] Roberto Malatesta.

judging that they could no longer make use of both, agreed that the marquis of Ferrara with his troops should go back home.

16

THUS, since that army was weakened, and left without a head, and was conducting itself in a disorderly way in every regard, the duke of Calabria, who was with his army near Siena, took spirit to come and meet it. And when it was done just as it had been thought, the Florentine troops, seeing themselves attacked, had confidence neither in their arms nor in their number,[1] which was superior to the enemy's, nor in the site, where they were because it was very strong; but without waiting even to see the enemy, they fled at the sight of its dust and left to the enemy their munitions, wagons, and artillery. Armies then were filled with such poltroonery and disorder that whether a horse turned its head or tail decided the victory or loss of a campaign. This rout filled the king's soldiers with booty and the Florentines with terror; for not only was their city at war, but also it was afflicted by a very grave pestilence, which had taken possession of it in a manner so that all the citizens, to escape death, had retired to their villas. This made the rout even more terrible, because those citizens having properties in the Val di Pesa and Val d'Elsa, who had withdrawn to them, after the rout hastened as quickly and as best they could to Florence not only with their children and belongings but with their laborers as well, so that it seemed they feared that at any hour the enemy could appear in the city. Those who had been put in charge of the war, seeing this disorder, commanded the troops who had been victorious around Perugia to drop the campaign against the Perugians and come to Val d'Elsa to oppose the enemy, which after its victory was raiding the countryside without any opposition. And although they had pressed the city of Perugia so that at any hour victory might be expected, nonetheless the Florentines wanted to defend their own before seeking to seize that of others. So that army, removed from its prosperous successes, was brought to San Casciano, a fortified town eight miles from Florence,[2] as it was judged that they could not make a stand elsewhere until the remnants of the routed army were together. The enemy, for its part—those who were freed at Perugia by the departure of the Florentine troops—became bold and took much booty in the territory of Arezzo and Cortone every day; and the others, who under Alfonso, duke of Calabria, had won

---

[1] Lit.: multitude.
[2] See *FH* VI 34.

at Poggibonsi, first made themselves lords of Poggibonsi and then of Vico and sacked Certaldo. And when these captures and plunders were done, they went to camp at the fortified town of Colle, which in those times was considered very strong; and having men faithful to the state of Florence, it could hold the enemy at bay until troops could be brought together. Thus, when the Florentines had gathered all their men at San Casciano, while the enemy was attacking Colle with all its might, the Florentines decided to draw near to them and give spirit to the people of Colle to defend themselves. And that the enemy might be more hesitant to offend them since adversaries were nearby, when this decision was made, the Florentines broke up their camp at San Casciano and put it at San Gimignano, five miles from Colle, from which with light horse and other light armed soldiers they harassed the duke's camp every day. Nonetheless, this relief was not sufficient for the people of Colle; because they were lacking in necessities, they surrendered on the thirteenth day of November, to the dismay of the Florentines and to the greatest joy of the enemy, especially the Sienese, who besides the common hatred they bear for the city of Florence particularly hated the people of Colle.

17

IT was already mid-winter and a bad time for war, so the pope and king, moved by the wish either to give hope of peace or to enjoy more peacefully the victories already won, offered the Florentines a three-month truce and gave them ten days' time to respond. The truce was accepted immediately. But, as it happens to everyone that wounds are felt more as the blood cools than when they are received, this brief respite made the Florentines realize more the anxieties they had sustained. The citizens accused one another freely and without respect; they brought out the errors committed in the war; they showed the expenses made in vain, the taxes unjustly imposed. Such things were spoken of not only within the circles of private individuals but spiritedly in the public councils. And there was one so bold as to turn to Lorenzo de' Medici and say to him: "This city is weary and wants no more war." And thus it was necessary for him to think about peace. Hence, having recognized this necessity, Lorenzo consulted with those friends he thought most faithful and wisest, and they concluded first, seeing the Venetians cold and little faithful and the duke a ward and involved in civil disorders, that they must seek new fortune with new friends. Yet they were doubtful into whose arms they should put themselves—those of the pope or those of the king. And when all had been examined, they approved the friendship of the king as being more stable and more safe: for the shortness of life of popes,[1] the change through succession, the slight fear that the Church has of princes, and the few scruples it has in adopting courses require that a secular prince cannot have entire confidence in a pontiff or safely share his fortune with him. For in wars and dangers, whoever is friend of the pope will be accompanied in victories and be alone in defeats, since the pontiff is sustained and defended by spiritual power and reputation. Having thus decided that it would be of greater benefit to gain the king to themselves, they judged that it could not be better done or with more certainty than by the presence of Lorenzo, because the more one used liberality with that king, the more, they believed, they could find remedies for past enmities. Therefore Lorenzo, having made up his mind to his journey, entrusted the city and the state to Messer Tommaso Soderini, who was at that time Gonfalonier of Justice, and at the beginning of December he departed from Florence. When he arrived in Pisa, he wrote to the Signoria the cause of his departure. To honor him and to enable him to negotiate for peace with the king with greater reputation, the Signori made him spokesman for the Florentine people and gave him authority to make an alliance with the king such as might appear to him best for their republic.

18

IN these same times, Signor Roberto da San Severino, together with Ludovico and Ascanio, because their brother Sforza was dead,[1] again attacked the state of Milan so as to return to governing it. When they had seized Tortona and when Milan and all that state were in arms, Duchess Bona was advised to repatriate the Sforzas and to receive them into the state so as to dispose of these civil contentions. The principal author[2] of this advice was Antonio Tassino of Ferrara. Born in base condition, he came to Milan and fell into the hands of Duke Galeazzo, who gave him to his wife the duchess as her chamberlain. Either because this man was handsome in body or for some other secret virtue, after the death of the duke he rose to such high reputation with the duchess that he almost governed the state. This very much displeased Messer Cicco,[3] a man most excellent in prudence and in long practice, so that in those things he could, he strove to diminish the authority of Tassino with the duchess and with others of the government. When Tassino became aware of this,

---

[1] Cf. *FH* I 23; *P* 11.
[1] Sforza Maria Sforza, duke of Bari, had died on July 27, 1479.
[2] Lit.: the prince.
[3] Cicco Simonetta, the secretary of state; *FH* VIII 13.

to get revenge for these injuries and to have close to him someone who could defend him against Messer Cicco, he encouraged the duchess to repatriate the Sforzas; she followed his advice and, without consulting in anything with Messer Cicco, repatriated them. Whereupon he said to her, "You have taken a decision that will take my life from me and your state from you." These things did happen soon afterward; for Messer Cicco was done to death by Signor Ludovico; and after some time Tassino was driven out of the dukedom, at which the duchess was so indignant that she left Milan and surrendered the government of her son into the hands of Ludovico. Thus, as Ludovico remained sole governor of the dukedom of Milan, he was, as will be shown, the cause of the ruin of Italy.[4] Lorenzo de' Medici had left for Naples and the truce between the parties was in force when, beyond all expectation, Ludovico Fregoso, who had a certain understanding with some Sarzanese, entered Sarzana by stealth with armed men, seized that town, and took prisoner the person who was there on behalf of the Florentine people. This incident greatly displeased the princes of the state of Florence, because they were convinced that everything had taken place by order of King Ferdinand. And they complained to the duke of Calabria, who was with the army in Siena, that during the truce they had been attacked in a new war. He made every showing, both with letters and with embassies, that such a thing had arisen without his father's or his consent. Nonetheless, to the Florentines it appeared they were in the worst situation, as they saw themselves void of money, the head of the republic in the hands of the king, an old war to be waged with the king and the pope and a new one with the Genoese, and themselves without friends. For they had no hope in the Venetians and rather feared the government of Milan because it was changeable and unstable. The only hope left to the Florentines was in what Lorenzo de' Medici had to negotiate with the king.

19

LORENZO had arrived by sea in Naples, where he was received honorably and with great expectation not only by the king but by all the city; for since so great a war had arisen to crush him alone, the greatness of his enemies had made him very great. But when he arrived in the presence of the king, he discussed the conditions in Italy, the humors of its princes and peoples, and what could be hoped for in peace and feared in war, in

[4] How Ludovico was "the cause of the ruin of Italy" by calling Charles VIII into Italy in 1494 is not in fact shown by NM. Cf. *P* 3.

such a mode that the king marveled more, after he had heard him, at the greatness of his spirit, the dexterity of his genius and gravity of his judgment, than he had marveled before at his being able to sustain so great a war alone. So he redoubled the honors to him and began to think he had rather have him leave as friend than hold him as enemy. Nonetheless, by various causes he entertained him from December to March, so as to make a double trial not only of him but of the city, because Lorenzo did not lack enemies in Florence who would have desired the king to detain him and treat him as he had Jacopo Piccinino.[1] Under the pretense of lamenting it, they spoke of it throughout the city, and in public deliberations they opposed whatever was favorable for Lorenzo. And by such modes they had spread the rumor that if the king were to hold him in Naples for a long time the government in Florence would change. This made the king postpone sending him back for that time to see if any tumult would arise in Florence. But when he saw that things went quietly, on the sixth day of March 1479, he let him go; but first, with every kind of benefit and demonstration of love, he won Lorenzo over, and between them perpetual accords for the preservation of their common states arose. Therefore Lorenzo, if he had left as great, returned to Florence very great, and he was received by the city with the joy that his great qualities and recent merits deserved, as he had exposed his very life to gain peace for his fatherland. For, two days after his arrival, the accord between the republic of Florence and the king was made public, by which each was obliged to the preservation of their common states. And as for the towns taken in the war from the Florentines, it was left to the will of the king to restore them; the Pazzi kept in the tower of Volterra were to be freed;[2] and certain sums of money should be paid to the duke of Calabria for a certain time. As soon as this peace was announced, it filled the pope and Venetians with indignation, because to the pope it appeared that the king had taken little account of him, and to the Venetians that the Florentines had taken little account of them; for as both one and the other had been companions in the war, they complained that they had had no part in the peace. When this indignation was understood and credited in Florence, it immediately gave everyone the suspicion that from the peace that had been made a greater war might arise. So the princes of the state decided to restrict the government and that the making of important deliberations should be reduced to a smaller number; they made a council of seventy citizens with the greatest authority they could give it in principal actions. This new order put a check on the spirit of those who were seeking new

[1] See *FH* vii 8.
[2] Guglielmo de' Pazzi and his cousins; see *FH* viii 9.

things. And to give themselves reputation, before everything the seventy accepted the peace made by Lorenzo with the king; they appointed as spokesmen to the pope and to the king Messer Antonio Ridolfi and Piero Nasi. Nonetheless, notwithstanding this peace, Alfonso, duke of Calabria, did not depart with his army from Siena, pretending that he was being held back by the discords of those citizens, which were so many that, although he was quartered outside the city, they brought him back into it and made him the arbiter of their differences. The duke, taking this opportunity, punished many of those citizens with fines and condemned many of them to prison, many to exile, and some to death. As a result of these modes, he became suspect not only to the Sienese but to the Florentines, who did not want to make him prince of that city. Nor was any remedy discovered, since the city of Florence had a new friendship with the king, and the pope and the Venetians were hostile. This suspicion appeared not only generally in the people[3] of Florence, subtle interpreters of all things, but in the princes of the state; and everyone affirmed that our city had never been in such danger of losing its liberty. But God, who in such extremities has always had a particular care for it, made an unhoped-for accident arise that gave the king, the pope, and the Venetians something greater to think about than Tuscany.

20

MAHOMET the Grand Turk had gone to encamp at Rhodes with a very great army and had attacked it for many months; nonetheless, although his forces were great and his obstinacy for the capture of that town very great, he found even greater obstinacy in the besieged, who defended themselves with such virtue from such force that Mahomet was forced to depart from that siege in shame. When he had left Rhodes, therefore, a part of his fleet under Pashaw Ahmet came toward Valona, and, whether he saw the ease of the undertaking or his lord commanded him to it, in sailing along the coast of Italy at a stroke he put four thousand soldiers on land; and after attacking the city of Otranto, he took it quickly, sacked it, and killed all its inhabitants. Then, with the best modes he had at hand, he fortified himself in the city and in the port; and since he had brought good cavalry with him, he raided and plundered the surrounding countryside. When the king saw this attack and realized how great was the prince whose undertaking it was, he sent messengers everywhere to make it known and to ask assistance against the common enemy; and with great

---

[3] Lit.: in the universal people.

urgency he recalled the duke of Calabria and his troops, who were at Siena.

21

AS much as this assault upset the duke and the rest of Italy, so much did it make Florence and Siena rejoice, for to Siena it appeared that it had regained its liberty and to Florence that it had escaped those perils that had made it fear it would lose liberty. The lamentations of the duke in leaving Siena enhanced this opinion, as he accused the fortune that with one unhoped-for and unreasonable accident had taken from him the empire of Tuscany. The same chance made the pope change his plan: whereas at first he had never wanted to listen to any Florentine spokesman, he became so much milder that he listened to anyone who would reason about universal peace with him. So the Florentines were assured that if they would bend to ask pardon from the pope, they would find it. Thus, to the Florentines it appeared that this opportunity should not be allowed to pass, and they sent twelve ambassadors to the pontiff. After they had arrived in Rome, the pope kept them waiting with various dealings before giving them an audience. Yet, finally, it was established between the parties how in the future they would have to live and how much each of them would have to contribute in peace and how much in war. The ambassadors then came to the feet of the pontiff, who awaited them in the midst of his cardinals, with exceeding pomp. They made excuses for the things that had happened, now accusing necessity, now the malignity of others, now the popular fury and their just anger; and they said that those are unprosperous who are forced either to fight or to die. And because anything must be endured so as to escape death, they had endured the war, the interdicts, and other inconveniences that had been drawn in the train of past events so that their republic might escape slavery, which is customarily the death of free cities. Nonetheless, if indeed they had been forced to make some mistake, they were ready to make amends for it, and they trusted in his clemency who, by the example of the Supreme Redeemer, would be ready to receive them in his most merciful arms. To their excuses the pope answered with words full of pride and wrath, reproving them for all they had done against the Church in times past; nonetheless, to preserve the precepts of God, he was content to give them that pardon they asked for. But he must make them understand that they had to obey; and if they were to discontinue their obedience, the liberty that they nearly lost now they would lose then, and justly, because those are deserving of liberty who exert themselves in good and not wicked deeds; for liberty badly used offends oneself and others, and to esteem God little and the Church less is the office not of a free man but of a dissolute one more inclined to evil than good, whose correction belongs not only to princes but to any Christian whatever. Consequently, in regard to past events, they had to blame themselves; they had given cause for war with wicked deeds and nourished it with the worst; the war had been eliminated more by the kindness of others than by their own merits. Then a formal statement of their accord and the benediction was read, to which the pope added, apart from the things negotiated and established, that if the Florentines wanted to enjoy the fruits of this benediction they must keep armed, with their money, fifteen galleys for the whole time the Turk should fight against the Kingdom.[1] The spokesmen complained very much about this burden imposed on top of the accord that had been made, but they were unable to lighten it in any part by any means or favor or by any complaint. But when they returned to Florence, the Signoria, to confirm this peace, sent as spokesman to the pope Messer Guidantonio Vespucci, who a short while ago had returned from France. He with his prudence reduced everything to tolerable terms and obtained many favors from the pontiff, which was the sign of greater reconciliation.

22

THEREFORE, after the Florentines had settled things with the pope, and after Siena and they had been freed from fear of the king by the departure of the duke of Calabria from Tuscany, and as the war with the Turks continued, they pressed the king in every way to restore to them the fortified towns that the duke of Calabria on departing had left in the hands of the Sienese. Hence the king feared that the Florentines might detach themselves from him in his great necessity and, by starting a war against the Sienese, impede the assistance to him from the pope and from other Italians for which he was hoping. Therefore, he was content that the fortified towns be restored to them and with new obligations again obligated the Florentines to him. And so force and necessity, not written documents and obligations, make princes keep faith. Thus, when the fortified towns had been received and this new confederation settled, Lorenzo de' Medici reacquired the reputation that first the war and then the peace, when there was fear of the king, had taken from him. There had been no

---

[1] The kingdom of Naples.

lack in those times of anyone to slander him openly, saying that to save himself he had sold his fatherland and that their towns had been lost in war and their liberty would be lost in peace. But once the towns were held again, an honorable accord settled with the king, and the city restored to its former reputation, in Florence, a city eager to speak, which judges things by results and not by advice, the reasoning turned around; and it celebrated Lorenzo to the sky, saying that his prudence had known how to gain in peace what bad fortune had taken from it in war and that he had been able to do more with his advice and his judgment than the arms and forces of the enemy. The attacks of the Turk had postponed the war that was about to arise on account of the indignation that the pope and the Venetians felt for the peace that had been made; but as the beginning of that attack was unexpected and the cause of much good, so the end was unexpected and the cause of much evil: for when Mahomet the Grand Turk died, beyond every expectation, and discord broke out among his sons, those who were in Puglia, abandoned by their lord, ceded Otranto by an accord to the king. Thus, since the fear that had held in check the spirits of the pope and the Venetians had been taken away, everyone feared new tumults. On one side, the pope and Venetians were leagued; with them were the Genoese, Sienese, and other minor powers; on the other side were the Florentines, the king, and duke,[1] to whom were allied the Bolognese and many other lords. The Venetians desired to become lords of Ferrara, and it appeared to them they had reasonable cause for the enterprise and certain hope of concluding it. The cause was that the marquis[2] declared that he was no longer bound to receive the vicedominus and salt[3] from them since, by past agreement, after seventy years that city was to be free from both burdens. The Venetians responded on their side that as long as he held the Polesine he must accept the vicedominus and the salt. And since the marquis was unwilling to agree to this, it appeared to the Venetians they had just occasion for taking up arms and a convenient time for doing it, as they saw that the pope was full of indignation against the Florentines and the king. And further to gain the pope's favor, when Count Girolamo[4] went to Venice, he was very honorably received by the Venetians, and they granted him their citizenship and gentleman's rank, always a sign of very great honor to whomever they gave it. To be ready for that war, they had levied new taxes and made captain of their armies Signor Roberto da San Severino,

[1] The duke of Milan.

[2] Ercole d'Este, duke (not marquis) of Ferrara.

[3] The vicedominus was an official sent by the Venetians to protect their subjects. Salt mined from Ferrarese territory was a Venetian monopoly.

[4] Girolamo Riario.

who, angry with Signor Ludovico, governor of Milan, had fled to Tortona; and having made some tumults there, he had gone to Genoa. He was called from there by the Venetians and made prince of their army.

23

WHEN these preparations for new movements became known to the opposing league, they made it too prepare for war; the duke of Milan chose as his captain Federico, lord of Urbino; the Florentines, Signor Costanza[1] of Pesaro. And to test the intent of the pope and to make it clear whether the Venetians were making war on Ferrara with his consent, King Ferdinand sent Alfonso, duke of Calabria, with his army to the Tronto and asked the pope for passage so as to go to Lombardy in aid of the marquis—which the pope altogether refused. So as it appeared to the king and the Florentines that they had confirmed the pope's intent, they decided to press him with their forces so that he must become their friend by necessity, or at least to give him such hindrance that he could not furnish aid to the Venetians. For the Venetians were already in the field and had opened war on the marquis and first raided the countryside; then they laid a siege to Ficarolo, a fortified town very important to the state of that lord. As the king and the Florentines, therefore, had decided to attack the pontiff, Alfonso, duke of Calabria, hurried toward Rome and with the help of the Colonna, who had joined him because the Orsini had taken the side of the pope, did a great deal of damage in the countryside; and from the other side the Florentine troops, with Messer Niccolò Vitelli, attacked Città di Castello, seized that city, and drove from it Messer Lorenzo,[2] who was holding it for the pope, and set up Messer Niccolò as its prince. The pope, therefore, was in the greatest anxiety, because Rome was agitated within by the party[3] and outside the country was overrun by its enemies. Nonetheless, as a spirited man who wanted to conquer and not yield to the enemy, he engaged as captain the Magnificent Roberto of Rimini;[4] and having had him come to Rome, where all the pope's men at arms had gathered, he showed him how much honor would be his if, against the forces of a king, he would liberate the Church from those troubles in which it found itself and how great an obligation not only he but all his successors would have to him and that not only men but God would be ready to be grateful to him. The Magnificent Roberto, having

[1] Costanza Sforza.
[2] Lorenzo Giustini; see *FH* VIII 15.
[3] The Colonna.
[4] Roberto Malatesta.

first considered the pope's men at arms and all his weaponry, urged him
to get as much infantry as he could, which was put into effect with all
zeal and speed. The duke of Calabria was near Rome, so that every day
he raided and plundered up to the gates of the city. This so angered the
Roman people that many offered voluntarily to join with the Magnificent
Roberto in the liberation of Rome, all of whom were thanked and accepted by that lord. When the duke heard of these preparations, he moved
somewhat away from the city, thinking that if he were at some distance
the Magnificent Roberto would not be of a mind to go out and meet him;
and in part he was waiting for his brother Frederick, who had been sent
by his father with new troops. The Magnificent Roberto, seeing he was
almost equal to the duke in men at arms and superior in infantry, went
out of Rome in array and placed his quarters two miles from the enemy.
When the duke saw his adversaries close upon him, beyond his every
expectation, he judged it proper for him either to fight or to flee as defeated; hence, almost compelled, so as not to do a thing unworthy of the
son of a king, he decided to fight. And facing the enemy, each ordered
his troops in the mode that they then used to do, and they joined in a
battle that lasted until noon. And this battle was fought with more virtue
than any other that had been fought for fifty years in Italy, for in it, between one side and the other, more than a thousand men died. The outcome was glorious for the Church, because the multitude of its infantry
thrust against[5] the ducal cavalry so that it was forced to turn about, and
the duke would have been taken prisoner if he had not been saved by
many Turks from among those who had been at Otranto and had fought
with him then. This victory won, the Magnificent Roberto returned in
triumph to Rome. It was a triumph he was able to enjoy little, because,
having drunk a great deal of water as a result of the oppressiveness of the
day, a flux began in him that in a few days killed him. His body was
honored by the pope with every kind of honor. Having won this victory,
the pontiff immediately sent the count[6] toward Città di Castello to see to
the restoration of that town to Messer Lorenzo and in part to try for the
city of Rimini. For after the death of the Magnificent Roberto, there remained of him, in the keeping of his wife, his little son, and the pontiff
thought it would be easy to seize that city. It would have turned out successfully for him if the widow had not been defended by the Florentines,
who opposed him with such force that he could effect nothing against
either Castello or Rimini.

[5] Lit.: offended.
[6] Count Girolamo Riario.

24

WHILE these things were toiling on in Romagna and in Rome, the Venetians had seized Ficarolo and with their troops had crossed the Po. The camps of the duke of Milan and of the marquis were in disorder because Federico, count of Urbino, had become ill, and although he had himself carried to Bologna to be cured, he died; so the affairs of the marquis went on declining, and in the Venetians the hope of seizing Ferrara grew every day. On the other side, the king and the Florentines were making every effort to bring the pope to their will, and as they had not succeeded in making him yield to arms, they threatened him with the council that already had been convoked by the emperor at Basel. Hence, through the king's spokesmen, who were in Rome, and through the chief cardinals, who desired peace, the pope was persuaded and forced to think about peace and the union of Italy. Hence, the pontiff, out of fear and also because he saw that the greatness of the Venetians would be the ruin of the Church and of Italy, turned to make an accord with the league. He sent his nuncios to Naples, where they made a league for five years between the pope, the king, the duke of Milan, and the Florentines, reserving a place for the Venetians should they accept it.[1] This done, the pope let the Venetians know that they should abstain from war on Ferrara. The Venetians did not want to consent to this; indeed, they prepared for the war with even greater forces; and when they had defeated the men of the duke and of the marquis at Argenta, they were so close to Ferrara that they put their camp in the marquis's park.

25

HENCE, it appeared to the league that it could no longer postpone furnishing vigorous help to that lord, and they had the duke of Calabria come into Ferrara with his troops and with those of the pope; and likewise the Florentines sent all their troops there. And so as to arrange the order of the war better, the league held a diet at Cremona, to which came the pope's legate with Count Girolamo, the duke of Calabria, Signor Ludovico, and Lorenzo de' Medici with many other Italian princes; there the princes divided among themselves all the modes of the future war. And because they judged that Ferrara could not be relieved better than by making a bold diversion, they wanted Signor Ludovico to agree to make war against the Venetians for the state of the duke of Milan. That lord did

---

[1] On the situation in the "province" of Italy reflected in this league, see *P* 11.

not want to agree to this, as he feared he might bring a war on himself that he could not end when he pleased. And so it was decided to halt with all their troops at Ferrara; and having put together four thousand men of arms and eight thousand infantry, they went to meet the Venetians, who had two thousand two hundred men of arms and six thousand infantry. To the league it appeared that the first thing to do was to attack the fleet that the Venetians had on the Po; and having attacked it near Bondena, they routed it with a loss of more than two hundred boats, taking prisoner there Messer Antonio Giustinian, overseer of the fleet. After the Venetians had seen all Italy united against them, they had hired the duke of Lorraine with two hundred men at arms to improve their reputation. Hence, when their fleet received this damage, they sent him with a part of their army to hold the enemy at bay. And they had Signor Roberto da San Severino cross the Adda with the rest of their army and approach Milan, shouting out the name of the duke and of his mother, Madonna Bona; for they believed they would stir up something new in Milan in this way, since they considered that Signor Ludovico and his government were hated in that city. This attack brought with it great terror at its beginning and put the city in arms; nonetheless, it produced an outcome contrary to the design of the Venetians, because this injury was the cause of Signor Ludovico's consenting to that which he had not wanted to consent to. And so, having left the marquis of Ferrara to the defense of his own things with four thousand cavalry and two thousand infantry, the duke of Calabria with twelve thousand cavalry and five thousand infantry entered the territory of Bergamo and from there went to that of Brescia and then to the territory of Verona; and those three cities, without the Venetians' having any remedy for it, he deprived of almost all their countryside; for Signor Roberto with his troops was hardly able to save the cities. On the other side, the marquis of Ferrara had recovered a great part of his thing, since the duke of Lorraine, who was against him, was unable to resist him, as he had no more than two thousand cavalry and a thousand infantry. And so all the summer of the year 1483 was fought prosperously for the league.

26

WHEN spring of the following year came, winter having passed quietly, the armies took to the field; and to overcome the Venetians with more haste, the league put all its army together. And if the war had been maintained as in the past year, the league would easily have taken from the Venetians all of the state they held in Lombardy, for the Venetians were reduced to six thousand cavalry and five thousand infantry and had to oppose thirteen thousand cavalry and six thousand infantry, because the duke of Lorraine, the year of his contract having finished, had gone home. But as often happens where many of equal authority compete, disunion among them most times gives victory to the enemy. After the death of Federico Gonzaga, marquis of Mantua, who with his authority had kept the duke of Calabria and Signor Ludovico faithful, differences began to arise between them and from differences, jealousy, because Gian Galeazzo, duke of Milan, was already of an age to take the government of his state; and since his wife was the daughter of the duke of Calabria,[1] the duke desired that not Ludovico but his son-in-law govern the state. But Ludovico, recognizing this desire of the duke's, decided to take from him the opportunity of executing it. This suspicion of Ludovico's, known to the Venetians, was taken by them as an opportunity, and they judged they could win by peace after they had lost by war, as they always had done. And having secretly negotiated an accord between themselves and Signor Ludovico, they concluded it in August of 1484. When this accord came to the notice of the other confederates, it displeased them very much, especially after they saw that they had to restore to the Venetians the towns taken from them and leave them Rovigo and the Polesine, which they had seized from the marquis of Ferrara, and even let them have back all the privileges that they had formerly held in that city. And it appeared to everyone that a war had been waged in which very much had been spent, and that in waging it honor had been acquired and in ending it, shame, since the towns taken had been returned and the losses not recovered. But the allies were constrained to accept this because they were wearied by the expenses, and they were not willing, because of the defects and ambitions of others, to make any further test of their fortune.

27

WHILE in Lombardy things were being governed in this form, the pope through Messer Lorenzo pressed Città di Castello so as to drive out Niccolò Vitelli, who had been abandoned by the league so as to attract the pope to its purpose. And while the pope was pressing that town, those within it who were Niccolò's partisans made a sortie and, coming to grips with the enemy, routed them. Hence, the pope recalled Count Girolamo from Lombardy and had him come to Rome to build his forces and return to that campaign; but judging then that it was better to gain over Messer

[1] Isabella of Aragon.

Niccolò to himself with peace rather than to attack him again with war, he made an accord with him and, in the best mode he could, reconciled him with Messer Lorenzo, his adversary. He was compelled to this more by a suspicion of new tumults than by love of peace, because he saw malign humors awakening between the Colonna and the Orsini. The king of Naples had taken the country around Tagliacozzo from the Orsini in the war between himself and the pope and had given it to the Colonna, who were taking his side. Then, when peace was made between the king and the pope, the Orsini asked for it by virtue of these agreements. The pope indicated many times to the Colonna that they should restore it, but neither by the begging of the Orsini nor by the threats of the pope would they condescend to restore it; indeed, they offended the Orsini anew with looting and other similar injuries. Hence, the pontiff, unable to put up with them, moved all his forces together with those of the Orsini against the Colonna and sacked the houses they had in Rome, and whoever defended them he killed and arrested; and he stripped them of the greater part of their fortified towns. So those tumults were put to rest not by peace but by the affliction of one party.

28

THINGS were not yet quiet in Genoa and in Tuscany, because the Florentines kept Count Antonio da Marciano with troops on the frontiers of Sarzana, and while the war lasted in Lombardy, they harassed the Sarzanese with raids and similar light engagements. In Genoa, Battistino Fregoso, the doge of that city, trusting in Archbishop Pagolo Fregoso, was arrested with his wife and his children by him; and Pagolo made himself prince of the city. The Venetian fleet also had attacked the Kingdom, seized Gallipoli, and harassed other places around it.

But when peace came in Lombardy, all tumults were set at rest except in Tuscany and Rome. For the pope, having pronounced peace, died five days later, either because the end of his life had come or because his sorrow over the peace that was made—as he was an enemy of peace—killed him. This pontiff, therefore, left in peace that Italy which he had always kept at war while he lived. Upon his death, Rome was immediately in arms. Count Girolamo withdrew with his troops near the Castello;[1] the Orsini feared that the Colonna might want to avenge their recent injuries; the Colonna asked again for their houses and their fortified towns: hence, in a few days murders, robberies, and fires followed in many places of

[1] Castel Sant'Angelo in Rome.

that city. But when the cardinals had argued to the count that he should have the Castello returned to the hands of the College, go off to his own states, and free Rome of his arms, the count, who desired to make the future pontiff benevolent toward him, obeyed and, having restored the Castello to the College, went to Imola. Thus, since the cardinals had been freed of this fear and the barons freed of the assistance in their differences they hoped for from the count, they turned to the creation of the new pontiff. After some dispute, Giovan Battista Cibo, cardinal of Malfetta and a Genoese, was elected; and he called himself Innocent VIII. With his easy nature, for he was a humane and quiet man, he had arms put aside and for the time pacified Rome.

29

AFTER the peace in Lombardy, the Florentines were unable to quiet down, as they thought it a shameful and ugly thing that a private gentleman had despoiled them of the town of Sarzana.[1] And because in the articles of the peace it was stated not only that one could ask for the return of things lost but that one could make war on anyone who hindered their acquisition, they immediately ordered themselves with money and men for that undertaking. Hence, as it did not appear to Agostino Fregoso, who had seized Sarzana, that he could sustain such a war with his private forces, he gave that town to San Giorgio. But since one must mention San Giorgio and the Genoese many times, it does not seem unfitting for me to set forth the orders and modes of that city, as it is one of the principal cities of Italy. Since the Genoese had made peace with the Venetians, after the very important war that had taken place between them many years ago,[2] their republic had been unable to repay those citizens who had loaned a great sum of money, and it had granted them the income from the customs and declared that each should share according to his credit in the receipts of the principal sum until they had been entirely satisfied by the Commune; and so that the creditors could meet together, the palace that is above the customhouse was assigned to them. These creditors thus ordered among themselves a mode of government, making a council of a hundred of themselves to deliberate public affairs and a magistracy of eight citizens as head of all to execute them; they divided their credits into parts, which they called "places"; and they entitled their whole body after San Giorgio. When their government was thus apportioned, new needs

[1] See *FH* VIII 18.
[2] The war of Chioggia and the peace of Turin, in 1381; see *FH* I 32.

occurred to the Commune of the city; so it had recourse for new assistance to San Giorgio, which, being rich and well administered, could be
of service to the Commune. And in the bargain, as the Commune had
first granted the customs receipts to San Giorgio, it began, as a pledge of
the money it had had, to grant San Giorgio some of its towns. And the
thing had gone so far, arising from the needs of the Commune and the
services of San Giorgio, that the Commune had put under the administration of San Giorgio the greater part of the towns and city subject to the
empire of Genoa, which San Giorgio governs and defends and each year
by public suffrage sends them its rectors without the Commune's being
involved in it in any degree. From this it arose that the citizens took away
their love from the Commune, as something tyrannical, and placed it in
San Giorgio, as a party well and equitably administered; and from this
arose easy and frequent changes of state and the fact that the Genoese
obey sometimes one of their own citizens and sometimes a foreigner, because not San Giorgio but the Commune changes its government. Thus,
when the Fregosi and Adorni fought over the principate, since they were
fighting over the state of the Commune, the greater part of the citizens
drew aside and left it as prey to the winner. Nor does the company of San
Giorgio do otherwise when someone has taken over the state than make
him swear to observe its laws, which have not been altered up to these
times, because San Giorgio has arms, money, and government, and one
cannot alter the laws without danger of a certain and dangerous rebellion.
An example truly rare, never found by the philosophers in all the republics they have imagined and seen:[3] to see within the same circle, among
the same citizens, liberty and tyranny, civil life and corrupt life, justice
and license, because that order alone keeps the city full of its ancient and
venerable customs. And if it should happen—which in time it surely
will—that San Giorgio should take over the whole city, that would be a
republic more memorable than the Venetian.

30

TO this San Giorgio, therefore, Agostino Fregoso granted Sarzana. San
Giorgio received it willingly and undertook its defense, immediately put
the fleet to sea, and sent troops to Pietrasanta so as to prevent anyone
from going to the camp of the Florentines, which was already near Sarzana. The Florentines, on the other side, desired to seize Pietrasanta; for

---

[3] Cf. the phrase in *P* 15, which contrasts "imagined" republics and principalities to those
that have been "seen."

not having that town made the acquisition of Sarzana less useful, since Pietrasanta was located between Sarzana and Pisa. But the Florentines could not reasonably besiege Pietrasanta unless they were hindered in the acquisition of Sarzana either by the people of Pietrasanta or by whoever was inside there. And so that this might happen, the Florentines sent a large amount of munitions and provisions from Pisa to the camp with a weak escort so that whoever was in Pietrasanta would fear less because the guard was small and, because the booty was sizable, would be more desirous of attacking it. The thing then went according to plan, because those who were in Pietrasanta, seeing so much booty right before their eyes, snatched it. This gave legitimate cause to the Florentines to undertake their campaign; and so, putting Sarzana aside, they encamped at Pietrasanta, which was full of defenders who defended it vigorously. The Florentines, after placing their artillery on the plain, made a bastion of the mountain so as to be able to bear down from that side as well. Jacopo Guicciardini was commissioner of the army; and while the fighting went on at Pietrasanta, the Genoese fleet seized and burned the fortress of Vada, and its men, put on land, overran and plundered the countryside around it. To oppose them, Messer Bongianni Gianfigliazzi was sent with infantry and cavalry; he partly checked their pride, so that they did not raid with such license. But the fleet, continuing to harass the Florentines, went to Leghorn and with pontoons[1] and other devices drew close to the new tower and attacked it for many days with artillery; but when the fleet saw it was not getting any benefit, it turned back from Leghorn with shame.

3 1

IN the meantime, at Pietrasanta the fighting was sluggish; so the enemy took up spirit, attacked the bastion, and seized it. This resulted in so much reputation for them and so much fright in the Florentine army that it nearly routed itself; so it moved four miles from the town, and its heads judged that, since it was already the month of October, it was well to withdraw to quarters and save that siege for another time. As soon as this disorder was learned in Florence, it filled the princes of that state with indignation; and immediately, so as to restore the reputation and force of the camp, they elected Antonio Pucci and Bernardo del Nero as new commissioners. These men went to the camp with a large sum of money and explained to its captains what would be the indignation of the Signoria, of the state, and of the whole city if they did not return with the

---

[1] Excavating machines.

army to the walls, and what a disgrace would be theirs if such captains, with such an army, having against them nothing but a small garrison, could not capture so vile and so weak a town. They pointed out the present advantage of such an acquisition and what they could hope for in the future from it, so that the spirits of all were rekindled to return to the walls; and before everything else, they decided to acquire the bastion. In acquiring it, one learned how much humanity, affability, and gracious greetings and words can do for the spirits of soldiers; for Antonio Pucci, by urging on this soldier, promising something to the other, by shaking the hand of one, embracing another, made them go to the attack with such forcefulness that they acquired that bastion in a moment. The acquisition was not without loss, inasmuch as Count Antonio da Marciano was killed by an artillery shot. This victory gave such terror to those in the town that they began to reason about surrender; hence, so that things might be concluded with more reputation, it appeared to Lorenzo de' Medici that he himself should go to the camp, and not many days after he had arrived, the fortified town was taken. Winter had come now, and so to the captains it appeared that they should not proceed any further with the campaign but should wait for another time, especially since in that autumn, on account of the bad air, the army had been weakened and many of its heads were gravely ill; among them, Antonio Pucci and Messer Bongianni Gianfigliazzi not only sickened but died, to the sorrow of everyone, such was the grace that Antonio had acquired for himself by the things he had done at Pietrasanta. After the Florentines had acquired Pietrasanta, the Lucchese sent spokesmen to Florence to ask for it as a town that already belonged to their republic, for they alleged that it was among the obligations[1] that all the towns that were recovered by one from another ought to be restored to their first lord. The Florentines did not deny the agreements, but they answered that they did not know if by the peace that was being negotiated between themselves and the Genoese they had to restore that town; and therefore they could not make a decision about it before that time; and even if they did not have to return it,[2] it was necessary for the Lucchese to think about satisfying them for the expenses made and the damage received through the deaths of so many of their citizens; and if they should do this, they could easily hope to get it back. So all that winter was consumed in negotiations between the Genoese and Florentines for the peace that was being negotiated in Rome through the pontiff. But as there was no conclusion, the Florentines, when spring came, would have attacked Sarzana if they had not been pre-

[1] Of the treaty of Bagnolo; *FH* VIII 26.
[2] To Genoa.

vented by the illness of Lorenzo de' Medici and by the war that arose between the pope and King Ferdinand. For Lorenzo not only was afflicted by gout, which he had as an inheritance from his father, but was attacked by very grave stomach pains, which necessitated his going to the baths to be cured.

32

BUT a more important cause was the war, the origin of which was this. The city of l'Aquila was subject to the kingdom of Naples in such a mode that it lived almost free. In this city the count of Montorio[1] had much reputation. The duke of Calabria was near the Tronto with his men at arms under color of wanting to put down certain tumults that had arisen in those parts among the peasants. Since he was scheming to bring l'Aquila back to obeying the king entirely, he sent for the count of Montorio as if he wished the count to serve him in the things he was doing then. The count obeyed without any suspicion, and when he arrived at the duke's, he was made a prisoner by the duke and sent to Naples. As soon as this thing was known in l'Aquila, it angered the whole city; and, the people having taken up arms, Antonio Concinello, commissioner for the king, was killed and with him some citizens who were known to be partisans of his majesty. And so that the people of l'Aquila might have someone to defend them in their rebellion, they raised the banners of the Church and sent spokesmen to the pope to give him the city and themselves, begging him to help them as something of his own against tyrannical rule. The pontiff took up their defense spiritedly, since he hated the king for private and public causes; and as Signor Roberto da San Severino was hostile to the state of Milan and unemployed, he took him for his captain and had him come with utmost speed to Rome. Besides this, he urged all friends and relatives of the count of Montorio to rebel against the king, so that the princes of Altamura, of Salerno, and of Bisignano took up arms against him. The king, seeing himself attacked by so sudden a war, fell back on the Florentines and the duke of Milan for help. The Florentines were in doubt as to what they ought to do, because to them it appeared difficult to drop their own enterprises for another's, and to take up arms once again against the Church appeared dangerous to them. Nonetheless, since they were in league, they put their faith ahead of convenience and danger to themselves and hired the Orsini; and in addition, they sent all

[1] Pietro Camponeschi.

their troops under the count of Pitigliano[2] toward Rome in aid of the king. The king then made two armies: one under the duke of Calabria he sent toward Rome, which together with the Florentine troops opposed the army of the Church; with the other, under his own command, he opposed the barons. And on one side and the other this war was waged with varying fortune. In the end, as the king came out on top in every place, in August of 1486, through the spokesmen of the king of Spain,[3] a peace was concluded, to which the pope agreed because he had been beaten by fortune and did not want to try it further. All the powers of Italy united in the peace, leaving only the Genoese apart as rebels against the state of Milan and seizers of towns belonging to the Florentines. Peace having been made, Signor Roberto da San Severino, who in the war had been hardly faithful to the pope and hardly a formidable enemy to the others, left Rome as though driven out by the pope and was pursued by the soldiers of the duke and the Florentines. When he had passed Cesena, seeing he would be overtaken, he took to flight and with less than a hundred cavalry brought himself to Ravenna. Of the rest of his troops, part were accepted by the duke, part undone by peasants. The king, when peace was made and he was reconciled with the barons, had Jacopo Coppola and Antonello d'Anversa killed with their children, as the ones who in the war had revealed his secrets to the pontiff.

33

THE pope had learned from the example of this war with how much promptness and zeal the Florentines keep their friendships; so whereas at first he hated the Florentines, both because of his love for the Genoese and because of the aid the Florentines had provided to the king, he began to love them and to show greater than the usual favor to their spokesmen. This inclination, recognized by Lorenzo de' Medici, was assisted with all his industry; for he judged it to be of great reputation to himself if to the friendship of the king he could add that of the pope. The pontiff had a son called Francesco, and, desiring to honor him with states and with friends so that after his death his son could maintain himself, he knew of no one in Italy with whom he could more securely unite his son than with Lorenzo; so he worked it out that Lorenzo gave a daughter of his as wife to him. This alliance accomplished, the pope desired the Genoese to agree to cede Sarzana to the Florentines, as he pointed out to them that they

[2] Niccolò Orsini, condottiere; see P 12.
[3] Ferdinand the Catholic, king of Aragon.

could not keep what Agostino had sold, nor could Agostino donate to San Giorgio what was not his.[1] Nonetheless, he could never make any headway; indeed, the Genoese, while these things were being negotiated in Rome, armed many of their boats, and without anything being known of it in Florence, they put three thousand infantry on land and attacked the fortress at Sarzanello, situated above Sarzana and possessed by the Florentines; and they plundered and burned the village next to it; and afterward, having placed artillery before the fortress, they attacked it with all intensity. This new attack was unexpected by the Florentines; hence, they immediately assembled their men under Virginio Orsini at Pisa, and they complained to the pope that while he was negotiating peace the Genoese had started a war with them. Then they sent Piero Corsini to Lucca to keep that city faithful; they sent Paolantonio Soderini to Venice to test the spirits of that republic; they asked aid from the king and from Signor Ludovico, and got none from anyone: for the king said he was afraid of the fleet of the Turk, and Ludovico with other caviling postponed sending any. And so the Florentines are almost always alone in their wars; nor do they find anyone to aid them with the spirit with which they help others. Nor were they frightened this time by having been abandoned by their allies, since it was not new to them. They made a large army under Jacopo Guicciardini and Piero Vettori and sent it against the enemy; they made their camp by the Magra River. In the meantime, Sarzanello was hard pressed by the enemy, who were besieging it with mines and with every kind of force. So the commissioners decided to relieve it; nor did the enemy refuse battle, and when they came to grips, the Genoese were defeated; Messer Luigi dal Fiesco was taken prisoner there with many other heads of the enemy army. This victory did not frighten the Sarzanese in any mode that might make them want to surrender; indeed, they prepared obstinately for defense and the Florentine commissioners for offense: so Sarzana was vigorously attacked and defended. And as this siege went on at length, it appeared to Lorenzo de' Medici that he should go to the camp. When he arrived there, our soldiers took spirit and the Sarzanese lost it; for when they saw the obstinacy of the Florentines in attacking[2] them and the coolness in the Genoese for rescuing them, they put themselves in the hands of Lorenzo freely and without other conditions. When they had come under the power[3] of the Florentines, they were treated humanely, except for the few authors of the rebellion. During the siege, Signor Ludovico had sent his men at arms

[1] See *FH* VIII 18, 29.
[2] Lit.: offending.
[3] *Potestà*; or *podestà* in the Casella text: under the podestà of the Florentines.

to Pontremoli to make a show of coming in our favor; but with his fore-knowledge in Genoa, the party opposed to those who were ruling rose up and with the help of the duke's men gave themselves over to the duke of Milan.

34

IN these times, the Germans had started a war against the Venetians; and in the Marches, Boccolino da Osimo[1] had made Osimo rebel against the pope, and he set up a tyranny over it. After many accidents he was content, having been persuaded by Lorenzo de' Medici, to give up that city to the pontiff. And he came to Florence, where he lived for a long time very honorably under the faith of Lorenzo, then went to Milan, where, not finding the same faith, he was put to death by Signor Ludovico. The Venetians, attacked by the Germans, were defeated near the city of Trento and their captain, Signor Roberto da San Severino, killed. After this loss, the Venetians, in accordance with the order of their fortune, made an accord with the Germans, not as losers but as winners, so honorable was it for their republic.

Also in these times very important tumults arose in Romagna. Francesco d'Orso of Forlì was a man of great authority in that city; he came under the suspicion of Count Girolamo so that he was threatened many times by the count. Hence Francesco, living in great fear, was encouraged by his friends and relatives to anticipate; and since he feared being killed by the count, he should kill him first and escape his own dangers by another's death. Thus, his decision made and his mind intent on the undertaking, they chose the market day at Forlì as the time, because many of their friends from the countryside would be coming to the city on that day, and they thought they could make use of them for their deed without having to make them come. It was the month of May, when the greater part of Italians are in the habit of dining by daylight. The conspirators thought that the convenient hour to kill him would be after his dinner, at which time, while his servants were dining, he would be left almost alone in his room. With this thought, at the appointed hour, Francesco went to the houses of the count, and, having left his companions in the first rooms and come to the room where the count was, he told one of the servants to let the count know that he wished to speak to him. Francesco was brought in, and, finding the count alone, after a few words of pretended reasoning he killed him; then, his companions having been called, they

[1] Boccalino Guzzoni from Osimo.

killed the servant too. The captain of the town, by chance, was coming to speak to the count, and when he came into the room with a few of his men, he too was put to death by the killers of the count. These homicides done, a great tumult was raised, and the head of the count was thrown out of the window; and shouting "Church and Liberty," they had the whole people, who hated the avarice and cruelty of the count, armed. After his houses were sacked, they made prisoners of Countess Caterina[2] and all her children. Only the fortress remained to be taken if they wanted their enterprise to have a prosperous end. As the castellan was not willing to yield it, they begged[3] that the countess be content to induce him to give it up. This she promised to do if they would allow her to enter the fortress; and as pledge of her faith they would keep her children. The conspirators believed her words and permitted her to enter it. As soon as she was inside, she threatened them with death and every kind of punishment in revenge of her husband; and when they threatened to kill her children, she said she had with her the mode of producing more of them. The conspirators, therefore, seeing that they were not being assisted by the pope and hearing that Signor Ludovico, uncle of the countess, was sending troops to her assistance, became frightened; and taking away what property of theirs they could carry, they went to Città di Castello. Then the countess, having retaken the state, avenged her husband's death with every kind of cruelty. The Florentines, learning of the count's death, took the opportunity to recover the fortress of Piancaldoli, which had been seized from them in the past by the count. After they sent their men there, they recovered it, with the death of Cecca,[4] a very famous architect.

35

TO this tumult in Romagna was added another in that province of no less moment. Galeatto, lord of Faenza, had as wife the daughter of Messer Giovanni Bentivoglio, prince in Bologna. Whether out of jealousy or because she had been badly treated by her husband or by her own wicked nature, this woman hated her husband. And she went so far in hating him that she decided to take his state and his life from him. Feigning a certain illness, she went to bed, where she ordered that when Galeatto came to visit her, he should be killed by certain confidants of hers whom she had

---

[2] Caterina Sforza, natural daughter of Galeazzo Maria. For this story see also *D* III 6 and *P* 20.

[3] Or prayed.

[4] Francesco d'Angelo (1447–1488).

hidden in her room to this effect. She had made her father share in this thought, since he was hoping, after his son-in-law was dead, to become lord of Faenza. Therefore, when the appointed time came for this homicide, Galeatto entered his wife's room according to his custom, and when he had been with her a while to reason, the killers came out of secret places in the room and killed him without his being able to find any remedy. After his death there was a great uproar: his wife fled to the fortress with her small son dubbed Astorre; the people took up arms; Messer Giovanni Bentivoglio, together with one Bergamino, a condottiere of the duke of Milan, having first prepared themselves with many armed men, entered Faenza, where Antonio Boscoli was still Florentine commissioner. As all those heads congregated together during the tumult, and while they were speaking of the government of the town, the men of Val di Lamona, who had run to the noise as a people, started fighting against Messer Giovanni and Bergamino, killing Bergamino and taking Giovanni prisoner. Shouting the name of Astorre and of the Florentines, they entrusted the city to the Florentine commissioner. When this event was known in Florence, it displeased everyone very much; nonetheless, they set Messer Giovanni and his daughter at liberty; and by the will of the whole people, they undertook the care of the city and of Astorre. Besides these, very many tumults followed in Romagna, in the Marches, and in Siena for many years after the principal wars among the greater princes were settled. Because they were of little moment, I judge it superfluous to recount them. It is true that those in Siena, since the duke of Calabria had departed after the war of '78, were more frequent; and after many changes, in which sometimes the plebs and sometimes the nobles dominated, the nobles were left superior. Among these, Pandolfo and Jacopo Petrucci seized more authority than the others: they became like princes of that city, one from prudence, the other from spirit.

36

BUT after the war in Sarzana had ended, the Florentines lived in very great prosperity until 1492, when Lorenzo de' Medici died. For when the arms of Italy, which had been stayed by Lorenzo's sense and authority, had been put down, he turned his mind to making himself and his city great. To Piero, his eldest son, he joined in marriage Alfonsina, daughter of the knight Orsino; then he raised his second son, Giovanni, to the dignity of the cardinalate.[1] This was the more noteworthy since, beyond

---

[1] Later he became Pope Leo X.

every past example, he was brought to such rank when not yet fourteen years of age. It was a ladder enabling his house to rise to heaven, as happened later in the times that followed. For Giuliano, his third son, because of his slight age and the short time Lorenzo lived, he was not able to provide any extraordinary fortune. Of his daughters, one was married to Jacopo Salviati, another to Francesco Cibo, and the third to Piero Ridolfi; the fourth, whom he married to Giovanni de' Medici so as to keep his house united, died. In his other private things, he was very unprosperous in trade; for through the disorder of his agents, who administered his things not as private men but as princes, in many regards much of his movable property was eliminated; so it was required that his fatherland help him with a great sum of money. Hence, so as not to try the same fortune further, he set aside his mercantile interests and turned to landed property as a more stable and fixed kind of wealth; and around Prato, Pisa, and Val di Pesa he developed properties that for their utility, the quality of their buildings, and their magnificence were those not of a private citizen but of a king.

After this, he turned to making his city more beautiful and greater; and for this, since there was much space in it without dwellings, he ordered new streets to be lined with new buildings: hence, the city became more beautiful and greater. And so that he might live in his state more quietly and safely and that his enemies could be fought or held off at some distance from himself, toward Bologna, in the midst of the mountains, he fortified the town of Firenzuola; toward Siena, he began to establish the Poggio Imperiale and to make it very strong; toward Genoa, the acquisition of Pietrasanta and Sarzana closed that way to the enemy. Then, with stipends and pensions, he maintained his friends the Baglioni in Perugia and the Vitelli in Città di Castello; and he held the government of Faenza personally: all of which things were like solid ramparts to the city. Also, in these peaceful times, he kept his fatherland always in festivities: there frequent jousts and representations of old deeds and triumphs were to be seen; and his aim was to keep the city in abundance, the people united, and the nobility honored. He loved marvelously anyone who was excellent in an art; he favored men of letters—of which Messer Agnolo da Montepulciano,[2] Messer Cristofano Landino, and Messer Demetrio, a Greek,[3] can give firm testimony. Hence, Count Giovanni della Mirandola,[4] a man almost divine, left all the other parts of Europe where he had traveled and, attracted by the munificence of Lorenzo, made his home

[2] Angelo Ambrogini, il Poliziano.
[3] Demetrio Chalcondylas.
[4] Giovanni Pico della Mirandola.

in Florence. Lorenzo took marvelous delight in architecture, music, and poetry; and many poetic compositions not only composed but also commented on by him are in existence. And so that the Florentine youth might be trained in the study of letters, he opened in the city of Pisa a school to which the most excellent men in Italy then were brought. He built a monastery near Florence for Fra Mariano da Genazzano, of the order of Saint Augustine, because he was a very excellent preacher.[5]

Lorenzo was loved by fortune and by God in the highest degree, because of which all his enterprises had a prosperous end and all his enemies an unprosperous one. For besides the Pazzi, Battista Frescobaldi wanted to kill him in the Carmine and Baldinotto di Pistoia in his villa; and each of them, together with those who knew their secrets, suffered the very just penalties of their evil thoughts. His mode of life, his prudence and fortune, were known and held in admiration by princes not only in Italy but far away from it. Matthias, king of Hungary, gave him many signs of the love he bore for him; the Sultan sent him his spokesmen and presented his gifts; the Grand Turk put into his hands Bernardo Bandini, the killer of his brother. These things caused him to be considered wonderful in Italy. His reputation grew every day because of his prudence; for he was eloquent and sharp in discussing things, wise in resolving them, quick and spirited in executing them. Nor can vices of his be adduced to stain his great virtues, even though he was marvelously involved in things of Venus and he delighted in facetious and pungent men and in childish games, more than would appear fitting in such a man. Many times he was seen among his sons and daughters, mixing in their amusements. Thus, considering both his voluptuous life and his grave life, one might see in him two different persons, joined in an almost impossible conjunction. In his last days he lived full of distress caused by the illness that held him marvelously afflicted; he was oppressed by intolerable stomach pain, which so racked him that in April of 1492 he died, in the forty-fourth year of his life. Nor did anyone ever die, not only in Florence but in Italy, with such fame for his prudence and so much mourned in his fatherland. And that very great disasters[6] must arise from his death, heaven showed many very evident signs, among which was the following: the highest tip of the church of Santa Reparata was struck by lightning with such fury that a great part of the pinnacle was ruined, to the amazement and marveling of everyone.[7] Thus, all the citizens and all the princes of Italy mourned his death, of which they made manifest signs, because there was

[5] Also because he was a determined opponent of Savonarola, whom NM does not mention.

[6] Lit.: ruins.

[7] Cf. *D* I 56.

no one who did not signify through his spokesmen the grief felt at such an event. But whether they had just cause to mourn him, the effect of his death demonstrated shortly after; for when Italy was left deprived of his advice, no mode was found for those who remained either to satisfy or to check the ambition of Ludovico Sforza, governor of the duke of Milan. Therefore, as soon as Lorenzo was dead, those bad seeds began to grow which, not long after, since the one who knew how to eliminate them was not alive, ruined and are still ruining Italy.

Anselmi, Gian Mario. *Ricerche sul Machiavelli Storico*. Pisa: Pacini, 1979.

Baron, Hans. *From Petrarch to Leonardo Bruni*. Chicago: University of Chicago Press, 1968.

Bondanella, Peter E. *Machiavelli and the Art of Renaissance History*. Detroit: Wayne State University Press, 1973.

Brucker, Gene A. *Renaissance Florence*. Berkeley: University of California Press, 1983.

Cabrini, Anna Maria. *Per una valutazione delle "Istorie Fiorentine" del Machiavelli*. Florence: La Nuova Italia, 1985.

Cochrane, Eric. *Historians and Historiography in the Italian Renaissance*. Chicago: University of Chicago Press, 1981.

Dionisotti, Carlo. "Machiavelli Storico." In Dionisotti, *Machiavellerie*. Turin: Einaudi, 1980.

Gaeta, Franco. "Machiavelli Storico." In *Machiavelli nel V Centenario della Nascita*. Bologna: Massimiliano Boni, 1973.

Garosci, Aldo. *Le Istorie Fiorentine del Machiavelli*. Turin: Giappichelli, 1973.

Geerken, John H. "Machiavelli Studies since 1969." *Journal of the History of Ideas* 37 (1976): 351–368.

Gilbert, Felix. *Machiavelli and Guicciardini*. Princeton: Princeton University Press, 1965.

———. "Machiavelli's *Istorie Fiorentine*: An Essay in Interpretation." In Felix Gilbert, *History; Choice and Commitment*. Edited by Franklin L. Ford. Cambridge, Mass.: Harvard University Press, 1977.

Hale, J. R. *Florence and the Medici*. New York: Thames and Hudson, 1978.

Kent, Dale. *The Rise of the Medici: Faction in Florence, 1426–1434*. Oxford: Oxford University Press, 1978.

Machiavelli, Niccolò. *Istorie Fiorentine*. 2 vols. Edited by Plinio Carli. Florence: Sansoni, 1927.

———. *Istorie Fiorentine*. Books I–III. With commentary by Vittorio Fiorini. Florence: Sansoni, 1894.

———. *Istorie Fiorentine*. Edited with an introduction by Franco Gaeta. Milan: Feltrinelli, 1962.

Machiavelli, Niccolò. *The Letters of Machiavelli.* Translated by Allan Gilbert. New York: Capricorn, 1961.

——. *Tutte le Opere.* Edited by Mario Martelli. Florence: Sansoni, 1971.

——. *Tutte le opere storiche e letterrarie di Niccolò Machiavelli.* Edited by Guido Mazzoni and Mario Casella. Florence: Barbera, 1929.

Mansfield, Harvey C., Jr. "On the Impersonality of the Modern State: A Comment on Machiavelli's Use of *Stato.*" *American Political Science Review* 77 (1983): 849–857.

——. "Party and Sect in Machiavelli's *Florentine Histories.*" In Martin Fleisher, ed., *Machiavelli and the Nature of Political Thought.* New York: Atheneum, 1972.

Marietti, Marina. "Machiavel historiographe des Médecis." In André Rochon, ed., *Les écrivains et le pouvoir en Italie à l'époque de la Renaissance.* Paris: 1974.

Münkler, Herfried. *Machiavelli: Die Begründung des politischen Denkens der Neuzeit aus der Krise der Republik Florenz.* Frankfurt: Europäische Verlagsanstalt, 1982.

Najemy, John M. "*Arti* and *Ordini* in Machiavelli's *Istorie Fiorentine.*" In S. Bertelli and G. Ramakus, eds., *Essays Presented to Myron Gilmore.* Florence: Sansoni, 1978.

——. "Machiavelli and the Medici: The Lessons of Florentine History." *Renaissance Quarterly* 35 (1982): 551–576.

Phillips, Mark. "Barefoot Boy Makes Good: A Study of Machiavelli's Historiography." *Speculum* 59 (1984): 585–605.

——. "Machiavelli, Guicciardini, and the Tradition of Vernacular Historiography in Florence." *American Historical Review* 84 (1979): 86–105.

Ridolfi, Roberto. *The Life of Niccolò Machiavelli.* Translated by Cecil Grayson. Chicago: University of Chicago Press, 1963.

Rubinstein, Nicolai. *The Government of Florence under the Medici 1434–1494.* Oxford: Clarendon Press, 1966.

——. "Il Poliziano e la questione delle origini di Firenze." In *Il Poliziano e il suo tempo.* Atti del IV Consegno Internazionale di Studi sul Rinascimento. Florence, 1957.

——. "Machiavelli e le origini di Firenze." *Rivista Storica Italiana* 79 (1967): 952–959.

Skinner, Quentin. *The Foundations of Modern Thought.* 2 vols. Cambridge: Cambridge University Press, 1978.

——. *Machiavelli.* New York: Hill and Wang, 1981.

Stephens, J. N. *The Fall of the Florentine Republic 1512–1530*. Oxford: Clarendon Press, 1983.

Strauss, Leo. *Thoughts on Machiavelli*. Glencoe, Ill.: The Free Press, 1958.

Villari, Pasquale. *The Life and Times of Niccolò Machiavelli*. Translated by L. Villari. London: Fisher Unwin, 1898.

INDEX OF PERSONS

References are to book, chapter, and page of the translation. The Letter Dedicatory and Preface are abbreviated as LD and P respectively. Names and descriptions are as given in the text, with additional information, if any, in parentheses.

Abati, the, Florentine family, II 4.57, 17.70, 21.74

Abati, Neri, a prior, dissolute and eager for evil, II 21.74

Acciaiuoli, the Florentine family, II 33.90; VII 11.289, 18.297

Acciaiuoli, Agnolo, archbishop of Florence, conspired against the duke of Athens, Rinaldo degli Albizzi, and Piero de' Medici, II 36.95–96, 40.101; IV 30.180; VI 4.234, 31.266; VII 11.288–289, 17.295, 18.296, 19.297, 23.302

Acciaiuoli, Alamanno, III 15.127

Acciaiuoli, Donato di Jacopo, recklessly threatened revolt against Maso degli Albizzi and was banished, III 25.139–140, 26.141–142

Acciaiuoli, Donato (di Neri), VIII 14.333

Acciaiuoli, Michele, III 26.141

Acciaiuoli, Raffaello, son of Agnolo, deprived of his wife's dowry by Cosimo de' Medici, VII 11.288

Acquasparta, Matteo d', papal legate, II 17.70, 19.72

Adimari, the, Florentine family, II 4.57, 17.70; III 27.142

Adimari, Andrea, III 24.138

Adimari, Antonio, conspired against the duke of Athens, II 36.96–97, 37.98

Adimari, Bernardo, III 28.144

Adimari, Forese, II 14.66

Adolf (I) of Saxony, emperor, I 25.36

Adorni, the, Genoan family, enemies of the Fregosi, V 6.192; VI 35.271, 38.274; VII 7.285; VIII 29.352

Adorno, Prospero, VIII 13.332–333

Adrian V, pope, brought Emperor Rudolf into Italy against Charles I of Anjou, I 23.34

Agapetus (II), pope, urged Emperor Otto (I) to free Italy from the Berengars, I 12.24

Agli, the, Florentine family, II 4.57

Agnoli, the, Florentine family, III 10.118

Agolanti, the, Florentine family, II 4.57

Ahmet, Pashaw, captain for Mahomet the Grand Turk, his attack on Italy saved Florence from losing its liberty, VIII 20.341

Aistulf, king of the Longobards, made war on pope Gregory III, I 10.20–21

Alamanni, Boccacino, count, IV 24.170

Alans, I 1.10, 2.10, 4.13

Alaric, king of the Visigoths, I 1.10

Alberic, duke of Tuscany, Rome saved from the Saracens through his virtue, I 12.23

Alberigo da Conio, Count. See Conio, Ludovico da

Albert, son of Berengar III (II), I 13.24

Albert (I), king of Germany, II 25.80

Alberti, the Florentine family, III 8.114, 23.137, 24.138, 25.139, 26.141, 28.144, 29.144–145; IV 2.147, 9.154; V 4.189

Alberti, Alberto degli, III 25.139

Alberti, Andrea degli, III 25.139

Alberti, Antonio degli, incriminated in a conspiracy by the confession of a monk, banished, III 14.125, 23.137, 28.144

Alberti, Benedetto, rich, humane, severe, a lover of liberty and a hater of tyranny; became the object of envy and suspicion after the Guelfs regained the state and was banished, III 9.116, 10.117, 14.125, 15.127, 18.130, 19.131, 20.133–134, 22.136, 23.137, 25.139; IV 10.155

Alberti, Jacopo, II 32.87

Albizzi, the, Florentine family, enemies of